THE COMPLETE GUIDE TO

BED &
BREAKFASTS,
INNS & GUESTHOUSES

PAMELA LANIER

The information in this book was supplied in large part by the innkeepers themselves, and is therefore subject to change without notice. We strongly recommend that you call ahead and always verify the information in this book before making your plans. We cannot be held responsible in the event that any information listed here is incorrect.

Cover by Jim Wood

Published by: John Muir Publications, Inc.
           P.O. Box 613
           Santa Fe, NM 87504

Library of Congress Catalogue No. 84-42648

ISBN 0-912528-35-4

First edition May 1984

Book trade distributor: W.W. Norton & Co., Inc.
                     New York, NY

Printed in the United States of America

For J.C. Dolfin Valdes

Acknowledgements

Corinne Rednour, George Lanier, Venetia Young, Vincent Yu, Lucy Rush for your help, love, and support—thank you.

To my friends who were so generous with their time and skills:

Marguerite Tafoya, Peggy Dennis, Megan Daane, Adele Novelli, Dorina Sarkis, Judy Jacobs, Carol McBride, Betty Parfitt, Kitty, Donald Pettyjohn, Jane Foster, Lita Hernandez, Nancy Ebert, Ruth Young, Carol Lehman, Mrs. Gieselman (the best English teacher ever), Mary Institute, Sheila Gorsuch, Mary Ellen Mort, Ingrid Head, Sumi Timberlake, Thomas Patterson.

Special thanks to Richard Paoli and all the travel writers who provided us with so much information and enthusiasm.

To the great folks in the Chambers of Commerce, State and Regional Departments of Tourism, and, especially to the helpful people at AAA. I am most grateful.

To the innkeepers themselves who are so busy, yet found the time to fill out our forms and provide us with all sorts of information. I wish you all great success.

At JMP—Ken Luboff, Eve Muir, Ada Browne, Lisa Cron, John Stick, Jeanne Flannery, Joan Kafri, Charles Wolff, Richard Polese, Curly Caffal, Peter Aschwanden, Deborah Reade, Jim Wood and Richard Harris.

Alfred, Cindy, Roy and Lloyd at Alfred's Palace, Negril - thank you for the food of body and spirit.

Contents

Part I: Introduction & How To Use This Book . 1

Part II: Bed & Breakfast Inns 29

Part III: Reservation Service Organizations . .279

Part IV: B&B Inns with Special Amenities . . .306

Part V: Some Favorite B&B Recipes 338

Vote
For Your Choice of
"Inn of the Year"

Did you find your stay at a Bed & Breakfast, Inn or Guesthouse listed in this Guide particularly enjoyable? Use the form in the back of the book or just drop us a note and we'll add your vote for the "Inn of the Year."

The winning entry will be featured in the next edition and receive a free copy of *The Complete Guide to Bed & Breakfasts, Inns and Guesthouses in the U.S. and Canada.*

Please base your decision on:

- **Helpfulness of Innkeeper**
- **Quality of Service**
- **Cleanliness**
- **Amenities**
- **Decor**
- **Food**

Look for the winning Inn in the next Updated & Revised edition of *The Complete Guide to Bed & Breakfasts, Inns and Guesthouses in the U.S. and Canada.*

Part I

Introduction
and
How To Use This Book

Introduction

There was a time, and it wasn't that long ago, when bed and breakfast inns were a rarity in the United States. Travelers made do at a hotel or motel; there was no alternative. The few bed and breakfast inns were scattered across the rural areas of New England and California. They were little known to most travelers; often their only advertisement was by word of mouth.

But in a few short years that has changed, and changed in a way that could only be called dramatic. There has been an explosion in the number of bed and breakfast inns. Today, inns can be found in every state, and often in cities; they have become true alternatives to a chain motel room or the city hotel with its hundreds of cubicles.

This sudden increase in bed and breakfast inns started less than a decade ago when Americans, faced with higher costs for foreign travel, began to explore the backroads and hidden communities of their own country.

American bed and breakfast inns have older and similar cousins in Europe and England. The Zimmer frei in Germany, usually a room and breakfast, is one example. The better known cousin in England is the private home with a "Bed and Breakfast" sign in the window. Guests pay a small sum to sleep in the extra bedroom and take breakfast with the household in the morning. The American translation has expanded on this tradition of offering hospitality in a private home.

Other factors have influenced the growth and popularity of bed and breakfast inns. Among them, the desire to get away from the daily routine and sameness of city life; the desire to be pampered for a few days; and also the desire to stay in a place with time to make new friends among the other guests.

The restored older homes that have become bed and breakfast inns answer those desires. The setting most often is rural; the innkeepers provide the service — not a staff with name tags — and the parlor is a gathering place for the handful of guests. They are a home away from home.

The proliferation of these inns as an alternative lodging has created some confusion. It's been difficult to find — in one place — up-to-date and thorough information about the great variety of inns.

Some books published in the past five or six years have tried to provide this information. But those books focused on one region of the country or named too few inns. While some earlier books gave detailed descriptions of the inns, few bothered to provide information about the type of breakfast served, whether there are rooms for non-smokers, and such things as whether the inn offered free use of bicycles or whether it had a hot tub.

An effort to collect as much information about as many inns as possible in one book has been overdue. Now that has been remedied. You hold a copy of the result in your hands.

—*Richard Paoli,*
Travel Editor
San Francisco Examiner

How To Use This Guide

How It's Organized

This book is organized alphabetically by state and, within a state, alphabetically by city or town. The inns appear first. Following the state list of inns is a listing of the reservation service organizations serving each state and lists of inns with special characteristics.

Check the table of contents for the location of our special lists, recipes, and other features.

Three Types of Accommodations

Inn: Webster's defines an inn as a "house built for the lodging and entertainment of travelers." All the inns in this book fulfill this description. Many also provide meals, at least breakfast, although a few do not. Included are inns with no more than 30 guest rooms.

Bed and Breakfast: Can be anything from a home with three or more rooms to, more typically, a large house or mansion with eight or nine guest accommodations which serves breakfast in the morning.

Guest Houses: Private homes welcoming travelers, some of which may be contacted directly but most you reserve through a reservation service organization. More on this later.

Breakfasts

We define a **Full Breakfast** as one being along English lines, including eggs and/or meat as well as the usual breads, toast, juice and coffee.

Continental Breakfast means coffee, juice, bread or pastry.

Continental Plus is a breakfast of coffee, juice and choice of several breads and pastry and possibly more.

Meals

Bear in mind that inns which do not serve meals are usually located near a variety of restaurants.

Can We Get a Drink?

Those inns without a license will generally chill your bottles and provide you with set-ups upon request.

Prices

Prices quoted in the book should be used as guidelines so you may compare establishments, but they are subject to change. Generally, where not specified, the lower price is for a comfortable single and the highest price is for the best double. Where only one price appears, you may assume it is for an average double.

Appearing next to the price is a code indicating the type of food services available:

B&B: Breakfast included in quoted rate.

EP (European Plan): No meals.

MAP (Modified American Plan): Includes breakfast and dinner.

AP (American Plan) Includes all three meals.

Be sure to confirm prices and services when you make your reservation.

Credit Cards and Checks

If an establishment accepts credit cards, it will be listed as **Visa, MC** or **Amex**. Most inns will accept your personal check with proper identification but be sure to confirm when you book.

Reservations

Reservations are essential at most inns, particularly during busy seasons, and are appreciated at other times. Be sure to reserve even if only a few hours in advance, to avoid disappointment. When you book, feel free to discuss your requirements and confirm prices, services and other details. We have found innkeepers to be delightfully helpful.

Arriving late: Most inns will hold your reservation until 6 p.m. If you plan to arrive later, please phone ahead to let them know.

Deposits or advance payment are required at some inns.

Children, Pets and Smoking

Children, pets and smoking present special difficulties for many inns. To let you know whether they are allowed, limited, or not permitted, it is noted as follows:

	Yes	Limited	No
Children	C-yes	C-ltd	C-no
Pets	P-yes	P-ltd	P-no
Smoking	S-yes	S-ltd	S-no

Handicap Accessibility

Because many inns are housed in old buildings, access for handicapped persons in many cases is limited. Where this information is available, we have noted it in the same line as limitations on children, pets and smoking. Be sure to confirm your exact requirements when you book.

Big City

In many big cities there are very few small, intimate accommodations. We have searched out as many as possible. We strongly advise you to investigate the guest house alternative, which can provide you with anything from penthouse in New York to your own quiet quarters with a private enterance in the suburbs. See our RSO listings at back of the book.

Farms

Many B&Bs are located in a rural environment, some on working farms. We have provided a partial list of farm vacation experiences.What a restorative for the city-weary. They can make a great family vacation—just be sure to keep a close eye on the kids around farm equipment.

Bathrooms

Though shared baths are the norm in Europe, this is sometimes a touchy subject in the U.S.A. We list the number of private baths available directly next to the number of rooms. Bear in mind that those inns with shared baths generally have more than one.

Manners

Please keep in mind when you go to an inn that innkeeping is a very hard job. It is amazing that innkeepers manage to maintain such a thoroughly cheerful and delightful presence despite the long hours. Do feel free to ask your innkeeper for help or suggestions, but please don't expect him to be your personal servant. You may have to carry your own bags.

When in accommodations with shared baths, be sure to straighten the bathroom as a courtesy to your fellow guests. If you come in late, please do so on tiptoe, mindful of the many other patrons visiting the inn for a little R 'n'R.

Lastly, when in the country, take nothing but photographs and leave nothing but footprints.

Sample Bed & Breakfast listing

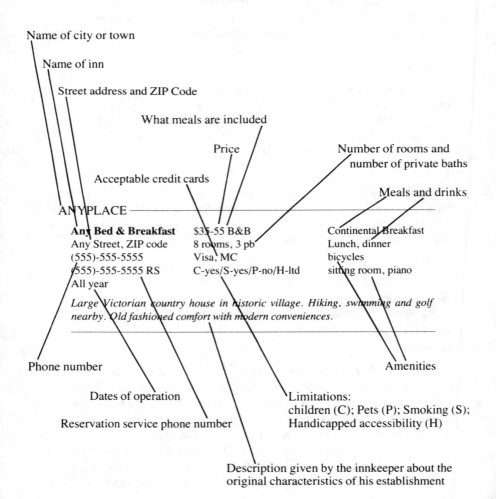

Name of city or town

Name of inn

Street address and ZIP Code

What meals are included

Price

Number of rooms and number of private baths

Acceptable credit cards

Meals and drinks

ANYPLACE ——————————————————————

Any Bed & Breakfast $35-55 B&B   Continental Breakfast
Any Street, ZIP code   8 rooms, 3 pb   Lunch, dinner
(555)-555-5555   Visa, MC   bicycles
(555)-555-5555 RS   C-yes/S-yes/P-no/H-ltd   sitting room, piano
All year

Large Victorian country house in historic village. Hiking, swimming and golf nearby. Old fashioned comfort with modern conveniences.

——————————————————————

Phone number

Amenities

Dates of operation

Limitations:
children (C); Pets (P); Smoking (S);
Handicapped accessibility (H)

Reservation service phone number

Description given by the innkeeper about the original characteristics of his establishment

Introdución

Hasta muy poco tiempo, era raro encontrar en Estados Unidos posadas que ofrecieran cama y desayuno. Los viajeros no tenían otra posibilidad que arreglarse con hoteles o moteles. Pero esto ha cambiado dramáticamente en unos pocos años gracias a la proliferación de una nuevo tipo de alojamiento. Hoy en día las posadas con cama y desayuno se encuentran en todos los estados y se han convertido en verdaderas alternativas a las cadenas moteleras para automovilistas o al hotel céntrico con sus cientos de cubículos.

Las posadas norteamericanas tienan sus raíces en Europa e Inglaterra. Un ejemplo es el Zimmer frei alemán, casi siempre consistente en un cuarto con desayuno. Su pariente más conocido en Inglaterra es la casa particular con el letrero *Bed & Breakfast* en la ventana. La versión americana ha ensanchado esta tradición hospitalaria mediante la inclusión de fondas y hoteles pequeños.

El crecimiento y la popularidad de estas posadas se debe también a otros factores: el deseo de escapar de la rutina y la monotonía de la vida en la ciudad, el querer darse el gusto durante unos días, y también el afán de alojarse en un sitio donde es posible conocer a los otros huéspedes y hacer nuevos amigos.

Las casas viejas restauradas y convertidas en posadas con dormitorios y servicio de desayuno dan repuesta a esas necesidades. A menudo estas casas se encuentran en zonas rurales y los dueños se encargan de todas las tareas. No hay sirvientes de uniforme, los huéspedes son contados, y el cuarto de recibo es centro de encuentros y conversaciones. Para el viajero es como una segunda casa.

Hasta ahora hacía falta un libro que reuniera tanta información sobre estas posadas como fuera posible. Eso se ha remediado con la copia que tiene usted en sus manos.

—*Richard Paoli,*
Editor
Sección de Viajes
del periódico
San Francisco Examiner

Como utilazar esta guía

Este libro está organizado alfabéticamente por estado y, dentro del estado, alfabéticamente por ciudad o pueblo. Primero aparecen las posadas. A continuación de la lista de las posadas para los estados hay una lista de las organizaciones encargadas del servicio de reservas para cada estado.

Consulte la tabla de materias para encontrar nuestros listados especiales, las recetas y las otras secciones, incluyendo una lista de mesoneros que hablan lenguas extranjeras.

Tres clases de alojamente

Inn (Posada): "Una casa para el hospedaje y el etretenimiento del viajero." Todas las posadas de este libro se ajustan a esta descripción. Muchas también ofrecen comidas, o por lo menos el desayuno; otras no. Se incluyen posadas con menos de treinte cuartos.

Bed & Breakfast (Cama y Desayuno): Puede ser una casa de tres o más cuartos, o una mansión con ocho o nueve dormitorios y servicio de desayuno.

Guest Houses (Casas de Huéspedes): Se trata de una casa particular que da hospedaje a los viajeros. En algunos casos puede uno comunicarse con ellas directamente, pero en la mayoría es necesario hacerlo a través del servicio de reservaciones. Esto se detalla más adelante.

Desayunos

La clase de desayuno que se sirve en cada caso viene indicada en el ángulo superior derecho del listado:

El **Full Breakfast** (desayuno completo) es un desayuno que incluye huevos y/o carne así como pan, tostadas, jugo y café.

El **Continental Breakfast** (desayuno continental) consiste de café, jugo, pan o pasteles.

El **Continental Plus** (desayuno continental plus) tiene café, jugo, y un surtido de panes, pasteles y en ocasiones algunas cosas más.

En la parte superior de la columna central, al lado del precio del quarto, se indica si el precio del desayuno está *incluido*.

Comidas

Debajo de la información sobre las desayunos, en la parte superior de la columna derecha, se explica si la posada o casa de huéspedes ofrece otras comidas además del desayuno. Por lo general, las posadas que no ofrecen de comer están ubicadas en la proximidad de varios restaurantes.

¿Qué hay de beber?

Para saber si la posada tiene bar, fíjese en la misma línea de las comidas, o sea en el ángulo superior de la columna derecha. Las posadas que no tienen licencia para servir vinos casi siempre están despuestas a enfriar las botellas de los huéspedes y proveer los servicios de mesa necesarios.

Precios

Los precios de los cuartos se indican en la parte superior de la columna central. Estos son precios suministrados por los mesoneros y sirven de guía para comparar establecimientos, pero pueden cambiar. Generalmente, cuando no se especifica, el precio más bajo se refiere a un cuarto sencillo confortable, y el más alto al mejor cuarto doble. Cuando se da un precio solamente, puede usted suponer que se refiere a un cuarto doble corriente.

Junto al precio se ofrece, cuando es posible, la información sobre los términos de los servicios de comida, de acuerdo con lo siguiente:

B&B (Cama y Desayuno): El desayuno está incluído en el precio. La clase de desayuno se indica en la parte superior de la columna derecha.

EP (Plan Europeo): No se ofrecen comidas.

MAP (Plan Americano Modificado): Incluye desayuno y cena.

AP (Plan Americano): Incluye las tres comidas.

Verifique los precios y la clase de servicios en el momento de hacer las reservaciones.

Reservaciones

Las reservaciones son indispensables en casi todas las posadas, especialmente durante la temporada. Para evitar desilusiones, haga sus reservas aunque sólo se trata de unas cuantas horas por adelantado.

Organizaciones para el Servicio de Reservas

Estos negocios permiten reservar un cuarto en cualquiera de miles de casas particulares. Los procedimientos varían. Algunas organizaciones se encargan sólo de una ciudad o estado; otras, de todo el país. Hay quienes requieren una pequeña cuota de socio. Otras venden la lista de las casas hospederas. Muchas tratarán de encontrarle exactamente el lugar que usted busca y se les puede pagar directamente por el alojamente.

Estas organizaciones funcionan por lo general durante las horas de servicio público de acuerdo con los usos horarios. Hemos obtenido tanta información como fue posible sobre estos servicios. Al terminar la guía se halla una lista de las organizaciones para el servicio de reservas (RSO).

Los niños, los animales domésticos y los cigarrillos

Los niños, los animales domésticos y los cigarrillos son motivo de dificultades especiales para muchas posadas. Las limitaciones y las restricciones se indican en la parte inferior de la columna central de la manera siguiente:

	Sí	Limitados	No
Niños	C-yes	C-ltd	C-no
Animales domésticos	P-yes	P-ltd	P-no
Fumar	S-yes	S-ltd	S-no
Minusválidos	H-yes	H-ltd	

Modales

Cuando se aloje en una posada tenga en cuenta el trabajo que representa ese negocio. Es sorprendente que a pesar de trabajar largas horas los dueños de las posadas siempre tienen una disposición entusiasta y amigable. No dude en pedirles ayuda o sugerencias pero no espere que sean sus criados personales. Es posible que usted mismo tenga que acarrear su equipaje.

Si comparte el uso de un baño, déjelo limpio para la persona siguiente. Si regresa tarde a la posada, entre sin molestar a los demás. Por último, cuando esté en el campo, no se lleve más recuerdos que sus fotografías y no deje más rastros que sus huellas.

¿Qué le aguarda?

Una experiencia agradable. Un restaurativo para cuerpo y alma. Una oportunidad de hacer nuevos amigos en un ambiente propicio. Una ocasión para estar solos, los dos, en un retiro romántico. Las posadas ofrecen todo eso y mucho más. ¡Diviértase!

Esta guía es para ustedes…

Familias que salende vacaciones en un ambiente de descanso sin formalidades.

Visitantes extranjeros que quierien descubrir los *verdaderos* Estados Unidos.

Parejas que salen pasar el fin de semana juntos

Escápense a gozar la belleza del campo

Comerciantes viajeros que desean pasar un rato apacible después de trabajar todo el día

Gente jubilada que desea explorar el continente, bien sea en plan de lujo o módicamente

Ejemplo de una entrada para las posadas con cama & desayuno

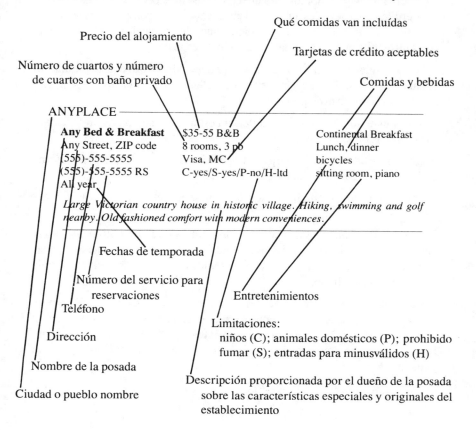

Qué comidas van incluídas

Precio del alojamiento

Tarjetas de crédito aceptables

Número de cuartos y número de cuartos con baño privado

Comidas y bebidas

ANYPLACE

Any Bed & Breakfast
Any Street, ZIP code
(555)-555-5555
(555)-555-5555 RS
All year

$35-55 B&B
8 rooms, 3 pb
Visa, MC
C-yes/S-yes/P-no/H-ltd

Continental Breakfast
Lunch, dinner
bicycles
sitting room, piano

Large Victorian country house in historic village. Hiking, swimming and golf nearby. Old fashioned comfort with modern conveniences.

Fechas de temporada

Número del servicio para reservaciones

Entretenimientos

Teléfono

Limitaciones:
    niños (C); animales domésticos (P); prohibido
    fumar (S); entradas para minusválidos (H)

Dirección

Nombre de la posada

Descripción proporcionada por el dueño de la posada
    sobre las características especiales y originales del
    establecimiento

Ciudad o pueblo nombre

Introduction

Il n'y a encore pas si longtemps, les auberges avec lit et petit déjeuner étaient trés rares aux Etats-Unis. Les voyageurs devaient aller à l'hotel du au motel. Il n'y avait pas le choix.

Mais, depuis quelques années, tout cela a changé, et on peut dire, d'une façon dramatique. Le nombre des auberges avec lit et petit déjeuner a explosé. Aujourd'hui on trouve ces auberges dans chaque état et souvent dans les villes; elles sont devenues une alternative bienvenue à la chaine de motel ou à l'hotel du centre-ville avec ses centaines de petites cages.

Les auberges américaines avec lit et petit déjeuner ont des cousins similaires et plus agés en Europe. Le Zimmer frei en Allemagne, par exemple, généralement une chambre avec petit déjeuner.

Son cousin mieux connu en Angleterra est une maison privée avec la pancarte *Bed & Breakfast* à la fenêtre.

La version américaine a élargi cette tradition d'offrir l'hospitalité dans une maison privée en petites auberges et hotels.

D'autres facteurs ont influencé la croissance et la popularité de ces auberges:

Le désir d'échapper à la routine quotidienne et à la monotonie de la vie citadine; le désir de se laisser choyer pendant quelques jours; et aussi le désir de rester dans un endroit précis avec le temps de se faire de nouveaux amis parmi les autres clients.

Les vieilles demeures restaurées en auberges avec lit et petit déjeuner répondent à ces désirs. Elles se trouvent souvent à la campagne, les aubergistes font le service—pas tout un personnel avec etiquette; et la salle commune est un lieu de rencontre pour les quelques clients. Ils sont à la maison, loin de la maison.

On aurait du depuis longtemps faire l'effort d'assembler en un livre le plus d'information possible sur le plus grand nombre d'auberges possible.

Nous l'avons fait, vous avez dans les mains un exemplaire du résultat.

—Richard Paoli,
Editeur des voyages
San Francisco Examiner

Comment utiliser ce guide

Organisation

Ce livre est organisé en ordre alphabétique par état, et à l'intérieur de chaque état, en ordre alphabétique pour les villes.

Regardez dans la table des matières nos listes spéciales, recettes, particularités, y compris la liste des aubergistes qui parlent les langues étrangères.

Trois genres d'accomodation

Inns (Les auberges): "Maison qui héberge et distrait le voyageur." Toutes les auberges listées dans ce livre répondent à cette description. Certaines servent les repas, au moins le petit déjeuner, d'autres ne le font pas. Listées sont les auberges qui ont trente chambres maximum.

Bed & Breakfast (Lit et petit déjeuner): Peut être une maison avec trois ou quatre chambres, ou, plus certainement, une large demeure ou hotel particulier avec huit ou neuf chambres d'amis qui sert le petit déjeuner le matin.

Guest Houses (Maisons d'amis): Maisons privées qui acceuillent le voyageur. Vous pouvez prendre contact directement avec certaines d'entre elles, mais la plupart du temps, il faut passer par l'agence de réservation. On reparlera de ça plus tard.

Les petits déjeuners

Le choix des différents petits déjeuners se trouve en haut et à droite de la liste.

Par **full breakfast** (petit déjeuner complet), nous entendons un repas, style anglais, avec oeufs, avec ou sans viande, en plus du pain, toasts, jus de fruit et café habituels.

Continental breakfast (petit déjeuner continental) veut dire café, jus de fruit, pain ou gateau.

Continental plus consiste de café, jus de fruit et le choix de plusieurs pains et patisseries, peut-être plus encore.

Vous trouverez si le petit déjeuner est inclu dans le prix de la chambre dans la colonne du milieu, à coté du prix de la chambre.

Les repas

La possibilité de prende les autres repas à l'auberge ou maison d'amis est listée en haut dans la colonne de droite, juste sous la liste des petits déjeuners. Les auberges qui ne servent pas de repas se trouvent souvent à proximité de restaurants variés.

Peut-on boire quelque chose?

La présence d'un bar est notée sur la même ligne que les repas en haut dans la colonne de droite. Les auberges qui ne servent pas d'alcool vous refroidiront quand-même vos bouteilles et vous procureront verres, glace, sodas et autres, à la demande.

Les prix

Le prix des chambres est listé en haut dans la colonne du milieu. Les prix donnés par les aubergistes servent de réference pour comparer les établissements, mais ils peuvent changer. Généralement, le prix le plus bas est pour une chambre simple, confortable, et le plus haut prix pour la meilleure chambre à deux. Quand il n'y a qu'un prix, c'est pour une chambre à deux, moyenne. Les renseignements au sujet des repas servis se trouvent à côté du prix.

B&B (lit et petit déjeuner): Petit déjeuner inclu dans le prix, décrit en haut dans la colonne de droite.

EP (plan européen): Pas de repas.

MAP (plan américain modifié): Petit déjeuner et diner compris.

AP (plan américain): Trois repas compris.

Confirmez les prix et services quand vous faites vos réservations.

Réservations

Les réservations sont nécessaires dans la plupart des auberges, surtout en pleine saison, et elles sont bien apprèciées entre saison.

Réservez quelques heures d'avance pour eviter toute déception.

Les agences de réservation

Agences par lesquelles vous pouvez réserver une chambre dans des milliers de maisons privées. Elles ne fonctionnent pas toutes de la même façon: Certaines représentent une seule ville, ou un seul état, d'autres servent tout le pays. Certaines demandent une petit somme pour faire partie de leur organisation, d'autres vendent la liste de leurs maisons d'acceuil. La plupart essayera de vous trouver juste le genre d'arrangement que vous cherchez et vous pouvez y payer votre pension directement.

Ces agences fonctionnent aux heures de travail régulières dans leur zone horaire. Nous avons receuilli autant d'information possible sur ces agences.

Enfants—Animaux—Fumeurs

Les enfants, animaux, fumeurs présentent certains problèmes pour un grand nombre d'auberges. S'ils sont limités ou exclus, nous l'avons noté en bas, dans la colonne du milieu.

	Oui	Limité	Non
Enfants	C-yes	C-ltd	C-no
Animaux	P-yes	P-ltd	P-no
Fumeurs	S-yes	S-ltd	S-no
Handicappés	H-yes	H-ltd	

Savoir-vivre

N'oubliez pas quand vous allez dans une auberge, que le métier d'aubergiste est très difficile. Il est remarquable que les aubergistes arrivent à maintenir une atmosphère réconfortante et agréable malgré leurs longues heures de travail. Votre aubergiste est là pour vous aider et répondre à vos questions, mais, s'il vous plait, ne leur demandez pas d'être votre valet. Vous aurez peut-être à porter vos propres bagages.

Quand vous partagez une salle de bain, laissez la en ordre, par considération pour les autres pensionnaires. Si vous rentrez tard, faites le sur la pointe des pieds s'il vous plait, par égard pour les clients venus à l'auberge pour se reposer.

Enfin, quand vous êtes à la campagne, ne prenez que des photos et ne laissez que l'empriente de vous souliers.

A quoi peut-on s'attendre?

A une expérience très agréable. Un réconstituant pour le corps et l'âme. Une occasion de se faire de nouveaux amis dans une atmosphère chaude et décontractée. La chance d'être seuls, juste vous deux, en séclusion romantique. Les auberges peuvent vous procurer tout cela et plus encore. Amusez-vous bien!

Ce guide est pour vous…

Couples qui veulent passer un week-end ensemble

S'évader pour admirer la beauté de la campagne,

Hommes d'affaire qui voyagent et voudraient un peu de chaleur et d'amitié après une dure journée de travail.

Retraités qui explorent le continent en luxe ou en budget limité.

Familles qui veulent prendre leur vacances dans une atmosphère décontractée et famille.

Visiteurs étrangers qui explorent la vraie amérique —

Mode d'emploi

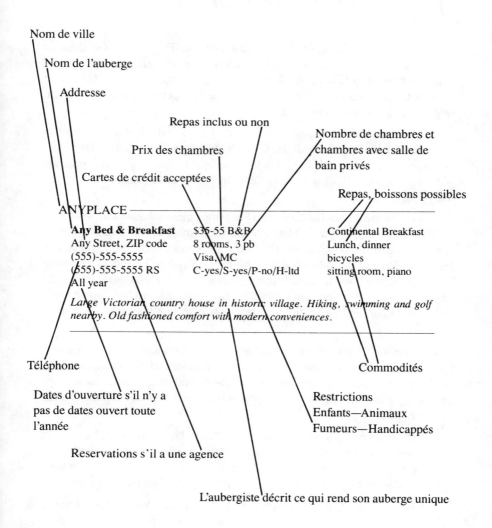

Nom de ville

Nom de l'auberge

Addresse

Repas inclus ou non

Prix des chambres

Nombre de chambres et chambres avec salle de bain privés

Cartes de crédit acceptées

Repas, boissons possibles

ANYPLACE

Any Bed & Breakfast $35-55 B&B   Continental Breakfast
Any Street, ZIP code   8 rooms, 3 pb   Lunch, dinner
(555)-555-5555   Visa, MC   bicycles
(555)-555-5555 RS   C-yes/S-yes/P-no/H-ltd   sitting room, piano
All year

Large Victorian country house in historic village. Hiking, swimming and golf nearby. Old fashioned comfort with modern conveniences.

Téléphone

Commodités

Dates d'ouverture s'il n'y a pas de dates ouvert toute l'année

Restrictions
Enfants—Animaux
Fumeurs—Handicappés

Reservations s'il a une agence

L'aubergiste décrit ce qui rend son auberge unique

Vorwort

Es ist noch nicht lange her, das "Zimmer-mit-Frühstück" Gasthöfe in Amerika eine Rarität waren. Der Reisende musste sich mit einem Hotel oder Motel zufrieden geben, ohne Alternative. Es gab nur eine handvoll Gasthöfe mit Bett und Frühstücksmöglichkeit, und die in abgelegenen Gegenden von Neu-England und Kalifornien.

Jedoch in den letzten paar Jahren hat sich das auf dramatische Weise verändert. Bett-und-Frühstücks-Gasthöfe tauchten überall auf. Man findet sie heute in allen Staaten, und oft in Grosstädten. Sie bieten eine erfrischende Alternative zu den Reihenzimmern der Motels oder zu den langen Korridoren der Hotels.

Die amerikanischen Gasthöfe, die Frühstück bieten, haben ihre Vorläufer in England und Europa. In Deutschland sieht man zum Beispiel "Zimmer frei", was gewöhnlich Bett und Frühstück bedeutet. Noch bekannter ist das Schild "Bed and Breakfast" im Fenster der englischen Privathäuser. Gäste schlafen für eine bescheidene Summe in dem extra Schlafzimmer und essen morgens mit der Familie zum Frühstück. In der amerikanischen Fassung sind nicht nur Familienhäuser einbegriffen, sondern auch Gasthöfe und kleine Hotels.

Der Zuwuchs an Bett-und Frühstücks-Unterkunft schuldet seine Beliebtheit auch unserem Verlangen, vom Einerlei des Stadtlebens fortzukommen, sich ein paar Tage lang verwöhnen zu lassen, und andererseits auch lange genug am gleichen Ort zu sein, um mit den anderen Gästen Bekanntschaften anzuknüpfen.

Die restaurierten, älteren Häuser, die "Bett-und-Frühstück" Gasthöfe geworden sind, entsprechen diesem Verlangen. Dort ist ein freundlicher Gastwirt zur hand — keine "Bedienung" mit Namensschildern. In dem grossen Zimmer treffen sich die paar Gäste und machen es sich gemütlich.

Es ist höchste Zeit, sich daran zu machen, ein Verzeichnis solcher Herbergen, und was sie bieten, in einem Band zusammenzufassen. Sie halten das Ergebnis in Ihrer Hand.

—Richard Paoli,
Reise-Redakteur des
San Francisco Examiner

Hinweise Zum Gebrauch Dieses Reiseführers

Gliederung des Verzeichnisses:

Die staaten sind alphabetisch verzeichnet, und die Orte innerhalb der einzelnen Staaten sin ebenfalls alphabetisch angegeben. Gasthöfe werden zuerst angegeben.

Unser Inhaltsverzeichnis weist Sie auch auf andere Sonderartikel hin, zum Beispiel auf die Sammlung von Rezepten. Oder das Verzeichnis fremdsprachiger Gastwirte.

Drei Arten von Unterkunft:

Inns (Gasthaus): Websters Englisches Wörterbuch gibt als Bedeutung an: "Ein Haus zur Unterkunft und Unterhaltung Reisender". Alle Gasthöfe im Verzeichnis fallen in diese Gruppe, und die meisten bieten auch Mahlzeiten, zumindest Frühstück. Ein paar haben keine Verpflegung. Nur Gasthäuser mit höchstens 30 Zimmern sind mit einbegriffen.

Bed & Breakfast (Bett und Frühstück): Manchmal ist das ein Familien-Haus mit 3 oder 4 Zimmern zu vermieten, aber meist handelt es sich hier um ein grosses Haus oder eine Villa mit 8 oder 9 Unterkünften für Gäste, und Frühstück wird dort morgens serviert.

Guest Houses (Privatunterkunft): Es handelt sich hier um Logier bei Privatleuten. An einige kann man sich direkt wenden, aber die meisten werden durch Buchungsagenturen vermittelt. Mehr davon später.

Das Frühstück

Was für ein Frühstück serviert wird, ersehen Sie aus der Angabe rechts oben in der jeweiligen Anzeige.

Full Breakfast ist Frühstück auf Englische Art mit Eiern und/oder Fleisch sowie das übliche Brot, Toast, Saft und Kaffee.

Continental Breakfast besteht aus Kaffee, Saft, und Brot oder andere Backwaren.

Continental Plus beitet zum Frühstück Kaffee, Saft, und eine Auswahl von mehreren Sorten Brot und anderem Gebäck, und manchmal noch weiteres.

Ob das Frühstück im Preis für das Zimmer mit einbeschlossen ist, geht aus der obersten Mittelsparte gleich neben dem Preis für das Zimmer hervor.

Andere Mahlzeiten:

Ob es auch andere Mahlzeiten dort gibt, ersehen Sie unter der Auskunft übers Frühstück oben in der rechten Spalte. Denken Sie bitte daran, dass Gasthäuser, in denen es kein Essen gibt, gewöhnlich in unmittelbarer Nähe von mehreren Gaststätten liegen.

Gibt's was zu trinken?

Bars sind in der gleichen Rubrik wie Mahlzeiten angebracht, rechts oben. Sollte Ihre Gastwirtschaft nicht zum Verkauf von Spirituosen zugelassen sein, stellen sie Ihnen Ihre Getränke doch kalt und geben auch Bestellungen für Sie auf.

Preise:

Wie teuer ist es? Die Zimmerpreise, die in der ersten Reihe der Mittlesparte angegeben sind, wurden uns von den Gastwirten als Richtlinien für Vergleichszwecke angegeben, und können sich verändern. Wo nicht anders vermerkt, ist der niedrigere Preis für ein bequemes Einzelquartier, und der höchste für das beste Zimmer für zwei. Ist nur ein Preis angegeben, nehmen Sie ruhig an, dass er für ein Doppelzimmer ist.

Neben dem Zimmerpreis in der Mittelsparte geben wir Auskunft über die Mahlzeiten, und inwiefern sie im Zimmerpreis einbegriffen sind.

B&B (Bett und Frühstück): Frühstück ist im Zimmerpreis einbeschlossen. Art des Frühstücks, oben rechts verzeichnet.

EP (Europäischer Plan): Keine Mahlzeiten einbegriffen.

MAP (Modifizierter Amerikanischer Plan): Frühstück und Abendbrot sind einbegriffen.

AP (Amerikanischer Plan): Alle drei Mahlzeiten sind im Preis einbegriffen.

Bitter vergewissern Sie sich der laufenden Preise beim Buchen.

Vorherbestellung

Die meisten Gastwirte oder ihre Agenturen verlangen, dass man weit voraus bucht, besonders während der Hochsaison, und auch zu anderen Zeiten wird das geschätzt.

Machen Sie unbedingt Vorherbestellung, selbst wenn es nur ein paar Stunden vor geplanter Ankunft ist, um sich spätere Enttäuschung zu sparen. Wir haben die Gastwirte auf erfrischende Weise hilfsbereit gefunden; also zögern Sie nicht, sich beim Buchen nochmals nach laufenden Preisen und gebotenen Bequemlichkeiten zu erkundigen.

Wenn man zu spät ankommt—Die meisten Gästehäuser erwarten Sie vor 18 Uhr. Bitte telefonieren Sie, wenn Sie nach 18 Uhr ankommen werden. In manchen Fällen wird eine Anzahlung oder Vorherbezahlung verlangt.

Buchungsdienstvereine (Reservation Service Organizations):

Durch die RSO-Büros können Sie ein Zimmer in tausenden von Angeboten mieten. Manche RSO-Büros vertreten einen ganzen Staat, oder eine Stadt. Andere haben Verbindugen über ganz Amerika. Manche verkaufen ein Verzeichnis der Gästhäuser. Wieder andere versuchen, genau das Passende für Sie su finden, und Sie zahlen dann die Zimmergebühr direkt an das RSO-Büro.

Die meisten RSO-Büros sind nur zur üblichen Geschäftszeit ihrer Gegend zu erreichen. Wir haben so viel wie möglich über die RSO-Büros erkundschaftet.

Am Ende des Reiseführers verzeichnen wir auch die RSO-Büros, die Verbindungen über ganz Amerika haben, sowie internationale RSO-Büros.

Kinder, Haustiere und Rauchen:

Kinder, Haustiere und Rauchen sind nicht überall gestattet. Wo sie beschränkt zugelassen (ltd.) oder verboten (no) sind, wird das im unteren Teil der Mittelspalte folgenderweise vermerkt:

	Ja	Beschränkt	Verboten
Kinder	C-yes	C-ltd	C-no
Haustiere	P-yes	P-ltd	P-no
Rauchen	S-yes	S-ltd	S-no

Bemerkung

Soweit wir zur Zeit des Buchdrucks wissen, sind alle Angaben hierin richtig. Preisänderungen sind jedoch vorbehalten. Wir sind auch nicht für Fehler oder unvollständige Angaben verantwort lich, noch für Anderungen in den Angaben oder für ihre grundsätzliche Zuverlässigkeit.

Die Angaben, die wir hier zusammengestellt haben, kommen von verschiedenen Quellen, aber hauptsächlich von den Gastwirten, und auch von persönlicher Kenntnis und von der Empfehlung zuverlässiger Bekannter.

Benehmen:

Bitte denken Sie daran, wenn Sie in einer Gaststätte einkehren, dass der Gastwirt einen schwierigen Berauf hat. Es ist erstaunlich, dass Gastwirte trotz der langen Arbeitszeit so wohlgemut und heiter sind. Sie geben gern Rat oder Hilfe, aber erwarten Sie bitte keinen Diener. Man muss möglicherweise sein eigenes Gepäck tragen. Bei geteiltem Bad verlangt es die Höflichkeit, nach sich aufzuräumen. Wenn Sie spät nachts ankommen, nehmen Sie bitte auf die schlafenden Gäste Rücksicht, die ihre Ruhe haben wollen.

Wenn Sie auf dem Land sind, nehmen Sie bitte nichts als nur Bilder, und hinterlassen Sie nichts weiter als Ihre Fusspur.

Was erwartet uns?

Ein herrliches Erlebnis. Ein Wiederaufleben des Körpers und der Seele. Die Gelegenheit, in entspannter, herzlicher Atmosphere neue Freundschaften anzuschliessen. Die Chance, allein zu sein, oder allein zu zweit, in romantischer Zurückgezogenheit.

Erläuterung der Eintragungen der Unterkunfsstätte

Name der Stadt oder Ortschaft
Name der Unterkunft
Adresse
Welche Kreditkarten akzeptiert werden

Preis für die Unterkunft, und welche Mahlzeiten im Preis einbegriffen sind
Anzahl der Zimmer, und wieviel mit eigenem Badezimmer (=pb)

Was für ein Frühstück?

ANYPLACE

Any Bed & Breakfast
Any Street, ZIP code
(555)-555-5555
(555)-555-5555 RS
All year

$35-55 B&B
8 rooms, 3 pb
Visa, MC
C-yes/S-yes/P-no/H-ltd

Continental Breakfast
Lunch, dinner
bicycles
sitting room, piano

Large Victorian country house in historic village. Hiking, swimming and golf nearby. Old fashioned comfort with modern conveniences.

Telefon-Nummer
Nummer der zuständigen Buchungsagentur

Zu welcher Jahreszeit offen?

Beschreibung des Gastwirts, was an diesem Gästehaus einmalig oder besonders bemerkenswert ist

Andere Mahlzeiten und Bars

Was gibt's sonst noch?

Beschränkungen in Bezug auf Kinder, Haustiere, Rauchen, oder für Behinderte geeignet (yes=ja; ltd=beschränkt; no=nicht zugelassen)

はじめに

　日本の国では昔から、旅館や民宿といった食事付の宿が数多くありますが、長い間アメリカには、泊まるだけのホテルかモーテルしかなく、食事付の宿は、ニューイングランド地方の田舎と、カリフォルニア州にほんのいくつか在っただけでした。

　アメリカではこの食事付の宿を、"ベットに朝食付のイン"（Bed ＆ Breakfast Inn）と呼んでいます。このタイプのインは、ここ数年の間に急激に増加して、今日ではアメリカの至る所に見られるようになり、都会のホテルやモーテルチェーンに並ぶものになりました。

　アメリカの"ベットに朝食付のイン"は、ヨーロッパのそれとよく似ています。例えば、ドイツのチマフライ（The Zimmer Frei）は、一部屋に朝食付ですし、英国の場合は、"ベットと朝食"（Bed & Breakfast）という看板が、民家の窓に出ています。旅行者は、安い宿賃を払って、客室で眠むり、翌朝、その家の人達と共に朝食を食べるのです。アメリカの"ベットに朝食付のイン"とは、こういった民宿タイプに、小さなインやホテルまで含まれたものだと解釈して下さい。

　毎日の仕事や都会の生活の単調さから解放されたい、二、三日ゆったりと優雅にくつろぎたい、そんな環境の中で新しい友人に出会えたら、などの人々の欲求が、このタイプのインの人気と増加に大きな影響を与えました。今やインキーパーとなった民家の主人は、その居間を一握りのお客達が楽しく集まれる場所にしようと自ら世話をするので、そこには家庭を離れた家庭の暖かい雰囲気が流れます。

　この"ベットに朝食付のイン"について、可能な限りの情報を収めた一冊の本が、待望の末に出版されました。

　その努力の成果が、今、貴方の手に握られているのです。

サンフランシスコ・エグザミナー新聞社
旅行編集部主任
リチァード・パオリ

ガイドブックの使い方

内 容

　アルファベット順に各州について記載され、州内においても同様に、各都市或いは町について載っています。

　更に、特製のリストには、外国語を話すインキーパーの名簿や、食事内容、その他の特色などが載っていますから、目次の項目を見て確かめて下さい。

三つのタイプ別宿泊設備

　Inn（イン）: 辞書によると、インとは"旅行者をもてなし、泊める家"とあります。例外を除いては、普通朝食と夕食付で、客室の数はおよそ30室以内です。

　Bed & Breakfast（ベットと朝食）: 3部屋以上の家から10室近くの客室設備のある大きな家などで、略してB & Bと呼ばれ朝食付です。

　Gest Houses（ゲストハウス）: 旅行者歓迎の個人宅で、そのほとんどがRSOを通して予約を受け付けますが、なかには旅行者が直接予約をする所もあります。

朝 食

　提供される朝食のタイプは、リストの右上の角に記載されています。

　Full Breakfast（フル・ブレックファスト）: 卵とハムかソーセージかベーコンに、パンとトーストとジュースとコーヒーが出されます。

　Continental Breakfast（コンチネンタル・ブレックファスト）: コーヒーとジュースに、パンかペストリーのどちらかを選びます。

　Continental Plus（コンチネンタル・プラス）: コーヒーとジュースに、何種類かあるパンとペストリーの中から好きな物を選び、その他にもおまけが付くかもしれないというブレックファストです。

　何れの朝食も、料金は中欄の一番上にある部屋代に含まれています。

昼食と夕食

　朝食以外の食事については、リストの右上の角にある朝食のタイプのすぐ下に記載されています。何も書いてない場合は、近くにいくつも良いレストランがあると思ってよいでしょう。

お酒は飲めるのでしょうか？

バーが有るときは、食事と同一の欄に記載してあります。無い場合でも普通は、ボトルを冷やしてくれたり、注文に応じて用意したりしてもらえます。

宿泊代

中欄の一番上にあるのが宿泊代です。金額は時々変化する事もあるので、他の所の宿泊代と比較して、宿を選ぶ時の目安にして下さい。金額の安い方は普通のシングルで、高い方は一番良いダブルです。一つしか金額が載っていない場合は、普通のダブルです。

宿泊代の右隣りにある略語は、食事のサービスについて意味しています。

B & B (Bed & Breakfast)：朝食付。朝食のタイプは右欄の上に記入されています。**EP (European Plan)**：食事無し。**MAP (Modified American Plan)**：朝食、夕食の二食付。**AP (American Plan)**：三食付。宿泊料金や食事のサービスについては、予約をする時に必ず確認して下さい。

リザベーション

予約は大抵のインで必要です。特にシーズン中は必ずするべきで、シーズン以外でもした方が喜ばれますし、後でがっかりしない為にも、少くとも数時間前までにすると良いと思います。その際に、料金やサービス、その他の詳細や特に要求したい事などを相談すると、インキーパーが気軽に応じてくれるでしょう。

遅く到着する場合：大抵のインは何の連絡も受けない時は、午後6時に予約を取り消しますから、前もって分っている場合は、インに電話をして知らせておいて下さい。

インの中には、予約金や前払いを要求する所もあります。

リザベーション・サービス・オーガニゼーション

旅行者の希望に応じてインを探し、部屋を予約する代理店です。通称、ＲＳＯと呼ばれ、限られた都市や州内だけで運営しているものから、全国に支店のあるものまで色々です。なかには、小額の入会金を必要としたり、インのリストを売ったりするＲＳＯもあり、又、宿泊代を直接Ｒ

ＳＯに支払う場合もあります。ＲＳＯの営業時間は、その地域時間の朝9時から午後5時ぐらいまでです。このガイドブックには、各州の終りの項にＲＳＯについてのインフォメーションがたくさん載っています。更に、一番最後の項には国内中にあるＲＳＯのリストと、外国旅行の時の為に国際的にも仕事をしているＲＳＯのリストが載せてあります。

子供とペットと喫煙について

多くのインにとってこの三つは難題です。もし、制限又は許可されない場合は、中欄の中程に、次の様に記入されています。

C —Children: 子供に制限有り、又は否。
P —Pets: ペットに制限有り、又は否。
S —Smoking: 喫煙に制限有り、又は否。

バスルーム

プライベートバス（浴室付部屋）の数を、中欄の二段目にある部屋数の隣りに記入しました。
例: 20 rooms, 18 P B（プライベートバス）。共同風呂は普通、複数以上あります。

注　解

このガイドブックの内容は、編集された1983年末の時点で正確ですが、料金、詳細等は、予告なしに変わる事がありますので御了承下さい。
収められたインフォメーションは、それぞれのインのインキーパーから集められただけでなく、信頼出来る人々からの知識や推薦などにもよりました。

マナー

インの運営というのは大変な仕事にも拘らず、キーパー達は何故あれ程長い間、いつも快活で愛嬌良くいられるのか、とても不思議です。インキーパーに援助を求めるのはもちろん自由ですが、彼らを召使いの様には思わないで下さい。自分の荷物は自分で持たなければならないかもしれません。
共同のバスルームを使った後は、次に使う人の事を思いやって、必ずきれいにしておいて下さい。夜遅くなってインに着いた時は、他のお客達の事を考えて、そーっと歩きましょう。

　最後に、田舎では写真以外は何もとらずに、足跡以外は何も残さない様にしましょう。

期待出来る事

　愉快至極な経験、心身のリフレッシュ、ゆったりした暖い雰囲気の中での新しい友人との出会い、一人になるチャンス、ロマンチックな土地に二人だけ。そして、もっともっと他にも。さあ、出発しましょう!!

各イン又はB & Bについて──記載事項の説明

　宿泊料とそれに含まれる食事

　部屋数と浴室付部屋数（P 6）

　使用できるクレジットカード

　子供（C）、喫煙（S）、ペット（P）の制限、又、身体障害者用の設備

　このイン又はB & Bのユニークな特徴に関する経営者の記述

　加えて、色々な地方への楽しいツアーを計画してみました。例としては、サンフランシスコとナッパヴァリー、古いニューイングランド地方、ロッキー山脈など、その他各地です。広大な自然を持つ素晴しいアメリカと、そこに生きる魅力的な人々に出会う素敵なチャンスです。詳細については、このガイドブック宛に、次の住所までお問い合わせ下さい。

P. O. Box. 20467, Oakland, California 94620-0467 U. S. A.

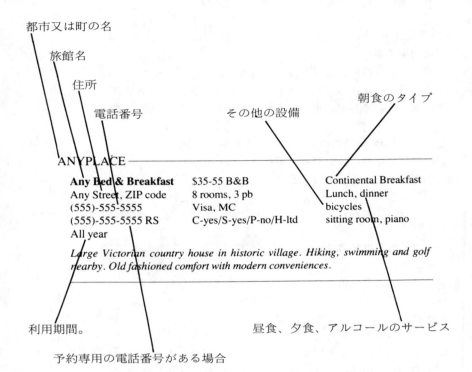

都市又は町の名

旅館名

住所

電話番号

その他の設備

朝食のタイプ

ANYPLACE ——————————————————————————————

Any Bed & Breakfast $35-55 B&B Continental Breakfast
Any Street, ZIP code 8 rooms, 3 pb Lunch, dinner
(555)-555-5555 Visa, MC   bicycles
(555)-555-5555 RS C-yes/S-yes/P-no/H-ltd sitting room, piano
All year

*Large Victorian country house in historic village. Hiking, swimming and golf
nearby. Old fashioned comfort with modern conveniences.*

——————————————————————————————

利用期間。

昼食、夕食、アルコールのサービス

予約専用の電話番号がある場合

Part II

Bed & Breakfast Inns

ALABAMA

MOBILE

Kraft Korner
90 Carlile Dr., 36619
(205)-666-6819

All year

$15/$20
2 rooms, 2 pb
none
C-yes/S-no/P-no

Full breakfast
Lunch, Dinner
piano
sitting room & library
games

We spoil folks, Southern style, in our quiet country home. 5 miles from I-10, 10 miles from Bellingrath Gardens.

SCOTTSBORO

The Brunton House
112 College Ave., 35768
(205)-259-1298

All year

$22.50-29.50
6 rooms, 0 pb

C-2 up/S-ltd/P-ltd/H-yes

Full breakfast
Complimentary tea, wine
bicycles
living room

Hospitality plus, excellent food. Country setting 2 blocks from Historic Square and 1st Monday Trade Days. YOU are our SPECIAL GUEST!

ALASKA

GUSTAVUS

Gustavus Inn
Box 31-B, 99826
(907)-697-3311
(907)-586-2006
April-October

$36 pp, AP
7 rooms, 0 pb
no
C-yes/S-ltd/P-ltd

Full breakfast
Lunch, tea, dinner, bar
bicycles

Your home in Glacier Bay features garden fresh produce and local seafood in a family-style homestead atmosphere.

JUNEAU ───────────────────────────────────

Mullins House $40-45 B&B Full breakfast
526 Seward St., 99801 4 rooms, 0 pb Complimentary wine
(907)-586-2959 sitting room
  C-yes/S-yes/P-no entertainment
All year

Old Miners home, redecorated in turn-of-the-century style in downtown Juneau. Complimentary sherry & cake each evening.

SKAGWAY ───────────────────────────────────

Skagway Inn $37.10-42.40 EP none
POB 192, 99840 15 rooms, 0 pb
(907)-983-2289 Visa, MC piano
  C-yes/S-yes/P-no/H-yes sitting room
All year

ARIZONA

CHANDLER ───────────────────────────────────

Cone's Tourist Home $26 Continental breakfast
2804 West Warmer, 85224 2 rooms, 1 pb
(602)-839-0369 no piano
  C-yes/S-yes/P-yes sitting room
Sept-June

Country living 18 miles from downtown Phoenix. Close to ASU, golf courses, & fine restaurants.

COCHISE ───────────────────────────────────

The Cochise Hotel $14-23 Full breakfast
Box 27, 85606 5 rooms, 5 pb Lunch, dinner
(602)-384-3156 sitting room
  C-yes/H-yes piano
All year

100 yr. old railroad hotel furnished in mostly original turn-of-the-century antiques. Built of thick adobe walls.

CORNVILLE ──

Point Willow $45-55 B&B   Brunch
POB 81, 86325   3 rooms, 0 pb   Dinner, wine
(602)-634-6152   no
                          C-no/S-yes/P-no

All year

Heart of Arizona on Oak Creek guest ranch house accented with antiques, full brunch included. 12 miles south of Sedona, Arizona.

FLAGSTAFF ──

Rainbow Ranch $20/person   Full breakfast
2860 N. Fremont, 86001   3 rooms, 0 pb   snacks
none   no   tennis courts
                          C-yes/S-yes/P-yes   sitting room

All year

Solar dried linens in a room with a view. Fresh eggs for breakfast and the Grand Canyon, too.

**Be sure to call the Inn to verify details and prices
and to make your reservation**

Copper Queen Hotel, Bisbee, Arizona

SEDONA

Garland's Oak Creek Lodge
POB 152, 86336
(602)-282-3343

Apr. 1—Nov. 15

$66-88 B&B
15 rooms, 15 pb
Visa, MC
C-yes/S-yes/P-no/H-ltd

Full breakfast
Dinner, bar
piano
sitting room

Rustic lodge, fruit orchards, Oak Creek, excellent food, homemade breads, fabulous soups — from our orchards, organic vegetable, and herb gardens.

TUCSON

Birdsall's
6750 Mamaronick, 85718
(602)-299-9242

Except August

$35/dbl B&B
2 rooms, 1 pb
no
C-yes/S-yes/P-no/H-yes

Full breakfast

piano

In beautiful desert foothills — many birds to watch — fine place to walk. Very quiet.

Myer's Blue Corn House
4215 E. Kilmer, 85711
(602)-327-4663

Closed in summer

$20-30 B&B
2 rooms, 0 pb
no
C-yes/S-no/P-yes

Full breakfast

bicycles
piano
sitting room

Myer's private home, yard for pets & children, breakfast, municipal golf & tennis, museums, shopping mall, city buses. Rooms quiet, clean, reasonable.

WICKENBURG

Kay El Bar Ranch
Rincon Rd., Box 2480,
85358
(602)-684-7593

Oct 15—May 15

$75-125 B&B
10 rooms, 10 pb
Visa, MC
C-yes/S-ltd/P-no/H-ltd

Full breakfast

Lunch, dinner, bar
swimming pool
piano
entertainment

Desert oasis w/grass, trees, flowers—scenic horseback rides included—National Historic Site w/old adobe buildings—excellent meals.

Our listings, supplied by the innkeeper, are as complete as possible. Many of the inns have more features — amenities or food and beverage service — than we list. Be sure to inquire when you book.

Fayetteville

Jonesboro

Fort Smith **Conway**

Little Rock

Hot Springs N.P.

ARKANSAS

El Dorado

EUREKA SPRINGS

Dairy Hollow House	$45-59 B&B	Continental breakfast
Rt. 2 Box 1, 72632	2 rooms, 2 pb	
(501)-253-7444	Visa, MC, AmEx	sitting room
	C-10 up/S-yes/P-no	

All year

Restored Ozark farmhouse in historic district. Antiques, flowers, great breakfasts, "Noveau'Zarks" French Country Dinners (by reservation, guests only).

Devon Cottage	$38-45 B&B	Full breakfast
26 Eureka St., 72632	2 rooms, 1 pb	
(501)-253-9169		
	C-yes/S-ok/P-no	

All year

Hilltop Edwardian cottage overlooking unique Victorian mountain village, surrounded by great natural beauty. Cheerful rooms furnished with antiques. Gourmet breakfast.

FORT SMITH

Merry Go Round Cottage	$25-35 B&B	Full breakfast
412 North 8th,	3 rooms, 1 pb	
(501)-783-3472	Visa, MC, AmEx	sitting room
(800)-643-2131	C-yes/S-yes/P-yes/H-yes	
All year		

Restored home, circa 1900, in Ft. Smith's Historic District. Across from restaurant famed for stained glass. Free stained glass manufacturing tour.

HELENA

Edwardian Inn	$45-50 B&B	Continental breakfast
317 Biscoe, 72342	12 rooms, 12 pb	Wine & cheese sometimes
	Visa, MC, AmEx	sitting room
	C-yes/S-yes/P-no	

All year

The Edwardian Inn offers twelve antique guest rooms, private bath and continental breakfast. Elegance and romance from the turn of the century.

HOT SPRINGS NP ───────────────────────────────

Williams House Inn
420 Quapaw St., 71901
(501)-624-4275
(800)-547-1463 RS
All year

$35-65 B&B
5 rooms, 3 pb
no
C-7 up/S-ltd/P-no

Full breakfast
Afternoon tea
sitting rooms
baby grand piano

Williams House shows Victorian flair for convenience and elegance. Your home away from home, nestled in Ouachita Mountains.

WASHINGTON ───────────────────────────────

The Old County Jail
POB 157, 71862
pay phone only
(501)-983-2178
All year (except 1/1-14)

$35-55 EP
6 rooms, 6 pb
no
C-no/S-yes/P-no

Full breakfast
Lunch, dinner
piano
parlor

Jail built in 1872, era is depicted throughout. In historic state park. Gourmet food. Reservations.

CALIFORNIA

ALAMEDA ───────────────────────────────

Garratt Mansion
900 Union St., 94510
(415)-521-4779

C-yes/S-no/P-no

All year

$45 dbl B&B
3 rooms, 0 pb

Full breakfast
Afternoon tea
bicycles
sitting room

An elegant Victorian in a quiet island community just 20 min. from downtown San Francisco offering personalized attention.

ALLEGHANY

Kenton Mine Lodge
P.O. Box 942, 95910
(916)-287-3212

$45 pp AP
25 rooms, 6 pb

C-yes/S-yes/P-no

Full breakfast
lunch, dinner, bar
gold panning, fishing
hiking, campfire

All year

Restored mining camp. Furnished in 1900 era, antiques, 3500 ft. elev., fishing, gold panning, hiking in the High Sierras.

AMADOR CITY

Mine House Inn
P.O. Box 226, 95601
(209)-267-5900

$45-55 B&B
8 rooms, 8 pb

C-yes/S-yes/P-no/H-yes

Continental breakfast

swimming pool

All year

Former Keystone Gold Mining Company office building, all rooms furnished in Victorian antiques. Relive a page from the gold rush days.

ANAHEIM

Anaheim Country Inn
856 S. Walnut, 92802
(714)-778-0150

$60-110 B&B
8 rooms, 1 pb
Visa, MC
C-12 up/S-ltd/P-no

Full breakfast
Complimentary tea, wine
hot tub
sitting room
organ

All year

Large historic house hear Disneyland—garden & trees, off street parking, antiques, warm homey atmosphere. Complimentary appetizers before dinner.

ANGWIN

Big Yellow Sunflower
235 Sky Oaks, 94508
(707)-965-3885

$65-105 B&B
1 room, 1 pb

C-6 up/S-ltd/P-ltd/H-yes

Full breakfast
Light supper
piano

All year

Secluded, spacious suite above Napa Valley. Private entrance, deck, bath, fireplace and kitchenette. Country cooking, charm and hospitality.

Forest Manor
415 Cold Spgs. Rd, 94508
(707)-965-3538

$65-115 B&B
4 rooms, 4 pb

C-no/S-no/P-no/H-yes

Continental plus
Tea, fruit basket
private jacuzzi in suite
sitting room, piano
bicycles

All year

Beautiful secluded 20 acre English Tudor forested estate in Napa Wine Country. Massive carved beams, fireplaces, decks, air-conditioned, game rooms.

APTOS

Apple Lane Inn
6265 Soquel Drive, 95003
(408)-475-6868

$60 B&B
4 rooms, 2 pb
Visa, MC
C-no/S-yes/P-no

Continental plus
Complimentary wine
sitting room, library
player piano
cider room

All year

Victorian farmhouse furnished with beautiful antiques offers country charm & seclusion, yet close to everything, including fine restaurants.

Mangels House
P.O. Box 302, 95003
(408)-688-7982

All year

$65-80 B&B
2 rooms, 0 pb

C-12 up/S-ltd

Continental plus
Complimentary wine
sitting room
piano

Country elegance in historic home. Gourmet breakfast served in your room or on the porch.

ARCATA

Plough and the Stars
1800 27th St., 95521
(707)-822-8236

All year

$32-60 B&B
5 rooms, 0 pb

C-no/S-yes/P-no/H-yes

Continental plus
Complimentary wine
sitting room, library

1860's farmhouse on two acres of pastoral grounds; casual, country atmosphere; first class hospitality.

ARROYO GRANDE

Rose Victorian Inn
789 Valley Rd., 93420
(805)-481-5566

All year

$60-80 B&B
6 rooms, 1 pb
Visa, AmEx
C-16 up/S-ltd/P-no/H-ltd

Full breakfast
Restaurant, bar
sitting room, piano

Majestic 98-year-old mansion; Pacific Ocean, sand dune views; gourmet breakfast of Eggs Benedict in crystal chandeliered dining room.

AVALON

Glenmore Plaza Hotel
120 Sumner Ave., 90704
(213)-510-0017

All year

$55-200 EP
26 rooms, 26 pb
Visa, MC, AmEx
C-yes/S-yes/P-no

whirlpool tub in room

Est. 1891 on island paradise. ⅓ blk. from beach amid shops & rest. Golf, tennis, diving, fishing, horseback riding, scenic island tours.

BEN LOMUND

Fairview Manor
245 Fairview Ave., 95005
(408)-336-3355

All year

$50-65 B&B
5 rooms, 3 pb
Visa, MC
C-no/S-yes/P-no/H-yes

Continental plus
Complimentary wine
sitting room

Romantic country styled redwood home, majestic stone fireplace, 2½ wooded acres Santa Cruz Mountains. Total privacy. Walk to town. Champagne.

BENICIA

Union Hotel
401 First St., 94510
(707)-746-0100

All year

$63.60-111.30 B&B
12 rooms, 12 pb
credit cards accepted
C-yes/S-yes/P-no/H-yes

Continental breakfast
Lunch, dinner, bar
jacuzzi bathtubs
entertainment

Sleep in the 19th Century. Antique rooms, queen sized beds, jacuzzi private bathtubs, menus based on Fannie Farmer's recipes.

38 California

French Hotel
1538 Shattuck Ave.,94709
(415)-548-9930

$55-85 EP
17 rooms, 17 pb
Visa, MC, AmEx
C-yes/S-yes/P-no/H-yes

Continental plus

All year

Urban hotel—balconies, modern French high-tech furniture, silk comforters, room service, concierge 24 hrs., complimentary parking, near retail stores.

Gramma's B&B Inn
2740 Telegraph, 94705
(415)-549-2145

$58-85 B&B
19 rooms, 19 pb
credit cards accepted
C-6 up/S-yes/P-no/H-yes

Full breakfast

sitting room

All year

Old Tudor Mansion refurbished. Some rooms overlook wonderful English garden. 8 have private fireplaces. 8 blocks from University of California.

BOLINAS ─────────────────────────────

Wharf Road B&B
11 Wharf Rd., 94924
(415)-868-1430

$45
2 rooms, 2 pb

C-8 up/S-no/P-no

Cafe downstairs

All year

Clean and interestingly decorated, close to beach & National Seashore, quiet, simple & inexpensively priced.

BOONVILLE ─────────────────────────────

Toll House Inn
PO Box 268, 95415
(707)-895-3630

$60-86 B&B
4 rooms, 2 pb
none
C-ltd/P-no/H-yes

Complimentary breakfast
dinner by reservation
complimentary wine
sitting room, library
hot tub, piano

All year

Mendocino wine country—flocks of sheep, deer, wild pig—540 acres of pasture—Built in 1912 in the Bell Vallley, the folk language Boonthing began here.

BURBANK ─────────────────────────────

Belair
941 N. Frederic, 91505
(213)-848-9227

$35 B&B
2 rooms, 1 pb

C-yes/S-yes/P-no

Continental plus

hot tub
sitting room, piano

All year

Near the glamour of Los Angeles and Hollywood.

CALISTOGA ─────────────────────────────

Calistoga Inn
1250 Lincoln, 94515
(707)-942-4101

$25-30 B&B
15 rooms, 0 pb
Visa/MC
C-yes/S-yes/P-no/H-ltd

Continental plus
Dinner, bar

All year

Small, affordable country hotel- "Johns-Down-the-Hill" -nationally recognized restaurant & pub-like bar in the heart of California's premium wine country.

The Gingerbread Mansion, Ferndale, California

Foothill House
3037 Foothill Blvd,94515
(707)-942-6933

All year

$65-85 B&B
3 rooms, 3 pb
Visa, MC
C-12 up/S-no/P-no/H-yes

Continental plus
Complimentary wine
hot tub
bicycles
sitting room

In a country setting, foothill House offers 3 spacious rooms individually decorated with antiques, each with private bath, entrance and fireplace.

Larkmead Country Inn
1103 Larkmead Ln., 94515
(707)-942-5360

All year

$85 B&B
4 rooms, 4 pb

C-no/S-yes/P-no

Continental plus
Complimentary tea, wine
sitting room
antique organ

Tranquil vinyard setting. Elegant Italianate Victorian house with broad porches shaded by old sycamores. Lovely antique furnishings, Persian carpets.

Please mention this guide when you make your booking

Mount View Hotel
1457 Lincoln, 94515
(707)-942-6877

$45-75 B&B
34 rooms, 34 pb

C-yes/H-yes

Continental breakfast
Lunch, dinner, bar
jacuzzi
swimming pool

All year

Napa Valley resort complete with exquisite dining room, lounge, pool-jacuzzi. Art Deco style modeled after the '30s & '40s. Complimentary breakfast.

Scarlett's Country Inn
3918 Silverado Tr, 94515
(707)-942-6669

$65
2 rooms, 2 pb

C-yes/S-yes/P-no/H-yes

Continental plus
Complimentary wine
swimming pool
sitting room

All year

Secluded French country farmhouse overlooking vineyards in famed Napa Valley. Breakfast served by woodland swimming pool. Close to spas and wineries.

Silver Rose Inn
351 Rosedale Rd., 94515

B&B
5 rooms, 4 pb

C-no/S-yes/P-no

Continental plus
Complimentary wine
hot tub
swimming pool
sitting room

Walk or jog thru adjacent vineyards & enjoy Calistoga's famous mud & mineral baths.

Wine Way Inn
1019 Foothill Blvd,94515
(707)-942-0680

$60-80 B&B
6 rooms, 4 pb
Visa, MC
C-10 up/S-yes/P-no

Continental plus
Complimentary wine
living room, fireplace
mineral baths nearby

Feb.—Nov. & Xmas wk.

Country charm in town; hillside borders spacious multi-level deck; central location to explore renowned vineyards of Napa/Sonoma.

CARMEL

Happy Landing Inn
Box 2619, 93921

$50-85 B&B
7 rooms, 7 pb
credit cards ok
C-no/P-no/H-ltd

Continental plus
Afternoon tea
sitting room

All year

Old Carmel charm, Hansel & Gretel acrhitecture—antique-filled rooms, flowers & sherry. Breakfast served to your rom with morning paper.

Holiday House
Camino Real & 7th, 93921
(408)-624-6267

$46-53 dbl. B&B
6 rooms, 2 pb
none
C-6-up/S-no/P-no/H-ltd

Full breakfast
complimentary wine
piano
sitting room, library

All year

Quiet and homey, in residential area, walking distance to town and beach. Ocean views; large beautiful garden.

**Be sure to call the Inn to verify details and prices
and to make your reservation**

Mission Ranch
26270 Dolores, 93921
(408)-624-6436

All year

$48.75—70.00
25 rooms, 25 pb
all credit cards
C-yes/S-yes/P-yes/H-yes

Continental plus
Dinner, bar
tennis courts (10)
piano bar

Country setting with ocean view just blocks from the beach, hiking trails and shopping.

Sea View Inn
Camino Real, 93921
(408)-624-8778

All year

$45-65 B&B
8 rooms, 6 pb
Visa, MC
C-12 up/S-no/P-no

Continental plus
Complimentary wine
sitting room

Intimate Victorian country inn, furnished with antiques in a cozy atmosphere with personal attention to your comfort.

Stonehouse Inn
Monte Verde & 8, 93921
(408)-624-4569

All year

$60-75 B&B
6 rooms, 0 pb

C-12 up/S-no/P-no

Continental plus
afternoon tea, sherry
sitting room

Historic Carmel house built in 1906, traditional Bed & Breakfast. Within walking distance of shopping, restaurants, beach.

Sundial Lodge
7th & Monte Verde, 93921
(408)-624-8578

All year

$60-70 B&B
19 rooms, 19 pb
Visa, MC, AmEx
C-yes/S-yes/P-yes

Continental breakfast
French restaurant
sitting room

European style inn with easy access to shops, restaurants & recreation areas. Your private retreat in old Carmel.

Vagabond House
4th & Dolores, 93921
(408)-624-7738

All year

$60-95
11 rooms, 11 pb
Visa, MC
C-no/S-yes/P-yes

Full breakfast
Complimentary tea, wine

Antique clocks & pictures, quilted bedspreads. Fresh flowers, plants, shelves filled with old books. Sherry by the fireplace. 2 blks. from downtown Carmel.

CARMEL-BY-THE-SEA

House of England
25020 Valley Way, 93923
(408)-624-3004

All year

$40-50
4 rooms, 1 pb

C-yes/S-ltd/P-no/H-yes

Full breakfast

hot tub
bicycles

Attractive, spacious accomodation, complimentary full breakfast, hot tubs—a real find.

**Enter your favorite inn in our "Inn of the Year" contest
(entry form is in the back of the book).**

Sandpiper Inn
2408 Bayview Ave., 93923
(408)-624-6433

$55-85
15 rooms, 15 pb
Visa, MC
C-12 up/S-yes/P-no

All year

Continental plus
Coffee, tea, sherry
tennis, golf, bicycles
fireplace lounge
library

Fifty yards from Carmel Beach. European style country inn, filled with antiques and fresh flowers. Ocean views, fireplaces, garden.

CHICO ————————————————————

Bullard House
256 E. 1st Ave.
(916)-342-5912

$50-60 B&B
4 rooms, 0 pb

C-no/S-no/P-no

All year

Continental plus
Complimentary wine
bicycles
sitting room
piano

Bullard House is a beautifully restored country Victorian centrally located to University, hospitals and downtown.

CLOVERDALE ————————————————

Old Crocker Inn
1116 Palomino Rd., 95425
(707)-894-3911

$50-70 B&B
10 rooms, 10 pb
Visa, MC
S-yes/P-no/H-yes

All year

Full breakfast
Complimentary wine
swimming pool
sitting room

Quiet charm and seclusion on five country acres. Beautiful views of the Alexander Valley and Russian River. Wine tasting, canoe trips, and lots more.

Vintage Towers
302 N. Main St., 95425
(707)-894-4535

$35-65 dbl B&B
7 rooms, 4 pb
Visa, MC
C-10 up/S-ltd/P-no

All year

Full breakfast
Complimentary wine
4 sitting rooms, piano
bicycles

A towered mansion on a quiet tree lined street, in a wine country town. Walk to river, wineries, and fine dining.

COLFAX ————————————————————

Bear River Mt. Farm
21725 Placer Hills Rd.
(916)-878-8314

$40 cpl B&B
3 rooms, 1 pb

C-yes/S-yes/P-yes/H-yes

All year

Continental plus

Separate cottage on 4 rural acres with equipped kitchen, fireplace, stereo, color TV, stream, fresh eggs, honey, in historic gold country.

COLOMA ————————————————————

Sierra Nevada House
P.O. Box 268, 95613
(916)-622-5856
(916)-933-0547
All year

$50-65 B&B
9 rooms, 9 pb
AmEx
C-yes/S-yes/P-no

Continental breakfast
Lunch, dinner, bar
piano, entertainment

Old fashioned soda parlor; 80 person capacity dining room; near state park highlighting gold discovery; whitewater rafting nearby.

Vineyard House
Cold Spring Rd., 95613
(916)-622-2217

All year

$40-50 B&B
7 rooms, 0 pb
Visa, MC, AmEx, BA
C-16 up/S-yes/P-no

Continental plus
Dinner, saloon
sitting room, piano

Country charm in the middle of Coloma's picturesque river valley, featuring antique-filled rooms and full dining room service.

COLUMBIA ─────────────────────────────────────

City Hotel
POB 1870, 95310
(209)-532-1479

All year

$52.50-59.50
9 rooms, 9 pb
Visa, MC, BA
C-yes/S-yes/P-no/H-ltd

Continental plus
Lunch, dinner, bar
sitting room, piano

Historical location in a State preserved goldrush town; 9 antique appointed rooms; small elegant dining room and authentic saloon.

Mt. Holly Estate
P.O. Box 787, 95310
(209)-532-0542

All year

$48 B&B
2 rooms, 0 pb

C-no/S-ltd/P-no

Full breakfast
Complimentary tea, wine
swimming pool
sitting room
piano

Located one mile from historic Columbia and Gold Rush State Park, country living at its best. Complimentary wine. Furnished in Antiques.

CORONADO ─────────────────────────────────────

Carolyn's B&B Homes
POB 943, 92118
(207)-548-2289

All year

$38-45 dbl B&B
6 rooms, 1 pb
major credit cards
C-yes/S-yes/P-yes

Continental plus
Afternoon tea
hot tub
bicycles

COULTERVILLE ─────────────────────────────────

Jeffrey Hotel
P.O. Box 4, 95311
(209)-878-3400

All year

$26-72
18 rooms, 7 pb
credit cards accepted
C-yes/S-yes/P-no

Full breakfast
Lunch, dinner, bar
swimming pool
tennis courts
sitting room, piano

Restored Gold Rush era hotel, dining room and saloon at entrance to Yosemite. Surrounded by all year recreational facilities.

DAVENPORT ─────────────────────────────────────

New Davenport B&B
31 Davenport Ave., 95017
(408)-425-1818

All year

$45-75 B&B
8 rooms, 8 pb
Visa, MC, AmEx
C-yes/S-no/P-no/H-yes

Continental breakfast
Lunch, dinner, beer/wine
sitting room

Charming colorful rooms decorated with antiques, handcrafts and ethnic treasures. Complimentary champagne.

Please mention this guide when you make your booking

44 California

DINSMORE ───────────────────────────────

Dinsmore Lodge
95526
(707)-574-6466

$50
7 rooms, 0 pb
Visa, MC
C-yes/S-yes/P-no

Continental plus
Complimentary wine
hot tub
sitting room

Except Christmas

Historic stagecoach stop in remote and beautiful setting. Swimming, fishing in Van Duzen River—430 acres to roam. Public air strip.

DOWNIEVILLE ───────────────────────────

Sierra Shangri-La
Rte. 49, 95936
(916)-289-3455

$40-85 EP
8 rooms, 8 pb

C-yes/S-yes/P-no/H-yes

All year

Private cottages on the banks of the Yuba River blending beautiful landscaping into the surrounding forest, provide peace and tranquility.

EL CAJON ───────────────────────────────

Bud & Dot Shackelford
11532 Rolling Hills Dr.
(619)-442-3164

3 rooms, 2 pb

C-yes/S-yes/P-no

Full breakfast
snacks, bar service
swimming pool
piano

All year

San Diego area, nearby club membership. Breakfast—homemade pastries. Children accepted.

ELK ─────────────────────────────────────

Elk Cove Inn
POB 367, 95432
(707)-877-3321

$46-126 B&B or AP
9 rooms, 6 pb

C-8 up/S-ltd/P-no/H-yes

Full breakfast
Dinner (wknds), bar
sitting room, piano
library, stereo &
record library

All year

1883 Victorian—original old-fashioned country inn, outstanding dramatic ocean views; specializing in German and French cuisine and personal service.

Green Dolphin Inn
6145 S. Hwy. 1, 95432
(707)-877-3342

$65 B&B
3 rooms, 3 pb

C-no/S-yes/P-no

Full breakfast
Complimentary cider
Sitting room, piano
library

All year

Homey atmosphere, room furn. in antiques, gourmet breakfast in dining room overlooking ocean.

Harbor House by the Sea
5600 S. Hwy. 1, 95432
(707)-877-3203

$100-150 dbl MAP
13 rooms, 13 pb

C-no/S-yes/P-no

Full breakfast
Full dinner, wine list
sitting room, piano
private beach

All year

EUREKA

Carter House Inn
1033 Third St., 95501
(707)-445-1390

All year

$55-65 B&B
3 rooms, 1 pb
Visa, MC, AmEx
C-yes/S-ltd/P-no

Full breakfast
Complimentary wine
sitting room
bicycles

New Victorian. Enjoy wines & hors d'ouevres before dinner, cordials or teas & cookies at bedtime. Warm hospitality and a breakfast you will never forget.

The Mansion, San Francisco, California

Eagle House B & B
Second & C, 95501
(707)-442-2334

All year

$60-80
10 rooms, 10 pb
credit cards accepted
C-no/S-no/P-no/H-yes

Continental plus
Complimentary tea, wine
entertainment
sitting room

The Eagle House Bed & Breakfast Inn provides a panoramic view of Humboldt Bay, the fishing fleet & the city of Eureka.

Old Town B&B Inn
1521 Third St., 95501
(707)-445-3951

All year

$45-55 B&B
5 rooms, 3 pb
Visa, MC
C-yes/S-no/P-no

Full breakfast
Complimentary wine
bicycles
sitting room w/fireplace

Historic 1871 home, graciously decorated with antiques. Warm hospitality. Quiet location close to Old Town, restaurants, antique shops, museums, etc.

FERNDALE

Gingerbread Mansion
400 Berding St., 95536
(707)-786-4000

All year

$45-65 B&B
4 rooms, 2 pb
Visa, MC
C-10 up/S-no/P-no

Continental plus
Afternoon tea & cake
sitting room
bicycles

Victorian splendor & romance await you in one of Northern California's most photographed homes, in the irresistible fairytale village of Ferndale!

Shaw House Inn
703 Main St., 95536

All year

$55-65 B&B
5 rooms, 2 pb

C-older/S-ltd/P-no

Full gourmet breakfast
Complimentary wine
sitting room, library
organ

Ferndale's elegant Inn—first house built in Ferndale (1854). Antiques, fresh flowers, wine, join other guests in library, parlor, enclosed deck.

FORT BRAGG

Casa del Noyo Inn
500 Casa del Noyo, 95437
(707)-964-9991

All year

$50-70 B&B
6 rooms, 6 pb
Visa, MC
C-yes/S-yes/P-no/H-ltd

Continental Plus
Bar service (wknds)
12-stool bar

Fine food and lodging. Turn of the century elegance, spacious rooms.

Cleone Lodge
24600 N Hwy. Blvd, 95437
(707)-964-2788

All year

$38.50-58.50
10 rooms, 10 pb
Visa, MC
C-yes/S-yes/P-yes

Continental plus

hot tub
picnic area
sun decks

A ranch style country inn. 5½ acres of beautiful grounds close to sandy beaches, small lake & riding stables.

Country Inn
632 N. Main St., 95437
(707)-964-3737

$45-50 B&B
8 rooms, 8 pb
Visa, MC, AmEx
C-15 up/S-ltd/P-no/H-yes

Continental plus
Complimentary wine
sitting room

All year

Built in 1800's, sun deck, sloping ceilings, floral wallpapers—close to Skunk R.R., restaurants, beach, galleries, shops.

Glass Beach Inn
726 N. Main St., 95437
(707)-964-6774

$48-63 B&B
7 rooms, 7 pb
Visa, MC
C-no/S-yes/P-no/H-ltd

Full breakfast
Complimentary wine
hot tub
sitting room

All year

Several of our rooms have their own fireplace, decor ranges from very elegant Victorian to all wood sailing ship theme complete with hanging queen size bed.

Grey Whale Inn
615 N. Main St., 95437
(707)-964-0640

$40-65 B&B
13 rooms, 11 pb
Visa, MC, AmEx
C-yes/S-ok/P-no/H-yes

Continental plus

sitting room

All year

Historic Northcoast landmark. Comfortably furnished, some antiques. Ocean view suites/rooms, wheelchair suite, three kitchens. Extensive art collection.

Pudding Creek Inn
700 N. Main St., 94537
(707)-964-9529

$37-65 B&B
10 rooms, 10 pb
Visa, MC
C-10 up/S-no/P-no

Continental plus
Complimentary wine
sitting room

Except 1st 2 wks. Jan.

1884 Victorian built by Russian count. Enclosed garden court—fuschias, begonias, ferns. Country gift shop. Restaurants, beaches, tennis courts nearby.

FRENCH GULCH

French Gulch Hotel
P.O. Dr. 6B, 94603
(916)-359-2114

$30-50
7 rooms, 1 pb
Visa, MC
C-yes/S-no/P-no/H-ltd

Continental plus
Dinner, Sunday brunch
sitting room, piano
entertainment

All year

Early gold country hotel. Jazz on Saturday night. Great food in the Feeney Room.

GASQUET

Patrick Creek Lodge
95543
Idlewild Toll Sta. 5

$29 dbl
16 rooms, 16 pb
Visa/MC
C-yes/S-yes/P-yes/H-yes

Full breakfast
Lunch, dinner
hot tub, swimming pool
sitting room, piano
weekend entertainment

All year

Rustic hideaway nestled in the Six Rivers National Forest. Enjoy the peace and quiet of the log lodge built in 1925. Fishing and hiking available.

48 California

GEORGETOWN —————————————————————————————————

Woodside Mine
P.O. Box 43, 95634
(916)-333-4499

All year

$40-60 B&B
9 rooms, 0 pb
Visa, MC
C-no/S-yes/P-no/H-yes

Continental plus
Cocktail hour
swimming pool, hot tub
sitting room, piano
bicycles

Jewel of the Mother Lode Country—elegantly restored Victorian Inn. To be open by June 1984. Elegant grounds and mountain spring pool.

GEYSERVILLE —————————————————————————————————

Campbell Ranch Inn
1475 Canyon Rd., 95441
(707)-857-3476

February—November

$75 B&B
3 rooms, 2 pb

C-teens/S-no/P-no

Full breakfast
Complimentary wine
swimming pool
tennis court, bicycles
sitting room, piano

Three bedroom hilltop ranch home with tennis court & swimming pool. Fresh flowers, wine & homemade pie.

Hope-Merrill House
21253 Geyserville, 95441
(707)-857-3356
(800)-USA-INNS RS
All year

$50-60 B&B
5 rooms, 2 pb
Visa, MC, AmEx
S-no/P-no/H-yes

Full breakfast
Complimentary wine
sitting room

Award-winning restored Eastlake Victorian; heart of Sonoma County premium wine country; old fashioned hospitality; delicious food.

Isis Oasis
20889 Geyserville, 95441
(707)-857-3525

All year

$35-47 B&B
12 rooms, 0 pb
Visa
S-yes/H-yes

Full breakfast
Complimentary wine
hot tub, sauna
swimming pool
bicycles

Unique Wine Country lodge surrounded by acres of trees, foliage and lawn—exotic animals and birds—artistically decorated, comfortably casual.

GRASS VALLEY —————————————————————————————————

Purcell House
119 N. Church St., 95945
(916)-272-5525

All year

$40-65 B&B
6 rooms, 6 pb
Visa, MC, HE
C-no/S-no/P-no

Continental plus
Complimentary wine
sitting room, piano

6 rooms, each with its own bath, furnished in the elegance of the 1800's. Breakfast is a delicious treat of croissants & danish, fresh fruit & beverage.

GROVELAND —————————————————————————————————

Hotel Charlotte
Rte. 120
(209)-962-6455

All year

$35-50 EPB
12 rooms, 8 pb
Visa, MC
C-yes/S-yes

Breakfast, lunch, dinner
Beer & wine
pool, tennis courts
entertainment

Charming old historical hotel. Iron bedsteads. Near Yosemite National Park, one mile to airport, golf. Fishing, swimming, tennis, horseback, water skiing.

GUALALA

Gualala Hotel
95445
(707)-884-3441

All year

$27.50—55.00 EP
19 rooms, 5 pb
Visa, MC
C-yes/S-yes/P-no

Breakfast, lunch, dinner
Complimentary wine
sitting room, piano

Historic 1903 Hotel, overlooking the ocean, furnished with original antiques. Extensive wine shop, family style meals.

Old Milano Hotel
38300 Hwy. 1, 95445
(707)-884-3256

Wknds only Dec.-Mar.

$55-85 B&B
9 rooms, 3 pb
Visa, MC
C-no/S-no/P-no

Continental plus
Beer & wine
hot tub
sitting room, piano

Country retreat on the Mendocino Coast; ocean view rooms, Victorian antiques, gourmet breakfast served in room, garden or parlor; country recreation.

Saint Orres
36601 Hwy. 1, 95445
(707)-884-3303

All year

$54-102
11 rooms, 3 pb
Visa, MC
C-yes/S-yes/P-no/H-ltd

Continental plus
Dinner, beer, wine
lobby with fireplace
bar with solarium

Uniquely handcrafted rooms. Intimate hideaway. Ocean views. Accomodations: The Cabin, The Tree House, The Cottage. With continental breakfast.

Whale Watch Inn
35100 Hwy. 1, 95445
(707)-884-3667

All year

$75-135 B&B
6 rooms, 6 pb
Visa, MC
C-no/S-ltd/P-no

Continental plus
Complimentary wine
lounge w/fireplace

A getaway like no other, six luxurious, contemporary cliffside accomodations with dramatic ocean views and beach access; fireplaces and kitchens in four.

GUERNEVILLE

Ridenhour Ranch House
12850 River Rd., 95446
(707)-887-1033
(800)-USA-INNS RS
Closed Dec. & Jan.

$49.75-69.75
7 rooms, 4 pb
Visa, MC
C-10 up/S-ltd/P-no/H-yes

Continental plus
Complimentary wine
hot tub
sitting room

Country Inn on the Russian River in the heart of the lush and lovely Sonoma wine country. Adjacent to historic Korbel Champagne Cellars.

HALF MOON BAY

Mill Rose B & B Inn
615 Mill St., 94109
(415)-726-9794

All year

$65-95 B&B
6 rooms, 6 pb
all credit cards
C-no/S-no/P-no/H-yes

Full breakfast
Complimentary tea, wine
bicycles
entertainment
sitting room

Exquisitely appointed flower filled rooms & suites with private bath, entrance. English country garden by the sea. Perfect for weddings, business meetings.

San Benito House
356 Main St., 94019
(415)-726-3425

$29-70 B&B
12 rooms, 9 pb
credit cards ok
C-yes/S-yes/P-no

Continental breakfast
Lunch, dinner, bar
sauna, sun deck
croquet, gardens

All year

A romantic bed and breakfast just south of San Francisco. Historic inn, gourmet restaurant, western style saloon and garden-deli cafe.

HEALDSBURG

Belle de Jour
16276 Healdsburg, 95448
(707)-433-7892

$65-75 B&B
5 rooms, 1 pb

C-no/S-yes/P-no

Continental plus
Complimentary wine
sitting room, piano

All year

A little farm with the ambiance of the French countryside. Separate cottages, perfect hideaway in the beauty of the Russian River Wine Valley.

Camellia Inn
211 North St., 95448
(707)-433-8182

$37-70 B&B
6 rooms, 4 pb
Visa, MC
S-yes/P-no

Full breakfast
Comp. wine & cheese
swimming pool
sitting room

All year

Elegant Italianate Victorian, built 1869, near Sonoma's finest wineries—beautifully restored, furnished with antiques, oriental rugs.

Grape Leaf Inn
539 Johnson St., 95448
(707)-433-8140

$45-95 B&B
7 rooms, 7 pb
Visa, MC
C-12 up/S-no/P-no/H-yes

Full breakfast
Complimentary wine
sitting room
jacuzzis in some rooms

All year

Victorian elegance in the midst of Sonoma County's finest wineries. Generous full breakfast, complimentary premium wines, private baths and more!

Healdsburg Inn
P.O. Box 1196, 95448
(707)-433-6991

$55-70 B&B
8 rooms, 8 pb
Visa, MC, AmEx
C-10 up/S-ltd/P-no

Continental plus
Wine tasting (Fri. eve.)

All year

Madrona Manor
1001 West Side Rd.,95448
(707)-433-4231
(800)-547-1463 RS
All year

$75-125 B&B
16 rooms, 16 pb
Visa, MC, AmEx
C-yes/S-yes/P-yes/H-yes

Full breakfast
Gourmet restaurant
music room
antique rosewood piano

Circa 1881, furnished with antiques. All rooms with private baths. Carriage house. Wine country, canoeing, bicycling, historical points of interest.

Please Mention *The Complete Guide* **to the innkeeper when you reserve your room**

Raford House
10630 Wohler Rd., 95448
(707)-887-9573

All year

$53-69
7 rooms, 5 pb
Visa, MC
C-older/S-yes/P-no

Continental plus

bicycles
dining room

Victorian farmhouse overlooks the vineyards of Sonoma County. Country setting just½ hour away from San Francisco.

INVERNESS

Blackthorne Inn
P.O. Box 712, 94937
(415)-663-8621

All year

$50-90 B&B
5 rooms, 0 pb
Visa, MC
C-12 up/S-ltd/P-no

Continental plus
Complimentary tea/sherry
hot tub
sitting room w/fireplace

Sunset Magazine (April '83) describes the Inn as "a carpenter's fantasy, with decks, hot tub, foreman's pole, and spiral staircase."

We want this guide to be as complete as possible, so if you know of an inn (30 rooms or less), bed & breakfast or guesthouse we don't list, please send us their name on the form in the back of the book.

Elk Cove Inn, Elk, California

Inverness Lodge
Callendar & Argyle,94937
(415)-669-1034

Jan. 1 to Nov. 30

$32.50—45.00 EP
9 rooms, 9 pb
Visa, MC, AmEx, DC, CB
C-ok/S-yes/P-no

Full breakfast
Dinner

Secluded family operated country hideaway in old world atmosphere; gourmet Czech cuisine, extensive wine list, Czech & Viennese background music; romantic.

MacLean House
P.O. Box 651, 94937
(415)-669-7392
(415)-663-1420 RS
All year

$54 B&B
2 rooms, 2 pb

C-yes/S-yes/P-no

Continental plus
Complimentary wine

A small Scotish guesthouse, nestled in the trees overlooking Tomales Bay; shortbread and sherry to greet you.

Ten Inverness Way
10 Inverness Way, 94937

All year

$48-55 B&B
5 rooms, 0 pb

S-ltd/P-no

Full breakfast
Complimentary sherry
sitting room, piano
library

A classic bed and breakfast inn for lovers of handmade quilts, hearty breakfasts, great hikes and good books.

IONE

Heirloom Inn
214 Shakley Ln.
(209)-274-4468

All year

$45-65 B&B
5 rooms, 2 pb

C-12 up/S-yes/P-no

Full breakfast
Complimentary tea, wine
sitting room, piano
bicycles

Petite colonial mansion, 1863, in private garden setting—verandas, fireplaces, heirloom antiques, French country breakfast, comfort, gracious hospitality.

JACKSON

Ann Marie's Lodgin
410 Stasel St., 95642
(209)-223-1452

All year

$60 B&B
3 rooms, 2 pb

C-yes/S-ltd/P-no

Full breakfast
Complimentary wine, tea
swimming pool
sitting room, parlor

Overlooking historic Jackson—1892 Victorian Country Inn, calico curtains, old lace, linens, antiques, 9 AM harvest breakfast. Air cond., children welcome.

Court Street Inn
215 Court St., 95642
(209)-223-0416

All year

$45-145 B&B
7 rooms, 4 pb

C-12 up/S-yes/P-no/H-yes

Full breakfast
Complimentary wine, tea
sitting room, piano

Located in the heart of the Mother Lode country, Century-old inn offers the charm of yesteryear.

Gate House Inn
1330 Jackson Gate, 95642
(209)-223-3500

$45-75 B&B
5 rooms, 5 pb

C-no/S-no/P-no

All year

Continental plus
Complimentary wine
swimming pool
sitting room, organ
green house

Stately 1900 Victorian in original prime condition with one acre of beautiful landscaped gardens. The only one of its kind in county.

JAMESTOWN

National Hotel
Box 502, 95327
(209)-984-3446

All year

$38-49 B&B
11 rooms, 5 pb
Visa, MC, AmEx
C-8 up/S-yes/P-no

Continental plus
Full restaurant, bar

JENNER

Murphy's Jenner
P.O. Box 69, 95450
(707)-865-2377

All year

$35-125 B&B
11 rooms, 11 pb
credit cards accepted
C-yes/S-yes/P-no/H-yes

Full breakfast
Restaurant, bar
hot tubs
piano, entertainment
sitting room

Peaceful, romantic, outstanding country, river and ocean views; Sunset weddings by the sea, Mercedes Winery tours, eight beautiful sandy beaches.

Stillwater Cove Ranch
95450
(707)-847-3227

Except Christmas

$29.20-55.00 EP
6 rooms, 6 pb

C-yes/S-yes/P-yes/H-ltd

library

Private beautiful retreat on rugged Sonoma Coast—redwood forest, stream and accessible coves.

JULIAN

Julian Gold Rush Hotel
2032 Main St., 92036
(619)-765-0201

All year

$38-52 B&B
15 rooms, 3 pb

C-wkdys/S-ok/P-no

Full breakfast

sitting room, piano

Sole surviving hotel in the southern Mother Lode of California, restored to its full glory in genuine American antiques.

Pine Hills Lodge
92036
(619)-765-1100

All year

$30-85
17 rooms, 12 pb
Visa, MC, AmEx, DC, CB
C-yes/S-yes/P-yes/H-ltd

Continental plus
Dinner, bar
swimming pool
sitting room
dinner theater (wknds)

Built in 1912, the lodge displays a warmth not readily found in today's hustle-bustle world—a rustic refuge from plastic and glitter.

Advance reservations are essential at most inns during busy seasons and appreciated at other times

Shadow Mountain Ranch　$45-55 B&B　　Complimentary breakfast
2771 Frisius Rd., 92036　4 rooms, 0 pb　　complimentay wine
(619)-765-0323　　　　none　　　　　　hot tub
　　　　　　　　　　　C-no/S-no/P-no/H-yes　entertainment
All year

Ore house from San Diego in rustic mountain mining town. Real ranch feeling.

LAGUNA BEACH ───────────────────────────────

Carriage House　　$60-80　　　　　Continental plus
1322 Catalina St., 92651　6 rooms, 6 pb　Complimentary wine
(714)-494-8945　　　　　　　　　　　bicycles
　　　　　　　　　C-yes/S-yes/P-no　ocean swimming
All year

Colonial New Orleans-style carriage house with central brick courtyard, tropical land-scaping. Six suites each with sitting room, bedroom, bath.

Eiler's Inn　　　　$85-135 B&B　　Full breakfast
741 S. Coast Hwy., 92651　12 rooms, 12 pb　Complimentary wine
(714)-494-3004　　　　Visa, MC, AmEx　sitting room
　　　　　　　　　　S-yes/P-no
All year

Romantic country inn, ocean ½ block, walking distance to village. Courtyard and foun-tain where breakfast, wine & cheese are served.

LITTLE RIVER ───────────────────────────────

Glendeven　　　　$40-75 B&B　　　Continental plus
8221 N. Hwy. 1, 95456　6 rooms, 4 pb　Complimentary wine
(707)937-0083　　　　　　　　　　　sitting room
　　　　　　　　　C-7 up/S-ltd　　baby grand piano
All year　　　　　　　　　　　　　bicycles

A special country inn close to Mendocino, the serenity of a fern canyon or Glendeven's gardens and lovely views.

Victorian Farmhouse　$60 B&B　　　Continental plus
7001 N. Hwy 1, 95456　4 rooms, 4 pb　Sherry in parlor
　　　　　　　　　　　　　　　　　sitting room
　　　　　　　　　C-16 up/S-ltd/P-no/H-yes
All year

We are in the country. Please enjoy our orchard, flower gardens, and picnic on the other side of School House Creek.

LOS ALAMOS ───────────────────────────────

Union Hotel　　　$65-90 B&B　　　Full breakfast
P.O. Box 616, 93440　14 rooms, 3 pb　Dinner, bar
(805)-344-2744　　　　　　　　　　　hot tub
　　　　　　　　　C-no/S-yes/P-no　swimming pool
Fri-Sat-Sun year-round　　　　　　　sitting room, piano

Prices quoted are the most current available. However, due to increases and seasonal fluctuations, they may have changed. Be sure to check when you make your reservations.

LOS ANGELES

Salisbury House
2273 West 20th, 90018
(213)-737-7817

All year

$40-60 B&B
5 rooms, 3 pb

C-12 up/S-yes/P-no

Full breakfast
Complimentary wine
sitting room

Experience the ultimate in Bed and Breakfast luxury and turn of the century charm. Has been used as location for movies and commercials.

LOS GATOS

La Hacienda Inn
18840 Saratoga Rd.,95030
(408)-354-9230

All year

$45-85 B&B
20 rooms, 20 pb
Visa, MC, AmEx, DC
C-yes/S-yes/P-no

Continental breakfast
Restaurant/bar
hot tub
swimming pool

On historic site of Rinconada Land Grant and Overland Express stage stop, inn draws a diverse clientele appreciative of gracious California hospitality.

MAMMOTH LAKES

Tamarack Lodge Resort
Tamarack Lodge Rd.
(619)-934-2442

All year

$30 B&B
15 rooms, 3 pb
Visa, MC, AmEx
C-yes/S-yes/P-yes/H-yes

Continental plus
Dinner
sitting room, piano

On Twin Lakes in the Mammoth Lakes Sierra. Great fishing, hiking, cross-country & downhill skiing. Rustic, well-kept year-round resort—something for everyone.

MENDOCINO

Agate Cove Inn
Box 1150
(707)-937-0551

All year

$49 up B&B
7 rooms, 7 pb
Visa, MC, AmEx
C-10 up/S-no/P-no

Full breakfast
Complimentary wine
piano

Private cottages, each with fireplace & views of the ocean. Near the village of Mendocino—center for arts on the North Coast. Whale watching Nov.-March.

Ames Lodge
42287 Little Lake Rd., 95460
(707)-937-0811

Except Dec.-Jan.

$25-40 B&B
7 rooms, 2 pb

C-yes/S-yes/P-no/H-yes

Continental plus
Complimentary wine
sitting room
piano

Originally built as a retreat, three miles east of Mendocino. Ideal for small groups, individuals, couples or families.

Big River Lodge
POB 487, 95460
(707)-937-5615

All year

$80-86
23 rooms, 23 pb
Visa, MC, AmEx, CB, DC
C-yes/S-yes/P-yes/H-yes

Continental plus
Complimentary wine
sitting room
bicycles

A truly elegant country inn in a pastoral setting. All accomodations with fireplaces, ocean views, decks, antiques, four-posters and TVs.

Headlands
PO Box 132, 95460
(707)-937-4431

$57-70 B&B
6 rooms, 6 pb
none
C-no/S-yes/P-no

Continental plus
complimentary wine
common room

All year

Completely restored Victorian home located in picturesque Mendocino village. All rooms have private baths and fireplaces. Many have ocean views.

Joshua Grindle Inn
44800 Little Lake Rd., 95460
(707)-937-4143

$50-63 B&B
7 rooms, 7 pb

C-no/S-yes/P-no/H-yes

Continental plus
Complimentary wine
sitting room, piano
bicycles

All year

Historic country charm in coastal village of Mendocino. Antiques, fireplaces, private baths, breakfast, art galleries, shops, restaurants.

MacCallum House
740 Albion St., 95460
(707)-937-0289

$34.50-95.00 B&B
21 rooms, 8 pb
Visa, MC
C-yes!/S-yes/P-dep

Continental plus
Restaurant, bar
sitting room

All year

The MacCallum House provides friendly, personal attention to guests in handsome, authentically restored Victorian home in the village of Mendocino.

Mendocino Hotel
45080 Main St., 95460
(707)-937-0511

$45-165 B&B
26 rooms, 13 pb
Visa, MC, AmEx
C-14 up/S-yes/P-no/H-ltd

Continental breakfast
Lunch, dinner, bar
sitting room

All year

Victorian hotel, all rooms furnished with antiques. Breakfast, lunch served in beautiful Garden Room. Dinners served main Victorian Dining Room.

Whitegate Inn
499 Howard St., 95460
(707)-937-4892

$49-80 B&B
6 rooms, 4 pb

C-15 up/S-ok/P-no

Continental plus
Complimentary wine
sitting room, old organ

All year

Located in historic Mendocino, one of the town's more elegant homes, all rooms furnished with antiques.

MIDDLETOWN

Harbin Hot Springs
P.O. Box 782, 95461
(707)-987-2477

$16 up EP
25 rooms, 0 pb

S-ltd/P-no

Full breakfast
Lunch, dinner
hot springs
swimming pool
sitting room, piano

All year

1,100 acres of peaceful natural surroundings, large natural hot baths, sprawling sundecks (bathing suits optional), massage, mud baths, hiking.

Nethercott Inn
18750 S. Patah Ln.,95461
(707)-987-3362

$35
3 rooms, 0 pb
Visa, MC
C-yes/S-ltd/P-no/H-yes

Continental breakfast

sitting room

All year

Historic farm house in lake country — a classic Bed and Breakfast Inn.

MOKELUMNE HILL ─────────────────────────────

Hotel Leger
P.O. Box 50
(209)-286-1401

$27-47 EPl B&B
13 rooms, 6 pb

C-yes/S-yes/P-no

Dinner (French), bar

swimming pool
pianos
entertainment

All year

Up-country hideaway, genuine antiques, French dining. Close to skiing, tennis, golf, 3 large lakes; built-in pool.

MONTEREY ─────────────────────────────────

Iris Inn
P.O. Box 2495, 93942
(503)-488-2286

$40-45 B&B
4 rooms, 0 pb
Visa, MC
C-yes/S-no/P-no

Full breakfast
Complimentary wine
sitting room

May 15—Sept. 30

Lovely turn-of-the-Century inn located four blocks from the Shakespearean Festival which features summer-long award-winning plays. Gourmet breakfasts.

Jabberwock
598 Laine St., 93940
(408)-372-4777

$75-120 B&B
5 rooms, 3 pb

C-no/S-yes/P-no

Continental plus
Sherry & hors d'ouevres
sitting room

All year

Once a convent, this Victorian home is above "Cannery Row". Sherry on the sunporch overlooking Monterey Bay, gardens & waterfalls.

Old Monterey Inn
500 Martin St., 93940
(408)-375-8284

$95-160 B&B
10 rooms, 8 pb

C-no/S-yes/P-no

Continental plus
Complimentary tea, wine
sitting room

All year

Tudor country house, magnificent gardens, luxurious accomodations, fireplaces, complimentary wine & cheese, breakfast in bed, secluded garden cottage.

MUIR BEACH ───────────────────────────────

The Pelican Inn
94965
(415)-383-6000

$90
6 rooms, 6 pb
Visa, MC
C-yes/S-yes/P-ok/H-yes

Full English breakfast
Full restaurant, bar
sitting room
piano
entertainment

All year

A romantic country inn in the English mode.

**Enter your favorite inn in our "Inn of the Year" contest
(entry form is in the back of the book).**

58 California

Dunbar House
271 Jones St., 95247
(209)-728-2897

All year

$45-55 B&B
5 rooms, 0 pb

C-10 up/S-no/P-no

Continental plus
Complimentary wine
sitting room
bicycles

Restored 1880 home with historical designation located in Murphys, Queen of the Sierra. Walking distance to Main Street.

Murphys Hotel
POB 329, 95247
(209)-728-3444

All year

$35-60
9 rooms, pb
Visa, MC, AmEx
C-yes/S-yes/P-yes/H-yes

Full breakfast
Lunch, dinner, bar

Historic country inn located in the Mother Lode. 9 guest rooms, dining room, banquet rooms, and saloon are all Nineteenth Century.

Arbor Guest House
1436 G Street, 94559
(707)-252-8144

except Christmas week

$55-85 B&B
4 rooms, 4 pb
Visa, MC
C-10-up/S-no/P-no/H-ltd

Complimentary breakfast
continental plus
tennis nearby
sitting room, library
Spanish spoken

Beautifully restored 1906 home and carriage house with period furnishings in serene garden setting. Convenient to wineries and fine restaurants.

Beazley House
1910 1st St., 94558
(707)-257-1649
(707)-257-1051 RS
All year

$60-100 B&B
8 rooms, 5 pb
MC, Visa
C-12-up/S-no/P-no/H-ltd

Continental breakfast
complimentary wine
hot tub
entertainment
sitting room, library

The Beazley House is a colonial revival. Relax in old fashioned comfort...breakfast, complimentary sherry.

Gallery Osgood
2230 First St., 94559
(707)-224-0100
(800)-833-1111 RS
All year

$60
2 rooms, 0 pb
Visa, MC
C-no/S-yes/P-no

Continental plus
Complimentary wine
sitting room

Intimate 1898 Queen Anne home combining B&B with fine art/craft gallery. Enjoy conversation with artist/gourmet cook owners.

Goodman House
1225 Division St., 94558
(707)-257-1166
(707)-257-1051 RS
All year

$55-75 B&B
4 rooms, 1 pb

S-no/P-no

Continental plus
Complimentary wine
sitting room
piano

"A Stay with a Difference." Preserving more than a century of Napa Valley hospitality. One of Napa's stately old homes with a prestigious past.

La Residencia Inn	$60-95 B&B	Continental plus
4066 St. Helena Hwy. N.,	7 rooms, 4 pb	
94558	Visa, MC, AmEx	Complimentary wine
(707)-253-0337	C-no/S-yes/P-no/H-yes	hot tub
(707)-257-1051 RS		sitting room
All year		

Built 1870, gracious Victorian in park-like setting, furnished with most comfortable beds, air conditioned; winery tours individually arranged.

Napa Inn	$50-80 B&B	Continental plus
1137 Warren St., 94558	4 rooms, 2 pb	
		sitting room
	C-yes/S-yes/P-no	
All year		

Elegant restored mansion in the heart of the wine country. Quiet residential area. Golf, ballooning, fine restaurants, winery tours nearby.

Old World Inn	$50-90 B&B	Continental plus
1301 Jefferson, 95449	8 rooms, 8 pb	Complimentary tea, wine
(707)-257-0112	Visa, MC, AmEx	jacuzzi
	C-no/S-no/P-no	sitting room
All year		

Run with old world hospitality by its English innkeepers, this Victorian inn is uniquely decorated throughout in bright Scandinavian colors.

Sybron House	$70-90 B&B	Continental plus
7400 St Helena Hwy,94558	4 rooms, 2 pb	Complimentary wine
(707)-944-2785		hot tub
	C-no/S-no/P-no	tennis courts
All year		sitting room, piano

New Victorian on hill commanding best view of Napa Valley. First-class tennis court & spa.

Village Inn		Continental breakfast
1012 Darms Ln., 94558	8 rooms, 8 pb	Complimentary wine
	C-yes/S-yes/P-yes	

Country retreat, newly renovated cottages, bike and jogging lanes, nearby shopping, dining, balloon flights, wineries, tennis, antique shops, picnics.

Yesterhouse Inn	$55-75 B&B	Continental plus
643 Third Street, 94559	6 rooms, 1 pb	Complimentary wine
(707)-257-0550	Visa, MC	sitting room, library
(707)-257-1051 RS	C-yes/S-yes/P-no	antique pump organ
All year		

Victorian home built in 1896.

Advance reservations are essential at most inns during busy seasons and appreciated at other times

NEVADA CITY ───────────────────────────────────

Red Castle Inn
109 Prospect St., 95959
(916)-265-5135

$45-75 B&B
8 rooms, 6 pb

S-ok/P-no

Continental plus
Complimentary sherry
parlor
very old organ

All year

Gothic revival, elegant, homey, lush grounds, on the edge of a nature lovers' dream, in a sophisticated mountain town.

**Enter your favorite inn in our "Inn of the Year" contest
(entry form is in the back of the book).**

Bed & Breakfast aboard a yacht (American Family Inn), San Francisco, California

OLEMA

Olema Inn
10000 Sir Francis Drake
(415)-663-8441
(415)-663-1420 RS
All year

$50-70 B&B
3 rooms, 1 pb
Visa, MC
C-yes/S-ltd/P-no/H-yes

Continental breakfast
Full restaurant
sitting room
entertainment

Century-old, fully restored restaurant and antique-filled lodging—gateway to Pt. Reyes National Seashore.

OLYMPIC VALLEY

Christy Hill
1650 Squaw Valley Rd.
(916)-583-8551

All year

$50-85
7 rooms, 7 pb
Visa, MC, AmEx
C-yes/S-ok/P-no/H-yes

Continental breakfast
Lunch, dinner, bar

An intimate old family home, with ski area views, at Squaw Valley, serving gourmet meals year round.

OROVILLE

Jean's Riverside B&B
P.O. Box 2334, 95965

B&B
7 rooms, 3 pb

C-ok/S-ltd/H-yes

Continental breakfast
Lunch, dinner, wine
river waterfront

Waterfront hideaway (canoes available). Near Feather River Canyon, I-5, Oroville Dam, historical sites, golfing, fishing, hunting.

ORSI

Valley View Citrus Ranch
14801 Ave. 428, 93647
(209)-528-2275
(800)-USA-INNS RS
All year

$32-35
4 rooms, 2 pb

C-yes/S-yes/H-yes

Full breakfast
Complimentary wine
tennis courts
sitting room, organ

Colorful garden, clay tennis court, breakfast in gazebo, air conditioning, fireplace, antiques, sunsets, serenity. 45 min. to Sequoia National Parks.

PACIFIC GROVE

Centrella Hotel
Box 884, 93950
(408)-372-3372

All year

$50-135
27 rooms, 23 pb
Visa, MC, AmEx
S-ltd/P-no/H-yes

Continental plus
Tea/wine/hors d'oeuvres
sitting room

Restored Victorian—award winner for interior design. Ocean, lovers point and many attractions of the Monterey Peninsula. Fireplaces in suites.

Gosby House Inn
643 Light House Av, 93950
(408)-315-1287

All year

$50-75 B&B
19 rooms, 13 pb

C-12 up/S-no/P-no

Continental plus

sitting room

Gracious accomodations in one of nature's most magnificent meetings of land and sea—the Monterey Peninsula. Warmth, hospitality and fine appointments.

Green Gables Inn
104 5th St., 93950   7 rooms, 4 pb
(408)-375-2095

S-no/P-no

All year

Continental plus
Complimentary tea, wine
bicycles

Inn on Monterey Peninsula, decorated to complement the beautiful views; generous continental breakfast; near Cannery Row, Carmel, Monterey.

House of Seven Gables $65-95 dbl B&B
555 Ocean View, 93950   12 rooms, 12 pb
(408)-372-4341

C-12 up/S-no/P-no

All year

Continental plus
Afternoon tea
sitting room

Splendid Victorian. Our old family home. On the very edge of Monterey Bay. Only minutes to Monterey, Carmel, Pebble Beach, Big Sur.

Martine Inn $75-150 B&B
255 Oceanview Blvd,93950   19 rooms, 19 pb
(408)-373-3388   Visa, MC, AmEx
C-yes/S-no/P-no/H-yes

All year

Continental plus
Afternoon tea
jacuzzi, sauna, bicycles
sitting room, library
piano, organ, game room

A magnificent mansion overlooking the Pacific Grove shoreline of Monterey Bay. Walk to Cannery Row, Cal-Rep Theater, and the Aquarium.

Roserox Country Inn $65-145 B&B
557 Ocean View Blvd.   8 rooms, 0 pb
(408)-373-ROSE   no
C-13-up/S-ltd/P-no

All year

Continental plus breakft
Comp full bar, tea, wine
bicycles, horeseshoes,
croquet, sitting room w/
fireplaces, library

Intimate historic Victorian on shores of the Pacific. Honeymoon Suite, antique brass beds, feather quilts, clawfoot tubs. Breakfast in bed. Spectacular ocean views.

PALM SPRINGS

Ingleside Inn $85-500 B&B
200 W. Ramon Rd., 92262   28 rooms, 28 pb
(619)-325-0046   Visa, MC, AmEx
C-16 up/S-yes/P-ltd/H-yes

All year

Continental plus
Restaurant
hot tub, sauna
piano, entertainment
swimming pool

Genuine antiques; continental breakfast, private patio, pool, completely private although in heart of city; steam bath & whirlpool tub in all rooms.

PASADENA

Crown B&B Inn $55-75 B&B
530 S. Marengo, 91101   5 rooms, 2 pb
(818)-792-4031   Visa, MC
C-12 up/S-no/P-no

Except Christmas

Continental plus
Complimentary wine
sitting room

Convenient to downtown Los Angeles and Rose Bowl. Craftsman style house on the National Register of Historic Places.

Donnymac Irish Inn
119 N. Meridith, 91106
(213)-440-0066

$50-70 B&B
5 rooms, 1 pb

C-12 up/S-ltd/P-no/H-ltd

Continental plus
Complimentary wine
hot tub
bicycles
parlor

All year

American Craftsman home on beautiful tree-lined street in good area. Wine, fresh fruit, flowers, spa-in-gazebo, hammocks, waterfall in meditation corner.

PLACERVILLE

Combellack Blair House
3059 Cedar Ravine, 95667
(916)-622-3764

$55
2 rooms, 0 pb

C-no/S-no/P-no

Full breakfast
Complimentary wine
sitting room, piano

All year

Elaborate 1895 Queen Anne Style Victorian furnished in genuine antiques, where memories might have otherwise faded and been lost forever.

**Fleming Jones
Homestead**
3170 Newtown Rd., 95667
(916)-626-5840

$45-65 dbl B&B
5 rooms, 3 pb

C-12 up/S-yes/P-no/H-ltd

Continental plus
Complimentary sherry
sitting room, library
farm animals

All year

1883 farmhouse on 11 acres; balcony overlooks meadows, woods for hiking; wicker porch swings, historic rose garden, vegetable garden; in gold rush country.

James Blair House
2985 Clay St., 95667
(916)-626-6136

$35-55 B&B
3 rooms, 0 pb

C-yes/S-no/P-no

Continental plus
Complimentary wine

All year

Romantic 1901 Queen Anne Victorian with 3-story turret, conservatory and wine cellar. Breakfast served in country kitchen in front of fireplace.

Morey House
805 Lilac Ln., 95667
(916)-621-1186

$50-70 B&B
3 rooms, 3 pb

C-yes/S-no/P-no

Full breakfast
Complimentary tea, wine
sitting room

Feb.–Dec.

This home (circa 1860's) is nestled on a secluded knoll overlooking Old Town. Furnished with an eclectic collection of antiques.

River Rock Inn
1756 Georgetown Dr,95667
(916)-622-7680

$50-60 B&B
4 rooms, 1 pb

C-yes/P-no/H-yes

Full breakfast
Complimentary sherry
sitting room

All year

Relax on the 110' deck overlooking the American River, fish and pan for gold in the front yard. Quiet and beautiful.

Rupley House Inn
95667
(916)-626-0630

All year

$50-85 B&B
6 rooms, 2 pb

C-12 up/S-ltd/P-no/H-ltd

Continental plus
Complimentary wine
sitting room
50 acres
gold panning

Surrounded by 50 acres, Pennsylvania Dutch ranchhouse (1929) welcomes guests to an informal atmosphere of champion Quarter Horses, antiques, homemade quilts.

POINT REYES

Holly Tree Inn
3 Silverhills Rd., 94956
(415)-663-1554

All year

$50-60 B&B
4 rooms, 2 pb

C-yes/S-ltd/P-no

Continental plus
Complimentary wine
sitting room

A romantic country inn in a valley on the coast near San Francisco. Cozy fireplaces and delicious breakfasts await you.

Thirty-Nine Cypress Way
P.O. Box 176, 94956
(415)-663-1709

All year

$42-47 B&B
3 rooms, 0 pb

C-no/S-no/P-no/H-yes

Full breakfast
Complimentary wine
sitting room
bicycle

Antiques, original art, oriental rugs, spectacular view! Close to beaches, 140 miles of hiking trails. Horseback riding arrangements available.

POINT RICHMOND

East Brother Light Station
117 Park Place, 94801
(415)-233-2385

All year

$155-175 dbl MAP
3 rooms, 3 pb

C-8 up/S-ltd/P-no

Continental plus
Dinner, wine
parlor

Escape to an island within sight of the San Francisco skyline. Share the history of a 110 year old lighthouse.

POPE VALLEY

James Creek Ranch B&B
2249 James Crk., 94567

All year

$85
5 rooms, 5 pb

C-yes/S-yes/P-yes/H-yes

Full breakfast
Complimentary wine
lake swimming, fishing

This country hideaway is your retreat from the world. A quiet time to enjoy lakes, creeks, sunsets and sunrises.

RUTHERFORD

Rosi's of Rutherford B&B
P.O. Box 243, 94573
(707)-963-3135

All year

$75-90 B&B
2 rooms, 2 pb
Visa, MC
C-no/S-ltd/P-no

Continental plus
Wine & cheese
spa
sitting room

Casual comfort in heart of exciting Napa Valley wine country — fireplace, wine/cheese in garden, hot tub/spa, fresh baked croissants.

SACRAMENTO

Amber House B&B
1315 22nd St., 95816
(916)-444-8085

$65-75 B&B
4 rooms, 2 pb
Visa, MC, AmEx
C-no/S-no/P-no

Full breakfast
Complimentary wine, tea
sitting room, library
bicycles

All year

"Tailored Elegance" framed by towering old elm trees. Beautifully appointed bedrooms, wine presented in gracious living room.

Aunt Abigail's B&B
2120 G St., 95816
(916)-441-5007

$50-60 B&B
5 rooms, 2 pb
credit cards accepted
C-yes/S-yes/P-no

Continental plus
Complimentary tea, wine
hot tub
sitting rooms

All year

Grand old mansion in heart of State Capitol. Family memorabilia and artifacts from Aunt Abigail's many travels decorate every room.

Bear Flag Inn
2814 I St., 95816
(916)-448-5714

$40-50 B&B
2 rooms, 2 pb
Visa, MC
C-yes/S-yes/P-no

Continental plus
Complimentary wine
sitting room
piano

All year

Antiques, wine, books, fireplace & conversation await guests in restored downtown Arts & Crafts home. Walk to restaurants & tourist spots.

Briggs House
2209 Capitol, 95816

$45-90 B&B
6 rooms, 3 pb
Visa, MC, AmEx
S-ltd/P-no

Full breakfast
Comp. wine, nuts & fruit
hot tub, sauna, bicycles
sitting room, library
piano

All year

This elegantly restored Victorian is just a few blocks from the State Capitol, with spa, sauna, and bicycles available for guests. Gourmet breakfast.

Morning Glory
700 22nd St., 95815
(916)-447-7829

$45-75 B&B
4 rooms, 2 pb

C-yes/S-ltd/P-no

Full breakfast
Complimentary tea, wine
sitting room
piano

All year

Turn-of-the-Century colonial revival finely appointed with antique furniture, lace curtains, patchwork quilts, vintage magazines and items of nostalgia.

SAINT HELENA

Ambrose Bierce House
1515 Main St., 94574
(707)-963-3003
(707)-963-7756 RS
All year

$70-80 B&B
4 rooms, 2 pb
AmEx
C-no/S-yes/P-no

Continental plus
Complimentary wine
bicycles
sitting room

History and wine country charm combined amid brass beds and claw foot tubs; complimentary bottle of Ambrose Bierce wine.

Bale Mill Inn
3431 N St. Helena Hwy.,
94574
(707)-963-4545

$55-60 B&B
5 rooms, 0 pb
Visa, MC, BA
C-6 up/S-yes/P-no

Continental plus

Complimentary wine
sitting room

All year

Chosen best country inn in Napa County for its interiors, also best continental breakfast by L.A. Times.

Bartels Ranch
1200 Conn Valley Rd.,94574
(707)-963-4001

All year

$75-110
3 rooms, 3 pb

S-yes/P-no/H-yes

Continental plus
Complimentary wine
hot tub, swimming pool
bicycles, sitting room
piano, entertainment

Secluded romantic country estate offers the perfect wine country weekend. Recreation room w/fireplace, pool table, pool/jacuzzi. Warm hospitality.

Bell Creek B & B
3220 Silverado Tr.,94574
(707)-963-2383
(707)-257-0557 RS
All year

$40 B&B
2 rooms, 0 pb

C-yes/P-no

Full breakfast
Afternoon tea
swimming pool
sitting room

Country farmhouse tucked away in walnut orchard. Continental atmosphere, simple, clean, comfortable. Close to wineries & restaurants. Swimming pool.

Chalet Bernensis
225 St. Helena Hwy,94574
(707)-963-4423

All year

$45-68 B&B
9 rooms, 4 pb
Visa, MC
C-no/S-no/P-no

Continental plus
Complimentary wine
sitting room

Century old Victorian—handmade quilts, Victorian or turn-of-the-century oak furniture, iron & brass beds (queen size). Center of wine country.

Chestelton House
1417 Kearney St., 94574
(707)-963-2238

All year

$50-90 B&B
4 rooms, 2 pb

C-no/S-no/P-no

Continental plus
Complimentary wine
sitting room

Elegant, romantic, and quiet—in the very heart of the wine country—quaint town and wonderful restaurants nearby.

Cinnamon Bear
1407 Kearney St., 94574
(707)-963-4653

All year

$65-75 B&B
4 rooms, 4 pb
Visa, MC, AmEx
C-10 up/S-ltd/P-no

Continental plus
Complimentary wine
sitting room, piano

Homesick for a visit to your favorite aunt's house? Bring your teddy & come to the Napa Valley wine country.

Erika's Hillside
285 Fawn Park, 94574
(707)-963-2887

All year

$65-110 B&B

C-yes/S-yes/P-no

Continental plus
Complimentary wine
sitting room

18th-Century hillside chalet with European hospitality, breakfast served on patio, deck or garden room. Anniversary and wedding parties welcome.

The Farmhouse
300 Turpin Rd., 94574
(707)-944-8430
(707)-257-1051 RS
All year

$60-80 B&B
3 rooms, 1 pb

C-12 up/S-ltd/P-no

Continental plus
Complimentary wine
swimming pool
studio grand piano
sitting room

Quiet and secluded country farmhouse surrounded by vineyards, within walking distance of two of the best known wineries in the area.

Ink House
1575 St. Helena Hwy.
(707)-963-3890

All year

$70-80 B&B
4 rooms, 4 pb

C-12 up/S-no/P-no

Continental plus
Complimentary wine
parlor
antique pump organ

The Ink House, private, in beautiful St. Helena, antiques, parlor, continental breakfast with homemade pastries. Up from Napa Valley.

Judy's Bed & Breakfast
2036 Madrona Ave., 94574
(707)-963-3081

All year

$65 B&B
1 room, 1 pb

C-no/P-no

Continental breakfast
Complimentary wine
swimming pool
color TV

Quiet country atmosphere yet walking distance to town. Surrounded by vineyards. Breakfast is served in your room or outside by the pool.

Oliver House B & B
2970 Silverado Tr.,94574
(707)-963-4089
(707)-963-7756 RS
All year

$45-95 B&B
5 rooms, 3 pb
Visa
C-12 up/S-no/P-no

Continental plus

sitting room

Warm intimate country atmosphere. Picturesque Swiss chalet overlooking acres of vineyard. Fireplaces, private baths, queen size beds, balconies with view.

Villa St. Helena
2727 Sulpher Spgs.,94574
(707)-963-2514

All year

$65-150 B&B
4 rooms, 4 pb
Visa, MC, AmEx
C-no/S-yes/P-no/H-yes

Continental plus
Complimentary wine
swimming pool
library

Secluded Mediterranean villa overlooking Napa Valley. Romantic antique-filled rooms, fireplaces, private entries; hiking, picnics, Gourmet breakfast.

White Ranch
707 White Lane, 94574
(707)-963-4635

$70 B&B
1 room, 1 pb

C-no/S-no/P-no

Continental plus
Complimentary wine
sitting room

All year

Historic farmhouse among the vineyards—parlor with fireplace—country atmosphere yet close to wineries and restaurants. Personal, intimate, relaxing.

Wine Country Inn
1152 Lodi Ln., 94574
(707)-963-7077

$78-110 B&B
25 rooms, 25 pb
Visa, MC
C-12 up/S-yes/P-no/H-yes

Continental plus

sitting room

Except pre-Christmas

Beautiful Country Inn furnished with antiques and nestled in the heart of the wine country.

SAN DIEGO

Britt House
406 Maple St., 92103
(619)-234-2926

$63-95 B&B
9 rooms, 1 pb
Visa, MC
P-no

Full breakfast
Afternoon tea
sitting room, piano
sauna

All year

Queen Anne Victorian home with 2-story stained glass windows. Homemade breakfast & afternoon tea. 2 blocks from Balboa Park.

St. Orres, Gualala, California

SAN FRANCISCO —————————————————————————

Alamo Square Inn
719 Scott St., 94117
(415)-922-2055

All year

$45-175 B&B
5 rooms, 0 pb
Visa, MC, AmEx
C-12 up/S-ok/P-no

Full breakfast
Complimentary tea, wine
sitting room
bicycles
entertainment (harpist)

Fine restoration of a magnificent mansion. Graced by European furnishings and Oriental rugs, flowers from the garden and host committed to excellence.

Albion House
135 Gough Street, 94102
(415)-621-0896

All year

$55-125 B&B
8 rooms, 8 pb
Visa, MC, AmEx
C-12 up/S-yes/P-no

Full breakfast
Complimentary wine
sitting room

An elegant city hideaway conveniently located near the Opera House, just moments away from Union Square and other tourist attractions.

Archbishop's Mansion
1000 Fulton St., 94117
(415)-563-7872

All year

$90-165 B&B
15 rooms, 15 pb
Visa, MC, AmEx
P-no

Continental plus
Wine, tea, bar
sitting room, piano

An historic French chateau on the park—luxurious lodging in the "Belle Epoque" style. Beautiful conference & reception rooms. VIP service.

Bed & Breakfast Inn
4 Charlton Ct., 94123
(415)-921-9784

All year

$53-163 B&B
9 rooms, 5 pb

C-no/S-yes/P-no

Continental breakfast
Complimentary wine
sitting room

San Francisco's first "Country Inn"; nine unique accomodations are romantic hideaways. Brew a cup of tea, or have continental breakfast.

Casa Arguello
225 Arguello Blvd.,94118
(415)-752-9482
(415)-386-9918
All year

$30-45 B&B
5 rooms, 2 pb

C-7 up

Continental plus

sitting room

Casa Arguello offers reasonable, comfortable rooms in a cheerful spacious townhouse 10 min. from the center of the city.

Casita Blanca
330 Edgehill Way, 94127
(415)-681-4393
(415)-654-9339 RS
All year

$50 B&B
2 rooms, 1 pb

S-ok

Continental breakfast

Casita Blanca is a detached cottage in a secluded forest area. View of Golden Gate. Fireplace, patio, completely furnished. 2 adults.

Clementina's Bay Brick
1190 Folson St.
(415)-431-8334

All year

$25-55 EP
15 rooms, 0 pb
Visa, MC, AmEx
C-to 12/S-yes/P-no

2 bars, disco
piano, entertainment

Entertainment complex for women—although we cater to women regardless of sexual preference, we retain a very open policy to ALL people.

Fay Mansion Inn
834 Grove St., 94117
(415)-921-1816
(800)-547-1463 RS
All year

$58-108 B&B
5 rooms, 0 pb

C-12 up/S-no/P-no

Continental plus
Afternoon tea
sitting room, piano

Affordable luxury—French antiques, marble fireplaces, original gas chandelier and hand-painted and stencilled ceiling. Excellent service.

Hermitage House
224 Sacramento, 94115
(415)-921-5515

exc. Christmas season

$45-90 B&B
10 rooms, 8 pb
Visa, MC
C-ltd/S-yes/P-no

Full breakfast
complimentary wine
tennis nearby
piano, sitting room
library

Greek Revival, country kitchen for snacks. Fireplaces; antique furnishings. Minutes by bus to Nob Hill and downtown.

Hotel Edward II
3155 Scott St., 94123
(415)-921-9776
(800)-547-1463 RS
All year

$32.50-$55.00 B&B
30 rooms, 5 pb
Visa, MC
C-yes/S-yes/P-no

Continental breakfast
Italian dinner, bar

Perched atop a tidy Italian Bakery and a delightful Italian restaurant... a fully refurbished European style pension in San Francisco's Marina district.

Hotel Louise
845 Bush St., 94108
(415)-775-1755

All year

$50-65
25 rooms, 25 pb
Visa, MC, AmEx
C-yes/P-no

Continental breakfast
Complimentary wine
sitting room

Early 20th Century, marble-facaded building—Rooms are custom decorated with wallpaper, chintz fabrics and comfortable furnishings. Kitchen, TV, phone.

The Inn San Francisco
943 S. Van Ness, 94110
(415)-641-0188

All year

$46-106 B&B
15 rooms, 10 pb
Visa, MC, AmEx
C-12 up/S-yes/P-no

Full breakfast

hot tub
3 sitting rooms
sun deck

A grand 27 room 1872 Victorian mansion furnished in 19th-Century antiques. Garden room, hot tub, fresh flowers in rooms.

Inn at Union Square
440 Post St., 94102
(415)-397-3510
All year

$90-150 B&B
27 rooms, 27 pb
Visa, MC, AmEx
C-yes/S-yes/P-no

Continental plus
Complimentary wine

Georgian antiques by San Francisco designer Nat Rosenblatt. Terry cloth robes, complimentary shoeshine. Suitable for business travelers.

Inn on Castro
321 Castro St., 94114
(415)-861-0321
All year

$60-75 B&B
5 rooms, pb
Visa, MC, AmEx
C-no/S-ltd/P-no

Continental plus
Complimentary tea, wine
sitting room
bicycles

Restored Victorian, lush contemporary interiors, filled with an abundance of art, accessories, plants, flowers, and especially friendliness.

Jackson Court
2198 Jackson St., 94115
(415)-929-7670
All year

$75-140 B&B
10 rooms, 10 pb
Visa, MC, AmEx
C-16 up/S-ok/P-no

Continental plus
Complimentary wine
sitting room

A stately brownstone in the heart of San Francisco, distinguished by its luxurious amenities and attention to comfort and hospitality.

Lyon Street B & B
120 Lyon St., 94117
(415)-552-4773
(800)-547-1463 RS
All year

$60-65 B&B
4 rooms, 4 pb

C-yes/S-yes/P-no

Continental plus
Complimentary wine
sitting room
piano
bicycles

Sunny, spacious suite of 4 rooms—queen size bed in bedroom, queen-size sofa bed in double parlor. Next to Golden Gate Park, great restaurants & shops.

Mansion Hotel
2220 Sacramento, 94115
(415)-929-9444

All year

$79-200 B&B
19 rooms, 19 pb
Visa, MC, AmEx, DC
C-yes/S-yes/P-yes

Full breakfast
Dinner, tea, wine
sitting room, piano
park next door
Mansion Magic Concerts

Breakfast in bed, fresh flowers in your room, nightly concerts, billiard room, Bufano gardens, superb dining. San Francisco landmark.

Monte Cristo
600 Presidio Ave., 94115
(415)-931-1875
(415)-626-8777 RS
All year

$45-75 B&B
14 rooms, 11 pb
Visa, MC, AmEx
C-yes/P-no/H-yes

Full breakfast
Complimentary tea, wine

1875 hotel-saloon-bordello, furnished with antiques. Each room decorated differently—Georgian four-poster, Chinese wedding bed, spindle bed, etc.

Obrero Hotel
1208 Stockton St., 94133
(415)-986-9850

All year

$25-45 B&B
12 rooms, 0 pb

C-yes/S-no/P-no

Full breakfast
Dinner

Friendly slice of life in bustling Chinatown adjacent to North Beach, within walking distance of Union Square and Fisherman's Wharf.

Pension San Francisco
1668 Market St., 94102
(415)-864-1271

All year

$23-33 EP
30 rooms, 0 pb
Visa, MC, AmEx
C-yes/S-yes/H-yes

sitting room

European tradition in an affordable hotel. Charming rooms, central location, good public transportation; perfect home base for your San Francisco visit.

Petite Auberge
863 Bush St., 94108
(415)-928-6000

All year

$75-150 B&B
26 rooms, 26 pb
credit cards accepted
C-yes/S-yes/P-no

Continental plus
Complimentary wine, tea
sitting room

Surround yourself with the romantic ambiance of a french country inn snuggled in downtown area of S.F. Tastefully appointed rooms. Fireplaces.

The Red Victorian Inn
1665 Haight St., 94117
(415)-864-1978
(415)-864-1906
All year

$35-65 B&B
16 rooms, 2 pb
Visa, MC
C-yes/P-no

Continental breakfast
"Tea'n'Tapes"
"Pink Parlor"
art gallery

Near Golden Gate Park in colorful Haight-Ashbury, our "New Age" hotel welcomes creative thinkers, friendly people. 35 restaurants nearby.

Riley's Bed & Breakfast
1322-24 6th Ave., 94122
(415)-731-0788

All year

$30-35
5 rooms, 0 pb

C-yes/S-ltd/P-no

Continental plus
Complimentary tea, wine
sitting room

1908 Victorian furnished with antiques. 2 blocks to Golden Gate Park and Univ. of Calif. Medical Center. Public transportation, 15 minutes to downtown.

Spreckels Mansion
737 Buena Vista W, 94117
(415)-861-3008

All year

$75-225 B&B
10 rooms, 8 pb
Visa, MC, AmEx
S-yes/P-no

Continental breakfast
Complimentary wine
sitting rooms, piano

Victorian Landmark Mansion with luxurious suites romantically furnished for special city nights. Fireplace, breakfast in bed. Views, phones, easy parking

Stewart-Grinsell House
2963 Laguna St., 94123
(415)-346-0424

All year

$65-95 B&B
5 rooms, 3 pb
Visa, MC, AmEx
C-Yes!/P-no

Continental plus
Complimentary tea, wine
sitting room
outdoor deck

Victorian retreat—quiet block off Union Street blends city sophisticated room appointments with country hospitality on the serene outdoor deck.

Union Street Inn
2229 Union St., 94123
(415)-346-0424

All year

$75-145 B&B
6 rooms, 3 pb
Visa, MC, AmEx
C-yes/S-yes/P-no

Continental plus
Complimentary wine
sitting room

Charming, elegant inn located in a lively shopping/entertainment area of San Francisco; romantic old-fashioned garden, private carriage house w jacuzzi.

Victorian Inn on the Park
301 Lyon St., 94117
(415)-931-1830

All year

$75-95 B&B
6 rooms, 6 pb
Visa, MC, AmEx
C-10 up/S-yes/P-no

Continental plus
Complimentary wine
parlor
library

1897 Queen Anne Victorian — near Golden Gate Park, downtown. Antiques and private baths. A registered historic landmark.

Wamsley B & B Art Center
1902 Filbert St., 94123
(415)-567-1526

All year

$55-125 B&B
4 rooms, 3 pb
Visa, MC
C-yes/S-no/P-no

Full breakfast
picnic lunch, kitchens
studio room

We are an Art Center as well, with art classes/materials and shared studio. We offer an Art Package which includes a 3 day lodging, museum tour, buffet.

Warner Embassy
1198 Fulton St., 94117
(415)-931-6301

All year

$80-150 B&B
5 rooms, 1 pb
credit cards accepted
C-12 up/S-yes/P-no

Continental plus
Complimentary wine
2 pianos
sitting room

Centrally located Registered Landmark Victorian with dramatic ornate interior, large unique rooms, vista tower, rooms for special occasions and meetings.

Washington Square Inn
1660 Stockton St., 94133
(415)-981-4220

All year

$55-125 B&B
15 rooms, 11 pb
Visa, MC, AmEx
C-yes/S-yes/P-no

Continental plus
Wine & beer
sitting room

In San Francisco's North Beach—the essence of San Francisco. Near all attractions and many fine restaurants.

Willows B&B Inn
710 14th St., 94114
(415)-431-4770

$42-95 B&B
11 rooms, 0 pb
Visa, MC, AmEx, DC, CB
C-8 up/S-yes/P-no

Continental plus
Complimentary tea, wine
sitting room

All year

Laura Ashley decor throughout, each room has its own flowers, fruit, private telephone. European service, S.F. style. Convenient transportation, parking.

SAN JUAN BAUTISTA ────────────────────────────

**Bed & Breakfast San
Juan**
PO Box 613, 95045
(408)-623-4101

$45 B&B
4 rooms, 0 pb
none
C-ltd/S-yes/P-no/H-yes

Complimentary breakfast
complimentary wine
bicycles, tennis nearby
entertainment, library
Spanish & Chinese spoken

All year

National Register Home (1858) near cathedral of all California missions, Teatro Campesino (Luis Valdez) theatre group, fine restaurants.

SAN LUIS OBISPO ────────────────────────────

Heritage Inn
978 Olive Street, 93401
(805)-544-7440

$47-55 dbl. B&B
9 rooms, 1 pb
Visa, MC
C-no/S-no/P-no/H-yes

Continental plus
lunch, picnic lunches
complimentary sherry
library
bicycles

All year

Turn-of-the-century hostelry with homestyle hospitality. Nine antique-filled guestrooms with fireplaces, balconies and cozy window seats.

SAN RAFAEL ────────────────────────────

Ole Rafael B&B
528 C St., 94901
(415)-453-0414

$40-79 B&B
3 rooms, 1 pb

C-yes/S-yes/H-yes

Continental plus
Complimentary tea, wine
sitting room
piano, TV

All year

Charming rooms with antique furniture. In-between point for San Francisco and wine area of Napa.

SANTA ANA ────────────────────────────

Old Oak Table
809 Clemensen Ave.,92701
(714)-639-7798

$25-30 B&B
2 rooms, 0 pb

C-yes/S-ltd/P-no/H-yes

Full breakfast
Complimentary wine
swimming pool
sitting room

All year

Arty home—warm family atmosphere; close to Disneyland and Knotts Berry Farm. Gourmet breakfast; wine and fresh fruit in room.

SANTA BARBARA ────────────────────────────

Bath Street Inn
1720 Bath St., 93101
(805)-682-9680

$50-80 B&B
6 rooms, 4 pb
Visa, MC
C-no/S-yes/P-no

Continental plus
Complimentary wine
sitting room
bicycles

All year

Bayberry Inn
111 W. Valerio, 93101
(805)-682-3199
(805)-682-2121
All year

$45-85 B&B
6 rooms, 3 pb
Visa, MC
C-no/S-no/P-no

Continental breakfast
Complimentary wine
sitting room, piano
bicycles

A gracious in-town bed & breakfast inn within walking distance to shops, fine restaurants and entertainment, only 1-1/2 mi. to beach. Fireplaces.

Blue Quail Inn
1908 Bath Street, 93101

All year

$36-78 B&B
8 rooms, 2 pb
Visa, MC
C-12 up/P-no

Continental breakfast
Picnic lunches, cider
sitting room
bicycles

Charming country atmosphere in a quiet residential area of Santa Barbara. Guest rooms, suite and private cottages filled with antiques.

Glenborough Inn
1327 Bath St., 93101
(805)-966-0589

All year

$55-120
8 rooms, 4 pb
Visa, MC
C-12 up/S-ltd/P-no

Continental plus
Complimentary wine
sitting room

Lovely grounds, elegant antique-filled rooms & suites, breakfast in bed, enclosed jacuzzi create a relaxing romantic holiday or business trip.

Hitchcock House B&B
431 Corona del Mar,93103
(805)-962-3989

All year

$75-85 B&B
4 rooms, 4 pb
Visa, MC, AmEx
C-13 up/S-yes/P-no

Full breakfast
Complimentary wine
bicycles
private sitting rooms

Full breakfast is served in bed, on the patio, or guests may take their baskets to the beach for a breakfast or brunch picnic.

Old Yacht Club, Ltd.
431 Corona del Mar,93103
(805)-962-1277

All year

$45-75 B&B
5 rooms, 1 pb
Visa, MC, AmEx
C-12 up/S-ltd/P-no

Full breakfast
Dinner, beer & wine
bicycles

A 1912 California classic. Beautifully decorated antique-filled rooms. Gourmet breakfast. Dinner by reservation. 1/2-block to beautiful beach.

Olive House
1604 Olive St., 93101
(805)-962-4902

All year

$50-85 B&B
6 rooms, 5 pb
Visa, DC
C-yes/S-yes/P-no/H-yes

Full breakfast
Complimentary wine
sitting room, piano
entertainment
bicycles

Please Mention *The Complete Guide* **to the innkeeper when you reserve your room**

Parsonage
1600 Olive St., 93101
(805)-962-9336

$55-105
5 rooms, 2 pb

C-no/S-yes/P-no

Full breakfast
Complimentary wine
sitting room

All year

A beautifully restored Queen Anne Victorian. An oasis of elegance with ocean and mountain views. Close to everything. German spoken.

SANTA CRUZ

Babbling Brook Inn
1025 Laurel St., 95060
(408)-427-2437

$60-95 B&B
12 rooms, 12 pb
AmEx, Visa, MC
C-12-up/S-yes/P-no/H-yes

Complimentary breakfast
complimentary wine
hot tub, library
picnic baskets
French & Greek spoken

All year

European setting with gardens, gazebo, patio and covered footbridge. Laurel Creek. Complimentary wine in front of your own fireplace.

Chateau Victorian
118 1st St., 95060
(408)-458-9458

$55-95 B&B
7 rooms, 7 pb
AmEx, Visa, MC
C-no/S-no/P-no/

Complimentary breakfast
complimentary wine
bicycles, tennis nearby
hot tub nearby, piano
library, German spoken

All year

One block from the beach and the boardwalk...in the heart of the Santa Cruz fun area.

Cliff Crest
407 Cliff St., 95060
(408)-427-2609

$45-85 B&B
6 rooms, 6 pb
AmEx, Visa, MC
C-12-up/S-no/P-no/

Complimentary breakfast
complimentary wine
chocolates
sitting room
library

All year

Romantic Victorian mansion—six unique rooms with private baths. Fireplaces, solarium, gazebo and a sumptious breakfast. One block from beach & boardwalk.

Darling House
314 W. Cliff Dr., 95060
(408)-458-1958

$50-95 B&B
8 rooms, 2 pb
major
C-ltd/S-no/P-no/H-yes

Complimentary breakfast
comp. tea & wine
all meals by reservation
sitting room, library
hot tub, bicycles

All year

1910 ocean-side architectural masterpiece...beveled glass, Tiffany lamps, open hearths and the grace of genuinely open hearts. We also create sea adventures.

SANTA ROSA

Pygmalion House
331 Orange St., 95401
(707)-526-3407

$55-65 B&B
2 rooms, 0 pb

C-yes/S-yes/P-no

Full breakfast
Complimentary wine
sitting room

All year

Delightfully restored Queen Anne cottage central to Northern California wine country, San Francisco Bay area and North Coast resort areas.

SAUSALITO ————————————————————————————————

Casa Madrona Hotel
801 Bridgeway, 94965
(415)-332-0502

$60-140 B&B
30 rooms, 30 pb
Visa, MC, AmEx
C-6 up/S-yes/P-no/H-yes

Continental plus
Restaurant
hot tub

All year

Casa Madrona offers the privacy and coziness of a European country inn in individually decorated rooms.

Sausalito Hotel
16 El Portal, 94965
(415)-332-4155

$40-105
15 rooms, 8 pb
Visa, MC, AmEx
C-yes/S-yes

Continental breakfast

All year

Furnished in genuine antiques, a reasonably priced beautiful hideaway with a village feel, in colorful Sausalito, short ferry or drive to San Francisco.

SEAL BEACH ————————————————————————————————

Old Seal Beach Inn
212 5th St., 90740
(213)-493-2416

$45-90 B&B
23 rooms, 23 pb
Visa, MC, AmEx
C-yes/S-ltd/P-no/H-yes

Continental plus
Complimentary wine
swimming pool
sitting room

All year

Old world country style inn—antique street lights, ornate fences—cobblestone courtyard, private pool, garden; complimentary sherry in library.

SONOMA ————————————————————————————————

Chalet Bed & Breakfast
18935 5th St. W., 95476
(707)-938-3129
(707)-996-0190
All year

$55-75 B&B
5 rooms, 1 pb
major credit cards
C-yes/S-yes/P-no

Full breakfast
Complimentary wine
hot tub, bicycles
sitting room

Swiss-style chalet. Wine country farm setting, 3 acres—serve our own eggs, fruit, nuts. Rooms furnished in antiques. Delicious FULL breakfast.

Country Cottage Inn
291 1st St. East, 95476
(707)-938-2479

$50-75
2 rooms, 1 pb

C-yes/S-ok/P-no/H-yes

Champagne & fresh fruit
Kitchen facilities
sitting room

All year

Completely private two-bedroom garden cottage, circa 1899. One block from historic buildings and gourmet shops, restaurants and antiques.

Sonoma Hotel
110 W. Spain St., 95476
(707)-996-2996

$44-68 B&B
17 rooms, 5 pb
Visa, MC, AmEx
C-yes/S-yes/P-no

Continental breakfast
Full restaurant & bar
piano, lobby, patio

All year

Wine country hotel and restaurant furnished entirely in period antiques. Located on Sonoma's historic plaza—a perfect place for evening strolls.

Thistle Dew Inn
171 W. Spain St.
(707)-938-2909

$45-85 B&B
6 rooms, 2 pb
Visa, MC, AmEx
S-ltd/P-no/H-ltd

Continental plus
Complimentary sherry
sitting room
bicycles

All year

Just off historic Sonoma Plaza; furnished in original Gustav Stickley Mission furniture; air-conditioned, fireplaces, wine tours, hot air ballooning.

SONORA

Gunn House
286 S. Washington, 95370
(209)-532-3421

$36.72-66.96
25 rooms, 25 pb
Visa, MC, AmEx
C-yes/S-yes/P-no

Continental plus
Cocktail lounge
swimming pool

All year

Historic building, 1st 2-story adobe building in Sonora (1851) with Victorian furnishings & Victorian bar.

Jameson's
22157 Feather River, 95370
(209)-532-1248

$45-60 B&B
4 rooms, 0 pb

C-no/S-ltd/P-no

Continental plus
Afternoon tea
sitting room
bicycles

All year

Large elegant home built among huge oaks & boulders over running creek. Bridal suite with Scheherazade theme is incredibly lovely.

Lulu Belle's
85 Gold St., 95370
(209)-533-3455

$50-60 B&B
5 rooms, 5 pb

C-no/S-ltd/P-no

Full breakfast
Complimentary wine
sitting room
piano, organ
entertainment

All year

Lulu Belle's is: Old Fashioned Hospitality—Old Time Musical Entertainment & Fun— Excellent Food—Unique Rooms—Rare Antiques.

Ryan House
P.O. Box 416, 95370
(209)-533-3445

$45-55 B&B
4 rooms, 2 pb

C-6 up/S-no/P-no

Continental plus

sitting room

All year

Gold Rush romance in historic Mother Lode, close to fine dining and antique shops — we make you kindly welcome!!!

Serenity
P.O. Box 3484, 95370
(209)-533-1441

$50-60 B&B
4 rooms, 4 pb

S-yes/P-no

Full breakfast
Complimentary tea, wine
sitting room
piano

All year

Enjoy relaxed elegance in period home. Large rooms, library, veranda, and wooded grounds add to the serene ambiance.

Sonora Inn
160 S. Washington, 95370
(209)-532-7468
(800)-321-5261 RS
All year

$29-75
31 rooms, 31 pb
Visa, MC, AmEx
C-yes/S-yes/P-no

Full breakfast
Lunch, dinner, bar
hot tub, swimming pool
sitting room, piano

Historic hotel in continuous service since 1896, located in the heart of the gold country.

SUNNYVALE ———————————————————————————

Sunnyside
435 E. McKinley, 94086
(408)-736-3794

All year

$35 B&B
2 rooms, 2 pb

C-no/S-yes/P-no/H-yes

Full breakfast
Complimentary wine
sitting room

SUTTER CREEK ———————————————————————————

Foxes in Sutter Creek
POB 159, 95685
(209)-267-5882

All year

$65-115 B&B
3 rooms, 3 pb
AmEx
C-12 up/P-no

Full breakfast
Complimentary tea, wine
sitting room in 1 suite

Complimentary LOCAL wines, breakfast served on silver service to each suite or in the garden. Furnished with outstanding antiques.

Nine Eureka Street
P.O. Box 386, 95685
(209)-267-0342

All year

$45-65 B&B
5 rooms, 4 pb

C-wkdys/S-ltd/P-no

Continental plus
Complimentary wine
sitting room, organ
large front porch

Warm, friendly hospitality amidst antique furnishings, beautiful woods, stained glass windows within two blocks of unique shops, near Gold Country attractions

Sutter Creek Inn
75 Main St., Box 385, 95685
(209)-267-5606

All year

$35-75
17 rooms, 17 pb

C-no/S-yes/P-no/H-ltd

Full breakfast
Complimentary wine
sitting room, piano
library
tennis courts

3 golf courses, antique shops in town. Complete library in living room. Beautiful gardens. Handwriting analysis on request. Electric blankets.

TAHOE CITY ———————————————————————————

Mayfield House
236 Grove St., 95730
(916)-583-1001

All year

$50-70 B&B
6 rooms, 0 pb
Visa, MC
C-no/S-ok/P-no/H-yes

Continental plus
Complimentary wine

Within walking distance to shops and restaurants—each room individually decorated— "spit-spat" clean—convenient shuttle to skiing.

We want to hear from you — any comments regarding the inns or our publication may be noted on the form at the end of the book.

TEMPLETON ─────────────────────────────────

Country House Inn	$55 B&B	Continental plus
91 Main St.	6 rooms, 1 pb	Complimentary tea, wine
(805)-434-1598		sitting room
	C-no/S-no/P-no/H-yes	player piano
All year		

Home built in 1886 by founder of Templeton. 6 spacious bedrooms with antiques, fresh flowers, beautiful gardens. Near 6 wineries, Hearst Castle.

TOMALES ─────────────────────────────────

Byron Randall's	$35-50 EP	Continental plus
25 Valley St., 94971	8 rooms, 1 pb	Kitchen use
(707)-878-9992		sitting room, piano
(800)-547-1463 RS	C-10 up/S-yes/P-no	
All year		

Quiet, privacy on dead end street; large garden, patios, etc.

TRUCKEE ─────────────────────────────────

Bradley House	$30-60 B&B	Continental plus
POB 2011, 95734	6 rooms, 1 pb	Wine & cheese
(916)-587-5388		sitting room, library
	C-10 up/S-no/P-no	
All year		

Restored 1880's Victorian w/period furnishings in historic Truckee; walk to Amtrak or bus service, minutes to Tahoe north shore skiing.

Hilltop at Truckee	$29-55 B&B	Continental breakfast
Box 8579, 95737	24 rooms, 24 pb	Complimentary coffee
	Visa, MC, AmEx	jacuzzi
	C-yes/S-yes/P-yes/H-yes	parlour
All year		badmitten

Rustic ranch setting in the Sierras, nestled on 70 acres of pine covered hill, overlooking "Old Town Truckee". Come to HILLTOP!

TUOLUMNE ─────────────────────────────────

Oak Hill Ranch	$45-65 B&B	Full gourmet breakfast
P.O. Box 307, 95379	4 rooms, 1 pb	Complimentary tea, wine
(209)-928-4717		bicycles
	C-yes/S-ltd/P-no/H-yes	player piano, organ
All year		sitting room

"For a perfect sojourn into the past", spacious rural Victorian on 55 acres, near two State Parks and Yosemite. 3000' elevation in California Mother Lode.

TWAIN HARTE ─────────────────────────────────

Twain Harte B & B	$35-50 B&B	Continental plus
Box 1718, 95385	5 rooms, 1 pb	Complimentary wine
(209)-586-3311	Visa, MC	sitting room, piano
	C-yes/S-yes/P-no	pool table, rec room
All year		

Vacation hideaway in a quaint mountain village with a romantic and intimate atmosphere. Sunny breakfast room, antique furnishings.

VALLEY FORD

Inn at Valley Ford	$45-55	Continental plus
P.O. Box 439, 94972	4 rooms, 0 pb	Complimentary tea, wine
(707)-876-3182	Visa, MC	hot tub
	C-no/S-ltd/P-no/H-yes	bicycles
All year		sitting room

Comfortable Victorian farmhouse furnished with antiques, books and flowers located in pastoral hills minutes from the Pacific and Sonoma Wine Country.

VENICE

Venice Beach House	$50-125 B&B	Continental plus
15 30th Ave., 90291	8 rooms, 4 pb	Complimentary sherry
(213)-823-1966	Visa, MC, AmEx	sitting room, piano
	C-10 up/S-no/P-no	bicycles
All year		

A world of warmth and hospitality offered at this elegant 1911 historic landmark; secluded, but close to beach, galleries and restaurants.

VOLCANO

St. George Hotel	$70 MAP	Full breakfast
P.O. Box 9, 95689	20 rooms, 6 pb	Dinner, bar
(209)-296-4458		sitting room
	H-yes	pianos
Closed Jan.-early Feb.		

WEST COVINA

Hendrick Inn	$20-35 B&B	Full breakfast
2124 Merced Ave., 91791	4 rooms, 1 pb	dinner by reservation
(213)-919-2125 RS	none	hot tub, pool
	C-yes/S-yes/P-no/H-yes	bicycles, library
All year		tennis nearby

Featured in Life magazine, beautifully decorated ranch home features a hot tub, swimming pool, large porch and deck.

WEST HOLLYWOOD

La Maida House	$70-105 B&B	Continental plus
11154 La Maida St.,91601	6 rooms, 4 pb	Lunch, dinner, wine
(818)-769-3857		sitting room, den
	C-16 up/S-NO/P-no	solarium
All year		1881 grand piano

An elegant city hideaway in the midst of Los Angeles' many and diversified cultural and recreational attractions.

WESTPORT

Cobweb Palace Inn	$33-53 B&B	Continental plus
38921 N Hwy. 1, 95488	8 rooms, 5 pb	Dinner, bar
(707)-964-5588	Visa, MC	sitting room, piano
	C-16 up/S-yes/P-no	
All year		

A small Victorian western country inn located 200 yards from the ocean in a small village with secluded beaches.

Dehaven Valley Farm Inn $45-70 B&B Continental plus
POB 128, 95448 8 rooms, 2 pb Dinner, wine
(707)-964-2931 sitting room, piano
C-ltd/P-no/H-ltd
All year

Historic Victorian farmhouse nestled on 40 beautiful acres on Mendocino coast; sandy beach across the street. Gourmet dinners. Breakfast included.

Howard Creek Ranch $30-65 B&B Full ranch breakfast
P.O. Box 121, 95488 5 rooms, 0 pb Complimentary tea, wine
(707)-964-6725 hot tub, sauna
C-10 up/S-yes/H-yes swimming pool
All year sitting room, piano

Cozy inn filled with collectibles, antiques & memorabilia, unique health spa with privacy and dramatic views adjoining a wide beach.

WOODLAND HILLS

Baracco's $30/night, 200/wk B&B Continental plus
23026 Calvert, 91367 1 room, 1 pb
(213)-345-0652
C-yes/S-yes/P-no
All year

Located in San Fernando Valley, beautiful country home on ½ acre landscaped grounds. Private parking, nearby restaurants & shopping.

YOUNTVILLE

Bordeaux House $35-120 B&B Continental plus
6600 Washington, 94599 6 rooms, 6 pb Complimentary tea, wine
(707)-944-2855 Visa, MC, AmEx, DC
C-yes/S-yes/P-no/H-yes
All year

In the heart of Napa Valley wine country, north of San Francisco. Mobil 4-star rated. Fireplaces, air conditioning.

Burgundy House $40-105 B&B Continental breakfast
POB 2776, 94599 8 rooms, 4 pb Complimentary wine
(707)-944-2855 Visa, MC, AmEx, DC
C-yes/S-yes/P-no/H-yes
All year

A historic country inn with period antiques in the Napa Valley wine country north of San Francisco. Mobil 4-star rated. Air-conditioned.

Magnolia Hotel $65-135 Full breakfast
6529 Yount St., 94599 11 rooms, 11 pb Complimentary wine
(707)-944-2056 hot tub
C-no/S-no/P-no swimming pool
All year sitting room

110-year-old building, originally built as an hotel; furnished with antiques; extensive wine cellar; beautiful, relaxing deck and garden areas.

Oleander House
7433 St.Helena Hwy,94599
(707)-944-8315
(707)-257-0557 RS
All year

$85-95 B&B
4 rooms, 4 pb
credit cards accepted
C-no/S-no/P-no

Full breakfast
Complimentary wine
sitting room

Country French charm—antiques, brass beds—private decks, baths, fireplaces. Laura Ashley fabrics & papers. Wine & cheese in afternoon.

Webber Place
6610 Webber St., 94599
(707)-944-8384

$65-100 B&B
4 rooms, 2 pb
Visa, MC
C-no/S-yes/P-no

Continental plus
Complimentary tea, wine
sitting room

All year

Antique claw-legged bathtubs, which easily accomodate two, make an excellent setting for romance as well as relaxation.

COLORADO

Rocky
Mountain N.P. •

• Grand
Junction

• Denver

• Colorado
Springs

Pueblo •

• Durango

ASPEN ─────────────────────────

Christmas Inn
232 W. Main St., 81611
(303)-925-3822

21 rooms, 21 pb
Visa, MC, AmEx
C-yes/S-yes/P-no/H-ltd

Continental plus
(winter only)
hot tub, sauna
sitting room

May 28-Oct. 15, 11/20-4/15

Attractive, cozy, clean rooms with extra long beds. Excellent location. Cheerful lobby & sitting room for spectacular view of Aspen ski mountains.

Hearthstone House
134 E. Hymm St., 81611
(303)-925-7632
(303)-925-9000 RS

$96-120 B&B
18 rooms, 18 pb
Visa, AmEx
C-5 up/S-yes/P-no

Full breakfast
Afternoon tea
hot tub
sitting room, library

The preferred place to stay in Aspen.

Hotel Lenado
200 S. Aspen St., 81611
(303)-925-6246
(303)-925-9000 RS
All year

$90-300 B&B
19 rooms, 19 pb
Visa, MC, AmEx
C-yes/S-yes/P-no/H-yes

Full breakfast
Tea, appetizers, bar
hot tub, sauna, tennis
bicycles, swimming pool
library, piano

A new Aspen landmark — inventive architecture, romantic ambience, gracious service. Seventeen Guestrooms & suites furnished in applewood, ironwood, willow

Innsbruck Inn
233 W. Main St., 81611
(303)-925-2980
(303)-925-9000 RS
All year

$40-105 B&B
31 rooms, 31 pb
Visa, MC, AmEx, DC, CB
C-yes/S-yes/P-no/H-ltd

Continental buffet
Complimentary wine
Swimming pool, sauna
sitting room, piano

Charming, family-operated Tyrolean-style lodge located at skiers' bus stop. Generous, complimentary continental breakfast buffet and apres-ski refreshments

---

Little Red Ski Haus
118 E. Cooper, 81611
(303)-925-3333
925-9000 RS
Summer-Fall-Winter

$12-32 B&B
21 rooms, 4 pb

C-yes/S-yes/P-no/H-ltd

Full breakfast (winter)
Continental (summer)
hot tub
fireplace lounge
piano

Famous restored historic Victorian Inn/Lodge. 3 lounges, one with fireplace. Two blocks from center of town and main ski lift.

Molly Gibson Lodge
120 W. Hopkins, 81611
(303)-925-2580
(800)-922-9010
All year

$69-229 B&B
18 rooms, 18 pb
Visa, MC, AmEx
C-yes/S-yes/P-no

Continental breakfast
Bar service
hot tub, swimming pool
tennis
lounge, fireplace

Snow Queen Lodge
124 E. Cooper, 81611
(303)-925-9973
925-9000 RS
All year

$20-54 B&B
5 rooms, 0 pb
AmEx
C-yes/S-yes/P-no

Continental plus

We specialize in a friendly congenial atmosphere with western hospitality and inexpensive rates.

Ullr Lodge
520 W. Main St., 81611

All year

$37-65 B&B
23 rooms, 23 pb
Visa, MC, AmEx, DC
C-yes/S-yes/P-no

Full breakfast (winter)
Continental (summer)
hot tub, sauna
swimming pool
sitting room

Small European style lodge offering rooms and apartments. Free shuttle ski route. Walking distance to music festival & Aspen Institute.

BOULDER

Briar Rose B & B
2151 Arapahoe Ave.,80302
(303)-442-3007

All year

$49-75 B&B
11 rooms, 6 pb
Visa, MC, AmEx
C-yes/S-yes/P-ltd

Continental plus
Afternoon tea, wine
high tea—chamber music
poetry, drama readings
bicycles

Entering the Briar Rose is like entering another time when hospitality was an art and the place for dreams was a feather bed.

Prices quoted are the most current available. However, due to increases and seasonal fluctuations, they may have changed. Be sure to check when you make your reservations.

BUENA VISTA

Blue Sky Inn
719 Arizona St., 81211
(303)-395-8862

$38-48 B&B
6 rooms, 2 pb

C-yes/S-no/P-yes

All year

Full breakfast
Other meals(reservation)
bicycles
sitting room, library
w/ fireplaces

On Arkansas River, mountain views, fishing, bird watching, croquet, vegetable and flower gardens. Glorious ski-touring trails — December to May.

CENTRAL CITY

Two Ten Casey
POB 154, 80427
(303)-582-5906
(303)-333-3340 RS
All year

$25 plus $5pp B&B
1 room, 1 pb
no
C-yes/S-yes/P-no/H-yes

Continental breakfast

History and beauty surrounding this old mining town. Separate entrance and bath is very special.

CLARK

The Home Ranch
Box 822K, 80428
(303)-879-1780

$92 pp
7 rooms, 7 pb

C-yes/S-yes/P-no

All year

Full breakfast
Lunch, dinner
sitting room, piano

What's special? The food, the horses, the fishing, and the company.

COLORADO SPRINGS

Griffin's Hospitality Hs
4222 N Chestnut,80907
(303)-599-3035

$30-35 B&B
3 rooms, 0 pb
no
C-yes/S-yes/P-no

All year

Full breakfast

piano
sitting room
tennis nearby

"Look out our windows— you have a wonderful view of Pikes Peak." Air Force Academy, Royal Gorge, Olympic Training Center.

CRIPPLE CREEK

Imperial Hotel
Box 247, 80813
(303)-689-2922

$28-33
30 rooms, 16 pb
Visa, MC, AmEx, DC, CB
C-yes/S-yes/P-no

Mid-May to Mid-October

Full-service restaurant
Bar service
sitting room, piano
entertainment

Small intimate hotel, built in 1896, turn of century decor in public & private rooms, fine international cuisine, cabaret style melodrama theatre.

DEL NORTE

Balloon Ranch
Box 41, 81132
(303)-754-2533

$88 up B&B
14 rooms, 6 pb
Visa, MC, AmEx
C-yes/S-yes/P-ltd

May—November

Full breakfast
Lunch, dinner, bar
hot tub, sauna
swimming pool, tennis
sitting room

Mountain valley seclusion, hot air balloon trips, horses, dirt bikes, 4X4 tours, rafting, rock climbing, balloon pilot school.

86 Colorado

────────────────────────────────

Sheets Residence | $37 B&B | Breakfast
577 High St., 80218 | 4 rooms, 4 pb | Afternoon tea
(303)-329-6170 | no | bicycles
| C-yes/S-yes/P-no | piano
All year | | sitting room

From Better to Best to the ultimate in Perfection & Greatness.

DURANGO ────────────────────────────────

Tall Timber | $975 pp/week AP | All meals included
Box 90G, 81301 | 8 rooms, 4 pb | Bar service
(303)-259-4813 | | hot tubs, sauna
| C-yes/S-yes/P-no | swimming pool, tennis
May 15-Oct. 15; 12/10-2/1 | | sitting room

Remote luxury resort — accessible only by helicopter or narrow gauge train. 5-star accomodations in wilderness setting. Total escape.

The Victorian Inn | $35-55 B&B | Full breakfast
2117 W Second Ave.,81301 | 4 rooms, 2 pb | Complimentary wine
(303)-247-2223 | no | bicycles
| C-yes/S-yes/P-yes | sitting room

Beautifully decorated rooms, Eggs Benedict house specialty, skiing at Purgatory, Silverton narrow gauge train.

EMPIRE ────────────────────────────────

The Peck House | $30-60 | Lunch, dinner, bar
P.O. Box 428, 80438 | 10 rooms, 5 pb |
(303)-569-9870 | Visa, MC, AmEx, DC, CB | sitting room
| C-yes/S-yes/P-no |
All year | |

Country Inn of Victorian elegance filled with history and antiques, close by Colorado's Ski Country, serving superior continental dining.

ESTES PARK ────────────────────────────────

Aspen Lodge & Guest Ranch | | Full breakfast
Longs Peak Rte. 7,80517 | 23 rooms, 23 pb | Lunch, dinner, bar
| | swimming pool
| C-yes/S-yes/P-no | entertainment

Beautiful cozy lodge with magnificent view of Longs Peak and Rocky Mountain National Park. Exceptional meals and fine wine list.

Wanek's Lodge at Estes | $34/2 B&B | Continental breakfast
POB 898, 80517 | 6 rooms, 0 pb | Lunch, dinner, BYOB
| no | piano
| C-yes/S-ltd/P-no | sitting room
All year | |

A modern mountain inn, old-fashioned hospitality, great food, unparalleled panoramas; Rocky Mt. Nat'l Park, fish, golf, swim, tennis, hike, ski nearby.

GREEN MT. FALLS

Columbine Lodge
Box 267, 80819
(303)-684-9062

$18.50-52.50 EP
16 rooms, 16 pb
Visa, MC
C-yes/S-yes/P-yes

Breakfast, lunch, dinner

piano
sitting room
near pool, tennis

All year

Historic, rustic mountain lodge. Beautiful setting. Homecooked meals. Open all year with year round activities.

Outlook Lodge
6975 Howard, 80819
(303)-684-2303

$25-32 pp B&B
12 rooms, 2 pb
Visa, MC
C-yes/S-yes/P-yes/H-ltd

Continental plus

piano
sitting room

June-August

Victorian parsonage in mountain village, original furnishing. Fishing, hiking, swimming, tennis, horseback riding, only 15 minutes from Colorado Springs.

LA VETA

1899 Inn
314 S. Main, 81055
(303)-742-3576

$20.00-22.50 B&B
5 rooms, 2 pb

C-yes/S-no/P-sm

Full breakfast

sitting room
piano
bicycles

All year

Like walking into grandmother's home with family antiques and light airy rooms. A small town retreat in southern Colorado.

MANITOU SPRINGS

Nippersink Wimmersink
106 Spencer Ave., 80829
(303)-685-9211

$25 B&B
3 rooms, 1 pb
credit cards accepted
C-12 up/S-yes/P-no

Continental plus
Complimentary wine
sitting room

All year

At the base of Pikes Peak, 1885 Victorian offers spacious accomodations, complimentary evening sherry in the parlor. Most charming shops in the Rockies.

OURAY

Baker's Manor
317 Second St., 81427
(303)-325-4574

$16-19 B&B EP
6 rooms, 0 pb
no
C-yes/S-yes/P-no

Continental breakfast

June-Oct.

100 year old Victorian guest house 8,000 feet in San Juan Mountains. Quaint town with hot springs pool, hiking and jeeping.

St. Elmo Hotel
426 Main St., 81427
(303)-325-4318

$26-48 B&B
12 rooms, 6 pb
Visa, MC
C-yes/S-ltd/P-no/H-ltd

Continental plus
Dinner, bar
sitting room
piano

All year

Hotel & BonTon Restaurant surrounded by beautiful, rugged 14,000-ft. peaks. Furnished with antiques, honeymoon suite. Hot springs, jeeping.

88 Colorado

The House of Yesteryear
Box 440, 81427
(303)-325-4277

$25-45 B&B
8 rooms, 1 pb
no
C-yes/S-yes/P-no

Continental breakfast

June 10—Sept. 10

Overlooks Ouray. Beautiful view. Ouray—4 blocks—beautiful old town. Jeeping the mountains favorite sport. Hummingbirds.

Weisbaden Spa & Lodge
Box 349, 81427
(303)-325-4347

All year

$44-62 dbl B&B
16 rooms, 16 pb

C-yes/S-ltd/P-no/H-yes

Continental plus
Tea, coffee, hot cocoa
hot tub, sauna
swimming pool
sitting room

The Weisbaden has been called "a place of unequaled ambience." Unique natural vapor cave w/ 106-degree soaking pool. Cross-country right from the front door.

PONCHA SPRINGS —————————————————

Jackson Hotel
220 S. Main St., 81242
(303)-539-3122

All year

$18 up
11 rooms, 3 pb
Visa, MC
C-yes/S-yes/P-no

Full breakfast
Lunch, dinner, bar
sitting room, piano

Historic old west hotel—Jesse James slept, ate, and drank here. Friendly, comfortable. Summer whitewater rafting, winter alpine & X-C skiing.

REDSTONE —————————————————————

Historic Redstone Inn
82 Redstone Blvd.,81623
(303)-963-2526
(303)-945-4955 RS
All year

2/$42-48 EP
35 rooms, 30 pb
Visa, MC, AmEx
C-yes/S-yes/P-no/H-yes

Breakfast, lunch, dinner
Bar service
tennis courts
piano
sitting room

Country inn with unique history, beautiful setting, combines today's comfort with yesterday's charm. Notable for lovely decor, fine restaurant.

SILVERTON ————————————————————

Alma House
220 E. 10th St., 81433
(303)-387-5336

June 15—Labor Day

$30
10 rooms, 0 pb
credit cards accepted
C-yes/S-no/P-yes

Coffee/tea

sitting room
in-house movies

Completely restored 1898 hotel for non-smokers featuring soft water, huge towels, clock-radio, cable color TV, Beautyrest Queen in each room.

Teller House Hotel
1250 Greene St., 81433
(303)-387-5423

All year

$24 dbl B&B
9 rooms, 0 pb
credit cards accepted
C-yes/S-yes/P-yes

Full breakfast
Lunch, dinner, bar
piano in 1 room

Teller House Hotel—Step back 100 years in the heart of the San Juans—the "Mining Town that Never Quit."

STEAMBOAT SPRINGS —————————————————————————

Sky Valley Lodge
Box 2153, 80477
(303)-879-5158

Closed May 1-30

$57 dbl B&B
26 rooms, 26 pb
Visa, MC
C-yes/S-yes/P-yes

Full breakfast
Dinner, bar
hot tub, sauna
swimming pool, tennis
sitting room

A modern rustic lodge with cathedral ceilings and oversized fireplaces. Property includes 110 acres with horseback riding, river rafting.

The House on the Hill
POB 770598, 80477
(303)-879-1650

Except May

$40-75 B&B
3 rooms, 0 pb
Visa, MC
C-older/S-yes/P-ltd

Continental plus
Complimentary wine
hot tub
piano
sitting room

Elegant home, friendly atmosphere near downtown Steamboat and fine cuisine. Cross-country skiing, close proximity to all sporting activities.

TELLURIDE ————————————————————————————————

New Sheridan Hotel
231 Colorado Ave., 81435
(303)-728-4351
(800)-525-3455 RS
All year

$30-66
30 rooms, 9 pb
Visa, MC, AmEx
C-yes/S-yes/P-no/H-yes

Full breakfast
Lunch(summer),dinner,bar

Victorian elegance, relaxed, restored comfort, situated in the heart of Telluride—a national historic landmark, just minutes from Telluride Ski Area.

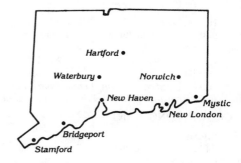

CONNECTICUT

CHESTER ——————————————————————————————————————

The Inn at Chester
318 W. Main St.,
(203)-526-4961

All year

$70 EP
22 rooms, 22 pb
Visa, MC, AmEx
C-yes/S-yes/P-yes/H-yes

Full breakfast
Lunch, dinner, bar
bicycles, tennis, sauna
sitting room, library,
piano, entertainment

The Inn, on 15 acres centered around a 1776 farmhouse, abounds with fireplaces, antiques, and public areas for resting, reading, refreshment.

EAST HADDAM

Bishop's Gate
Goodspeed Landing,06423
(203)-873-1677

All year

$40-85 B&B
6 rooms, 4 pb
no
C-6 up/S-yes/P-no/H-yes

Continental plus
Complimentary wine
sauna
piano
sitting room

1818 Colonial home with 6 charming guest rooms, open fireplaces, period pieces and fine antiques, near famous Goodspeed Opera House.

ESSEX

Griswood Inn
06426
(203)-767-0991

Except Christmas

$48-56 B&B
21 rooms, 21 pb
Visa, MC, AmEx, DC
C-yes/S-yes/P-yes

Continental plus
Lunch, dinner, bar
sitting room
entertainment

Continuous operation for 207 years. Country place. A myriad of Currier and Ives steamboat prints. On the banks of a beautiful river.

GLASTONBURY

Butternut Farm
1654 Main St.,06033
(203)-633-7197

All year

$32-38
4 rooms, 0 pb
no
C-yes/S-ltd/P-no

Complimentary wine

piano
sitting room

An 18th-Century jewel furnished with period antiques. Attractive grounds with herb gardens and ancient trees.

GREENWICH

Homestead Inn
420 Field Pt. Rd., 06830
(203)-869-7500

All year

$65-132 B&B
13 rooms, 13 pb
all
C-yes/S-yes/P-no/H-ltd

Continental breakfast
Lunch, dinner, bar
sitting room

Sophisticated country inn; 45 min. from NYC; built 1799, completely restored 1979; superb French cuisine for lunch & dinner; many antiques.

GROTON LONG POINT

Shore Inne
54 East Shore Rd.,06340
(203)-536-1180

April—Nov.

$32-45
7 rooms, 3 pb
Visa, MC
C-yes/S-ltd/P-no

Continental breakfast

tennis courts

Unique location on the water with splendid views. Residential area. 3½ miles from Mystic. Private beaches, fishing, tennis.

Our listings, supplied by the innkeeper, are as complete as possible. Many of the inns have more features — amenities or food and beverage service — than we list. Be sure to inquire when you book.

Stonehenge, Ridgefield, Connecticut

IVORYTOWN

Copper Beech Inn
Main Street, 06442
(203)-767-0330

5 rooms, 5 pb
all major
C-ltd/S-yes/P-no

Continental plus
Lunch, dinner, bar
bicycles
piano

All year (ex. Mondays)

entertainment

A hostelry where even a short visit is a celebration of good living. The only 4-star restaurant in Connecticut.

MYSTIC

1833 House
33 Greenmanville,06355
(203)-572-0633

$22-52 B&B
4 rooms, 2 pb

C-yes/P-yes

Continental plus

sitting room

All year

Proximity to world famous Mystic Seaport Museum, U.S. Coast Guard Academy, Mystic Marinelife Aquarium, one hour to Newport R.I.

Harbour Inne & Cottage
Edgemont St., 06355
(203)-572-9253

$25-60 EP
5 rooms, 3 pb
no
C-yes/S-yes/P-yes

sitting room

All year

Small Inne plus 3-room cottage on Mystic River. Walk to Seaport & all attractions. Water-front tables, cable TV, kitchen priv., canoeing & boating.

92　Connecticut

NEW MILFORD ──

Homestead Inn　　　　　$28-36
5 Elm St., 06776　　　　　15 rooms, 15 pb
(203)-354-4080　　　　　　Visa, MC, AmEx　　　　sitting room
　　　　　　　　　　　　　C-yes/S-yes/P-yes/H-ltd

All year

Located in the center of town, at the village green. Within two blocks of churches, banks, drug stores and fine restaurants.

NEW PRESTON ──

Hopkins Inn　　　　　　$33-38 EP　　　　　　Full breakfast
Hopkins Rd., 06777　　　9 rooms, 7 pb　　　　Luncheon, dinner, bar
(203)-868-7295　　　　　no　　　　　　　　　　sitting room
　　　　　　　　　　　　C-yes/S-ok/P-no

May—Oct.

A country inn overlooking Lake Waramaug — terrace dining in the summer.

**The Inn on Lake
Waramaug**　　　　　　　$60-83 MAP　　　　　Full breakfast
06777　　　　　　　　　25 rooms, 25 pb　　　Luncheon, dinner, bar
(203)-868-0563　　　　Visa, MC, AmEx, DC　　pool, sauna, tennis
(212)-724-8775　　　　C-yes/S-yes/P-no/H-yes　sitting room, piano
All year　　　　　　　　　　　　　　　　　　entertainment

Authentic colonial (1790) restored and furnished with pine and cherry antiques. Complete resort, private beach, indoor pool, Showboat Cruises, sleigh rides.

NORFOLK ──

The Blackberry River Inn $40-60　　　　　　Luncheon, dinner, bar
Route 44, 06058　　　　16 rooms, 7 pb
(203)-542-5100　　　　Visa, MC　　　　　　　swimming, tennis
　　　　　　　　　　　C-12 up/S-yes/P-no/H-yes　2 sitting rooms, piano
Except March　　　　　　　　　　　　　　　　library, fireplaces

Inn dates back to 1763 — Near all outdoor sports, state parks, antiquing, canoeing & horseback riding.

Mountain View Inn　　$52-57 B&B　　　　　Continental plus
Litchfield Rd., 06058　　11 rooms, 5 pb　　　Lunch, tea, dinner, bar
(203)-542-5595　　　　Visa, MC, AmEx　　　　bicycles
　　　　　　　　　　　C-yes/S-yes/P-ltd/H-yes　piano
All year　　　　　　　　　　　　　　　　　　sitting room

Romantic 1875 Victorian country inn located in picture perfect village. Central to musical concerts, antiquing, skiing and hiking.

OLD LYME ──

Bee and Thistle Inn　　$46-68　　　　　　Full breakfast
100 Lyme St., 06371　　10 rooms, 8 pb　　　Lunch, dinner, bar
(203)-434-1667　　　　Visa, MC, AmEx　　　　bicycles
　　　　　　　　　　　C-yes/S-yes/P-no　　　2 parlors, piano
All year　　　　　　　　　　　　　　　　　　harpist Saturdays

An Inn on 5½ acres in historic district. On the Lieutenant River set back amidst majestic trees. Sophisticated country cuisine.

Old Lyme Inn
85 Lyme St., 06371

$45-50
5 rooms, 5 pb
major credit cards
C-yes/S-yes/P-yes/H-ltd

Continental breakfast
Lunch, dinner

Exc. Mon. & Xmas wk.

RIDGEFIELD ———————————————————————————

The Elms Inn
500 Main St.,06877
(203)-438-2541

$55-95 B&B
20 rooms, 20 pb
Visa, MC, AmEx, DC
C-yes/S-yes/P-no

Continental breakfast
Bar service
lounge

All year

The 1760 Elms on Historical Site of Battle of Ridgefield; four-poster beds, fireplace each room, continental breakfast is an experience.

Stonehenge
Route 7, 06877
(203)-438-6511

$65-75 EP
8 rooms, 8 pb
Visa, MC, AmEx, DC, CB
C-yes/S-yes/P-no/H-yes

Continental breakfast
Lunch, dinner, wine
swimming pool
sitting room
piano

All year

Country inn located on 10 acres in densely wooded countryside. Idyllic seclusion with lake, inground pool. Restaurant has international reputation.

West Lane Inn
22 West Ln., 06877
(203)-438-7323

$85-95 B&B
20 rooms, 20 pb
Visa, MC, AmEx
C-yes/S-yes/P-no/H-yes

Full breakfast
Lunch, snacks, tea
bicycles
tennis courts
sitting room

All year

Elegant country inn, relaxing atmosphere, heated towel racks, bidets. A charming place to treat yourself to sheer luxury.

SALISBURY ———————————————————————————

White Hart Inn
Village Green, 06068
(203)-435-2511

$45-65 EP
25 rooms, 23 pb
Visa, MC, AmEx
C-yes/S-yes/P-yes/H-ltd

Full breakfast
Lunch, tea, dinner, bar
hot tub
sitting room, piano
entertainment

All year

Traditional country inn for all seasons, part of everyone's visit to New England. Enjoy fine dining, drinking, lodging & our country store.

WESTPORT ———————————————————————————

Cotswold Inn
76 Myrtle Ave., 06880
(203)-226-3766

$140-165 B&B
4 rooms, 4 pb
Visa, MC, AmEx
C-yes/S-yes/P-no/H-yes

Full breakfast
Wine & cheese
sitting room
entertainment (wknds)

All year

A lovely country retreat in the heart of what is considered the most sophisticated, cosmopolitan town in New England!

**Be sure to call the Inn to verify details and prices
and to make your reservation**

WOODBURY ——————————————————————————————

Curtis House
Main St., 06798
(203)-263-2101

$20-40 B&B
18 rooms, 12 pb
yes
C-yes/P-no

Continental breakfast
Luncheon, dinner, bar

All year

Connecticut's oldest Inn, most rooms with canopied beds.

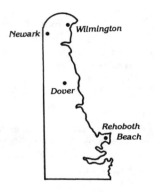

BETHANY BEACH ——————————————————————————

The Homestead Guests
721 Garfield Pkwy,19930
(302)-539-7248

$20-25
3 rooms, 0 pb
no
C-yes/S-yes/P-no

bicycles

May-Nov.

Country home, big yard, a beautiful location and a family beach.

Sea Vista Villa
Box 62, 19930
(302)-539-3354
(202)-232-8718 RS
May-Thanksgiving

$45-50 dbl B&B
3 rooms, 3 pb
no
C-no/S-yes/P-no

Full breakfast
Complimentary happy hour
swimming pool
tennis courts
bicycle rental

Small guest houses by the lake, full breakfast. Come spring, summer and fall. Near Washington & Baltimore.

NEW CASTLE ——————————————————————————————

William Penn Guest House
206 Delaware St.,19720
(302)-328-7736

$25-30 EP
4 rooms, 0 pb
no
C-yes/S-yes/P-no

living room

All year

The house was built about 1682. William Penn stayed overnight. Restored and located in the center of the Square.

REHOBOTH BEACH ──────────────────────────────

Beach House Bedroom $35-40 B&B   Continental breakfast
Box 138, 19971   2 rooms, 1 pb
(302)-227-0937   no   large porch
     C-no/S-yes/P-no
June-Sept.

Beach—2 blocks. Washington's summer capital. Fine dining, relaxed summer fun in a modern, airy beach cottage. Min. stay 2 nights.

The Corner Cupboard Inn   Full breakfast
50 Park Ave., 19971   18 rooms, 10 pb   Dinner (summer season)
     sitting room
     C-yes/S-yes/P-yes   piano

The Inn that was in before Inns were in! Fifty years at 50 Park Ave. as a summer retreat for Baltimore and Washington. B&B mid-Sept. to Memorial Day.

The Pleasant Inn $55 &up   Continental breakfast
1st St. & Olive, 19971   10 rooms, 10 pb
(302)-227-7311   Visa, MC
     C-no/S-yes/P-no

All year

Beach hideaway furnished in genuine antiques.

FLORIDA

AMELIA ISLAND ──────────────────────────────

1735 House $45-80 B&B   Continental plus
584 S. Fletcher, 32034   6 rooms, 6 pb
(904)-261-5818   Visa, MC, AmEx
     C-yes/S-yes/P-no/H-yes

All year

White frame house overlooking the Atlantic Ocean. Breakfast served with morning newspaper. Lighthouse.

BRADENTON

Banyan House
624 Fontana Ln., 33529
(813)-746-8633

$40-55 B&B
2 rooms, 2 pb
no
C-no/S-yes/P-no

Continental plus

sitting room

Nov.—May

Self-contained guest house, furnished with antiques, sleeps 2. Gulf beaches are 5 miles or walk to the bayou or river.

CABBAGE KEY

Cabbage Key Inn
33924
(813)-283-2278

$35
6 rooms, 2 pb
Visa, MC
C-yes/S-yes/P-no

Full breakfast
Lunch, dinner, bar
piano
sitting room

All year

Cabbage Key, a beautiful island with nature paths through exotic jungles and breathtaking waterfront, known by yachtsmen from many ports.

CEDAR

Island Hotel
Main St., 32625
(904)-543-5111

$30-50
10 rooms, 3 pb
no
C-yes/P-ltd

Full breakfast
Brunch, dinner, bar
sitting room, piano
jazz trio
bicycle-built-for-2

Except January

1850 Jamaican Architecture overlooking historic district. Homemade: bread, chowders, baked & poached seafood, fresh vegetables. Antiques.

ENGLEWOOD

Lemon Bay B&B
12 Southwind Dr., 33533
(813)-474-7571

$35 EP
1 room, 1 pb
no
C-yes/S-yes/P-no/H-yes

Continental breakfast

Organ

Oct.—June

Bayfront location offers views, fishing and boat dockage. Walk to P.O. and stores. Short drive to Gulf. Tennis/golf nearby.

EVERGLADES CITY

Rod & Gun Club
PO Box G, 33929
(813)-695-2101

$38 EP
17 rooms, 17 pb
Gulf
C-yes/S-yes/P-no

Full breakfast
Lunch, dinner, bar
Swimming pool
bicycles
tennis courts

All year

A charming building of the late 1800s. Paneled in pecky Cypress native to this section of Florida at that time. A genuine old Southern hostelry of that era.

Prices quoted are the most current available. However, due to increases and seasonal fluctuations, they may have changed. Be sure to check when you make your reservations.

FERNANDINA BEACH

Bailey House
28 S. 7th St, 32034
(904)-261-5390

All year

$45-75
4 rooms, 4 pb
AmEx
C-10 up/S-ltd/P-no

Continental breakfast

old pump organ
sitting room
air conditioned, heat

On National Historic Register in 30 block historic district. Walk to shopping, restaurants, marina & tennis. 5 min. to beach & golf.

Greyfield Inn
Box 878
Cumberland Is., 32034
(904)-261-6408
All year

$75 pp AP
9 rooms, 1 pb
Visa, MC
C-yes/S-ltd/P-no

Three meals included
Bar
hot tub
bicycles
sitting room

House built 1904 for Margaret Carnegie. Original furnishings and unspoiled island—no telephone, TV, etc. Beach. Seafood, everything homemade.

HAWTHORNE

The Yearling
Rte. 3 PO Box 123, 32640

All year

$16-18
7 rooms, 7 pb
yes
C-yes/S-yes/P-no/H-yes

Lunch, dinner, bar

Cabins on Cross Creek away from city traffic. Restaurant on property serving regional favorites.

INDIANTOWN

Seminole Country Inn
15885 Warfield, 33456
(305)-597-3786

All year

$29-34
28 rooms, 22 pb
credit cards accepted
C-yes/S-yes/P-no/H-yes

Full breakfast
Lunch, dinner, bar
hot tub, sauna
sitting room

INVERNESS

Crown Hotel
109 N. Seminole Av,32650
(904)-344-5555

All year

$48-100 B&B
34 rooms, 34 pb

C-yes/S-yes/P-no/H-yes

Full breakfast
Lunch, dinner, bar
swimming pool
entertainment
sitting room, piano

Fully restored Victorian hotel. Gourmet dining in restaurant and English Pub. Browse in out antique shop or relax by the pool.

KEY WEST

Eaton Lodge
511 Eaton St., 33040
(305)-294-3800

Mid-Oct.—early Sept.

$50-90 B&B
11 rooms, 11 pb
Visa, MC, AmEx
C-yes/S-yes/P-no/H-ltd

Continental plus
Refrigerators
hot tub
sitting room

Handsome Victorian home, in historic downtown, tastefully adapted; paddle fans and verandas; lush tropical gardens, whirlpool-spa & secluded terrace.

Eaton Lodge, Key West, Florida

Eden House
1015 Fleming, 33040
(305)-296-6868

Nov.–Aug.

$22-47 EP
30 rooms, 7 pb
yes
C-no/S-yes/P-no

Restaurant

swimming pool
sitting room
bicycles

In the heart of old Key West. Pool, garden cafe, Bermuda fans and lush flora set the mood at the Eden House. A step back in time.

Ellie's Nest
1414 Newton St., 33040
(305)-296-5757

All year

$38-53 B&B
6 rooms, 4 pb
Visa, MC
C-no/S-yes/P-no/H-ltd

Continental breakfast
Snacks, wine
hot tub
swimming pool
sitting room, library

Key West's only guest house for gay women where you can be yourself in a modern secluded tropical environment with friends.

LAKE WALES

Chalet Suzanne
PO Box AC, 33853
(813)-676-6011

All year

$45-70 EP
30 rooms, 30 pb
All major
C-yes/S-yes/P-yes/H-yes

Full breakfast
Lunch, dinner, bar
swimming pool
piano

Unique country inn centrally located for Florida attractions. Gourmet meals; private airstrip. A memorable experience.

LYNN HAVEN

Gulf Coast Inn
324 Bell Circle, 32444
(204)-265-5275

All year

$29 B&B
2 rooms, pb
no
C-yes/S-no/P-no

Full breakfast
Comp. tea & wine
sitting room
television
1 bicycle

Executive home ten minutes from Panama City Beach on the Gulf of Mexico and the nightlife of the Miracle Strip.

MARATHON

Hopp Inn Guest House
5 Man-O-War Dr., 33050
(305)-743-4118

All year

$35 B&B
5 rooms, 5 pb
no
C-yes/S-yes/P-no

Full breakfast
Afternoon tea
sitting room
bicycles

Oceanfront rooms, tastefully decorated, color TV, air conditioned, Bahama fans, tropical setting in the heart of Florida Keys. Rooms have separate entrances.

NAPLES

Feller House
2473 Longboat Dr., 33942
(813)-774-0182

Oct.–April

$23-30 B&B
2 rooms, 2 pb
no
C-6 up/S-yes/P-no

Continental plus
Wine or cocktails
swimming pool
tennis courts
sitting room, piano

Enjoy sunny weather in winter in homey atmosphere. Ten minutes to miles of beach on Gulf of Mexico.

100 Florida

PENSACOLA

Sunshine
508 Decatur Ave., 32507
(904)-455-6781

$17-28 B&B
2 rooms, 0 pb
no
C-yes/S-ok/P-no

Full breakfast

swimming pool
sitting room
TV

All year

Sunshine is 20 minutes from beautiful Gulf of Mexico — world's whitest beaches. We speak German. Free pickup from airport.

ST. AUGUSTINE

Kenwood Inn
38 Marine St., 32084
(904)-824-2116

$30-50 B&B
15 rooms, 13 pb
Visa, MC
C-older/S-yes/P-no

Continental breakfast

swimming pool
sitting room
piano

All year

19th-Century inn located in historic district of our nation's oldest city. Walk to attractions; beautiful beaches 5 minutes away.

St. Francis Inn
279 St. George St.,32084
(904)-824-6068

$20-60
10 rooms, 10 pb
no
C-yes/S-yes/P-no

All year

Built in 1791, located in Historic District, 1 block west of the Oldest House in U.S.A.

WAKULLA

Wakulla Springs & Lodge $29 EP
32305
(904)-640-7011

27 rooms, 27 pb
Visa, MC
C-yes/S-yes/P-no

Full breakfast
Lunch, dinner
sitting rooms

All year

Pleasant and spacious accommodations with fine dining. Jungle and glass-bottom boat tours through a wildlife sanctuary.

Our listings, supplied by the innkeeper, are as complete as possible. Many of the inns have more features — amenities or food and beverage service — than we list. Be sure to inquire when you book.

GEORGIA

• *Atlanta*

• *Macon*

• *Columbus*

Savannah •

• *Americus*

Okefenokee
Swamp •

CLARKESVILLE

LaPrade's
Rte. 1, Hwy 197N, 30523
(404)-947-3312

April—Dec.

$22 pp AP
20 rooms, 20 pb
no
C-yes/S-yes/P-no/H-yes

Full breakfast
3 meals included
game room
lake swimming

LaPrade's Restaurant, Cabins and Marina on Lake Burton, famous for bountiful southern cooking served family style. On prettiest lakes in Georgia.

COLUMBUS

Deloffre House
812 Broadway, 31901
(404)-324-1144

All year

$43-55 B&B
4 rooms, 4 pb
Visa, MC, AmEx
C-12 up/S-yes/P-no/no

Continental plus
Complimentary sherry
sitting room

An 1863 town house, elegantly restored and modernized, where guests may enjoy Victorian charm and gracious hospitality of the South.

DAHLONEGA

Forest Hills Mt. Resort
Rte. 3, 30533
(404)-864-6456

All year

$40-95
18 rooms, 18 pb
Visa, MC, AmEx
C-yes/S-yes/P-yes/H-yes

Full breakfast
Weekend family suppers
swimming pool
private hot tub

Family owned and operated mountain retreat offering private cabins, recreation facilities, and lots of room for your enjoyment.

Smith House
202 Chestatee SW, 30533
(404)-864-3566

All year

$35 EP
20 rooms, 20 pb
Visa, MC, AmEx
C-yes/S-yes/P-no/no

Full breakfast
Lunch, dinner
swimming pool

Old country inn. Big porch, rocking chairs, famous all-you-can-eat dining room service, one block from town square.

HELEN

Hilltop Haus
PO Box 154, 30545
(404)-878-2388

$25-45
4 rooms, 2 pb
no
C-yes/S-yes/P-no/H-yes

Full breakfast
Afternoon coffee
bicycles
sitting room

All year

Located within walking distance of alpine village, Helen. Country-style breakfast with buttermilk biscuits, Appalachian Trail nearby.

LAKEMONT

Lake Rabun Inn
30552
(404)-782-4946

$16.50-22.50
16 rooms, 0 pb
no
C-yes/S-yes/P-no/no

Continental breakfast

sitting room

April—Oct.

Charming, informal accomodations for nature lovers. Lobby has stone fireplace and handmade furniture. Spring water. Whitewater rafting, swimming, hiking.

MARIETTA

Arden Hall
1052 Arden Dr. SW, 30060
(404)-422-0780
(404)-422-0796
All year

$45-50 B&B
2 rooms, 2 pb
no
C-no/S-no/P-no/no

Full breakfast

sitting room
piano

Arden Hall was built in 1880 and is 18 miles from Atlanta. We offer elegant breakfasts, tour information and many continental restaurants nearby.

MOUNTAIN CITY

York House
Box 126, 30562
(404)-746-2068

$25-40 B&B
14 rooms, 14 pb
Visa, MC
C-yes/S-yes/P-no/no

Continental plus

sitting room
piano
video movies

All year

*Tranquil lodging, antiques. Breakfast served in room. White water rafting, skiing, rocking on porch, featured in movie **Deliverance**, picnic area.*

SAUTEE

Stovall House
Rt. 1 Box 103-A, 30571
(404)-878-3355

$25 pp
5 rooms, 5 pb
no
C-yes/S-ltd/P-no/no

Full breakfast
Afternoon tea
sitting room
piano

All year

Historic farmhouse in scenic mountain surroundings. Shopping, sightseeing, hiking & water sports available in area. A country experience.

SAVANNAH

17 Hundred 90 Inn
307 E. President, 31401
(912)-236-7122

$59-100
15 rooms, 15 pb
Visa, MC, AmEx, DC, CB
C-yes/S-yes/P-no/no

Continental breakfast
Lunch, dinner, wine, bar

All year

The only truly luxurious accomodations in historic Savannah combined with the finest in continental cuisine. Savannah's most elegant dining room.

Ballastone Inn
14 E. Oglethorpe, 31401
(912)-236-1484

All year

$95-190 B&B
19 rooms, 19 pb
Visa, MC, AmEx
C-yes/S-yes/P-yes/no

Continental plus
Bar
sitting room

In the center of Savannah's Historic District, offering the discriminating traveler the ultimate in luxurious accomodations.

Please mention this guide when you make your booking

The Foley House Inn, Savannah, Georgia

Bed and Breakfast Inn
117 Gordon St. W., 31402
(912)-238-0518
(912)-233-7666 RS
All year

$24-48 B&B
8 rooms, 4 pb
Visa, MC, AmEx
C-yes/S-yes/P-no/no

Continental breakfast
Complimentary sherry
sitting room
library

Two 1853 Federal townhouses in heart of Savannah's National Historic District; the graciousness of antebellum South refined by contemporary amenities.

Charlton Court
403 E Charlton St, 31401
(912)-236-2895

All year

$65 B&B
1 room, 1 pb

C-yes/S-yes/P-no

Continental plus
Complimentary wine
sitting room
bicycles

Private carriage house, c. 1850, in midst of Historic District. Extraordinary accomodations including wine, bicycles, breakfast.

Eliza Thompson House
5 W. Jones St., 31401

All year

$68-88
26 rooms, 26 pb
Visa, MC, AmEx
C-yes/S-yes/P-no/H-yes

Continental breakfast
Afternoon tea, bar
sitting room
entertainment sometimes

The Eliza Thompson House (1847) provides the opportunity to live Savannah's history. Carriage ride through historic district or evening in our courtyard.

Foley House Inn
14 W. Hull St., 31401
(912)-232-6622

All year

$85-135 B&B
11 rooms, 11 pb
Visa, MC, AmEx
C-yes/S-yes/P-no/H-yes

Continental plus
Complimentary wine
hot tubs
sitting room
bicycles available

A restored antebellum mansion, furnished with antiques, town-car limousine service, in-room video disc players. Truly "the best of two worlds".

Four Seventeen
417 E. Charleston, 31401
(912)-233-6380

All year

$60-125 B&B
2 rooms, 2 pb
no
C-yes/S-yes/P-extra/H-yes

Continental breakfast
Cocktails
private living room
bicycles
books, games, TV, radio

See historic Savannah from centrally located private suite. Guests of two or more days treated to cocktails. Antique collection.

Jesse Mount House
209 W. Jones St., 31401
(912)-236-1774

All year

$60 up B&B
3 rooms, 1 pb

C-yes/S-yes/P-no/

Continental plus
Complimentary wine
sitting room
piano
bicycles

Three-bedroom suite, TV sitting room, bath. Rare antiques; gilded harps as seen in the New York Times. Complimentary continental breakfast.

Liberty Inn
128 W. Liberty St.,31402
(912)-233-1007
(912)-233-7666 RS
All year

$70-120 B&B
4 rooms, 4 pb
Visa, MC, AmEx
C-yes/S-yes/P-no/ltd

Continental breakfast
kitchen
hot tub
receiving twin parlor

1834 Inn located in heart of historic Savannah, near the waterfront & shops. Garden, super spa, parking, continental breakfast. Peach cordial in each suite.

Mary Lee's House
PO Box 607, 31402
(912)-232-0891

All year

$50 B&B
3 rooms, 3 pb
no
C-yes/S-yes/P-no/no

Continental breakfast

private living rooms

Circa 1843. Comfortably furnished with country antiques. Complete privacy in the heart of the city's renowned historic district. Charming garden courtyard.

Remshart-Brooks House
106 W. Jones St., 31401
(912)-236-4337

All year

$50 B&B
1 room, 1 pb
Visa, MC
C-yes/S-yes/P-no/H-yes

Continental breakfast

sitting room

Experience the charm and hospitality of Historic Savannah while being "at home" in the garden suite of Remshart-Brooks House — built 1854.

Stoddard-Cooper House
19 W. Perry St., 31401
(912)-233-6809

All year

$75-125 B&B
2 rooms, 2 pb
no
C-yes/S-yes/P-no/H-yes

Continental breakfast
Complimentary wine

Restored historic home with a pedigree "as long as your arm". Freedom and privacy of your own apartment. Private hidden garden.

ST. MARY's —————————————————————————————

Riverview Hotel
105 Osborne St., 31558
(912)-882-3242

All year

$29-35 EP
18 rooms, 18 pb
Visa, MC, AmEx
C-yes/S-yes/P-no/no

Restaurant, bar

sitting room

Renovated, turn-of-the-century hotel, across street from Cumberland Island National Seashore ferry.

ST. SIMONS ISLAND ——————————————————————— ———————

Little St. Simons Island
PO Box 1096
(912)-638-7472

Jan.—Oct.

$130-200 AP
14 rooms, 10 pb
MC, AmEx
C-yes/S-ok/P-no/no

Full breakfast
Lunch, dinner inc.
swimming pool
sitting room

Excellent food, accommodations on secluded 12,000 acre island. Miles of unspoiled beaches, forests, marshes. Professional naturalists.

THOMASVILLE ──────────────────────────

Susina Plantation Inn   AP   Full breakfast
Rte. 3 Box 1010, 31792   8 rooms, 6 pb   Dinner complimentary
                                                             swimming pool
                                   C-yes/S-yes/P-yes/H-yes   tennis, bicycles
                                                             sitting room

Greek Revival mansion built 1840 furnished in antiques, a real Southern "Tara".

HAWAII

ALEA ──────────────────────────

Alohaland Guest House $25-35 B&B   Continental breakfast
98-1003 Oliwa, 96701   2 rooms, 1 pb   Afternoon tea
(808)-487-0482   no   sitting room
                                   C-no/S-no/P-no   piano

All year

Oriental hospitality in family-style atmosphere. Warm personal, friendly attention assured. Our home — your home away from home in Honolulu's suburbs.

KAILUA, OAHU ──────────────────────────

Pacific Hawaii B&B $20-40   Kitchen facilities
19 Kai Nani Pl., 96734   3 rooms, 2 pb
(808)-262-6026   no
                                   C-yes/S-yes/P-no/H-yes

All year

Spanish style home with court yard, large yard, and wide stretch of sandy beach. Private entrance to each room. Undiscovered by tourists.

Enter your favorite inn in our ''Inn of the Year'' contest (entry form is in the back of the book).

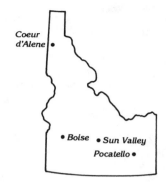

Coeur
d'Alene •

• Boise   • Sun Valley
Pocatello •

BONNER'S FERRY

Deep Creek Inn $22-36 EP   Full breakfast
83805   12 rooms, 12 pb   Lunch, dinner, bar
(208)-267-2373   Visa, MC   swimming pool
                           C-yes/S-yes/P-yes/H-yes bicycles
All year   piano

Sleep and eat by the creek. Country setting just as pretty in winter as summer, and fall is enchanting!

HAILEY

Ellsworth Inn $55-85   Full breakfast
715 3rd Ave. S., 83333   8 rooms, 8 pb   Afternoon tea
(208)-788-2298   Visa   sitting room
                           S-ltd/P-no
All year

Old World charm and hospitality, antiques and quilts in all the rooms. European sideboard breakfast—afternoon tea.

IDAHO CITY

Idaho City Hotel $20-22   Full breakfast
P.O. Box 70, 83631   5 rooms, 5 pb
(208)-392-4290   Visa, MC   lounge, cable TV
                           C-yes/S-yes/P-yes   near hot springs
All year

Old west hotel furnished with genuine antiques, in old mining town just 45 minutes from Boise.

MERIDIAN

The Home Place $23-38 B&B   Full breakfast
415 W Lk. Hazel Rd,83642   3 rooms, 1 pb
(208)-888-3857   swimming pool
(800)-547-1463 RS   C-yes/S-yes/P-no   sitting room
All year   piano

Rural setting, contemporary farmstead atmosphere, near National Birds of Prey Refuge.

STANLEY ———————————————————————————

Idaho Rocky Mtn. Ranch $36-45   Full breakfast
HC64 Box 9934, 83278   18 rooms, 18 pb   Dinner
(208)-774-3544   Visa, MC   sitting room, piano
                       C-no/S-yes/P-no/H-yes   natural hot pool
Mid-June—mid-September

*Log lodge and cabins hand built in 1930. View of the Sawtooth Mountains. Hiking,
boating, horseback riding near the Ranch.*

Redfish Lake Lodge $27-42   Full menu dining room
83278   32 rooms, 19 pb   Bar service
(208)-774-3536   Visa, MC   lake swimming
                       C-yes/S-yes/P-yes/H-yes   bicycles
Memorial wknd to Oct. 15

Reasonably priced rustic inn on Redfish Lake.

ILLINOIS

ELDRED ———————————————————————————

Hobson's Bluffdale $17.50 B&B   Full breakfast
Eldred-Hillview Rd,62027   5 rooms, 5 pb   Lunch, dinner
(217)-983-2854   no   hot tub, swimming
                       C-yes/S-ltd/P-no/H-yes   bicycles
April—Nov.   entertainment

*320 acre working farm. 160 year old stone ancestral farmhouse. 6 fireplaces. Yard shaded
by 300 year old trees. Towering bluffs.*

GALENA ———————————————————————————

Colonial Guest House $30-35 B&B   Continental breakfast
1004 Park Ave.   4 rooms, 4 pb   Afternoon tea
(815)-777-0336 RS   no   Bicycles
                       C-yes/S-yes/P-small/H-yes   sitting room
All year

*Antique lovers will enjoy the ambiance of this large, stately pillared 1826 mansion.
Moderate rates include continental breakfast.*

Stillman Manor $40.50-44.50 EP   Lunch & dinner only
513 Bouthillier,   7 rooms, 7 pb
(815)-777-0557   Visa, MC
                           C-yes/S-yes/P-no
All year

*Stillman Manor Estate, 1858. General Grant was a regular guest. Antiques & fireplaces,
crystal, porcelain. Riverboats.*

GRAND DETOUR ────────────────────────────────────

Colonial Inn $28 B&B   Continental breakfast
Rock & Green Sts., 61021   12 rooms, 4 pb
(815)-652-4422   no   sitting room
                           C-yes/S-ok/P-no   piano
All year

1850 Victorian charm in a New England type village in Illinois.

INDIANA

CHURUBUSCO ──────────────────────────

Sycamore Spring Farm $50-75 AP   Full breakfast
Box 224, 46723   2 rooms, 2 pb   All meals included
(219)-693-3603   no   living room, library
                           C-yes/S-no/P-no   piano & harpsichord
Jan.—Oct.   farm activities

*Sample rural life on a working midwestern farm. Williamsburg reproduction home.
Garden fresh produce. A book by the fireplace in winter.*

MICHIGAN CITY ──────────────────────────

Duneland Beach Inn $34-49 B&B   Full breakfast
3311 Potawatomi, 46360   12 rooms, 6 pb   Family style dinner
(219)-874-7729   Visa, MC   Bicycles, tennis courts
                           C-older/S-ltd/P-no/H-yes private beach
All year   sitting room

*Charm and elegance of quieter days at our year round Dunes Country hideaway; gourmet
Sunday brunch amid a gaslight setting.*

MIDDLEBURY

Patchwork Quilt
11748 C.R. –2, 46540
(219)-825-2417

$30-40 B&B
8 rooms, 2 pb
no
C-yes/S-ltd/P-no/H-yes

Continental plus
Dinner
Farm pond swimming
piano, sitting room

All year
Amish tours

Prepare to be pampered in gracious country home; patchwork quilts on all beds. In Amish country. Near Shipshewana Flea Auction.

WESTFIELD

Camel Lot
4512 W. 131st St, 46074
(317)-873-4370

$40-60
1 room, 1 pb
no
C-10 up/S-yes/H-yes

Full breakfast

sitting room
piano

All year

Have breakfast on the terrace overlooking the Siberian tiger's quarters — photograph zebras, llamas, deer at this exotic animal breeding ranch.

IOWA

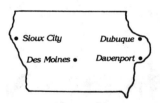

ANAMOS

The Inn at Stone City
52205
(319)-462-4733

$25 pp
6 rooms, 0 pb
Visa, MC
C-yes/S-yes/P-yes/H-yes

Full breakfast
Lunch, dinner, bar
bicycles, jacuzzi
cross-country skiing

All year
canoe rentals

Beautiful stone mansion and estate in former artists colony, Stone City. We take pride in our varied menus and personal service.

BENTONSPORT

Mason House Inn
RR 2, 52565
(319)-592-3113

$30-75 B&B
10 rooms, 2 pb
no
C-no/S-ltd/P-no/H-yes

Full breakfast
Dinner by reservation
bicycles

All year

Historic inn built in steamboat era located in designated National Historic District. Quiet, comfortable escape to bygone era.

Hotel Manning, Keosauqua, Iowa

BROOKLYN

Hotel Brooklyn
154 Front St., 52211
(515)-522-9229

All year

$12-36
10 rooms, 10 pb
no
C-yes/P-no

Continental breakfast

sitting room

Built in 1875. Beautiful marble fireplace, antiques. Very warm, homey place. 2 miles of 180, 1 mile off 6.

HOMESTEAD

Die Heimat
52236

All year

$21 up
19 rooms, 19 pb
Visa, MC
C-yes/S-yes/P-no

Continental plus
Beer & wine
sitting room

Stay overnight at our century old restored Inn. All rooms have private baths furnished with Amana furniture and antiques.

KEOSAUQUA

Hotel Manning
52565
(319)-293-3232

All year

$20-36
28 rooms, 10 pb
no
C-yes/S-yes/P-no/H-ltd

Full breakfast
Lunch, dinner, bar
sitting room
piano

Restored steamboat architecture hotel furnished with authentic antiques. Next to Des Moines River and Iowa's largest state park. Quiet atmosphere.

Please Mention *The Complete Guide* **to the innkeeper when you reserve your room**

KANSAS

KANSAS — Kansas City • / Topeka • / • Garden City / • Dodge City   • Wichita

HARPER

Rosalea's Hotel
121 W. Main St., 67058
none

May—October

$18-36
8 rooms, 4 pb
no
C-no/S-yes/P-no

Full breakfast
Bagel bar lunch
piano
sitting room
"swatting mosquitos"

America's most eccentric hotel — in the nicest possible sense of the word. An eclectic mix of Victorian antiques and Kansas hospitality. Membership.

WAKERFIELD

B&B on our Farm
Rt. 1, Box 132, 67487
(913)-461-5596

All year

$18-30 B&B
3 rooms, 0 pb
no
C-yes/S-yes/P-yes

Full breakfast

bicycles & Yamahopper

Real farm, modest; couple nearing retirement invite you to spend the night & have a hearty breakfast.

KENTUCKY

Louisville • / • Frankfort / • Lexington / • Paducah   • Mammoth / Cave N.P.   • Hazard

BARDSTOWN

Talbot Tavern
40004
(502)-348-3494

All year

$37.80 dbl
6 rooms, 6 pb
Visa, MC, AmEx
C-yes/S-yes/P-no

Lunch, dinner only
Bar
entertainment

1779 stone inn, one of first hostelries west, each room original, fireplaces, antiques. Wall paintings done by guest Prince Louis Phillipe of France.

BRANDENBURG

Doe Run Inn
Rte. 2, 90108
(502)-422-2982

All year

$15-24
12 rooms, 5 pb
Visa, MC
C-yes/S-yes/P-small

Full breakfast
Lunch, dinner
sitting room

Quiet country inn beside a running brook. Antiques. Breakfast, lunch & dinner daily, smorgasbords Friday night & Sunday noon. 1000 acres to wander in.

HARRODSBURG

Beaumont Inn
40330
(606)-734-3381

March—November

$40-60 EP
29 rooms, 29 pb
Visa, MC
C-yes/S-yes/P-no

Full Breakfast
Luncheon, dinner
swimming pool
tennis courts
sitting room, piano

Country Inn built in 1845 in the heart of Kentucky's Bluegrass Region, furnished with antiques, serving traditional Kentucky Southern cuisine.

LOUISIANA

CONVENT

Tezcuco Plantation Home
Rt. 1 Box 151, 70723
(504)-562-3929

All year

$65-95
10 rooms, 10 pb
Visa, MC, AmEx
C-yes/S-yes/P-no

Full breakfast
Restaurant

Stay in private cottages on the grounds of this restored 1855 plantation home on the Mississippi River. Tour of home included.

NEW IBERIA

Mintmere Plantation
1400 E. Main, 70560
(318)-364-6210

All year

$100 B&B
4 rooms, 4 pb
no
C-11 up/S-yes/P-no

Full breakfast

private sitting rooms
galleries, parlor
patio

Built in 1857, Mintmere is nestled among the oaks on historic Bayou Teche and furnished with elegant period antiques.

NEW ORLEANS

The Columns
3811 St. Charles, 70115
(504)-899-9308

All year

$35-75 B&B
25 rooms, 10 pb
Visa, MC, AmEx
C-yes/S-yes/P-no/H-yes

Continental breakfast
Lunch, dinner, bar
piano

Jazz every Wednesday in ballroom — no charge. Historic register. Garden District New Orleans, near Audubon Zoo, Universities.

Cornstalk Hotel
915 Royal St., 70116
(504)-523-1515

All year

$60-80 B&B
14 rooms, 14 pb
Visa, MC, AmEx
C-yes/S-yes/P-no

Continental breakfast
Complimentary tea & wine

Small, elegant hotel in heart of French Quarter. All antique furnishings. Complimentary wine/liquers on check-in, comp. breakfast, newspapers.

Lafitte Guest House, New Orleans, Louisiana

French Quarter Maisons
1130 Chartres St.,70116

Aug.—June

$36-45
7 rooms, 7 pb
no
C-12 up/S-yes/P-ok/H-ltd

Lafitte Guest House
1003 Bourbon St., 70116
(504)-581-2678

All year

$58-95 B&B
14 rooms, 14 pb
Visa, MC, AmEx
C-yes/S-yes/P-no

Continental breakfast

sitting room

Lamothe House
621 Esplanade Ave, 70116
(504)-947-1161

All year

$75-150 B&B
20 rooms, 20 pb
Visa, MC, AmEx
C-yes/S-yes/P-no/H-yes

Continental breakfast
Complimentary tea & wine
sitting room

An elegantly restored historic old mansion located on the eastern boundary of the French Quarter. This old mansion surrounds a romantic courtyard.

Maison de Ville
727 Toulouse St., 70130
(504)-561-5858

All year

$100-275 B&B
26 rooms, 26 pb
no
C-yes/S-yes/P-ltd/H-ltd

Continental breakfast
Tea, wine, bar
swimming pool
sitting room

A classic country inn located in the heart of the French Quarter. Rated the best small hotel in the country by Architectural Digest. Elegant atmosphere.

Noble Arms Inn
1006 Royal St., 70116
(504)-524-2222

All year

$51-133 B&B
16 rooms, 16 pb
Visa, MC, AmEx, CB, DC
C-yes/S-ok/P-no

Continental plus
Afternoon tea

Historic renovated twin townhouses built in 1820 offer accommodations with kitchenettes and lace wrought iron balconies. In the French Quarter.

Park View
7004 St. Charles, 70118
(504)-861-7564

All year

$30-45 B&B
25 rooms, 14 pb
Visa, MC, AmEx
C-yes/S-yes/P-no

Continental plus

bicycles
sitting room

Original high Victorian guest house on streetcar line, furnished with period antiques, verandas overlooking St. Charles Ave. and park.

We want this guide to be as complete as possible, so if you know of an inn (30 rooms or less), bed & breakfast or guesthouse we don't list, please send us their name on the form in the back of the book.

The Myrtles Plantation, St. Francisville, Louisiana

Soniat House
1133-35 Chartres, 70116
(504)-522-0570

All year

$85-135 B&B
25 rooms, 25 pb
Visa, MC, AmEx
C-yes/S-yes/H-yes

Continental plus
room service, bar
jacuzzis
sitting room
phones in bed and bath

A private hotel in the residential area of the French Quarter, furnished in period antiques offering modern amenities of telephones and jacuzzi baths.

OPELOUSAS

Estorge House
427 N. Market St., 70570
(318)-948-4592

All year

$100 B&B
2 rooms, 2 pb
no
C-11 up/S-yes/P-no

Full breakfast

sitting room in suite
galleries & main parlor

One of the more stately and impressive historic homes — built in 1827 — furnished with beautiful Louisiana antiques throughout.

ST. FRANCISVILLE

Myrtles Plantation
PO Box 387, 70775
(504)-635-6277

All year

$55-75 B&B
10 rooms, 10 pb
Visa, MC
C-yes/S-yes/P-yes/H-yes

Full breakfast
Bar service
bicycles
sitting room, piano
entertainment

Romantic 18th-century French-style plantation. Elaborate plaster friezework and faux bois; period furnishings; unique history includes ghosts; mint juleps.

WAKEFIELD ──────────────────────────────

Wakefield Plantation $40-50 B&B   Continental plus
PO Box 41, 70784   3 rooms, 1 pb
                                  no
                                  C-yes/S-yes/P-no
All year

Our home was built in 1834, is furnished with genuine antiques.

WHITE CASTLE ──────────────────────────

Nottoway $75-125   Full breakfast
PO Box 160, 70788   9 rooms, 9 pb   Lunch, dinner, bar
(504)-545-2730   Visa, MC   swimming pool
(504)-346-8263   C-12 up/S-yes/P-no   sitting room
All year   piano

WILSON ──────────────────────────────────

Glencoe Plantation $60-85 B&B   Full breakfast
PO Box 178, 70789   12 rooms, 12 pb   Bar
(504)-629-5387   Visa, MC   tennis court
                                  C-yes/S-yes/P-no/H-ltd   sitting rooms, piano
All year   swim, hike, fish

Spacious home on 1,000 acres. Original furnishings. Verandas with rocking chairs. Guests are invited to be comfortable, relax, enjoy themselves.

MAINE

BAR HARBOR ──────────────────────────────

Clefstone Manor $30-85 B&B   Continental plus
92 Eden St., 04609   18 rooms, 13 pb   Complimentary tea, wine
(207)-288-4951   Visa, MC, AmEx   sitting room
                                  C-yes/S-yes/P-no   library
Mid-May—mid-October   country club member

Clefstone Manor was built as a thirty room summer "cottage" for the historic Blair family. President Taft was a guest. Rooms filled with tranquility.

Dow Cottage Inn
227 Main St., 04609
(207)-288-3712

All year

$16-20 EP
9 rooms, 2 pb

C-yes/P-no

Hearthside Inn
7 High St., 04609
(207)-288-4533

June—October

$40-60 B&B
9 rooms, 7 pb
Visa, MC
C-10 up/S-yes/P-no

Continental breakfast
Complimentary tea, wine
sitting room w/fireplace
studio grand piano

Small pretty and gracious hostelry in quiet in-town location; come visit Bar Harbor and Acadia National Park.

Holbrook Inn
74 Mount Desert, 04609
(207)-288-4970

April 15-Nov.1

$35-55 B&B
11 rooms, 2 pb
AmEx,Visa,MC
P-no

Bar Harbor cottage built 1880, solarium where breakfast and wine are served. Antiques, oriental rugs. Large doll collection.

Ledgelawn Inn
66 Mount Desert, 04609
(207)-288-4596

April 15-Nov. 15

$45-100 B&B
22 rooms, 18 pb
MC, Visa, AmEx
C-yes/S-yes/P-no

continental breakfast
(comp.), bar service
pool, sauna, bicycles,
tennis nearby, piano
sitting room, library

A graceful turn-of-the-century mansion with lots of charm, antiques, sitting areas; in a quiet location only 5 minutes walk to downtown.

Manor House Inn
106 West St., 04609
(207)-288-3759

April 15—Nov. 15

$58-80 B&B
10 rooms, 10 pb
Visa, MC
C-no/S-ltd/P-no

Continental plus
Afternoon tea
sitting room, piano
swimming pool
tennis, bicycles

Lots of special touches — pool, 5 tennis courts, new Acadia National Park.

Mira Monte Inn
69 Mt. Desert St., 04609
(207)-288-4263

May—November

$45-65 B&B
10 rooms, 10 pb
Visa, MC, AmEx
C-yes/S-yes/P-no/H-yes

Full breakfast
Wine & cheese
sitting room, piano
tennis, swimming for
guests at nearby club

Renovated Victorian estate; period furnishings, fireplaces, one-acre grounds; quiet, in-town location, two king beds, walk to waterfront.

Enter your favorite inn in our "Inn of the Year" contest (entry form is in the back of the book).

Thornhedge
47 Mt. Desert St., 04609
(207)-288-5398

$45-65 B&B
14 rooms, 14 pb
Visa, MC, AmEx
C-yes/S-yes/P-no

Continental plus
Complimentary wine
sitting room, piano

March 15—Nov. 15

All rooms are furnished in antiques; all off street parking; close to shops, village green and restaurants; walking distance to shore.

Town Guest House
12 Atlantic Ave., 04609

$50-80
9 rooms, 9 pb
credit cards accepted
C-yes/S-yes/P-no

sitting room
bicycles

April—Oct.

A quiet in-town location; old fashion comfort with modern conveniences. Cable color TV, working fireplaces & porches.

BATH ———————————————————————————

Grane's Fairhaven Inn
N. Bath Rd., 04530
(207)-443-4391

$22-45 EP
9 rooms, 1 pb

C-yes/S-yes

Full breakfast

sitting room, piano
library, bicycles

All year

Old Country Inn—antique bed sets, quilts, etc. Hiking, swimming, golf nearby. Gourmet breakfasts available.

BELFAST ———————————————————————————

Chance Along Inn
Rt. 1, 04915
(207)-338-4785

$18-20 B&B
6 rooms, 0 pb

C-yes/S-ok/P-dogs

Continental plus

sitting room, piano
beach, sailing

All year

Closeness of beautiful Penobscot Bay and central location to Maine Coast's best features. Full sailing school. Sailing excursions available.

BETHEL ———————————————————————————

Norseman Inn
04217
(207)-824-2002

$28-32 EP
10 rooms, 1 pb

C-yes/S-yes/P-no

Full breakfast
Dinner, bar
sitting room, piano
bicycles

June—Aug., ski season

1783 farmhouse with old world charm. Reputation for quality. Lounge, fireplaces, rec. room, movies in winter season. Family oriented.

BLUE HILL ———————————————————————————

Altenhofen House
Peters Point, 04614
(207)-374-2116

$60-90 B&B
6 rooms, 6 pb
Visa, MC
C-yes/S-yes/P-ok

Full breakfast
Dinner, wine, tea
swimming pool
sitting room, piano

April—January

National Register of Historic Landmarks. Sailing, fishing, canoeing, windsurfing. Unique mansion with European charm.

Blue Hill Inn
04614
(207)-374-2844

All year

$43 dbl.
11 rooms, 9 pb
Visa, MC
C-yes/S-yes/P-no

full breakfast, dinner
continental breakfast
piano
sitting room
library

In continuous operation since 1840; nestled in picturesque village at head of Blue Hill Bay; mouth-watering Down East cooking. Hungarian spoken.

BOOTHBAY HARBOR

✓ **Green Shutters Inn**
P.O. Box 543, 04538
(207)-633-2646

May—September

$22-30 EP
22 rooms, 22 pb
Visa, MC, DC
C-yes/S-yes/P-yes

Full breakfast
Dinner
sitting room, piano

Home cooked food. Located in a quiet wooded area near the bay and 15 minute walk to the center of town.

✓ **Hilltop House**
McKown Hill, 04538
(207)-633-2941
(207)-633-3839
All year

$24-45 dbl
7 rooms, 3 pb

C-yes/S-yes/P-yes

Sits atop of McKown Hill overlooking town & harbor; walk to all activities. Parking in our lot.

Howard House Motor Lodge
Rte. 27, 04538

All year

$25-45 B&B
7 rooms, 7 pb
C-yes/S-ok/P-no

Continental breakfast

Relax in casual, quiet, country-like ambiance, away from crowds, but only about a mile from center of town.

✓ **Thistle Inn**
P.O. Box 176, 04538

All year

$28-35
10 rooms, 1 pb
C-yes/S-yes/P-yes

All meals served

Sea captain's home overlooking the harbor. Noted for New England country collectibles and excellent Down-East cuisine.

Topside
McKown Hill, 04538
(207)-633-5404

May—October

$45-80 EP
29 rooms, 29 pb

C-yes

Coffee only

Lodge/motel, sea in all directions (& nautical activities), true land & sea relaxation coupled with personal courtesy. Complimentary coffee.

Welch House $20-45 B&B Continental breakfast
36 McKown St., 04538 19 rooms, 11 pb
(207)-633-3431
  C-yes/S-yes/P-ltd/H-yes
March—November

Situated in town—near shops, restaurant, golf & swimming, summer stock. Beautifully furnished, sea views. Children welcome. Breakfast.

Westgate Guest House $35 dbl B&B Full breakfast
18 West St., 04538 8 rooms, 0 pb
(207)-633-3552
  C-yes/S-ok/P-no
Spring thru Fall

Walk to beautiful boat trips and all in-town activities. Hosts to two-week watercolor workshops for Skip Lawrence in June, July, August.

BUCKSPORT

Jed Prouty Tavern $23-33 EP
Box 550, 04416 18 rooms, 8 pb Bar service
(207)-469-2371 Visa, MC, AmEx, DC piano, entertainment
  C-yes/S-yes/P-yes/H-ltd
All year

America's fifth oldest continuously run Inn serving fine food & drink since 1798. Famous for Prime Rib & Seafood.

CAMDEN

Aubergine $50-60 B&B Continental plus
6 Belmont Ave., 04843 6 rooms, 4 pb Dinner, box lunch, bar
(207)-236-8053   sitting room
  C-yes/P-no harpsichord
May—November   lake, ocean swimming

Small romantic inn, new style French menu changes monthly, breakfast in bed featured in Gourmet Magazine.

Camden Harbor Inn $28-65 B&B Complimentary breakfast
83 Bayview St., 04843 18 rooms, 12 pb dinner, bar service
(207)-236-4200 MC, Visa entertainment
  C-12-up/S-yes/P-no library
All year

Historic inn built in 1873; near harbor, great views. Antique brass beds. Claw foot tubs.

High Tide Inn $45-55 EP Continental breakfast
04843 5 rooms, 1 pb
(207)-236-3742 Visa, MC sitting room
  C-no/P-no
May 15—Oct. 15

Seven panoramic acres, on ocean, at foot of mountain. Quiet, relaxing ambience within reach of exciting, varied activities. Former estate.

Owl and Turtle Bookmotel
8 Bay View, 04843
(207)-236-4769

All year

$45 B&B
2 rooms, 2 pb
credit cards accepted
S-no/P-no

Continental plus
Afternoon tea

Bookmotel overlooks Camden Harbor and Mt. Battie. Balconies, private baths, TV, radio, air conditioning, bookshop and tea room.

Whitehall Inn
52 High St., 04843
(207)-236-3391

Early spring—late fall

$50-80
10 rooms, 6 pb

C-yes/S-yes/P-no

Full breakfast
Dinner, tea, bar
sitting room, piano
tennis courts
bicycles

Two Victorian homes furnished with antiques. Water view room. Fine foods and wines since 1901.

CASTINE

Pentagoet Inn
P.O. Box 4, 04421
(207)-326-8616

March—December

$35-55 EP
14 rooms, 5 pb
Visa, MC, AmEx
C-5 up/S-yes/P-no

Full breakfast
Dinner, bar
sitting room, piano
chamber music

Situated in small history-oriented town. Home of Maine Maritime Academy. High level of intellectual conversation—probably most philosophical inn in America

CENTER LOVELL

Center Lovell Inn
Rte. 5, 04016
(207)-925-1575

May—Oct.

$70.50-105.00
5 rooms, 7 pb
Visa, MC
S-yes/H-yes

Full breakfast
Dinner, bar
sitting room

Country Inn, family oriented, surrounded by White Mountain National Forest, near Saco River for canoeing, Kezar Lake, foliage, Fryeburg Fair.

Westways on Kezar Lake
Rte. 5, 04016
(207)-928-2663
(800)-225-4897
5/15-10/31, 12/15-2/29

$71-96 EP, $95-120 MAP
7 rooms, 3 pb
Visa, MC
C-yes/S-yes/P-ltd/H-ltd

Full breakfast
Dinner, bar
sitting room, piano
tennis courts

Enjoy the splendor of the White Mountains. . . Let the haunting melody of the loon lull you to sleep. Complete recreational facilities.

CHEBEAGUE ISLAND

Chebeague Inn by-the-Sea
04017
(207)-846-9634

June—Columbus Day

$40-63 EP
14 rooms, 2 pb
Visa, MC
C-yes/S-ltd/P-no

Breakfast
Lunch, dinner, bar
sitting room, piano
bicycles

A step back in time, a romantic old Inn on an untouched island in Casco Bay, reached only by boat.

CLARK ISLAND

Craignair Inn
04857
(207)-594-7644

$40-45 B&B
17 rooms, 0 pb
Visa, MC
C-yes/S-yes/P-yes

Full breakfast
Dinner
bicycles

All year

Serenity, simplicity, seclusion—surrounded by woods and water, furnished with antiques. Dining room overlooks the sea.

DAMARISCOTTA

Brannon-Bunker Inn
Rt. 129 Box 245, 04543
(207)-563-5941
(617)-277-2292 RS
May—Columbus Day

$30-40 B&B
8 rooms, 5 pb
Visa, MC
C-yes/S-yes/P-yes

Continental plus

sitting room

Country B'n'B; charming rooms furnished with antiques; close to all mid-coast recreational facilities including ocean, beach, boating & golf; antiquing!

DEER ISLE

Pilgrim's Inn
Main St., 04627
(207)-348-6615

$55-60 MAP
12 rooms, 3 pb

C-yes/S-no/P-yes

Full breakfast
Supper, tea, bar
sitting room, piano
bicycles

May 20—Oct. 23

Idyllic location on Deer Isle. Elegant yet informal colonial inn, creative cuisine, rustic antique-furnished barn. Commons rooms w/ 8' fireplaces.

DENNYSVILLE

Lincoln House Inn
04628
(207)-726-3953

$45 dbl EP
6 rooms, 0 pb
Visa, MC
C-yes/S-yes/P-no

Full breakfast
Dinner, bar
sitting room, piano
river swimming

All year

A lovingly restored colonial in the northeastern coastal region of Maine.

EAST WATERFORD

Waterford Inne
Box 49, 04233
(207)-583-4037

$40-60 EP
9 rooms, 5 pb

C-yes/S-yes

Full breakfast
Dinner
sitting room
library

May—February

Country inning at its best! The hospitality, food and lovely surroundings will bring you back again and again and. . .

FIVE ISLANDS

Grey Havens Inn
Box 82, 04546
(207)-371-2616

$55-90 B&B
14 rooms, 5 pb

C-12 up/S-yes/P-no

Continental plus
Dinner
sitting room

May—October

Situated on a point overlooking Sheepscot Bay, we offer mooring facilities in Harmon's Harbor. 1-1/2 miles from Reid State Park.

124 Maine

GREENVILLE ─────────────────────────────

Greenville Inn　　　　$18-42 B&B　　　　Full breakfast
P.O. Box 1194, 04441　　12 rooms, 3 pb　　Lunch, dinner, bar
(207)-695-2206　　　　　Visa, MC
　　　　　　　　　　　　C-yes/S-yes/P-yes

All year

Restored lumber baron's mansion with unique embellishment on a hill in town overlooking Moosehead Lake and Squaw Mountain.

HANCOCK ──────────────────────────────────

Crocker House　　　　$32-50 B&B　　　　Continental breakfast
04640　　　　　　　　　10 rooms, 1 pb　　Dinner, bar
(207)-422-6806　　　　　Visa, MC　　　　　sitting room
　　　　　　　　　　　　C-yes/S-yes/P-yes

June—Columbus Day

Quiet traditional coastal inn offering simple elegant dining. A little out of the way, but way out of the ordinary.

LeDomaine　　　　　　$40-52 EP　　　　　Continental plus
US 1, Box 496, 04640　　7 rooms, 7 pb　　　Bar service
(207)-422-3395　　　　　Visa, MC, AmEx　　sitting room
　　　　　　　　　　　　C-yes/S-yes/P-yes　library
May 15—Oct. 31　　　　　　　　　　　　　badmitten

French Country Inn, dining room, fireplace, flowers everywhere, cordon bleu gourmet breakfast, private baths, porches.

KENNEBUNKPORT ──────────────────────────

1802 House　　　　　　$42-58 dbl B&B　　Full breakfast
Box 774　　　　　　　　6 rooms, 6 pb
(207)-967-5632　　　　　Visa, MC　　　　　sitting room
　　　　　　　　　　　　C-12 up/S-yes/P-no　pot belly stove

All year

Mulled cider/hot chocolate after x-country skiing. Gift certificates available for holidays & special occasions.

Breakwater　　　　　$35-70 B&B　　　　Continental breakfast
P.O. Box 816, 04046　　20 rooms, 20 pb　　Dinner (in season), bar
(207)-967-3118　　　　　Visa, MC
　　　　　　　　　　　　C-yes/S-ok/P-no

All year

Informal seacoast inn—country & antique furnishings—relaxing location on Kennebunk River—convenient to shops, lobster boats and picturesque walks.

Captain Jefferds Inn　$45-68 B&B　　　　Full breakfast
Box 691, 04046　　　　　11 rooms, 6 pb　　Afternoon tea
(207)-967-2311　　　　　　　　　　　　　sitting room
　　　　　　　　　　　　C-12 up/S-yes/P-yes/H-yes bicycles

All year

One of the most beautiful newly established Inns in America. Sea captain's mansion built 1804, furnished with antiques, folk art. See House Beautiful 1/83

Captain Lord Mansion
P.O. Box 527, 04046
(207)-967-3141

All year

$69-89 B&B
16 rooms, 16 pb

C-12 up/S-ltd/P-no

Full breakfast
Afternoon tea
sitting room, piano

An intimate Maine coast inn with working fireplaces in 11 guest rooms. Furnished in genuine antiques.

Chetwynd House
P.O. Box 130, 04046
(207)-967-2235

All year

$42-65 B&B
5 rooms, 2 pb
no
C-ltd/S-yes/P-no

Full breakfast
Complimentary tea, wine
sitting room, library

Kennebunkport—the village of Kenneth Roberts' historical novels. Take the beautiful staircase to beautiful rooms — view of harbor in this historic town.

English Robin
R1 Box 194, 04046
(207)-967-3505

May—October

$45-70 EP
2 rooms, 2 pb
Visa, MC
C-yes/S-yes/P-yes

swimming pool

Very private rooms. "The Barn" is self-contained. Near beaches and golf course.

Flakeyard Farm
RFD 2, 04046
(207)-967-5965

May—October

$50 B&B
3 rooms, 3 pb

C-yes/S-yes/P-no

Full breakfast

Rooms date to 1737, baths to 1983. Historic tree-shaded Georgian colonial close to shops and beaches.

Green Heron
Ocean Ave., 04046
(207)-967-3315

June to Columbus Day

$20.50-38.00 B&B
11 rooms, 11 pb

C-yes/S-yes/P-yes

Full breakfast

sitting room
bicycles

Older inn, many antique furnishings. Famous for breakfast. Fine ocean and river beaches, good fishing.

Old Fort Inn
P.O. Box 759, 04046
(207)-967-5353

May—October

$60-90 B&B
13 rooms, 13 pb
Visa, MC, AmEx
C-7 up/S-ltd/P-no

Continental breakfast

sitting room, piano
tennis, swimming pool
bicycles

A luxurious resort in a secluded charming setting. The Inn has yesterday's charm with today's conveniences. Within walking distance to the ocean.

Seaside Inn
Gooch's Beach, 04046
(207)-967-4461

$48-90 B&B
32 rooms, 32 pb

C-ltd/S-yes/P-ltd/H-yes

Continental plus
Box lunches in season
private ocean beach

All year

Seaside Inn and Cottage Colony located on oceanfront peninsula—private beach two hours from Boston. Since 1667.

White Barn Inn
Beach St., 04046
(207)-967-2321

26 rooms, 19 pb
Visa, MC, AmEx
C-yes/S-yes/P-no

Full breakfast
Dinner, bar
bicycles
entertainment

April—December

Restored Inn. Dining room set with pewter silver & linen. Architecturally preserved barn. Casual elegance. Recipient of 1983 Silver Spoon award.

KINGSFIELD

Country Cupboard
N. Maine St., 04947
(207)-265-2193

$32-79 pp MAP
7 rooms, 0 pb
Visa, MC
C-yes/S-ltd/P-no

Full breakfast
Dinner on request
hot tub, bicycles
swimming pool
sitting room

All year

Old farmhouse completely renovated and updated, tastefully furnished. Homelike atmosphere, home-cooked meals, amidst the beautiful western mountains.

Winter's Inn
P.O. Box 44, 04947
(207)-265-5421

$30-40 EP, $50-60 MAP
12 rooms, 6 pb
Visa, MC, AmEx
C-yes/S-yes/P-no

Full breakfast
Dinner, bar
swimming pool
entertainment

All year

On National Register of Historic Places, elegant Victorian mansion. Country Inn designed by the Stanley brothers of Stanley Steamer fame. Ski from doorstep.

LITTLE DEER ISLE

Eggemoggin Inn
04650
(207)-348-2540

$35-55 EP
10 rooms, 1 pb   4650
no
C-yes/S-yes/P-no

Full breakfast

sitting room, piano

May—October

Just one word — Maine!

MOUNT VERNON

Feather Bed Inn
Box 65, 04352
(207)-293-2020

$30-50 B&B
4 rooms, 1 pb

C-yes/S-yes/P-no

Continental plus
Dinner (reservation)
swimming pond
sitting room, piano

All year

1856 country charm, in a small New England village overlooking Lake Minnihonk. Homestyle cooking, intimate leisurely dining.

NAPLES ─────────────────────────────────────

Charmwoods
04055
(207)-693-6798

June 1—Oct. 15

$75-90 B&B
5 rooms, 5 pb

C-12 up/S-ltd/P-no

Continental plus
Complimentary wine
sitting room, piano
tennis courts

Unique mini-resort. Lakefront lodge overlooking mountains. Four-acre wooded estate with swimming, boating, canoeing and tennis. Golf, riding nearby.

NEW HARBOR ─────────────────────────────────

Bradley Inn
361 Pemaquid Pt., 04554
(207)-677-2105

All year

$28-40 B&B
11 rooms, 0 pb
Visa, MC, AmEx
C-yes/S-ltd/P-no

Continental breakfast
Dinner, bar
piano, sitting room
tennis courts nearby

Located on Pemaquid Point in the Atlantic—white sand and scenic woods, historic surroundings, near fishing, golfing, interesting areas.

Gosnold Arms
04554
(207)-677-3727

Mid-June—mid-Sept.

$35-72 MAP
24 rooms, 11 pb
Visa, MC
C-yes/S-yes/P-no/H-ltd

Full breakfast
Dinner, cocktails
sitting room

Charming country inn and cottages. All-weather dining porch overlooking harbor. Beaches, lobster pounds, parks nearby.

NEWCASTLE ──────────────────────────────────

Newcastle Inn
04553
(207)-563-5685
(207)-563-8878
All year

$30-45
20 rooms, 7 pb

C-yes/S-yes/P-ltd

Full breakfast
Afternoon tea
sitting room

Traditional New England surroundings and hospitality. Boating, beaches, restaurants, art galleries, golf, cross-country skiing are near by.

NORTH WATERFORD ────────────────────────────

Olde Rowley Inn
P.O. Box 87, 04267
(207)-583-4143

All year

$36 B&B
5 rooms, 1 pb
Visa, MC
C-ltd/S-yes/P-no/H-ltd

Full breakfast
Dinner, bar
sitting room

The Olde Rowley Inn built in 1790, served as a stagecoach inn. 5 quaint, cozy guestrooms. Fine country dining—breakfast or dinner.

NORTHEAST HARBOR ───────────────────────────

Grey Rock Inn
04662
(207)-276-9360

Mid-May—mid-June

9 rooms, 1 pb

C-12 up/S-ltd/P-no

Continental plus
Afternoon tea
sitting room

Elegant rooms with a view, hiking, boating, swimming, fishing, golf, antique & gift shops. Featured in Country Inns & Back Roads.

Harbourside Inn
04662
(207)-276-3272

$60-130 B&B
14 rooms, 14 pb

C-yes/S-no/P-no

Continental breakfast

June—September

Inn first opened in 1888. Near village of Northeast Harbor. Fireplaces, baths, trails to National Park, homemade blueberry muffins fresh each morning.

OGUNQUIT

Admiral's Loft
97 Main St.
(207)-646-5496

12 rooms, 5 pb

C-no/S-yes/P-no

Continental breakfast

May 15-Oct. 12

Berwick
Box 261, 03907
(207)-646-4062

$40-50 B&B
9 rooms, 9 pb
Visa, MC
C-no/S-yes/P-no

Continental breakfast

sitting room

All year

Walk to Beach—Restaurants—Shops.

Blue Shutters
6 Beachmere Pl., 03907
(207)-646-2163

$45-66 B&B
11 rooms, 11 pb

C-ltd/S-yes/P-no

Continental breakfast

sitting room

April—mid-November

Share the peacefulness and ocean view of this special guest house. Only a short amble to everything, including exquisite little beaches.

Captain Lorenz Perkins
P.O. Box 1249, 03907
(207)-646-7825

$30-60 B&B
13 rooms, 5 pb

C-3 up/S-yes/P-no

Continental plus
Complimentary wine
sitting room

April—October

Charming 18th-Century colonial home, furnished with antiques. Each is individually furnished. Walking distance to beach and shops.

Channing Hall
3 Pine Hill Rd., 03907
(207)-646-5222

$55-65 B&B
7 rooms, 7 pb
Visa, MC
C-no/S-yes/P-no

Continental plus
Complimentary liquors
sitting room

May—October

A quiet experience on spacious grounds in the elegance of a gracious mansion.

**Be sure to call the Inn to verify details and prices
and to make your reservation**

Clipper Ship Guest House
46 N. Main St., 03907
(207)-646-9735

April—October

$30-60 B&B
20 rooms, 6 pb
credit cards accepted
C-yes/S-yes/P-yes

Continental breakfast

sitting room
library

19th-Century guest house furnished in antique and modern exudes hospitality. In-town location, short walk to beach.

Dunelawn
Rte. 1, 03907
(207)-646-2403

January—November

$25-125 B&B
17 rooms, 6 pb
Visa, MC
C-yes/S-yes/P-no

Full breakfast
Dinner
piano, live jazz

Gorgeous mansion with incredible ocean and estate views—elegance in a relaxed atmosphere.

Hartwell House
116 Shore Rd., 03907
(207)-646-7210

All year

$85-95 B&B
9 rooms, 9 pb
Visa
C-no/S-yes/P-no

Continental plus

swimming, tennis
available

Elegantly furnished in Early American & English antiques. Set amid 2 acres of sculpted gardens, perfect for relaxing.

Inn at 77 Shore Road
77 Shore Rd., 03907
(207)-646-2933

May—October

$50-65 EP
7 rooms, 7 pb

C-yes/S-yes/P-no/H-ltd

1840 French Mansard mansion converted to comfortable fully equipped apartments. Sleep 3 or 4. Ocean views. Walk to beach, shops, restaurants.

Marimor Motor Inn
66 Shore Rd., 03907
(207)-646-7397

June—September

$24-35 dbl B&B
8 rooms, 0 pb
Visa, MC
C-no/S-yes/P-no

Continental breakfast

glass enclosed porch

Scenic Marginal Way, beaches & Perkins Cove nearby. Furnished in antiques. Backyard park with picnic tables under trees.

Sea Chimes
RD 1, Shore Rd., 03902
(207)-646-5378

May—September

$35-40 B&B
3 rooms, 0 pb

C-no/S-ltd/P-no

Continental breakfast

sitting room

Quiet, wooded setting, near the sea/shore road—between York Beach and Ogunquit, minutes to beaches, golf, tennis, theater, dining.

Seafair Inn
24 Shore Rd., 03907
(207)-646-2181

May 10—Oct. 10

$25-80 B&B
20 rooms, 16 pb
Visa, MC
C-ltd/S-yes/P-no

Continental breakfast

sitting room, piano

Restored Victorian inn furnished with period antiques. Walk to antique shops, restaurants, art galleries, sandy beach, and Maine's rocky coast.

RANGELEY ————————————————————————

Davis Lodge
Rte. 4, 04970
(207)-864-5569

5/15-10/15, 12/15-3/15

$25 pp
5 rooms, 4 pb
credit cards accepted
C-yes/S-no/P-no

Full Breakfast
Dinner, bar
Sitting room, piano
beach swimming

Secluded antique appointed log cabin. 2 massive fireplaces. Situated on Rangeley Lake overlooking mountains. Concerts in the summer.

Viola's Guest House
Pleasant St., 04970
(207)-864-5409

All year

$24-30 EP
4 rooms, 1 pb

C-yes/S-no/Pltd-

Full breakfast

Breakfast is served on sunny glass enclosed porch—8 tables, seats 25, home-made table cloths, place mats, valances—comfort at Ole Time Maine prices.

SEARSPORT ————————————————————————

Carriage House Inn
Rte 1, Box 238, 04974
(207)-548-2289

All year

$20-38 B&B
6 rooms, 1 pb
Visa, AmEx
C-yes/S-yes

Continental breakfast
Afternoon tea
sitting room
library

Homeport Inn
Box 148, 04974
(207)-548-2259

All year

$20-55 B&B
10 rooms, 6 pb
Visa, MC, AmEx, DC, CB
C-yes/S-yes/P-ltd/H-yes

Full breakfast
Tea, wine
sitting room

Listed Historic Register—Ideal mid-coast location for an extended stay to visit coast of Maine.

SO. BROOKSVILLE ————————————————————

Breezemere Farm
Box 290, 04617
(207)-326-8628

June—Columbus Day

$28 pp EP
13 rooms, 6 pb
Visa, MC
C-yes/S-ltd/P-yes

Full breakfast
Dinner
sitting room, piano
bicycles
ponies, pigs & goats

Unrivaled scenic beauty... coves, islands, rock ledges, trees, unparalled nature—bald eagles, seals, tidal life. Fine eating, sparkling accomodations.

SOUTH CASCO

Thomas Inn & Playhouse | $25 B&B | Complimentary breakfast
PO Box 128, 04077 | 10 rooms, 4 pb | all meals, full bar
| none | summer theatre
| C-yes/S-yes/P-no/H-ltd | piano bar, library
All year | | sitting room, billiards

Located in the Olde South Casco Village with frontage on Thomas Pond. Sandy beach, paved boat ramp.

SOUTHWEST HARBOR

Claremont | $52-90 MAP | Full breakfast
04679 | 29 rooms, 26 pb | Lunch, dinner, bar
(207)-244-5036 | | sitting room, piano
| C-yes/S-yes/P-no/H-ltd | tennis courts
May—October | | bicycles

On the shores of Somes Sound, the only fjord on the East Coast. Established 1884. Annual croquet tournament.

Harbor Lights Home | $12-28 EP
Rte. 102, 04679 | 9 rooms, 4 pb
(207)-244-3835 | Visa, MC | sitting room
| C-yes/S-yes/P-yes
All year

The inn is a big Victorian style home with some antique furnishings, in the center of town, beautiful state of Maine.

STRATTON

Widow's Walk | $10 B&B(summer), $24 MAP | Full breakfast
Box 150, 04982 | 6 rooms, 0 pb | Dinner (ski season)
(207)-246-6901 | | sitting room
| C-yes/S-yes/P-no
All year

Quaint Victorian mansion (1897) on Nat'l Reg. of Historic Places. Our best feature is our friendly homelike atmosphere.

SUNSET

Goose Cove Lodge | $50-60 B&B | Full breakfast
04683 | 21 rooms, 21 pb | Dinner, beer & wine
(207)-348-2508 | | beaches, sailboats
| C-yes/S-ltd/P-no | piano, sitting room
May-Oct. | | bicycles, entertainment

Seventy wooded acres with nature trails, half mile of oceanfront, sundecks, fireplaces, and peace at the end of beyond. Summer-weekly MAP only ($300-400)

SURRY

Surry House | $40-44 dbl. B&B | Complimentary breakfast
| 8 rooms, 6 pb   4684 | comp.tea, dinner, bar
(207)-667-5091 | VISA, MC | canoes, private beach
| C-yes/S-yes/P-no/H-yes | croquet, horseshoes
All year | | sitting room, library

Coastal country inn offering excellent cuisine, rolling lawns, private beach, spectacular sunsets, stenciled walls, New England charm and comfort.

TENANTS HARBOR ─────────────────────────────

East Wind Inn
P.O. Box 149, 04860
(207)-372-6366

All year

$32-38 EP
16 rooms, 2 pb
Visa, MC
C-12 up/S-yes/P-ltd/H-ltd

Full breakfast
All meals
sitting room
baby grand piano

Authentic country inn. Fishing boats unload at wharf. Antiques, telephones, color tv, and piano. Antique shops, movies, stores, museums nearby.

WATERFORD ─────────────────────────────

Artemus Ward House
04088
(207)-583-4106

May 15—Jan. 15

$35-40 B&B
4 rooms, 2 pb

C-yes/S-yes/P-no

Full breakfast
Tea, dinner
sitting room

Historic house in village listed on National Register. Antique furnishings, original stencils, private beach on lake, equestrian center adjoining.

WELD ─────────────────────────────

Weld Inn
Box 8, 04285
(207)-585-2429

All year

$16.50 pp B&B
13 rooms, 2 pb

C-yes/S-yes/P-no/H-ltd

Full breakfast
Lunch, dinner, bar

Country Inn, circa 1920's dining room, quiet, lake across street—mountain climbing, rock hounds, home cooking.

WELLS ─────────────────────────────

Grey Gull Inn
21 Webhannet,
04090
(207)-646-7501
April-October

$29-39

10 rooms, 0 pb
VISA, MC, AMEX

Food service varies

Country Inn directly on the ocean with outstanding views. Quiet Atlantic setting. Affordable. Chef-owned; dining in season.

Haven
Church St., 04090
(207)-646-4194

May 31—Oct. 15

$42 dbl B&B
6 rooms, 6 pb

C-yes/S-ltd/P-no/H-yes

Continental breakfast

sitting room
deck

Unique guest house formerly a country church. ½ block to the beach. Breakfast overlooking the ocean or wildlife preserve.

WEST FORKS ─────────────────────────────

Crab Apple Acres
Rte. 201, 04985

All year

$15 pp
7 rooms, 0 pb

C-yes/S-yes/P-no

Full breakfast
Dinner (reservation)
sitting room

1835 farmhouse on Kennebec River, offering homecooking & country hospitality. Professional whitewater outfitter—rafting daily all summer.

WISCASSET ──────────────────────────────

Roberts House $30-50 B&B   Continental breakfast
P.O. Box 413, 04578   3 rooms, 0 pb   tea, wine, beer
(207)-882-5055   library, grand piano
                          C-older/S-ltd/P-no   bicycles
All year sometimes

Roberts House in the old town of Wiscasset (1660)—furnished with antiques, quilts, continental breakfast with fresh fruit, homemade pastries.

Squire Tarbox $55 dbl B&B   Continental plus
RFD 2, Box 318, 04578   8 rooms, 2 pb   Dinner (res.), bar
                                                   sitting room, piano
                          C-ltd/S-yes/P-no
May 25—Nov. 1

Rural, wooded area on coastal Maine, convenient to Booth Bay, Wiscasset & Bath. A quiet interlude with a reputation for good food.

YORK ──────────────────────────────

Dockside Guest Qtrs. $29-71 EP   Continental plus
P.O. Box 205, 03909   20 rooms, 18 pb   Luncheon, dinner, bar
(207)-363-2868   Visa, MC   sitting room
                          C-yes/P-ltd/H-ltd   marina, boat rentals
June—Columbus Day

Super scenic location, several ocean beaches nearby. Historic District within walking distance. Rated 3 diamonds by AAA.

YORK BEACH ──────────────────────────────

The Bennetts $30-50
3 Broadway, 03910   7 rooms, 0 pb
(207)-363-5302   living room
                          C-yes/S-yes/P-no
May—Oct. 15

Guest house centrally located, ocean view. Quiet, clean atmosphere, fully equipped kitchen where people can prepare 3 meals a day.

Jo-Mar's Guest House $28-36 dbl B&B&B   Continental breakfast
Box 838, 03910   6 rooms, 0 pb
(207)-363-4826   sitting room
                          C-6 up/S-yes/P-no
mid-May—mid-Oct.

Oceanfront with spectacular views, quiet area overlooking Short Sands Beach. Friendly atmosphere, charming rooms. Convenient to the best of everything.

YORK HARBOR ──────────────────────────────

York Harbor Inn $40-60 B&B   Continental plus
P.O. Box 573, 03911   10 rooms, 0 pb   Lunch, dinner, bar
(207)-363-5119   Visa, MC, AmEx   sitting room, piano
                          C-yes/S-yes/P-yes   bicycles
All year   ocean swimming

Quiet, authentic Country Inn (circa 1637) listed in National Register of Historic Places; overlook the ocean and York Harbor Beach.

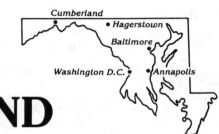

MARYLAND

ANNAPOLIS ───────────────────────────────────

Gibson's Lodging $33-38 B&B   Continental breakfast
110 Prince George, 21401   14 rooms, 0 pb
(301)-268-5555   no   sitting room
                            C-yes/S-yes/P-no/H-yes   piano

All year

Located in Historic District, near City Docks, adjacent to U.S. Naval Academy. Antique furnishings throughout. Offstreet parking. Daily maid service.

BETHESDA ───────────────────────────────────

Winslow Home $25-35 B&B   Breakfast
8217 Caraway St., 20818   2 rooms, 0 pb   No alcohol, please
(301)-229-4654   no   sitting room
                            C-yes/S-no/P-yes   piano

All year

National Capitol is 20 minutes away; Great Falls National Park is 10. Quiet residential home.

CHESTERTOWN ───────────────────────────────────

White Swan Tavern $55-80 B&B   Continental plus
231 High St., 21620   5 rooms, 5 pb   Afternoon tea
(301)778-2300   no   bicycles
                            C-yes/S-yes/P-no/H-ltd   sitting room

Except February

18th-Century Inn nestled in Maryland's historic eastern shore. Genuine antiques, homemade continental breakfast, tea, complimentary wine & fruit.

EASTON ───────────────────────────────────

Hynson Tourist Home $12-15 pp EP   none
804 Dover Rd., 21601   6 rooms, 2 pb
(301)-822-2777   no   piano
                            C-yes/S-yes/P-no

All year

The home of good seafood, golf courses. Close to Washington, D.C., Balto, Ocean City. Highly recommended.

**Be sure to call the Inn to verify details and prices
and to make your reservation**

ELLICOTT CITY

Hayland Farm
5000 Sheppard Ln., 21043
(301)-531-5593
(301)-596-9919
All year

$25-35
2 rooms, 0 pb
no
C-yes/S-no/P-no

Full breakfast

swimming pool
baby grand piano
library

Beautiful location, large pool, generous complimentary breakfast, baby grand piano, library. Bring children. Queen size & bunk beds.

FREDERICK

Spring Bank Farm Inn
7945 Worman's Mill,21701
(301)-694-0440

All year

$35-60 B&B
5 rooms, 1 pb
no
C-no/S-no/P-no

Continental plus

sitting room
piano

Stately home, period furnishings, elegant breakfasts at Spring Bank. Near Washington, DC; Baltimore; Harper's Ferry; Gettysburg; New Market & Leesburg.

GIRDLETREE

Stockmans
POB 125, 21829
(301)-632-3299
(301)-269-6232 RS
May—Nov.

$26-28 B&B
2 rooms, 0 pb
no
C-yes/S-no/P-no

Continental plus

living room, den
bicycles
piano

Large, comfortable, Victorian country house in a quiet residential village — on Maryland's lower Eastern Shore.

NEW MARKET

Strawberry Inn
Box 237, 17 Main, 21774
(301)-865-3318

All year

$45-60 dbl B&B
5 rooms, 5 pb
no
C-7 up/S-yes/P-no/H-ltd

Continental plus

sitting room

A country inn furnished with antiques. Less than one hour from Baltimore, Washington DC, Gettysburg. Continental breakfast served to your room.

PRINCESS ANNE

Washington Hotel & Inn
Somerset Ave., 21853
(301)-651-2525

All year

$20-30 EP
16 rooms, 16 pb
Visa, MC
C-yes/S-yes

Coffee shop
Dining rooms
sitting room

Historic Inn built 1744 — continuous operation — located in a historic town. A must for tourists. Bay trips and bicycling.

ST. MICHAELS

Kemp House
412 Talbot St. 21663
(301)-261-2243
(301)-261-2233 RS
All year

$35-55
6 rooms, 0 pb
Visa, MC
C-yes/S-yes/P-yes/H-yes

Continental plus

bicycles

1805 Georgian house with four-poster beds and working fireplaces in historic eastern shore village; close to restaurants, museums, harbor.

The Inn at Perry Cabin
21663
(301)-745-5178

All year

$80-120 B&B
6 rooms, 6 pb
Visa, MC, AmEx
C-yes/S-yes/P-no

Continental plus
Lunch, dinner
bicycles
entertainment
sitting room, piano

On the scenic Miles River in historic St. Michaels. Accessible to hunting, sailing, golfing and shopping. Seafood and wildlife abound.

VIENNA

Nanticoke Manor House
POB 156, 21869
(301)-376-3530

All year

$35-55 B&B
5 rooms, 2 pb
no
C-12 up/S-ltd/P-no

Continental plus
Complimentary wine
sitting room, piano
bicycles, fishing
croquet, badmitten

Authentic Victorian built 1861 overlooking the Nanticoke River. Spiral staircase, authentic furnishings, fireplaces. Near Blackwater Refuge.

WOODSBORO

The Rosebud Inn
4 N. Main St., 21798
(301)-845-2221

All year

$30-55
5 rooms, 3 pb
Visa, MC
C-yes/S-ltd/P-ltd

Continental plus

sitting room
organ

Only one hour's drive from Washington, D.C. and Baltimore — minutes from Camp David.

MASSACHUSETTS

BASS RIVER

Captain Isaiah's House
33 Pleasant St., 02664
(617)-394-1739

mid-May—mid-Oct.

$30 dbl B&B
6 rooms, 0 pb
no
C-yes/S-yes/P-no

Continental plus

sitting room

Charming, restored old sea captain's house in historic Bass River area. Most rooms have fireplaces, continental breakfast w/ homebaked breads, coffee cake.

BREWSTER

Bramble Inn
POB 159, 02631
(617)-896-7644

June—Oct.

$46-62 B&B
8 rooms, 3 pb
no
C-yes/S-yes/P-no/H-ltd

Continental breakfast
Lunch, dinner
sitting room
near beach, tennis

Romantic country inn in historic district of Cape Cod. Beach, tennis courts, and close to golf, fishing, and museums.

Inn of the Golden Ox
1360 Main St., 02631
(617)-896-3111

All year

$45
7 rooms, 0 pb
yes
C-12 up/S-yes/P-no

Full breakfast
Lunch, dinner, bar
Commons

Unique blend of New England and old world charm. Housed in 1828 church (decorated with antiques)—rated 3½ stars.

Old Manse Inn
POB 833, 02631
(617)-896-3149

All year

$40-60 dbl B&B
9 rooms, 9 pb
Visa, MC, AmEx
C-yes/S-yes/P-no/H-yes

Continental plus
Gourmet dinner, bar
sitting room, patio

Enjoy the salt air from your room in this sea captain's home. Walk to Cape Cod's attractions. Gourmet dining.

Old Sea Pines Inn
2553 Main St., 02631
(617)-896-6114

May—Oct.

$25-38 B&B
13 rooms, 8 pb
Visa, MC
C-10 up/S-yes/P-no

Continental plus
Snacks, wine & beer
sitting room

Newly redecorated turn-of-the-century mansion furnished with antiques. Near beaches, bicycle trails, quality restaurants and shops.

CAPE COD

Barnaby Inn
POB 151, West Harwich,
02671
(617)-432-6789

May—Oct.

$27-37 B&B

5 rooms, 3 pb
Visa, AmEx, BacAm
C-yes/S-yes/P-no

Continental plus

Dinner, bar
bicycle rental
tennis nearby

Barnaby's innkeepers make a special effort to treat their guests as part of the family sharing recipes, information and local history. We care.

Bay Breeze Guest House
POB 307, Monument Beach

$20-35 EP
7 rooms, 0 pb
no
S-no/P-no

tennis courts
sitting room

Comfortable informality at very moderate prices. Excellent swimming and good views.

Cobb's Cove
Rte. 6A, Barnstable Village,
02630
(617)-362-9356

$78-98
6 rooms, 6 pb
no
C-no/S-ltd/P-no

Full breakfast
dinner, comp. wine
whirlpool tubs
sitting room, library
piano

All year

For the discriminating traveler — secluded, beautifully appointed suites, whirlpool tubs. Stroll to the beach, shops and restaurants.

Country Inn
86 Sisson Rd., Harwich Port,
02646

$47 dbl
7 rooms, 7 pb
Visa, MC
C-yes/S-yes/P-no/H-ltd

Full breakfast
Dinner, bar service
swimming pool
tennis courts
sitting room, piano

All year

Country Inn is what its name implies—A lovely old Cape Cod home on six acres with the essence of yesteryear. An Inn of New England tradition.

Dunscroft Inn
24 Pilgrim Rd., Harwich
Port, 02646
(617)-432-0810

$50
6 rooms, 6 pb
no
C-ltd/S-yes/P-no

Continental plus
Wine
sitting room
piano

March—Dec.

Located 300 feet from a beautiful private beach on Nantucket Sound. Also within walking distance of restaurants, shops, theater. Residential area.

Lion's Head Inn
POB 444, West Harwich,
02671
(617)-432-7766

$38-50 B&B
5 rooms, 2 pb
no
C-no/S-yes/P-no/H-ltd

Full breakfast
complimentary tea, wine
sitting room

March—Dec.

Built as a Cape half-house in 1800, former sea captain's home, charming inn with sense of history, furnished in period antiques.

Nauset House Inn
POB 774, East Orleans,
02643
(617)-255-2195

$30-60 EP
14 rooms, 8 pb
Visa, MC
C-no/S-yes/P-no

Full breakfast
Hors d'ouvres, tea, wine
sitting room
piano

April—Nov. 20

Intimate 1810 Inn, unique turn of the century conservatory, warm ambience, a short walk to the sea.

Our listings, supplied by the innkeeper, are as complete as possible. Many of the inns have more features — amenities or food and beverage service — than we list. Be sure to inquire when you book.

CHATHAM

Seafarer Motel
Main St., 02546
(617)-432-1739

$52-62
20 rooms, 20 pb
Visa, MC
C-yes/S-yes/P-no/H-yes

Coffee only

sitting room

All year

Quiet location on 2 pretty acres, cozy accomodations, hand-stenciled decorative details, room coffee and the personal attentiveness of resident owners.

Ship's Knees Inn
Beach Rd., East Orleans,
02643
(617)-255-1312

$32-60
19 rooms, 5 pb
no
C-yes /S-yes/P-no

Continental breakfast

swimming pool

All year

A restored sea captain's house; surrounded by the charm of yesterday while offering the convenience of today.

CONCORD

Hawthorne Inn
462 Lexington Rd.,01742
(617)-369-5610

$55-75 B&B
5 rooms, 0 pb
no
C-yes/S-yes/P-no

Continental plus
Complimentary tea, wine
sitting room
bicycles

Except Jan.—Feb.

Located in the Historic Zone our rooms are appointed with antiques, quilts and artworks with the accent on New England comfort & charm.

DEERFIELD

Deerfield Inn
The Street, 01342
(413)-774-5587

$65-70 EP
23 rooms, 23 pb
Visa, MC, DC, AmEx
C-yes/S-yes/P-yes/H-yes

Full breakfast
Lunch, dinner, bar
sitting room

All year

Located in the center of Historic Deerfield with its 12 beautifully restored museum houses. 23 guest rooms, no two furnished alike.

EASTHAM

Whalewalk Inn
169 Bridge Rd., 02642
(617)-255-0617

$55-85 B&B
11 rooms, 11 pb
no
C-12 up/S-yes/P-no

Full breakfast

sitting room

March 1—Jan 4

A sophisticated Inn for the most discriminating traveler.

EDGARTOWN

Charlotte Inn
S. Summer St., 02539
(617)-627-4751

24 rooms, 22 pb
Visa, MC
C-no/S-yes/P-no

Full breakfast
Lunch, dinner
sitting room
piano

All year

Elegant Country Inn 1½ blocks from harbor, individually decorated rooms, some fireplaces — uncommon attention to detail — romantic setting.

Edgartown Inn　　　$55-95 EP　　　　　Full breakfast
N. Water St., 02539　　18 rooms, 12 pb
(617)-627-4794　　　　 no
　　　　　　　　　　　C-5 up/S-yes/P-no

April—Oct.

Historic Inn where Nathaniel Hawthorne, Daniel Webster, and John Kennedy stayed. Serving homemade cakes and breads for breakfast in garden.

FALMOUTH

Elm Arch Inn　　　　EP　　　　　　　　Coffee only
Elm Arch Way, 02540　 24 rooms, 12 pb
(617)-548-0133　　　　 no　　　　　　　　swimming pool
　　　　　　　　　　　C-yes/S-yes/P-no　 sitting rooms

All year

Bombarded by British War of 1812. Charming Colonial Inn — excellent location center of village. Convenient to all activities. Reasonable rates.

Merrell Tavern Inn, So. Lee, Massachusetts

Mostly Hall B&B Inn
27 Main St., 02540
(617)-548-3786

Except Feb.

$35-60 dbl B&B
7 rooms, 5 pb
no
C-16 up/S-yes/P-no

Full breakfast
Complimentary tea, wine
bicycles
sitting room

1849 sea captain's house on historic village green in charming town. Large rooms. Great restaurants, theater, the islands. Many guests from Europe.

GLOUCESTER ————————————————

Gloucester Traveler Inn
612 Essex Ave., 01930
(617)-283-2502

All year

$32-60
25 rooms, 25 pb
yes
C-yes/S-yes/P-yes/H-ltd

Full breakfast

swimming pool

An experience in true New England charm and hospitality.

Kris & Mike Schwartz
4 Bittersweet Ln., 01930
(617)-281-3376

May—October

$35 B&B
2 rooms, 0 pb
no
C-yes/S-yes/P-no

Continental plus

sitting room
piano

100-year-old Victorian home within walking distance of a beautiful beach & horseback riding. Homemade breakfast served on 40 ft. glass enclosed porch.

GREAT BARRINGTON ————————————————

**Seekonk Pines
GuestHouse**
Box 29AA,RD1,Rt.23,01230
(413)-528-4192

All year

$25-45
7 rooms, 1 pb
no
C-yes/S-ltd/P-no

Full breakfast

Swimming pool
bicycles
sitting room, piano

Former estate, close to Tanglewood, skiing, hiking. Hosts are artists and singers. Original artwork, homemade jams, produce for sale.

Turning Point
RD2 Box 140, 01230
(413)-528-4777

All year

$30-50 B&B
7 rooms, 1 pb
no
C-yes/S-no/P-no

Full breakfast
Complimentary tea, wine
sitting room
piano
bicycles

We offer a natural environment: whole grain vegetarian breakfast; no smoking; hiking/skiing; comfort in 18th Century Inn near Tanglewood, next to ski slopes.

HYANNIS ————————————————

Park Square Village
156 Main St., 02601
(617)-775-5611

All year

$34-49
13 rooms, 8 pb
Visa, MC, AmEx
C-yes/S-yes/P-no

Continental breakfast

swimming pool
screen tennis

Walk to Hyannis attractions, village setting w/trees & shrubs, motel efficiencies and family vacation apts, Capt. S. Baxter Hse 1855 & 1710 House.

142 Massachusetts

LAKEVILLE ————————————————————————

Pistachio Cove	$25-38 B&B	Gourmet breakfast
R.F.O. 5, 02346	4 rooms, 1 pb	Complimentary cocktail
(617)-763-2383	no	boats, lake
	C-yes/S-yes/H-ltd	sitting room
All year		color TVs

Savor country hospitality and informal elegance on scenic Lake Apponequet. Luxurious accomodations provide total relaxation.

LEE ————————————————————————————

Haus Andreas	$75-140 B&B	Continental breakfast
Stockbridge Rd., 01238	6 rooms, 6 pb	Afternoon tea
(413)-243-3298	Visa, MC	swimming, tennis
	C-10 up/S-yes/P-no	bicycles
All year		sitting room, piano

Historical revolutionary setting, heated pool, golf, tennis, luxury, comfort, local fine restaurants. Complimentary breakfast. Relax in old world charm.

LENOX ————————————————————————————

Candlelight Inn	$45-90 EP	
53 Walker St., 01240	5 rooms, 5 pb	Lunch, dinner, bar
(413)-637-1555	Visa, MC, DC, AmEx	entertainment
	C-yes/S-yes/P-no	
All year		

Beautiful summer courtyard service; Christmas time — a touch of splendor inside and out; enclosed porches for dining in all weather.

Garden Gables Inn	$28-80 EP	Full breakfast
141 Main St., 01240	11 rooms, 4 pb	
(413)-637-0193	Visa, MC	swimming pool
	C-yes/P-no	sitting room
Except March		library

Quiet, restful inn set away from the road on 4 acres of beautiful gardens, within comfortable walking distance to restaurant and shops.

Walker House	$40-95 B&B	Continental plus
74 Walker St., 01240	8 rooms, 8 pb	Complimentary tea, wine
(413)-637-1271	no	sitting room
	C-ltd/S-ok/P-ltd	piano
All year		bicycles

We make our guests feel like special pampered friends, in a lovely country atmosphere on 3 acres within walking distance of shops and restaurants.

Whistler's Inn	$45-100 B&B	Continental plus
5 Greenwood St., 01240	11 rooms, 11 pb	Afternoon tea
(413)-637-0975	Visa, MC	sitting room, piano
	C-yes/S-yes/P-no	library
May—October		bicycles, nearby lake

1820 Tudor mansion, old world charm, antiques, one block to center of Lenox, restaurants. Library & music room, continental breakfast.

NANTUCKET

Periwinkle Guest House
9 N. Water St., 02554
(617)-228-9267

$30-85 B&B
18 rooms, 8 pb
Visa, MC, AmEx
C-yes/S-yes/P-no

Continental plus

sitting room

All year

Several top floor rooms command a harbor view — all furnished with 1850 period antiques, private & semi-private baths — double backyard with picnic table.

Ships Inn
13 Fair St., 02554
(617)-228-0040
(617)-228-9559 RS
Mid-April—Mid-Dec.

$30-70
12 rooms, 10 pb
Visa, MC, AmEx
C-yes/S-yes/P-no

Continental plus
Dinner, bar
sitting room

Built 1812—whaling captain Obed Starbuck's mansion. Period furnishings—Birthplace Lucrica Coffen Mott. Centrally located.

West Moor Inn
Off Cliff Rd., 02554
(617)-228-0877

$25-85 EP
11 rooms, 6 pb
no
C-7 up/S-yes/P-no

Full breakfast
Other meals on occasion
sitting room
piano
bicycles

Except January

Gracious Federal style home—great views, quiet moors, distant sailboats, the historic town. A mile from bustling steamboat wharf.

Woodbox
29 Fair St., 02554
(617)-228-0587

$75-120 EP
9 rooms, 9 pb
no
C-yes/S-yes/P-no/H-yes

Full breakfast
Dinner
sitting room

June—October

Nantucket's oldest Inn built 1709, furnished with period antiques. Breakfast 8:30—10:30. Dinner—continental cuisine—7 and 9 pm.

NEW MARLBOROUGH

Old Inn on the Green
Star Rte. 70, 01230
(413)-229-7924

$50 B&B
4 rooms, 0 pb
no
C-yes/S-yes/P-no

Continental plus
Bar, Saturday dinner
sitting room

All year

1760 colonial inn on historic landmark register. 3 public rooms downstairs. Parlor, dining room, old tavern — inn furnished with antiques.

NEWBURYPORT

Benjamin Choate House
25 Tyng St., 01950
(617)-462-4786

$35-50 B&B
5 rooms, 2 pb
no
C-yes/S-yes/P-yes/H-ltd

Full breakfast
Complimentary tea, wine
bicycles
sitting room

All year

Herbert Fox's Benjamin Choate House: antiques, original art collection, hearty full breakfast at Newbury's largest kitchen hearths. Public boat landing.

Windsor House $47-80 Full breakfast
38 Federal St., 01950 6 rooms, 3 pb Tea, wine, supper
(617)-462-3778 Visa, MC Commons
C-yes/S-yes/P-yes organ
All year

Federalist mansion/ship's chandelry in restored historic seaport furnished in period antiques; explore our shops, museums, beaches and wildlife refuge.

NORTHFIELD ───

Northfield Country
House $30-60 Gourmet breakfast
School St., 01360 7 rooms, 3 pb Dinner (res.), wine
(413)-498-2692 no tennis court
C-yes/S-yes/P-no sitting room
All year piano

A country retreat; mountain views, lots of fresh air, horses grazing, typically New England, beautifully appointed rooms, some with working fireplaces.

PLYMOUTH ───

Colonial House Inn $50 dbl none
207 Sandwich St., 02360 6 rooms, 6 pb
(617)-746-2087 no
All year

Early American decor with private baths, air conditioning, TVs, pool, quiet secluded grounds, picturesque view of bay near historic sites.

PRINCETON ───

Country Inn at Princeton $95 B&B Continental plus
30 Mountain Rd., 01541 6 rooms, 6 pb Dinner, bar
(617)-464-2030 Visa, MC, AmEx parlor living room
C-no/S-ltd/P-no/H-yes
Except Mon., Tue.

1890 late Victorian Country Mansion. Romantic, elegant, intimate; couples only. 5-star gourmet cuisine. Spacious lodging quarters. Mountain view.

PROVINCETOWN ───

Bradford Gardens Inn $69-99 B&B Full gourmet breakfast
178 Bradford St., 02657 12 rooms, 12 pb
(617)-487-1616 Visa, MC, AmEx sitting room
C-yes/S-yes/P-no
April—Dec.

Charming country inn built in 1820. Working fireplaces in bedrooms. Extensive gardens, original paintings & antiques.

Hargood House $390-635/wk
493 Commercial St.,02657 17 rooms, 17 pb
(617)-487-1324
C-ltd

Unique self-contained apartments, private beach, waterfront garden, all rooms beautifully decorated and luxuriously outfitted.

The Wildwood Inn, Ware, Massachusetts

Land's End Inn
22 Commercial St., 02657
(617)-487-0706

All year

$33-70 B&B
15 rooms, 9 pb
no
C-ltd/S-yes/P-no/H-yes

Continental Breakfast

sitting room

Victorian summerhouse set high on a hill overlooking Provincetown and all of Cape Cod Bay. With a homelike and friendly atmosphere.

Rose and Crown
158 Commercial St.,02657
(617)-487-3332

All year

$30-75 B&B
8 rooms, 5 pb
no
C-yes/S-yes/P-no

Continental breakfast

sitting room

A relaxed, elegant 1780's Captain's House. Rooms feature antiques in a homey atmosphere. An unusual eclectic living room is featured.

ROCKPORT ─────────────────────────

Inn at Cove Hill
37 Mt. Pleasant, 01966
(617)-546-2701

Feb.–Oct.

$25-49 B&B
10 rooms, 7 pb
no
C-10 up/S-yes/P-no

Continental breakfast

living room

A 200 year old colonial home with period furnishings located in a New England village setting within walking distance of attractions.

Rocky Shores Inn
Eden Rd., 01966
(617)-546-2823

$46-57 B&B
22 rooms, 20 pb
no
C-yes/S-yes/P-no

Full breakfast

sitting room

May—Nov.

Inn and cottages with unforgetable views of Thacher Island lights and open sea. Complete complimentary breakfast included.

ROCKPORT GROVE

Addison Choate Inn
49 Broadway, 01966
(617)-546-7543

$55-95 B&B
9 rooms, 9 pb
no
C-13 up/S-yes/P-no

Continental plus

swimming pool
sitting room
library

Feb. 15—Nov. 30

Remarkably fine small country inn, cruise the coast on our private yacht the "Sweetwater". Antiques, flowers, a surprise on your pillow!

SALEM

Coach House Inn
284 Lafayette St., 01970
(617)-744-4092

$42-90
15 rooms, 12 pb
Visa, MC, AmEx
C-yes/S-yes/P-no

All year

Built in 1879 by Capt. E. Augustus Emmerton. Our guests enjoy comfortable rooms, the charm of his Victorian mansion.

Salem Inn
7 Summer St., 01970
(617)-741-0680

$50-75 B&B
12 rooms, 12 pb
all major
C-yes/S-yes/P-no

Continental breakfast

All year

Spacious, luxuriously appointed rooms in elegantly restored Federal mansion. In the heart of historic district, fine restaurants, harbor.

Stephen Daniels House
1 Daniels St., 01970
(617)-744-5709

$50 B&B
5 rooms, 5 pb
no
C-yes/S-yes/P-yes

Breakfast "sometimes"

sitting room
bicycles

All year

The house is 300 years old. Furnished with canopy beds and antiques throughout and fireplaces in every room.

Suzannah Flint House
98 Essex St., 01970
(617)-744-5281

$45 B&B
4 rooms, 0 pb
Visa, MC
C-yes/P-no

Continental plus

sitting room

March—Nov.

Located in Historic District, circa 1795 home maintains ambiance of bygone era. 4 air-conditioned rooms $45 each with breakfast.

SOUTH EGREMONT ───────────────────────

1780 Egremont Inn
Old Sheffield Rd.,01258
(413)-528-2111

$50-125
23 rooms, 23 pb
Visa, MC
C-8 up/P-no

Continental plus
Dinner, bar
Swimming pool
tennis courts

All year

sitting room, piano

One of a kind authentic inn, built as an inn in 1780. Nothing like it in the Berkshires.

SOUTH LEE ───────────────────────

Merrell Tavern Inn
Rt. 2, Main St., 01260
(413)-243-1794

$50-95 B&B
9 rooms, 7 pb
Visa, MC
C-yes/S-yes/P-no

Continental breakfast

sitting room

All year

New England setting of the 1800's in the heart of the Berkshire region, open fire in your room, continental breakfast.

STURBRIDGE ───────────────────────

Colonel Ebenezer Craft's
Box 1786, 01566
(617)-347-3313

$59-69 B&B
8 rooms, 6 pb
Visa, MC, AmEx
C-yes/S-yes/P-no

Continental plus
Lunch, dinner, tea, wine
swimming pool
sitting room, piano

All year

tennis courts

Colonial farmhouse built in 1786, antiques and four-poster beds, amenities include terry robes and jams or preserves at bedside.

Wildwood Inn
121 Church St., 01082
(413)-967-7798

$25-45 B&B
5 rooms, 0 pb
Visa, MC, AmEx
C-6 up/S-ltd/P-no

Continental plus
Tea, cider, restaurant
swimming hole, canoe
tennis courts

All year

sitting room

Relax—primitive antiques, heirloom quilts, firm beds... Enjoy Sturbridge, Deerfield, Amherst. Canoe, swim, bike, hike. Outstanding foliage. We spoil you.

WELLFLEET ───────────────────────

Inn at Duke Creeke
PO Box 364, 02667
(617)-349-9333

$35-60
25 rooms, 17 pb
Visa, MC, AmEx
C-yes/S-yes/P-no

Continental breakfast
Dinner, bar
piano
entertainment

Mid-May—mid-October

3 porches & lobby

Cozy Sea Captain's house in coastal fishing village. Close to beaches and Audubon Sanctuary. Overlooks salt marsh and duck pond.

WEST FALMOUTH ───────────────────────

Sjoholm B & B Inn
17 Chase Rd., 02574
(617)-540-5706

$18-49 B&B
18 rooms, 5 pb
Visa, MC
C-10 up/S-yes/P-no/H-yes

Full breakfast
Afternoon tea
bicycles
sitting room

All year

piano

Quaint 19th Century charm, peaceful country setting, caring innkeepers, make for a delightful stay. Stay in a fine English B & B. Rooms have fabric covered walls and are furnished with antiques and collectibles of wood, wicker, iron & brass.

148 Michigan

WHITINSVILLE ───────────────────────────────

Victorian
583 Linwood Ave., 01588
(617)-234-2500

$73-$88
8 rooms, 8 pb
Visa, MC, AmEx
C-yes/S-yes/P-yes

Full breakfast
continental plus

All year

lunch, dinner, full bar

23-room Victorian mansion with 12-foot ceilings. Marble fireplace. Antiques. 5 acre grounds complete the ambience.

WOODS HOLE ───────────────────────────────

Grey Whale Inn
565 Woods Hole, 02543
(617)-548-7692

$50 B&B
5 rooms, 2 pb
one
C-yes/S-yes/P-no

Complimentary breakfast
continental plus
bicycles, piano
sitting room

All year

library

Five room inn overlooking Martha's Vineyard on Cape Cod. Located in an historic district, the Grey Whale Inn was built during Thomas Jefferson's term as President.

Marlborough
320 Woods Hole, 02543
(617)-548-6218

$35 single B&B
7 rooms, 3 pb
none
C-yes/S-yes/P-ltd/H-ltd

Full complimentary
breakfast, afternoon tea
French spoken
games, TV, library

All year

pool, tennis, video

Rooms have fabric covered walls and are furnished with antiques of wood, wicker, iron and brass. The Marlborough is more than an inn, it's an experience!

MICHIGAN

DOUGLAS ───────────────────────────────

Rosemont Inn
83 Lake Shore Dr., 49406
(616)-857-2637

$45-70 B&B
8 rooms, 8 pb
Visa, MC
C-yes/S-yes/P-no/H-yes

Continental plus
Cheese & crackers
swimming pool
sitting room

All year

Victorian Inn on Lake Michigan. Furnished in antique reproductions, two parlors w/fireplace, large porches, Lake Michigan beach and heated pool.

LAKE LINDEN

Creative Holiday Lodge
1000 Calumet St., 49945
(906)-296-0113

All year

$14-26 B&B
4 rooms, 0 pb
no
C-yes/S-yes/P-no

Continental plus
Kitchen for use
swimming pool
sauna
sitting room, piano

Relish fresh blueberry muffins after your refreshing swim & sauna. Explore historic copper mines, beautiful waterfalls & enjoy great freshwater fishing.

LEXINGTON

Governor's Inn
7277 Simons St., 48450
(313)-359-5770

Memorial Day—October

$30 pp B&B
3 rooms, 3 pb

C-12 up/S-ltd/P-no

Continental plus

sitting room

Governor's Inn recreates the atmosphere of a turn-of-the-century summer home: wicker, iron beds, rockers on the shady porch.

MARSHALL

National House
102 S. Parkview, 49068
(616)-781-7374

All year

$45-75 B&B
16 rooms, 16 pb
Visa, MC, AmEx
C-yes/S-yes/P-no

Continental plus

sitting room

Michigan's oldest Inn lovingly restored with authentic antiques, located in Marshall, the midwest's most striking example of Victorian architecture.

MECOSTA

Blue Lake Lodge
P.O. Box 1, 49332
(616)-972-8391

April 1—November 25

$25
8 rooms, 0 pb
Visa, MC
C-yes/S-yes/P-yes/H-yes

sitting room
lake, boat, fishing

Sandy beach, fine fishing, beautiful, peaceful scenery.

PETOSKEY

Stafford's Bay View Inn
Box 3, 49770
(616)-347-2771

May 15—Oct. 30

$55-65 dbl B&B
21 rooms, 21 pb
Visa, MC, AmEx
C-yes/S-yes/P-small/H-yes

Full breakfast
Lunch, dinner, tea, wine
sitting room
piano

Michigan Historic Site overlooking Little Traverse Bay. Victorian charm, exceptional cuisine, scenic drives, shopping, summer and winter recreation.

PORT SANILAC

Raymond House Inn
M-25 1115 Ridge St,48469
(313)-622-8800
(800)-547-1436 RS
May thru October

$30-40 B&B
6 rooms, 4 pb

C-12 up/S-ltd/P-no

Continental plus

bicycles
sitting room

112-year-old Victorian home furnished in antiques; on Lake Huron; marina, boating, salmon fishing, swimming; owner-artist's gallery.

UNION CITY ───────────────────────────────

Victorian Villa
601 N. Broadway, 49094
(517)-741-7383

$40-65 B&B
5 rooms, 1 pb
Visa, MC
C-yes/S-no/P-no

Continental plus
Full Victorian tea
sitting room
piano

March 1—December 23

The Victorian Villa is an enchanting 19th Century guesthouse—romantic lodging—afternoon teas, a delicious continental breakfast—elegance of a century ago.

MINNESOTA

GRAND MARAIS ────────────────────────────

Gunflint Lodge
POB 100 GT, 55604
(218)-388-2294
(800)-328-3325 RS
All year

18 rooms, 18 pb
Visa, MC
C-yes/S-yes/P-yes/H-yes

Full breakfast
Lunch, dinner, tea
sauna
sitting room

Family style Northwest Country Inn, adjacent to famed Boundary Waters Canoe Area, hiking, fishing, wilderness activities program. Crosscountry skiing.

LITTLE FALLS ─────────────────────────────

Pine Edge Inn
56345
(612)-632-6681

$23.50-35.00 EP
30 rooms, 30 pb
Visa, MC, AmEx
C-yes/S-yes/P-yes/H-yes

Coffee shop

swimming pool
sitting room, piano

All year

Elegant New England Colonial, Lindbergs' home across the river, coach house dining room, main lobby sitting room—farmers, gov't people, housewives come.

MINNEAPOLIS ──────────────────────────────

Evelo's Bed & Breakfast
2301 Bryant Ave. S,55405
(612)-374-9656

$20-30 B&B
3 rooms, 0 pb
no
C-yes/S-no/P-no

Full breakfast

All year

1897 Victorian, period furnishings. Located on bus line, walk to Guthrie Theater, Mpls. Art Institute, childrens theater. Near historic Lake District.

NEW PRAGUE

Schumacher's New Prague
212 W. Main St., 56071
(612)-758-2133

All year

$59.95-79.95 EP
12 rooms, 12 pb
Visa, MC, AmEx
C-no/S-yes/P-no/H-ltd

Full breakfast
Lunch, dinner, bar
piano
sitting room

12 European decorated sleeping rooms named after the months of the year. Restaurant serves Czechoslovakian and German cuisine seven days a week.

NEWPORT

Schuyten Guest House
257 Third Ave., 55055
(612)-459-5698

All year

$30 B&B
2 rooms, 2 pb
none
C-yes/S-yes/P-yes

Full breakfast
Afternoon tea
bicycles

Tudor mansion on Mississippi River wooded lot. Filled with antiques. Near St. Paul, Minneapolis, International Airport, ski slopes. Dutch, German spoken.

OLD FRONTENAC

Lowell House B & B
531 Wood St., 55026
(612)-345-2456

May 1—November 30

$35-47 B&B
4 rooms, 1 pb

C-13 up/S-yes/P-no

Continental plus

sitting room

Enjoy Bed and Breakfast in a quaint and quiet corner of America's past—Mississippi River—near Rochester and Twin Cities.

SAUK CENTRE

Palmer House Hotel
56378
(612)-352-3431

All year

$16-30 EP
37 rooms, 4 pb
no
C-yes/S-yes/P-yes

Full service restaurant

tennis courts
sitting room, piano
dinner theatre

Historic site—the "original Main Street" home of Sinclair Lewis—first American author to win the Nobel Prize for Literature.

STACY

Kings Oakdale Park G.H.
6933 232nd Ave NE, 55029
(612)-462-5598

All year

3 rooms, 3 pb

S-yes/P-yes

Continental plus

Country lake area residence overlooks Typo Creek—volleyball, horseshoes. Short drive to scenic St. Croix River boat trip at Taylor Falls.

Prices quoted are the most current available. However, due to increases and seasonal fluctuations, they may have changed. Be sure to check when you make your reservations.

STILLWATER ─────────────────────────────

Lowell Inn
102 N. Second St., 55082
(612)-439-1100

$69-119 EP
21 rooms, 21 pb
Visa, MC, DC, AmEx
C-yes/S-ltd/P-no/H-yes

Full Breakfast
Lunch, dinner, bar
Jacuzzi

All year

Colonial country inn nestled in history-filled Stillwater, Minnesota near the bluff of St. Croix River. Elegant dining and accomodations.

WINONA ─────────────────────────────

Hotel and Zach's
3rd & Johnson, 55987
(507)-452-5460

$25-60
25 rooms, 25 pb
Visa, MC, AmEx
C-yes/S-yes/P-small

All year

Amidst the Mississippi River and valley bluffs—step into the world of Victorian Elegance.

MISSISSIPPI

NATCHEZ ─────────────────────────────

The Burn
712 N. Union St., 39120
(601)-445-8566

$75/dbl B&B
6 rooms, 6 pb
Visa, MC
C-6 up/S-yes/P-no/H-yes

Full breakfast
Complimentary wine
swimming pool
sitting room
piano

All year

The Burn (1832) is located in the oldest city on the Mississippi. Greek architecture, used as a hospital for Union soldiers.

Linden
1 Linden Place, 39120
(601)-445-5472

$70/dbl B&B
5 rooms, 5 pb
no
C-yes/S-yes/P-no

Full breakfast

sitting room
piano

All year

Antebellum Mansion furnished in antiques... in present owner's family for six generations. Southern breakfast served on gallery. AAA 4-diamond award.

Monmouth
POB 1736, 39120
(601)-442-5852

All year

$75-95 B&B
11 rooms, 11 pb
Visa, MC, AmEx
C-10 up/S-yes/P-no/H-ltd

Full breakfast
bar service
sitting room
piano

Ravennaside
601 S. Union St., 39120
(601)-442-8015

Except July—Aug.

$60/dbl B&B
5 rooms, 5 pb
no
C-yes/S-yes/P-yes/H-yes

Full breakfast
Bar, comp. cocktails
hot tub
sauna
sitting room, piano

Completely restored Gay Nineties Party House. Full breakfast served family style. Private tours given by owners.

Silver Street Inn
1 Silver St., 39120
(601)-442-4221

All year

$50-65
4 rooms, 2 pb
all
C-yes/S-yes/P-yes

Continental breakfast
Complimentary wine
sitting room

Live a bit of history on the Mighty Mississippi. Early country antique furnishings in a circa 1840 inn. Complimentary wine, muffins, coffee, juice.

Monmouth, Natchez, Mississippi

PORT GIBSON ─────────────────────────────────────

Oak Square
1207 Church St., 39150
(601)-437-4350
(601)-437-5771
All year

$50-65 B&B
8 rooms, 8 pb
Visa, MC, AmEx
C-yes/P-no/H-ltd

Full breakfast
Complimentary wine
large sitting room

Port Gibson, Mississippi, the town that General U.S. Grant said was "Too Beautiful to Burn." Plantation breakfast.

VICKSBURG ─────────────────────────────────────

Anchuca
1010 1st East St., 39180
(601)-636-4931

All year

$75-100 B&B
5 rooms, 5 pb
Visa, MC, AmEx
C-yes/S-yes/P-yes/H-ltd

Full breakfast
Comp. wine or mint julep
hot tub
swimming pool
sitting room, piano

Rooms furnished in beautiful antiques, one complimentary mint julep, sumptuous swimming pool, hot tub, breakfast served in magnificent dining room.

Cedar Grove
2200 Oak St., 39180
(601)-636-1605

All year

$75 dbl B&B
5 rooms, 5 pb
Visa, MC
C-10 up/P-no/H-ltd

Full breakfast
Complimentary wine
sitting room
piano

Antebellum mansion c. 1840—one of largest in the South—furnished in period. Guest rooms in mansion.

MISSOURI

ARROW ROCK ─────────────────────────────────────

Borgman's B&B
65320
(816)-837-3350

All year

$30-35 B&B
4 rooms, pb
no
C-yes/S-no/P-no/H-yes

Continental plus
Lunch, supper (arr.)
sitting room, porch
victrola

Enjoy antiques, crafts, theatre, and 1800 history in the warmth of the Borgmans century old home in historic Arrow Rock, Missouri.

Boscawen Inn	$18-55 EP	Full Breakfast
65320	18 rooms, 11 pb	Lunch, dinner, bar
(902)-634-3325	Visa, MC	sitting room
	C-yes/S-yes/P-no/H-ltd	
May—Oct.		

Elegantly restored late Victorian mansion, furnished with antiques, overlooking the historic and picturesque harbour of Lunesburg.

HERMAN

Der Klingerbau Inn	$47.50 B&B	Full breakfast
108 E. 2d St.	6 rooms, 4 pb	Fireside tea
(314)-486-2030	Visa, MC, AmEx	sitting room
	C-no/S-yes/P-no	piano
All year		

Authentic original German village with 108 buildings on National Register of Historic Places in heart of "Rhine Country of Missouri." Restaurant, antiques.

Schmidt's Guesthouse	$40-48 B&B	Continental plus
300 Market, 65041	5 rooms, 1 pb	Complimentary wine
(314)-486-2146		sitting room
(314)-965-4328 RS	C-yes/S-no/P-no	piano
March to Christmas		

Charming guest house furnished in Antiques. Hostess is a musician (German descent) and a knowledgable guide to this Old World town.

KANSAS CITY

Faust Townhouse	$15-20 B&B	Full breakfast
8023 N. Stoddard, 64152	2 rooms, 0 pb	Complimentary wine
(816)-741-7480	no	
	C-yes/S-yes/P-no	
All year		

Charming townhouse, close to everything; full breakfast served surrounded by genuine antiques. Complimentary wine. Come see our beautiful friendly city.

LATHROP

Parkview Farm	$15 pp B&B	Full breakfast
RR –1, Box 54, 64465	3 rooms, 0 pb	Limited bar service
(816)-664-2744	no	Sitting room
	C-yes/S-yes/P-no	piano
All year		farm tour

Located on a large farm with interesting work and livestock. Near a major interstate highway 40 miles from either Kansas City or St. Joseph, Mo.

STE. GENEVIEVE

Ste. Gemme Beauvais	$25-38 B&B	Full breakfast
78 N. Main St., 63670	8 rooms, 8 pb	Luncheon
(314)-883-5744	MC	
	C-yes/S-yes/P-no	
All year		

Charming little Victorian inn located just one hour from St. Louis in a small historic French town. Within walking distance of all restored French homes.

WASHINGTON ———————————————————————————————

Schewegmann House $35-50   Continental plus
438 West Frount   9 rooms, 7 pb
(314)-239-5025   Visa, MC   bicycles
                           C-yes/S-yes/H-yes   sitting room
All year   piano

A stately pre-Civil War Georgian style brick residence overlooking the Missouri River in the heart of Missouri's wine country.

MONTANA

Glacier N.P.

• Great Falls

• Missoula

• Helena   *Miles City •*

• Butte   *• Billings*

• Yellowstone N.P.

BIG SKY ———————————————————————————————

Lone Mountain Ranch $80 pp AP ($485/wk)   All meals included
Box 145, 59716   15 rooms, 15 pb   Bar service
(406)-995-4644   Visa, MC, AmEx   hot tub
                           C-yes/S-yes/H-yes   sitting room, piano
All year   entertainment

Historic guest ranch offering family vacations and Nordic ski vacations near Yellowstone National Park. Beautiful log cabins with fireplaces, conveniences.

BIG TIMBER ———————————————————————————————

Lazy K Bar Ranch $375-475/wk pp AP   All meals included
Box 550, 59011   18 rooms, 15 pb
(406)-537-4404   swimming pool
                           C-yes/S-yes/P-no   sitting room, piano
June 23—Labor Day   entertainment

100-year-old working dude ranch; isolated; totally different style. Rustic charm. Excellent service, horses, food, and company! References required.

ESSEX ———————————————————————————————

Izaak Walton Inn $25-33 EP   Full breakfast
Box 653, 59916   28 rooms, 4 pb   Dining room, bar
                           Visa, MC   sauna
                           C-yes/S-yes/P-no   sitting room
All year   piano

Wilderness inn; echoes past great days of transcontinental rail travel. Year-round retreat for hikers, X-country skiers, railfans; borders Glacier Natl. Pk.

NEVADA CITY ───────────────────────────────────

Nevada City Hotel $36-50
59755   14 rooms, 14 pb
(406)-843-5377   Visa, MC   sitting room
                     C-yes/S-yes/P-yes   piano
June 1—Labor Day

Truly western atmosphere of the Gold Rush Days. Two large rooms in the Hotel are completely furnished in exquisite 19th Century decor.

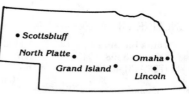

NEBRASKA

BELGRADE ───────────────────────────────────

Bel Horst Inn $20 EP   Dining room (Fri-Sun)
68623   14 rooms, 14 pb   Bar
(308)-357-1094   no   sitting room, piano
                     C-yes/S-yes/P-yes   entertainment
All year

Our authentically restored turn-of-the-century inn delights guests with its period items, wooden and brass furniture, and excellent cuisine.

CRAWFORD ───────────────────────────────────

Fort Robinson $16-36 EP   Cafeteria
Box 392, 69339   23 rooms, 23 pb
(308)-665-2660   Visa, MC   swimming, tennis
                     S-yes/P-ltd/H-yes   bicycles
Memorial Day—Labor Day   historical museum

Faithful visitors return year after year to Fort Robinson Inn. Former Cavalry headquarters evokes historical past in lovely setting.

Enter your favorite inn in our "Inn of the Year" contest (entry form is in the back of the book).

NEVADA

INCLINE VILLAGE

Haus Bavaria
PO Box 3308, 89450
(702)-831-6122

$45 dbl B&B
5 rooms, 5 pb
no
C-10 up/S-yes/P-no

Full breakfast
Complimentary wine
large family room
TV, fireplace

All year

There is much to do and see in this area; from gambling casinos to all water sports, golf, hiking, tennis and skiing at 12 different nearby sites.

NEW
HAMPSHIRE

ANTRIM

Maplehurst Inn
Route 202, 03440
(603)-588-2891

$35-45 dbl.
14 rooms, 14 pb
BAC, MC, VISA
C-yes/S-yes/P-yes

full breakfast, dinner
bar service
piano

All year

Located in the center of Antrim. Furnished with antiques including Avon Willard tall case clock. Best dining north of Boston.

ASHLAND ──

Cheney House	$24-30 B&B	full breakfast
PO Box 683, 03217	3 rooms, 0 pb	
(603)-968-7968	none	tennis, sitting room
	C-yes/S-yes/P-no	

May to mid-October

Victorian country home in lovely surroundings. Located in the heart of the N.H. Lakes Region, foothills of the White Mountains. Peaceful.

BENNINGTON ──

David's Inn	$40	Full breakfast
Bennington Sq., 03442	2 rooms, 2 pb	Luncheon, dinner, bar
(603)-588-2458	no	sitting room
	C-no/P-no/H-yes	

April—Nov.

1788 Cape Cod Inn furnished in antique period furniture. Recommended by Gourmet Magazine (Sept. 1980). Home cooking.

BRADFORD ──

Bradford Inn	$29.50-43.50	full breakfast,
Main Street, 03221	12 rooms, pb	dinner
(603)938-5309	none	bicycles, sitting room
	C-yes/S-yes/P-no	library

All year

There's simply nothing to do, but we have a fireplace, good books, three ski areas, and two lovely lakes nearby.

BRIDGEWATER ───

Pasquaney Inn	$34-76	Full breakfast
Newfound Lake,	28 rooms, 10 pb	Dinner, bar
(603)-744-2712	Visa, MC	lakefront, bicycles
	C-yes/S-yes/P-no	sitting room, piano
May 15—Oct. 15		recreation barn

An old New England Country Inn on the shores of Newfound Lake (since 1880). Comfortable rooms, excellent food.

CAMPTON VILLAGE ─────────────────────────────────────

Village Guest House	$24-32 EP	full breakfast,
PO Box 222, 03223	8 rooms, 1 pb	continental
(603)726-4449	MC, VISA	tennis nearby,
	C-yes/S-ltd/P-no	sitting room

All year

Warm hospitality in ski country locared in a small New England village about 10 minutes to Waterville Valley.

Our listings, supplied by the innkeeper, are as complete as possible. Many of the inns have more features — amenities or food and beverage service — than we list. Be sure to inquire when you book.

CENTER OSSIPEE

Hitching Post Inn	$30 B&B	full breakfast, dinner
Old Rte. 16, 03814	7 rooms, 0 pb	full bar
(603)539-4482	MC, VISA	entertainment, music
	C-yes/S-yes/P-no/H-yes	story telling, gift shop
Dec. 26-Oct.31		crafts & culinary class

Off the beaten path—close to lakes and mountains. Large rooms, homestyle cooking, smorgasbord, fireplaces, 4 dining rooms.

CONWAY

Darby Field Inn	$25-55 B&B. $35-65 MAP	Full breakfast
Bald Hill, 03818	11 rooms, 11 pb	Dinner, bar
(603)-447-2181	Visa, MC, AmEx	swimming pool
	C-yes/S-yes/P-dogs	sitting room
Nov—April		piano

Cozy little country inn situated on the north face of Bald Hill, overlooking the Mt. Washington Valley and Presidential Mountains.

DANBURY

Inn at Danbury	$30 up B&B	Full breakfast
Rte. 104, 03230	8 rooms, pb	Dinner, tea
(603)-768-3318	no	swimming pool (summer)
	C-yes/S-yes/P-no/H-yes	full bicycle shop
summer-fall, ski season		sitting room

Charming 19th century farm house; pleasant, quiet New England setting, skiing, biking & hiking. Wholesome hearty homemade meals.

EATON CENTER

Palmer House Inn	$30 B&B	full breakfast
Rte. 153, 03832	5 rooms, 1 pb	Dinner
(603)-447-2120	no	fireplace lounge
	C-yes/S-yes/P-yes	lake
All year		ski trails

Best of Both Worlds—a small, comfortable, antique-furnished country inn at scenic Crystal Lake — Mt. Washington Valley attractions and entertainments.

FITZWILLIAM

Fitzwilliam Inn	$28 dbl. EP	full breakfast,
03447	22 rooms, 12 pb	all meals, bar service
(603)-585-9000	all	swimming pool, sauna,
	C-yes/S-yes/P-yes/H-ltd	tennis nearby, piano
All year		sitting room, library

Old New England at its best—soft beds, good grog, fine food since 1796. Conference and meeting facilities. 14 mi. south of Keene, on bus line.

FRANCESTOWN

Inn at Crotched Mountain	$25-45	Full breakfast
Mountain Rd., 03043	14 rooms, 5 pb	Dinner, bar
(603)-588-6840	no	swimming pool
	C-yes/S-yes/P-yes/H-yes	tennis courts
June—Oct & ski season		sitting room

Mountains with outstanding views, some guest rooms have fireplaces. Excellent home cooked meals. Fireplaces in tavern, living room, and dining room.

FRANCONIA

Franconia Inn	$49pp-55pp MAP	full breakfast, dinner
Route 116, 03580	30 rooms, 16 pb	comp. tea, full bar
(603)-823-5542	Visa, AmEx, MC	bicycles, entertainment,
	C-yes/S-yes/P-no	hot tub, pool, tennis,
12/18-4/1, & 5/28-10/18		piano, sitting room

Located in the Eastin Valley—Mount Lafayette and Sugar Hill. Riding stable, ski center. All rooms beautifully decorated.

Horse and Hound Inn	$50-60	Continental breakfast
	7 rooms, 7 pb	
(603)-823-5501	no	
	C-no/S-yes/P-no	
May—Oct.		

Small, secluded inn on the valley slope of Cannon Mountain.

Pinestead Farm Lodge	$12 pp do	none
Rte 116, RFD 1, 03580	7 rooms, 1 pb	
(603)-823-5601	no	tennis court
	C-yes/S-yes/P-no	
All year		

A working family farn offering clean, comfortable, simple accomodations since 1899. Fully equipped kitchen for guests. Homemade quilts on beds.

Sugar Hill Inn	$23-35 B&B, $47-57 MAP	Full country breakfast
Rte 117, 03580	15 rooms, 9 pb	Dinner, wine/beer
(603)-823-5621	Visa, MC, AmEx	Queen Anne living room
	C-6 up/S-no/P-no	antique player piano
Mid-may-fall, ski season		

We are furnished with lovely antiques, located in the heart of skiing, antiquing, hiking, fishing, swimming & golfing. Built in 1748.

GLEN

Bernerhof Inn	$22.50 pp B&B	full breakfast, lunch,
Box 381, Rte. 302, 03838	10 rooms, 2 pb	dinner, bar service
(603)-383-4414	MC, VISA, AMEX	swimming pool, bicycles
	C-yes/S-ltd/P-no	entertainment, tennis,
Mid-Dec to Apr, June-Nov		piano, sitting room

Turn-of-the-Century Victorian featuring many period antiques; fine European cuisine in the Old World Tradition...The Taste of the Mountains Cooking School.

GOSHEN

Back Side Inn	$36-46 B&B	full breakfast, dinner
Rand Pond Rd., 03773	9 rooms, 4 pb	complimentary wine
(603)-863-5161	Visa, MC	piano, sitting room.
	C-yes/S-yes/P-yes/H-yes	library
Jan-Mar 18, Jun-Oct 18		

Big old farmhouse filled with antiques and country collectibles. Savory breakfasts included. Fieldstone fireplace where guests gather for conversation.

HAMPTON BEACH ─────────────────────────────────

Century House
552 Ocean Blvd., 03842
(603)-926-2931

$30-60 B&B
22 rooms, 22 pb
MC, VISA
C-yes/S-yes/P-no

full breakfast, lunch
dinner
swimming pool

All year

Two minute walk the the ocean shore.

HAVERHILL ─────────────────────────────────

Haverhill Inn
Dartmouth Col.Hwy.,03765
(603)-989-5961

$50 B&B
4 rooms, 4 pb

C-older/S-ltd/P-no/H-yes

Full breakfast
Complimentary tea, wine
grand piano
sitting room
library

All year

Built 1810, Haverhill Inn is beautiful. Every room is large, with fireplace. Bike tours, and canoeing inn-to-inn on the Connecticut River.

HENNIKER ─────────────────────────────────

Colby Hill Inn
The Oaks, Box 778, 03242
(603)-428-3281

$38-65
12 rooms, 8 pb
Visa, MC, AmEx
C-6 up/S-yes/P-no/H-yes

Full breakfast
Dinner, bar
swimming pool
sitting room

All year

Circa 1800 inn, antiques and good food, skiing, hiking, biking, canoeing, fishing and relaxing.

HILLSBOROUGH ─────────────────────────────────

Stonebridge Inn
Star Rte 3, Box 82,03244
(603)-464-3155

$30-40 B&B
4 rooms, 4 pb
Visa, MC
C-yes/S-yes/P-no

Continental plus
Lunch, dinner, bar
sitting room

All year

A mid-1800s colonial farmhouse, lovingly restored and redecorated, to create the kind of small country inn you've always hoped to find.

INTERVALE ─────────────────────────────────

Holiday Inn
Route 16A, 03845
(603)-356-9772

$30 B&B
10 rooms, 10 pb
Visa, MC, AmEx, CB, DC
C-yes/S-yes/P-no

Full breakfast
Dinner
swimming pool
sitting room, piano

summer-fall, ski season

If you want old-fashioned hospitality and a quiet place to relax, come to our Country Inn in the White Mountains.

JACKSON ─────────────────────────────────

Dana Place Inn
40 Pinkham Notch R,03846
(603)-383-6822

$30-78 EP
14 rooms, 8 pb
Visa, MC, AmEx
C-yes/S-yes/P-no/H-ltd

Full breakfast
Dinner, bar
hot tub, swimming pool
tennis, entertainment
sitting room, piano

May—Oct., Dec.—March

Country inn guest rooms, bright and cheerful. The original dining room features windows that look out over the grounds and flower gardens.

JACKSON VILLAGE

Village House	$32-46 B&B	Continental plus
Rte. 16A, 03846	10 rooms, 8 pb	
(603)-383-6666	Visa, MC	swimming pool
	C-yes/S-yes/P-no	tennis courts
June—Oct., Dec—March		sitting room

Beautiful village setting on 7 acres. Ten tastefully decorated rooms. Delux continental breakfast. Close to fine dining, hiking & golfing.

JAFFREY CENTER

Monadnock Inn	$23-42 B&B	Continental breakfast
Main Street	14 rooms, 7 pb	Lunch, dinner
(603)-532-7001	Visa, MC	sitting room, piano
	C-yes/S-yes/P-no	
All year		

Delightful inn, 14 rooms $23-42, some with private baths; complimentary breakfast. Lunch/dinner/Sunday brunch. Written up in Gourmet Magazine.

LACONIA

Hickory Stick Farm	$42-48 B&B	Full breakfast
R.F.D. –2, 03246	2 rooms, 2 pb	Dinner (Mem. Day—Oct.)
(603)-524-3333	Visa, MC, AmEx, DC, CB	sitting room
	S-ltd	
All year		

Early New England Colonial farm house furnished with antiques. Restaurant (Summer only) famous for roast duckling.

LITTLETON

Beal House Inn	$27-50 EP	Full breakfast
Main Street, 03561	15 rooms, 10 pb	Afternoon tea
(603)-444-2661	Visa, MC, AmEx, DC, CB	library
	C-yes/S-ok/P-ltd	sitting room
All year		piano

Intimate country inn furnished with comfortable antiques. Fireside country breakfast. Antique shop. Close to all White Mountain attractions. Skiing nearby.

Edencroft Manor	$30-50 EP	Full breakfast
Route 135, 03561	6 rooms, 4 pb	Dinner, bar
444-6776	Visa, MC, AmEx	sitting room
	C-yes/S-yes/P-yes	piano
All year		

Country inn with fireplaces. Lounge overlooking the mountains. Antiques, handmade comforters. Gourmet dinner, full breakfast, international coffees served.

LYME

Lock Lyme Lodge	$18-26 B&B	Full breakfast
Rte 10, 03768	29 rooms, 25 pb	Dinner (Summer only)
(603)-795-2141		tennis courts
	C-yes/S-ltd/P-ltd/H-ltd	lake, boats, canoes
All year		sitting room, piano

Unspoiled New Hampshire lake. Relax on Lodge grounds, enjoy the surrounding New England countryside. College town of Hanover eleven miles away.

Lyme Inn
Route 10, 03768

$40-65 B&B
15 rooms, 10 pb
Visa, MC, AmEx, DC, CB
C-8 up/S-yes/P-no

Full breakfast
Dinner, bar
sitting room

All year

Old country inn furnished in genuine antiques. Small New Hampshire town.

MILFORD

Ram in the Thicket
Off Rte. 101, 03055
(603)-654-6440

$25-35 B&B
9 rooms, 3 pb
Visa, MC
C-yes/S-yes/P-yes/H-ltd

Continental breakfast
Dinner, bar
hot tub
swimming pool
sitting room

All year

You will never eat a better dinner, than in this elegant, easy country Victorian setting, or sleep in sweeter surroundings.

NEW LONDON

Follansbee Inn
03260
(603)-927-4221

$25-38 EP
23 rooms, 11 pb
Visa, MC
C-yes/S-yes/P-no/H-ltd

Full breakfast
Dinner, bar
sitting room

All year

Picture perfect setting for a memorable visit. X-country & downhill skiing. Summer theater and great antiquing. 3 golf courses. 3-star Mobil rated dining.

Hide-Away Lodge
03257
(603)-526-4861

$30 dbl EP
7 rooms, 7 pb

C-yes/S-yes/P-yes

Full breakfast
Dinner, bar
sitting room, piano

Mid-May—October

Catering to peaceful people with pampered palates in woodland seclusion. Brook, lake, shady lawns, charming hospitality, meticulous housekeeping.

Pleasant Lake Inn
N. Pleasant St., 03257
(603)-526-6271

$34-40 B&B
12 rooms, 1 pb
Visa, MC
C-yes/S-yes/P-no

Continental plus
Dinner, bar
lake swimming
sitting room

All year

A country inn, built in the seventeen hundreds, overlooking a magnificent view of Pleasant Lake and Mt. Kearsage.

NORTH CHARLESTOWN

Indian Shutters Inn
Rt. 12, 03603
(603)-826-4445

$20-28 EP
12 rooms, 8 pb
Visa, MC
C-yes/S-yes/P-ltd/H-ltd

Full breakfast
Lunch, dinner, bar
piano
library

All year

Charming 1791 Stagecoach Inn, beautiful country setting. Superb New England fare—best beef, fresh seafood—all homemade. Lovely antique furnishings.

NORTH CONWAY

Cranmore Mountain Lodge
Kearsage Road,
(603)-356-2044

All year

$35-53 B&B
16 rooms, 6 pb
MC, BAm
C-yes/S-yes/P-no

Full breakfast
Dinner (winter only)
jacuzzi
swimming, tennis
sitting room

Authentic country inn located in the heart of the White Mts. Hearty country breakfast. Tennis court, pool, jacuzzi, toboganning, skating, x-c skiing.

Nereledge Inn
River Road, 03860

All year

$18-27 B&B
8 rooms, 0 pb
Visa, MC
C-yes/S-ok/P-no

Full breakfast
Lunch, dinner, bar
Sitting room
piano
entertainment

Cozy inn, five minutes walk from village, close to skiing areas & fishing, golf, climbing, canoeing... home cooked meals—country-style breakfast.

Stonehurst Manor
Off Rte. 16, 03860
(603)-356-3271

All year

$38-92 EP
24 rooms, 22 pb
Visa, MC, AmEx
C-yes/S-yes/P-no/H-yes

Full breakfast
Dinner, bar
swimming pool
tennis courts
library, piano

Turn-of-the-century mansion with old oak and stained glass. Relax by our fireplace in the library. Mt. Washington Valley close by.

NORTH WOODSTOCK

Cascade Lodge/B&B
Main St., POB 95, 03262
(603)-745-2722

All year

$14.50 pp B&B
12 rooms, 0 pb
AmEx
C-yes/S-yes/P-no

Full breakfast menu
Supper (res.)
sitting room

We spoil our guests and make them feel like family.

NORTHWOOD

Lake Shore Farm
Jenness Pond Rd., 03261
(603)-942-5521

All year

$20 EP
28 rooms, 20 pb

C-yes/S-yes/P-yes

Full breakfast
Lunch, dinner, bar
entertainment (winter)
tennis courts
sitting room

Your home away from home, all home cooking, family style service. Same family management since 1926.

PORTSMOUTH

Inn at Christian Shore
Maplewood Ave., 03801
(603)-431-6770

All year

$25-45 B&B
5 rooms, 3 pb
Visa, MC
C-yes/S-yes/P-yes

Full breakfast
Complimentary wine
sitting room

Federal house c. 1800 restored and decorated in that period. Walk to waterfront, shops, restaurants, historic sites.

Inn at Strawberry Banke $40 dbl B&B   Continental plus
314 Court St., 03801   4 rooms, 2 pb
(603)-436-7242   Visa, MC   bicycles
                           S-yes/P-no   sitting room
All year

This colonial inn charms travelers with its beautiful rooms and outdoor patio. Located near town, waterfront, and Prescott Park.

Martin Hill Inn $35-50   Full breakfast
404 Islington St., 03801   5 rooms, 5 pb   Complimentary port
(603)-436-2287   Visa, MC
                           C-no/S-yes/H-ltd
All year

1810 Colonial beautifully appointed rooms with period antiques. Elegant yet comfortable. Walk to waterfront. Lovely gardens.

RINDGE

Tokfarm Inn $15-28 B&B   Continental breakfast
P.O. Box 229, 03461   6 rooms, 0 pb
(603)-899-6646   swimming pool
                           C-no/S-no/P-no   sitting room
Spring/Summer/Fall   antique organ

Charming century-old hilltop farmhouse on Christmas Tree Farm. Spectacular tri-state view. Close by: Cathedral of the Pines, all sports.

SNOWVILLE

Snow Village Lodge $65-70 dbl B&B   Full breakfast
Foss Mt. Rd., 03849   14 rooms, 14 pb   Dinner, box lunch, bar
(603)-447-2818   yes   sauna
                           C-yes!/S-yes/P-yes!/H-yes tennis court
except 11/1—12/15   sitting room, piano

Secluded, spectacular view, exceptional food, warm, friendly inn, skiing (cross country) at the door, alpine nearby, cozy fireplace, lovely flowers.

SUGAR HILL

Sunset Hill House   B&B   Full breakfast
03585   35 rooms, 35 pb   Dinner, bar
(603)-823-5522   Visa, MC, AmEx   swimming pool
                          C-yes/S-yes/P-yes   parlors, library
All year

Ours is an old New England resort with one of the finest views in the White Mountains. We have a beautiful dining room that serves excellent food.

SUNAPEE

Dexter's Inn $60-85 B&B / $90-115 MAP Full breakfast
Stagecoach Rd., 03782   17 rooms, 17 pb   Lunch, dinner, bar
(603)-763-5571   tennis courts
                           C-yes/S-yes/P-yes/H-yes swimming pool
May—October   library, piano

Casual remote small tennis resort on 200 acres in mountains of Southern New Hampshire at 1400 feet overlooking Lake Sunapee.

TAMWORTH ────────────────────────────────

Tamworth Inn
Main Street, 03886
(603)-323-7721

$38-48 EP
22 rooms, 10 pb
Visa, MC
C-yes/S-no/P-no

Full breakfast
Bar service
swimming pool
entertainment

Nov.–Dec., March-April

sitting room, organ

1830 Tamworth Inn—a charming getaway in unspoiled Tamworth Village. First-class restaurant, cozy pub, a relaxing atmosphere for guests and local people.

TEMPLE ────────────────────────────────

Birchwood Inn
Rte. 45, 03084
(603)-878-3285

$34-40 B&B
7 rooms, 0 pb

C-yes/S-yes/P-no

Full breakfast
Dinner
bicycles, sitting room
1878 Steinway square

All year

grand piano

Original Rufus Porter murals in dining room. Summer stock theaters nearby & downhill & X-country skiing. Lakes nearby. Antiquing in area.

NEW JERSEY

AVON-BY-THE-SEA ────────────────────────────

Sands of Avon
42 Sylvania Ave., 07717
(201)-776-8386

$20-35 B&B
9 rooms, 0 pb

C-12 up/S-yes/P-no

Continental breakfast

sitting room

Summer

Lovely Victorian Inn with wrap around porches & rockers, ½ block to sandy beach and boardwalk. Relaxing tranquil atmosphere, a home away from home.

Please mention this guide when you make your booking

BAY HEAD

Conover's Bay Head Inn
646 Main Ave., 08742
(201)-892-4664

February—December

$42-85 B&B
12 rooms, 6 pb

C-teens/S-yes/P-no

Continental (summer)
Full breakfast (winter)
sitting room

Seashore hideaway furnished with antiques, handmade pillows, bedcovers, hand-crocheted wash cloths, framed old family pictures.

BEACH HAVEN

St. Rita Hotel
127 Engleside, 08008
(609)-492-9192

March—December

$46-58
25 rooms, 6 pb
Visa, MC
C-yes/S-yes/P-no/H-ltd

sitting room

½ block from ocean; oldest hotel on Long Beach Island; within walking distance to restaurants, shops, amusements, fishing, etc.

CAPE MAY

7th Sister Guesthouse
10 Jackson St., 08204
(609)-884-2280

All year

$46
6 rooms, 0 pb

C-7 up/S-yes/P-no

No meals

sitting room, piano

Original furniture plus an extensive wicker collection. Paintings by the owner /innkeeper, JoAnne Echevarria Myers, hang throughout. Ocean view rooms.

Abbey
Columbia & Gurney, 08204
(609)-884-4506

April—November

$50-75 B&B
7 rooms, 4 pb
Visa, MC
C-12 up/S-ok/P-no

Continental (summer)
Full breakfast(spr/fall)
sitting room, piano

Elegantly restored Victorian villa, with period antiques. One block from Atlantic Ocean, in the National Historic Landmark City of Cape May.

Abigail Adams B & B
12 Jackson St., 08204
(609)-884-1371

April—November

$40-60 B&B
6 rooms, 2 pb

C-14 up/S-ltd/P-no

Full breakfast
Tea, wine
sitting room
bicycles

Intimate, elegant country charm, ocean views, gourmet breakfast all located in historic Cape May and within 100 feet of beach.

Barnard-Good House
238 Perry St., 08204
(609)-884-5381

April—November

$50-70 B&B
6 rooms, 3 pb
Visa, MC
C-12 up/S-yes/P-no

Full breakfast(spr/fall)
Continental (summer)
sitting room, piano
bicycles

"Our breakfast and the warmth and love in our house is our hallmark. . . Oh the joy of our copper tub."

Brass Bed Inn
719 Columbia Ave., 08204
(609)-884-8075

All year

$35-60 B&B
8 rooms, 2 pb

C-12 up/S-ok/P-no

Full breakfast
Complimentary tea, wine
parlor, piano

Seashore Victorian home with a friendly atmosphere, original furnishings, family "treasures". Walk to ocean front, village shops, and restaurants.

Please Mention *The Complete Guide* **to the innkeeper when you reserve your room**

Humphrey Hughes House, Cape May, New Jersey

Captain Mey's Inn
202 Ocean St., 08204
(609)-884-7793

$50-70 B&B
9 rooms, 2 pb
Visa, MC
C-12 up/S-ltd/P-no

Full breakfast
Afternoon tea
sitting room

All year

Turn-of-the-century inn features spacious rooms furnished in antiques, private Delft Blue collection, Dutch artifacts, European accent throughout.

Gingerbread House
28 Gurney St., 08204
(608)-884-0211

$40-70 B&B
6 rooms, 3 pb

C-7 up/S-yes/P-no

Continental breakfast

sitting room

All year

The G.B.H. offers period furnished rooms—comfortable accommodations within walking to all major sights and restaurants. ½ block from the beach.

Humphrey-Hughes House
29 Ocean St., 08204
(609)-884-4428

$50-75 B&B
10 rooms, 3 pb
Visa, MC, AmEx
C-12 up/S-ltd/P-no

Continental plus
Afternoon tea
sitting room

May—October

Spacious Victorian accommodations in a quaint restored seaside resort designated a National Historical Landmark. Ideally located between beach & walking mall.

Mainstay Inn
635 Columbia Ave., 08204
(609)-884-8690

$40-72 B&B
12 rooms, 8 pb

C-no/S-no/P-no

Continental (summer)
Full breakfast(spr/fall)
sitting room, piano

April—October

Two wealthy 19th century gamblers spared no expense to build this luxurious villa. Victorian furnishings, garden, afternoon tea.

Poor Richard's Inn
17 Jackson St., 08204
(609)-884-3536

$24-52
8 rooms, 3 pb

C-ok/S-yes/P-no

Coffee only

sitting room

April—October

Classic gingerbread guest house offers accommodations with eclectic Victorian and country decor; near beach; friendly unpretentious atmosphere.

Queen Victoria
102 Ocean St., 08204
(609)-884-8702

$35-80 B&B
12 rooms, 4 pb
Visa, MC, AmEx
C-/S-ltd/P-no

Full breakfast
Afternoon tea
sitting room
library
bicycles

All year

A country inn located in the center of the nation's oldest seaside resort specializing in comfort & service. Large breakfast.

Windward House
24 Jackson St., 08204
(609)-884-3368

$50-60 B&B
7 rooms, 5 pb

C-yes/S-yes/P-no

Continental plus

library
bicycles

All year

Edwardian shingle cottage; sun and shade porches; spacious antique-filled guest rooms; massive oak doors with stained and leaded glass.

MILFORD

Chestnut Hill
63 Church St., 08848
(201)-995-9761

$50-65 B&B
5 rooms, 1 pb

C-yes/S-no/P-no

Full breakfast
Tea, mulled cider
sitting room, piano
bicycles
river swimming

All year

The peaceful beauty of the Delaware River is the perfect setting for our 1860 Victorian Inn overlooking the river.

OCEAN GROVE

Cordova
26 Webb Ave., 07756
201)-774-3084
(212)-751-9577 winter
Summer

$18-45 B&B
18 rooms, 1 pb

C-yes/S-ltd/P-no

Continental plus

sitting room
bicycles

Century old guest house in unspoiled Victorian beach community, friendly family atmosphere with old world charm; wooden boardwalk, sandy beach.

PRINCETON

Peacock Inn
20 Bayard Lane, 08504
(609)-924-1707

$40-65 EP
17 rooms, 6 pb
Visa, MC, AmEx, DC, CB
C-yes/S-yes/P-yes

Lunch, dinner, bar

All year

The Peacock Inn was built in 1775. Near the university, Governor's residence, which attracts distinguished guests. Hearty country breakfast.

RED BANK

Shaloum Guest House
119 Tower Hill, 07701
(201)-530-7759

$35 B&B
2 rooms, 1 pb

C-yes/S-yes/P-no

Continental breakfast

sitting room
swimming pool
tennis courts

All year

Modern facilities amidst landscaped setting—near beaches—easy access to New York City.

SPRING LAKE

Ashling Cottage
106 Sussex Ave., 07726
(201)-449-3553

$45-95 B&B
10 rooms, 8 pb
Visa, MC
C-yes/S-yes/P-no

Continental plus
Complimentary wine

April—December

Victorian gem furnished with oak antiques and solarium breakfast room, a block from the ocean, in a storybook setting.

Johnson House
25 Tuttle Ave., 07762
(201)-449-1860

$22-28 pp B&B
19 rooms, 9 pb

C-yes/S-ltd/P-no

Full breakfast

sitting room

All year

On the Jersey Gold Coast ("Finnish and Hungarian spoken"). Breakfast specials: Crepes and "Pannukakku".

Normandy Inn
21 Tuttle Ave., 07762

$38-70 B&B
18 rooms, 16 pb

C-yes/S-yes/P-no

Full breakfast
Complimentary tea, wine
sitting room
bicycles

All year

A New England Inn—many antiques and collectibles throughout the house. Some rooms have Victorian & brass beds. Near ocean.

STOCKTON

Colligan's Stockton Inn
Rte. 29, 08559
(609)-397-1250

$65-125 B&B
5 rooms, 5 pb
all credit cards
C-older/S-yes/P-no

Continental breakfast
Lunch, dinner, bar
sitting room, piano
entertainment

All year

Antique building with colonial charm of fireplaces and European touch of waterfall graced gardens to please winter and summertime guests.

Woolverton Inn
RD3, Box 233-A, 08559
(609)-397-0802

$45-60 B&B
9 rooms, 0 pb
AmEx
C-ok/S-yes/P-no

Continental plus
Afternoon tea
sitting room, piano

All year

1793 stone manor house set amidst formal gardens & stately trees, overlooking Delaware River Valley, famed for antiques & fine food.

NEW MEXICO

New Mexico map with: Taos, Gallup, Santa Fe, Albuquerque, Roswell, Silver City, Carlsbad Caverns, Las Cruces, N.P.

CHIMAYO

La Posada de Chimayo
Box 463, 87522
(505)-351-4605

All year

$55 dbl B&B
2 rooms, 2 pb

C-yes/S-yes

Full breakfast

private sitting rooms
fireplace

A traditional adobe guesthouse in beautiful Northern New Mexico, thirty miles north of Santa Fe on High Road to Taos.

ESPANOLA

La Puebla House
Rt. 1, Box 172A, 87532
(505)-753-3981

All year

$20-29 B&B
4 rooms, 0 pb
Visa, MC
C-yes/S-ok/H-yes

Continental plus
Afternoon tea
living room
library

Traditional adobe home located in small Spanish village between Santa Fe and Taos, near Espanola. Breakfast features home-baked delights.

GLENWOOD

La Casita
Rte. 10, Box 440, 88039

All year

$20-30 B&B
2 rooms, 1 pb
C-yes/S-yes/P-no/H-yes

Full breakfast
Dinner on request

Private self-contained guest house nestled beneath the Gila Wilderness in southwestern New Mexico. Big country breakfasts. A unique hideaway.

LOS ALAMOS

Los Alamos B & B
P.O. Box 1212, 87544
(505)-662-6041

All year

$25 up—B&B
3 rooms, 2 pb

C-yes/S-no/P-no

Full breakfast

sitting room
entertainment
bicycles

Furnished apartment sleeps 4; kitchenette, bath, patio. Hiking, skiing, Indian ruins minutes away—cool, pure air at 7500 feet elevation.

Orange Street B & B
3496 Orange St., 87544
(505)-662-2651

All year

$25-35 B&B
3 rooms, 0 pb

C-no/S-no/P-no

Full breakfast
Afternoon tea
sitting room, piano
bicycles
tennis, swimming nearby

Gourmet breakfast at the family's large antique oak table with view of pines & Jemez Mountains. 3 mi. to Pajarito Ski Area; hiking, bicycling.

PECOS ───────────────────────────────

Broken Drum Guest Ranch
Rt. 2 Box 100, 87552
(505)-757-6194

All year

$98-216 AP
11 rooms, 8 pb
Visa, MC
C-yes/S-yes/P-yes/H-yes

All meals included
Bar service
swimming pool
piano

Guest ranch in mountains of Santa Fe National Forest; 11 log cabins, 3 stocked fishing ponds, 1-1/2 miles of Pecos River, heated pool, horseback riding.

Las Palomas Conference Center (Mabel Dodge Luhan House), Taos, New Mexico

PILAR

The Plum Tree Hostel
By the Rio Grande, 87571
(505)-758-4696
(800)-USA-INNS RS
All year

$10.00-27.50 B&B
3 rooms, 3 pb
Visa, MC
C-yes/S-ltd/P-yes/H-yes

Full breakfast
Cafe
hot tub, sauna
swimming pool
sitting room

At the Plum Tree... you can hike, birdwatch, rockhound, swim, cross-country ski, raft, see petroglyphs, learn to kayak, study art, enjoy wholesome food.

SANTA FE

Casa Sibella
418-1/2 Montezuma, 87501
(505)-988-5248

All year

$12 pp B&B
4 rooms, 0 pb

C-yes/S-no/P-ltd

Continental plus
Afternoon tea
parlor

Unique cross between a hostel and a pension near center of town. Charming roof- top patio with mountain view available for picnics. Folk arts giftshop.

El Paradero
220 W. Manhattan, 87501
(505)-988-1177

All year

$32-64 B&B
9 rooms, 3 pb
Visa, MC
C-yes/S-yes/P-yes

Gourmet breakfast
Informal tea
piano, sitting room

A warm & friendly adobe in downtown Santa Fe. Nice guest rooms around a walled court- yard. Some fireplaces.

Grant Corner Inn
122 Grant Ave., 87501
(505)-983-6678

All year

$45-100 B&B
9 rooms, 5 pb
Visa, MC
C-3 up/S-yes/P-no/H-yes

Full breakfast
Gourmet picnic lunches
private club access
(hot tub, pool, sauna,
tennis, entertainment)

Elegant colonial home located in the heart of downtown Santa Fe, nine charming rooms furnished with antiques, friendly, warm atmosphere.

La Sala
643 Galisteo, 87501
(505)-983-2355
(800)-547-1463 RS
All year

$35-75
3 rooms, 1 pb
Visa, MC
C-no/S-yes/P-no

Continental breakfast

sitting room

Only 7 blocks from Santa Fe's famed Plaza. Minutes walk to galleries and restaurants.

Preston House
106 Faithway St., 87501
(505)-982-3465

All year

$35-90 B&B
5 rooms, 3 pb
Visa, MC
C-12 up/S-yes/P-yes

Continental plus
Complimentary tea, wine
sitting room
club membership
(tennis, swimming)

Historic 100 year old Queen Anne house on National Register with fireplaces and antiques; quiet location 3 blocks from Plaza.

Rancho Encantado
Box 57-C, 87501

$95-225 EP
22 rooms, 22 pb
credit cards accepted
C-yes/S-yes/P-yes/H-yes

April—New Years Day

All meals
Full service bar
sitting room, piano
hot tubs
swimming, tennis

A luxurious Mobil 4 Star guest ranch/resort tucked away in the foothills just eight miles north of Santa Fe's Plaza.

TAOS

La Fonda
Box 1447, 87571
(505)-758-2211

$35-60 EP
24 rooms, 17 pb
Visa, MC
C-yes/S-yes/P-yes

All year

no meals

sitting room

Family-owned and operated hotel in the great European tradition; host of many American and European celebrities for thirty years.

Las Palomas Conf. Center
P.O. Box 6689, 87571
(505)-758-9456

$40-70 B&B
9 rooms, 5 pb
Visa, MC
C-yes/S-yes/P-no

All year

Full breakfast

sitting room

The historic Mabel Dodge Lujan House. Come through the gates to a place where D.H. Lawrence, Georgia O'Keefe and others have stayed.

NEW YORK

AMAGANSETT

Mill Garth
Windmill Ln., 11930

11 rooms, 11 pb

C-yes/P-no/H-ltd

No food service
Private kitchens
bicycles

Ocean, fishing, sailing, tennis, horseback riding on beach while staying in the coziest suites on the south fork.

AMENIA

Troutbeck
Leedsville Rd., 12501
(914)-373-8580
(914)-373-3581
All year (wknds only)

$425-680/wknd dbl AP
30 rooms, 25 pb
AmEx
C-12 up/S-yes/P-no

All meals included
Open bar
public rooms, piano
tennis courts
swimming pool

Historical English country estate on 422 acres. Gold Standard for conference centers, praised by NY Magazine, NY Times, Good Housekeeping. Posh country inn.

AURORA

Aurora Inn
Main St., 13026
(315)-364-8842

April 1—Nov. 26

$37.45-$48.15 B&B
16 rooms, 8 pb
Visa, MC, AmEx
C-yes/S-yes/P-yes/H-ltd

Continental breakfast
Luncheon, dinner, bar
piano, sitting room
bicycles
lake swimming

Aurora is a small, historical village and is the home of Wells College. The Inn overlooks Cayuga Lake where radiant sunsets may be seen.

BARRYVILLE

All Breeze Farm
Star Rt. 234, 12719
(914)-557-8232

Jan. and Feb.

$25 dbl B&B
4 rooms, 4 pb

C-yes/S-yes/P-yes

Full breakfast
All meals
sitting room
2-seater bicycle

Small homestead on quiet, rural road offering modest accomodations and hearty meals for couples, families, groups. Canoeing, fishing, hayrides, & more.

BLUE MOUNTAIN LAKE

Hedges on Blue Mt. Lake
12812
(519)-352-7325

June 17—Oct. 11

$80-96 MAP
26 rooms, 26 pb

C-yes/S-yes/P-no/H-yes

Full breakfast
Dinner
sitting room, piano
tennis court
library

Awake to the call of a loon drifting across the lake, gear up for a day of hiking, boating & art classes.

CANAAN

Inn at the Shaker Mill
Cherry Ln., 12029
(518)-794-9345

All year

$30-35 pp
20 rooms, 20 pb

C-yes/S-ltd/P-yes

Full breakfast
Dinner, wine
sitting room
sauna
swimming pond

1824 Inn in the Berkshires. Open hearth in the lounge for sizzling steaks. Wooded acres, waterfalls, bountiful home-cooked meals.

We want this guide to be as complete as possible, so if you know of an inn (30 rooms or less), bed & breakfast or guesthouse we don't list, please send us their name on the form in the back of the book.

CAZENOVIA

Brae Lock Inn
5 Albany St., 13035
(315)-655-3431

$45-75
12 rooms, 12 pb
Visa, MC, AmEx
C-yes/S-yes/H-yes

Continental plus
Dinner
sitting room

All year

In our rooms we feature old-time charm. Our wee gift house offers antiques and unique gifts. Our restaurant has a varied menu.

Lincklaen House
79 Albany St., 93035
(315)-655-8171

$35-90
25 rooms, 25 pb

C-yes/S-yes/P-yes

Full breakfast
lunch, dinner, bar
Lake nearby, piano
tennis nearby, library
entertainment

All year

Built in 1835, stenciled rooms, courtyard for summer dining, 3 conference rooms, seasonal sports nearby. All meals served with fresh vegetables popovers.

CLARENCE

Asa Ransom House
10529 Main St., 14031
(716)-75902315

$60 B&B
4 rooms, 4 pb

C-yes/S-ltd/P-no

Full breakfast
Dinner, bar
sitting room
bicycles

Except January

Village Inn furnished with antiques—period reproductions, library, tap room, gift shop, herb garden, many regional dishes, own breads & desserts.

CLINTON

Clinton House
21 W. Park Row, 13323
(315)-853-5555

$35-40
5 rooms, 5 pb
Visa, MC, AmEx
C-yes/S-yes

Coffee & juice only
Dinner, bar
piano

All year

COLD SPRING

Antique Mews
73 Main St., 10516
(914)-265-3727

$65-85 B&B
2 rooms, 2 pb
Visa, MC
C-yes/S-yes/P-yes

Full breakfast

All year

1805 Federal townhouse. 40 antique shops in Cold Spring on Hudson's Main Street near West Point, Boscobel and Bear Mountain.

Hudson House
2 Main St., 10516
(914)-265-9355

$55-65 B&B
15 rooms, 13 pb
Visa, MC
C-yes/S-yes/H-yes

Continental breakfast
All meals, bar service
sitting room
bicycles

February—December

Historic landmark completely restored and furnished with pine antiques and adorned with antique toys & crafts. Overlooking the Hudson River.

One Market Street
1 Market St., 10516
(914)-265-3912

$45-55 B&B
1 room, pb
Visa, MC
C-yes/S-yes

Continental plus

All year

Built around 1810; one block from Hudson River; Storm King Mt. & West Point nearby.

COLDEN

Back of the Beyond
7233 East Hill Rd.,14033
(716)-652-0427

$40/cpl B&B
2 rooms, 1 pb

C-yes/S-no/P-no

Full breakfast
Complimentary wine
sitting room, piano
swimming pond

All year

Charming mini-estate 50 miles from Niagara Falls, skiing, swimming, hiking, organic gardens. Country breakfast served on deck/living room.

COOPERSTOWN

Hickory Grove Inn
Rte. 80 at Six Mile Pt.
(607)-547-8100

$25-35 B&B
4 rooms, 4 pb
Visa, MC, AmEx, DC
C-yes/S-ltd/P-no

Continental plus
Dinner
sitting room, piano

Easter—October

A 150-year old Inn, combined with a three-star restaurant, filled with antiques & local memorabilia. Lake swimming.

CORNING

Rosewood Inn
134 E. 1st St., 14830
(607)-962-3253

$9-40
5 rooms, 3 pb
none
C-yes/S-yes/P-yes

Continental plus

sitting room, library

EAGLE BAY

Big Moose Inn
Big Moose Lake, 13331
(315)-357-2042

$26-32 EP
14 rooms, 0 pb
credit cards accepted
C-yes/S-yes/P-no/H-ltd

Continental (wkdys)
All meals (wknds), bar
sitting room

May—Oct., Dec 26—Mar

Located on Big Moose Lake. Excellent dining. Overlooking the lake. Hiking trails; canoes; winter sports enthusiasts galore.

EAST CONCORD

Highland Springs
Allen Rd., 14055
(716)-592-4323

$30-35 B&B
3 rooms, 2 pb

C-yes/S-NO!/P-no

Continental plus

sitting room, piano
swimming pond

All year

Spacious, peaceful country home on 70 acres of rolling woods and meadows, 40 miles south of Buffalo/Niagara Falls.

We want to hear from you — any comments regarding the inns or our publication may be noted on the form at the end of the book.

EAST HAMPTON ─────────────────────────────

Bassett House
128 Montauk Hwy., 11937
(516)-324-6127

$445-95 B&B
12 rooms, 3 pb
most credit cards
C-yes/P-yes

Full breakfast
Complimentary tea, wine
sitting room, piano
library

All year
bicycles

A comfortable place with a rural inn atmosphere.

Hedges House
74 James Ln., 11937
(516)-324-7100

11 rooms, 11 pb
all major credit cards
C-no/S-yes/P-no

sitting room, piano

April—September

Incredible food, elegant atmosphere.

1770 House
143 Main St., 11937

$85-135 B&B
7 rooms, 7 pb
credit cards accepted
C-no/S-yes/P-no

Breakfast
Dinner (by res. only)
sitting room

All year

Enjoy the magnificent beaches of East Hampton; tennis, golf, fishing, riding. Let us share our lovely home with you.

ELKA PARK ─────────────────────────────

Redcoat's Return
Dale Ln., 12427
(518)-589-6379
(518)-589-9858
Closed Apr-May, Nov.

$60-70 B&B
14 rooms, 7 pb
Visa, MC, AmEx
C-yes/S-yes/P-no

Full breakfast
Dinner, tea, wine
sitting room

Cozy English-style country inn, scenically nestled in the heart of the Catskill Game Preserve. Abundant seasonal activities; excellent cuisine.

GARRISON ─────────────────────────────

Bird and Bottle Inn
Rte. 9, 10524
(914)-424-3000

$95-120
4 rooms, 4 pb
Visa, MC, AmEx
C-no/S-yes/P-no

Full breakfast
Dinner, bar

All year

Established in 1761, the Inn's history pre-dates the Revolutionary War. Each room has a working fireplace and four-poster or canopy bed.

Golden Eagle Inn
Garrison's Lndg., 10524
(914)-424-3067

$50-75 B&B
5 rooms, 3 pb
Visa, MC, AmEx
C-no/S-yes/P-no

Continental breakfast
Luncheon
Sitting room
canoes

Closed Feb.-March

New York's best kept secret—distinctive bed & breakfast on the banks of the Hudson River. Outdoor activities. Relaxing atmosphere.

GHENT

Cedar Hill
Tice Hill Rd., 12075
(518)-392-3923

All year

$72/cpl B&B	Full breakfast
11 rooms, 9 pb	Lunch, dinner, bar
Visa, MC	sitting room, piano
C-yes/S-yes/P-no	tennis, swimming,
	bicycles, entertainment

Country inn with a wealth of activity—pool, tennis court, near skiing, fishing, music and dance. Gourmet natural breakfast included.

GLEN FALLS

East Lake George House
492 Glen St., 12801
(518)-656-9452
(518)-792-9296
July—August

$50-80 B&B	Full breakfast
7 rooms, 5 pb	
Visa, MC	sitting room
C-yes/S-yes/P-no	lake swimming

Relaxing atmosphere at 100-year-old Inn directly on Lake George, swimming, canoeing, volleyball, etc. Other attractions nearby.

GREENPORT

Townsend Manor Inn
714 Main St., 11944
(516)-477-2000

All year

EP	Full breakfast
23 rooms, 23 pb	Lunch, dinner, lounge
all major credit cards	sitting room
C-yes/S-yes/P-no	swimming pool

Charming country Inn and Resort with all the modern conveniences and directly on the water. Excellent restaurant, full-service transient marina.

GREENVILLE

Greenville Arms
12083
(518)-966-5219

April—November

$50-60 B&B	Full breakfast
20 rooms, 13 pb	Dinner
	sitting room, piano
C-yes/S-yes/P-ltd	swimming pool

A Victorian country inn found in a quiet village in the Hudson River Valley. The former house of William Vanderbilt.

GROTON

Benn Conger Inn
206 W. Cortland, 13073
(607)-898-3282

All year

$45-75 B&B	Full breakfast
4 rooms, 2 pb	Dinner, nightcap
Visa, MC, AmEx	sitting room
C-12 up/S-ok/P-no	

Elegant and graceful Georgian-style mansion on quiet village sidestreet. Original cuisine. Distinctive accomodations. Convenient to I-81 (10 mi.)

Advance reservations are essential at most inns during busy seasons and appreciated at other times

182 New York

HIGH FALLS

Brodhead House
Rte. 213, 12440
(914)-687-7700
(914)-687-7777
All year

$42.80
3 rooms, 0 pb

C-yes/S-yes/P-yes

Continental breakfast

In the village of High Falls, turn time back 100 years at the Brodhead House. Overnight lodging in the Victorian manner.

House on the Hill
Box 86, Rte. 213, 12440
(914)-687-9627

All year

$45-70 dbl
5 rooms, 2 pb

C-yes/S-ltd/P-no

Full breakfast
Complimentary wine
sitting room, piano
lawn games

A beautiful unspoiled 1825 colonial; comfortable suites, private baths; public room with fireplace; historic High Falls, diner's delight, walk to creek, falls.

ITHACA

Elmshade Guest House
402 S. Albany St., 14850
(607)-273-1707

All year

$18 pp EP
8 rooms, 0 pb

C-yes/S-yes/P-no

No food service

The only tourist home in Ithaca. Very popular with parents of Cornell & Ithaca College students.

LAKE GEORGE

Corner Birches Guest House
86 Montcalm St., 12845

All year

$20.00-28.50 B&B
4 rooms, 0 pb

C-yes/S-yes/P-yes

Continental breakfast

sitting room

Since 1957, a tourist home that gives a feeling of a visit rather than just a stop-over.

LAKE PLACID

Interlaken
15 Interlaken Ave.,12946
(518)-523-3180

All year

$35-50 dbl B&B
8 rooms, 8 pb
Visa, MC
C-yes/S-yes/P-yes

Continental breakfast

sitting room

Adirondack Inn; heart of Olympic country; quiet setting—1/2 block from Main St. between Mirror Lake & Lake Placid; some rooms w/ balconies.

We want this guide to be as complete as possible, so if you know of an inn (30 rooms or less), bed & breakfast or guesthouse we don't list, please send us their name on the form in the back of the book.

South Meadow Farm
Lodge $18 pp B&B   Full breakfast
Cascade Rd., 12946   5 rooms, 0 pb   Trail lunch, farm dinner
(518)-523-9369   sitting room, piano
(800)-USA-INNS RS   C-yes/S-yes/P-no   swimming pond
All year

Enjoy the Olympic X-country ski trails that cross our small farm, the view, our fireplace, and home grown meals.

NEW YORK

Loretta & Wayne Caputo $50 dbl B&B   Continental plus
114 W. 87th St., 10024   1 room, 1 pb
787-7053
                              C-yes/S-yes/P-no
All year

Totally private studio apartment, bath, kitchenette, in renovated Brownstone, on third floor. Double bed plus 2 singles. Air conditioning.

NORTH RIVER

Garnet Hill Lodge $38-44 B&B   Full breakfast
13th Lake Rd., 12856   25 rooms, 14 pb   Lunch, dinner, bar
(518)-251-2821   sitting room, piano
                              C-yes/S-yes/P-no/H-yes   tennis courts
All year   beach-lake swimming

Mountain retreat with freshly baked breads, X-C skiing, hiking trails on premises. Alpine skiing and Adirondack Museum nearby.

ONEONTA

Agnes Hall Tourist Home $12-15 EP
94 Center St., 13820   3 rooms, 0 pb
(607)-432-0655
                              C-yes/S-yes/P-no
Except January

Cozy, quiet, clean inn with economical rates.

PINE HILL

Pine Hill Arms $30 dbl., $20 single   Full breakfast
12462   20 rooms, 20 pb   other meals, bar
(918)-254-9811   none   Pool, hot tub, sauna
                              C-yes/S-yes/P-no   tennis nearby, library,
All year   entertainment

Legendary 19th-Century Catskill Mountain inn with greenhouse restaurant. Minutes from skiing, trout streams, hiking trails and white water tubing.

White House Lodge $30 pp B&B   Complimentary breakfast
12465   15 rooms, 6 pb   dinner, comp. wine
(914)-254-4200   none   swimming pool
                              C-yes/S-yes/P-no/H-yes   tennis nearby
All year   piano, library

Homelike country atmosphere with fireside lounge. Property adjoins state forest, hiking trails, and two major ski centers.

PORTAGEVILLE

Genesee Falls Hotel
Rte. 436, 14536
(716)-493-2484

$18-33
12 rooms, 10 pb

C-yes/S-yes/P-no/H-ltd

February—November

Breakfast on weekends
Lunch, dinner except Tue
piano

Historic, Victorian hotel, comfortable, unpretentious. Close to Letchworth State Park, nature lovers delight. Good, reasonably priced food.

RENSSELAER

Tibbitt's House
100 Columbia Tpk., 12144
(518)-472-1348

$18-25 EP
5 rooms, 1 pb

C-no/S-yes/P-no

All year

Full breakfast

piano
enclosed porch

Comfortable, 126-year-old antiques-furnished farmhouse, 2 miles from Albany, State Museum, Hudson River, hiking/biking, old Dutch fort.

RHINEBECK

Beekman Arms
Rte. 9, 12572
(914)-876-7077

$45-65
30 rooms, 30 pb
Visa, AmEx
C-yes/S-yes/P-yes/H-ltd

All year

Full breakfast
Lunch, dinner, bar

"America's Oldest Inn" circa 1766.

SARATOGA SPRINGS

Adelphi Hotel
365 Broadway, 12866
(518)-587-4688

$45-95 B&B
20 rooms, 20 pb
Visa, MC, AmEx
C-yes/S-yes/P-no

May 1-Nov. 1

Continental plus
summer dinners, bar
piano
entertainment
sitting room, library

Charming accommodations. Opulently restored High Victorian Hotel located in the historic district of the renowned resort and spa of Saratoga Springs.

SAUGERTIES

A Secret Garden
6071 Malden Tpk., 12477
(914)-246-3338

$18-25
2 rooms, 1 pb

C-yes/S-ok/P-ltd

All year

Continental breakfast

sitting room
bicycles

Pre-Civil War home on two tree-shaded acres near the Catskill Mountains. We enjoy interesting guests. Coffee's always on.

SHELTER ISLAND

Bowditch House
166 N. Ferry Rd., 11965
(516)-749-0075

$40-65 B&B
9 rooms, 0 pb

C-8 up/S-ok/P-no

Summer; wknds thru Oct.

Full breakfast
Complimentary wine
sitting room

Century old farmhouse; peaceful, homey atmosphere; walk to shops, golf, restaurants, tennis, beaches, boating; antique decor; great food.

Chequit Inn
23 Grand Ave., 11965
(516)-749-0018

May—October

$30-40	Full breakfast
29 rooms, 19 pb	Lunch, dinner
Visa, MC, AmEx, DC	sitting room, piano
C-yes/S-yes/P-no/H-ltd	bicycles
	beach club membership

Victorian Inn (built in 1871) overlooking Dering Harbor, filled with antiques. Golf, tennis, swimming. Reserve 2-3 weeks in advance.

SKANEATELES

Sherwood Inn
26 W. Genesee St., 13152
(315)-685-3405

All year

$35-60 B&B	Continental breakfast
15 rooms, 15 pb	Lunch, dinner, bar
Visa, MC, AmEx, DC, CB	bicycles
C-yes/S-yes/P-yes	entertainment
	lake swimming

Beautiful old country inn located on gorgeous Skaneateles Lake and decorated in genuine antiques.

STAMFORD

Lanigan Farm House
R.D. 1, Box 399, 12167
(607)-652-7455
(607)-652-6263
All year

$30-35 B&B	Full breakfast
4 rooms, 0 pb	Complimentary tea, wine
	sitting room, piano
C-yes/S-yes/P-yes	

4 double rooms in a charming country home surrounded by scenic vacation area and cultural events.

STATEN ISLAND

Sixteen Firs
352 St. Paul Ave., 10304
(212)-727-9188

All year

$30-35 B&B	Continental breakfast
3 rooms, 0 pb	Coffee, tea anytime
	sitting room, piano
C-yes/S-yes/P-no	

Victorian, lovely grounds with historical background, air conditioning. Complimentary continental breakfast.

STEPHENTOWN

Millhof Inn
Rte. 43, 12168
(518)-733-5606

May 30—March 31

$50-80 EP	Full breakfast menu
12 rooms, 12 pb	Afternoon tea
Visa, MC, AmEx	piano, sitting room
C-12 up/S-ltd/P-no	swimming pool
	bicycles

Central European-style inn located in the Berkshires. Serene setting. Nearby skiing, Tanglewood and other resort attractions.

SYRACUSE

Ivy Chimney
143 Didama St., 13224
(315)-446-4199

All year

$20-35 B&B	Continental breakfast
3 rooms, 0 pb	
C-no/S-no/P-ok	

Clean, convenient, safe, reasonable. This is my own home. Very good for business travelers. Have cats in house.

TANNERSVILLE ───────────────────────────────

Washington Irving Lodge $20-24 pp | Full breakfast (summer)
Rte 23A | 28 rooms, 5 pb | Dinner (wknds), bar
(518)-589-5560 | | sitting room, 2 pianos
(518)-263-4208 RS | C-yes/S-yes/P-no/H-ltd | swimming pool
July, Aug., Nov.-April 15 | | tennis courts

Comfortable lodge 2 miles from Hunter Mtn. Ski Bowl. Festivals all summer long and best skiing at Hunter Mtn. each winter. Also open Columbus Day weekend & Memorial Day weekend.

THREE MILE BAY ──────────────────────────────

Le Muguet | | Continental breakfast
2553 Church St., 13693 | 2 rooms, 2 pb | on request
(315)-649-5896 | |
| C-ltd/S-no/P-ltd |
May—October

Two cozy apts. Hostess retired interior designer & decorator. Innovative ideas; green bottles; plants; antiques. St. Lawrence River Thousand Is. area.

TRUMANSBURG ─────────────────────────────────

Taughannock Farms Inn $28-45 | Continental plus
Rte. 89, 14886 | 6 rooms, 3 pb | Dinner, bar
(607)-387-7711 | | sitting room
| C-yes/S-yes/P-no/H-ltd | music box
Easter—Thanksgiving | | lake swimming

Next to spectacular Taughannock Falls & Gorge. Hiking trails, boat rentals, picnic grounds, marina. Overlooking Cayuga Lake.

TUCKAHOE ────────────────────────────────────

Bed & Breakfast $36-44 B&B | Full breakfast
82 Vermont Ter., 10707 | 5 rooms, 1 pb | Complimentary tea, wine
(914)-779-6411 | | sitting room
| C-yes/S-yes/P-no | bicycles
All year

30 minutes by car or train to Manhattan—1 block from station. Immaculate large home, free parking, quiet residential suburb.

WESTPORT ────────────────────────────────────

Inn on the Library Lawn $24-55 EP | Full breakfast
1 Washington St., 12993 | 20 rooms, 20 pb | Lunch, dinner, bar
(518)-962-8666 | credit cards accepted | swimming pool
| C-yes/S-yes/P-ltd | tennis courts
All year | | sitting room

North Country hospitality, comfortable accomodations, gourmet food, golf, tennis, year-around resort. Captivating vistas.

**Be sure to call the Inn to verify details and prices
and to make your reservation**

NORTH CAROLINA

ASHEVILLE

Flint Street Inn	$35-40	Full breakfast
116 Flint St., 28801	4 rooms, 0 pb	Complimentary wine
(704)-253-6723		sitting room
	C-12 up/S-yes/P-no	
All year		

Charming, turn-of-the-century style residence, located in historic district. Comfortable walking distance to town, restaurants, and shops.

Ray House	$25-35 B&B	Continental plus
83 Hillside St., 28801	3 rooms, 1 pb	
(704)-252-0106		library/music room
	C-yes/S-yes/P-no	grand piano
All year		

The Ray House, located in the city yet hidden among spruces and native trees. Interior has English country home feeling.

BAT CAVE

Stonehearth Inn	$25	Continental breakfast
Rte. 74, POB 9, 28710	4 rooms, 4 pb	Dinner
(704)-625-9990	Visa, MC	
	C-yes/S-yes/P-no	
All year		

Small family-run Inn, guestrooms right on the river. Informal, with a slower pace. Country cooking, restaurant specializes in rainbow trout.

BLOWING ROCK

Maple Lodge	$50/cpl B&B	Continental plus
P.O. Box 66, 28605	8 rooms, 8 pb	Complimentary wine
(704)-295-3331		sitting room, piano
	C-yes/S-yes/P-no	tennis courts
April—October		

"Grandmother's House" flavor. Two parlors, TV wicker room and sunporch for guests. Sherry and fruit bowls in rooms.

188 North Carolina

BREVARD ───

Colonial Inn	$24-38	Full breakfast
410 E. Main St., 28712	12 rooms, 10 pb	Afternoon tea
(704)-884-2105		sitting room—color TV
	C-yes/S-ok/P-no	
All year		

Antique furnishings, gracious hospitality, restful beauty. Main building recently placed on the National Register of Historic Places.

BRYSON CITY ───

Folkestone Lodge	B&B	Full breakfast
Rte. 1, Box 310, 28713	5 rooms, 5 pb	
	Visa, MC	sitting room, piano
	C-yes/S-no/P-no	library
All year		bicycles

Near Deepcreek Campground. Smoky Mountain National Park. Bed & Breakfast lodge— country flavor. Small, secluded, old fashioned.

───

Hemlock Inn	$49-66	Full breakfast
28713	25 rooms, 25 pb	Dinner
(704)-488-2885		sitting room
	C-yes/S-yes/P-no/H-ltd	
May—October		

Country Inn atmosphere, honest to goodness home cooking from Lazy Susan tables. Cool, quiet, restful on the edge of Great Smoky Mountains.

BURNSVILLE ──

Nu-Wray Inn	$28-40 EP	Full breakfast
P.O. Box 156, 28714	31 rooms, 25 pb	Supper, Sunday brunch
(704)-682-2329		sitting room
	C-yes/S-yes/P-no	
May—November		

Country Inn—operated by the same family for 4 generations. Specializing in fried chicken, country ham. Meals served family style. Reservations.

CLEMMONS ──

Tanglewood Manor House	$39-50 EP	Full breakfast
P.O. Box 1040, 27012	29 rooms, 27 pb	Lunch, dinner, bar
(919)-766-6461	Visa, MC, AmEx	swimming pool
	C-yes/S-yes/P-no/H-ltd	tennis courts
All year		bicycles

The Tanglewood Manor House and Lodge is located in Tanglewood Park which is a complete recreational resort for all ages.

DILLSBORO ───

Jarrett House	$25 up	Breakfast menu
P.O. Bos 219, 28725	18 rooms, 18 pb	Lunch, dinner
(704)-586-9964		
	C-12 up/P-no	
Easter—October		

The Jarrett House, famous for fine foods and lodging since 1890. Beautiful spring, porches w/ rocking chairs. Specializing in Southern foods.

EDENTON

Lord Proprietors' Inn
300 N. Broad St., 27932
(919)-482-3641

All year

$41-50 B&B
12 rooms, 21 pb

C-yes/S-yes/P-no

Continental plus

sitting room
bicycles

Two restored houses in the historic district of "the South's prettiest town." Furnished by area antiques dealers with all for sale.

FLAT ROCK

Woodfield Inn
P.O. Box 98, 28731
(704)-693-6016

All year

$72-90
18 rooms, 10 pb
credit cards accepted
C-yes/S-yes/P-yes/H-yes

Continental breakfast
Lunch, dinner, wine
sitting room, piano
tennis, hot tub, sauna
entertainment

A wonderful place to unwind and get away from everyday routine. Winner of Dinner Club of America Silver Spoon Award. Nature trail, golf.

FRANKLIN

Buttonwood Inn
190 Georgia Rd., 28734
(704)-369-8985

All year

$30-35 B&B
5 rooms, 5 pb

C-yes/S-no/P-no/H-ltd

Continental breakfast

sitting room, piano
golf

Completely surrounded by tall pines, small & cozy Buttonwood will appeal to the person who prefers simplicity and natural rustic beauty.

Poor Richards Summit Inn
P.O. Box 511, 28734
(704)-524-2006

All year

$35-40 B&B
14 rooms

C-no/S-no/P-no

Full breakfast
Dinner

Turn-of-the-century home; spacious, mountain vista, for those who seek serenity, beauty and old-fashioned hospitality.

GLENVILLE

Mountain High
Big Ridge Rd., 28736
(704)-743-3094

June—November

$15 B&B
3 rooms, 1 pb

C-no/S-no/P-no

Full breakfast

sitting room

High & cool, gorgeous Mountain views, horseback riding, fox hunting. All other sports close by plus whitewatering. Facilities for artists.

Advance reservations are essential at most inns during busy seasons and appreciated at other times

HENDERSONVILLE

Havenshire Inn
Rte. 4 Box 455, 28739
(704)-692-4097

May—October

$45-60 B&B
6 rooms, 3 pb
Visa, MC
C-yes/S-yes/P-no

Continental plus
Afternoon tea
sitting room, organ
pond, river, canoe
hiking trails

19th-Century English country manor house. Rich furnishings lend to atmosphere of comfortable elegance. Horses; pond; canoeing, fishing, picnicing.

HIGHLANDS

Highlands Inn
28741
(704)-526-9380

April 15—November 1

$50-92/cpl
35 rooms, 35 pb

C-yes/S-yes/P-no

Full breakfast
Lunch, dinner, tea
sitting room
piano, entertainment

1879-1880 Highland Inn: Excellence in gracious hospitality & food. Full breakfast, absolutely! Antique grand piano. Beautiful hills & sunsets.

Old Edwards Inn
Main St., 28741
(704)-526-5036

May—October

$50-60
21 rooms, 21 pb
Visa, MC, AmEx
C-yes/S-yes/P-no

Continental breakfast
Other meals served

100-year-old structure restored in a country manner with antiques—located in the town of Highlands, 4118 ft. elevation—very mild summers, exc. dining.

NAGS HEAD

Colony Beach Inn
P.O. Box 87, 27959
(919)-441-3666

All year

$34-75 EPP
30 rooms, 30 pb
Visa, MC, AmEx
C-yes/S-yes/P-no/H-yes

Full breakfast
Lunch, dinner, bar
sitting room, piano
swimming pool

Cedar shake giant of an oceanfront Inn, wood verandas, with a view of the ocean and hang gliding on Jockeys Ridge.

NEW BERN

Kings Arm Inn
212 Pollock St., 28560
(919)-638-4409

All year

$48-54 B&B
8 rooms, 8 pb
Visa, MC, AmEx
C-yes/S-yes/P-no/H-yes

Continental plus

In heart of historic district. Delicious hot breakfast. Southern hospitality. Information on sightseeing and dining.

PISGAH FOREST

Pines Country Inn
Hart Rd., 28768
(704)-877-3131

May—October

$40-58 MAP
26 rooms, 21 pb

C-yes/P-no/H-ltd

Full breakfast
Dinner (inc.)
sitting room, piano

Quiet, homey country inn, fantastic view. Where you come as guest and leave as our friend, part of our family.

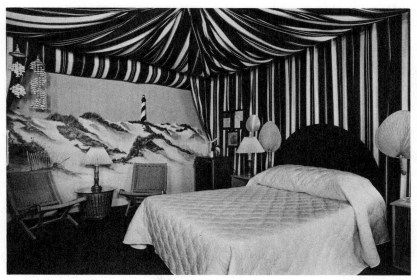

Tanya's Ocean House, Kill Devil Hills, North Carolina

POLLOCKSVILLE

Trent River Plantation
P.O. Box 154, 28573
(919)-224-3811

Except Jan/Feb

$38-48 EP
5 rooms

C-yes/S-yes/P-no

Continental plus
Complimentary wine
swimming pool
bicycles
sitting room

Luxurious rooms with canopy beds and antiques, Southern hospitality and all amenities.
See p. 67 Country Inns of the Old South, 1983 revised edition.

ROBBINSVILLE

Blue Boar Lodge
Kilmer Forest Rd., 28771
(704)-479-8126

May—September

$30 pp
8 rooms, 7 pb
Visa, MC
C-yes/S-ok/P-no

Full breakfast
Dinner
sitting room, piano
lake swimming
game room, boat rental

Secluded hideaway in the Smoky Mountains near beautiful hiking trails and lake activities;
family style meals.

**Snowbird Mountain
Lodge**
Kilmer Forest Rd., 28771
(704)-479-3433

May—October

$84/cpl AP
22 rooms, 20 pb
credit cards accepted
C-12 up/S-yes/P-no/H-yes

Full breakfast
Lunch, dinner included
sitting room, piano

Located in the heart of the National Forest. Fishing, hiking, mountain stream, swimming,
badmitten, archery & shuffleboard.

SALUDA ───

Orchard Inn	$60/cpl B&B	Full breakfast
P.O. Box 725, 28773	8 rooms, 8 pb	Lunch, dinner, tea
(704)-749-5471		library, living room
	C-no/S-yes/P-no	
All year		

Orchard Inn is a real country inn featuring quiet living with all the comforts and informal elegance of a mountain country house.

TRYON ──

Mill Farm Inn	$48 dbl B&B	Continental plus
P.O. Box 1251, 28782	8 rooms, 8 pb	
(704)-859-6992		sitting room
(800)-547-1463 RS	C-yes/S-yes/P-no	
March—November		

Fine guest Inn, including complementary breakfast—homelike atmosphere, bird watchers' paradise, plus cultural living experience.

Stone Hedge Inn	$42-62	Full breakfast
Box 366, 28782	4 rooms, 4 pb	Dinner (Wed-Sun)
(704)-859-9114	Visa, MC	swimming pool
	C-12 up/S-yes/P-no/H-ltd	
except Jan. 20-Feb. 15		

Enjoy a unique dining & lodging experience. Quaint & spacious rooms, each individually tailored for comfort. Beautiful, private mountain setting.

WAYNESVILLE ──────────────────────────────────────

Piedmont Inn	$33-45 B&B	Full breakfast
630 Eagles Nest, 28786	15 rooms, 15 pb	
(704)-456-8636	Visa, MC	swimming pool
	C-yes/S-yes/P-yes	tennis courts
All year		piano

Small friendly resort close to Blue Ridge Parkway and Smoky Mountain National Park. A perfect hideaway for anyone!

Swag	$72-98 MAP	Full breakfast
P.O. Box 280-A, 28786	12 rooms, 6 pb	Lunch (extra), dinner (inc)
(704)-926-0430	Visa, MC	library, piano
(404)-875-1632 OS	C-yes/P-no/H-ltd	racquet ball court
Late May—November 1		pond

At 5,000 feet, hand-hewn log lodge. Elegant, intimate hideaway. Twelve unique bedrooms. Excellent cuisine. Breathtaking views.

WINSTON-SALEM ────────────────────────────────────

Colonel Ludlow House	$40-90 B&B	Complimentary breakfast
Summit & W. 5th, 27101	12 rooms, 10 pb	complimentary tea & wine
(919)-777-1887	VISA, MC, AMEX	whirlpool tubs in room
	C-6-up/S-yes/P-no	sauna, bicycles, phones
All year		tennis nearby, piano

Historic National Register: 1887—unique guest rooms (pivate deluxe baths, som e with two person jacuzzi)—beautiful antiques—walk to restaurants, shops.

NORTH DAKOTA

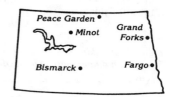

BUTTE

Long X Trail Ranch
58634
(701)-842-2128

All year

$19-26
6 rooms, 6 pb

C-yes/S-yes/H-yes

Full breakfast
Restaurant
sitting room
horses

A truly "real" Western experience—Friendly hospitality—clean, quiet accomodations— Relax and enjoy nature at its finest in North Dakota badlands.

OHIO

AKRON

Portage House
601 Copley Rd., 44320
(216)-535-9236

All year

$18-25 B&B
5 rooms, 1 pb

C-yes/S-yes/P-yes

Full breakfast
Lunch, dinner arranged
sitting room, piano

Old tudor-style house in historic setting of Indian Portage between 2 river systems and the site of Akron's founding family. Homemade breads & jam.

BAYFIELD

Greunke's Inn
17 Rittenhouse, 54814
(715)-779-5480

April—October

$38-42
6 rooms, 0 pb
Visa, MC
C-yes

Full breakfast
Lunch, dinner, beer

Like stepping into one of Norman Rockwell's Saturday Evening Post illustrations. Little has changed here since the late 1940s. Old jukebox is a gathering spot.

The Mansion	$40 B&B	Continental breakfast
7 Rice Ave., 54814	4 rooms, 0 pb	Complimentary wine
(715)-779-5508		sitting room, piano
	C-yes/S-no/P-yes/H-ltd	
All year		

Enjoy breathtaking views of Lake Superior through Tiffany stained glass windows before Edwardian dinners served in the dining room of this historic mansion.

BELLVILLE

Federick Fitting House	$28-38 B&B	Continental plus
72 Fitting Ave., 44813	3 rooms, 0 pb	
(419)-886-4283		sitting room, piano
	C-yes/S-no/P-yes	library
All year		bicycles

1863 Early Victorian home furnished with Ohio antiques; rural hospitality in a village setting. Just three miles east of I-71.

CLEVELAND

Tudor House	$25-55 B&B	Full breakfast
P.O. Box 18590, 44118	2 rooms, 2 pb	
(216)-321-3213		sitting room
	C-15 up/S-yes/P-no	
All year		

Lovely 1920's house on Register of Historic Places. Daily and extended stays. Kitchen privileges can be arranged.

FISH CREEK

White Gull Inn	$36-105 B&B	Full breakfast
Box 175	16 rooms, 9 pb	lunch, dinner
(414)-868-3517	none	bicycles
	C-yes/S-yes/P-no/H-ltd	entertainment
All year		piano

Situated between the bluff and the bay in Fish Creek on Wisconsin's Door Peninsula; charming turn-of-the-century inn.

LAPOINTE

Chateau Madeleine	$100-120 MAP	MAP
P.O. Box 27, 54850	12 rooms, 11 pb	
(715)-747-2463		sitting room, piano
	C-yes/S-yes/P-no	tennis, bicycles, beach
June 17—Oct. 23		entertainment

Chateau Madeleine is celebrating its 34th season as a country inn. Canoeing, sailing, swimming, tennis, golf, bicycling, hiking, birdwatching, relaxing.

POYNETTE

Jamieson House	$45-65 B&B	Full breakfast
407 N. Franklin, 53955	8 rooms, 7 pb	Restaurant, bar
(608)-635-4100	AmEx, DC	garden room
	C-yes/S-no/P-ltd/H-yes	piano, bicycles
All year		

The Jamieson House features intimate gourmet dining amid quiet Victorian elegance. Guest rooms have sumptuous velvet couches, sunken baths, antiques.

SPRING VALLEY ─────────────────────

3 B's Guest House $20-25 B&B   Full breakfast
103 Race St., 45370   3 rooms, 0 pb   Supper, tea, wine
(513)-862-424?   sitting room
                        C-yes/S-yes/P-no/H-yes bicycles
All year

Relax in this charming village home—owners retired Air Force couple. 20 miles from Dayton's Air Force Museum, King's Island.

ZOAR ─────────────────────────

Cider Mill $35 B&B   Full breakfast
P.O. Box 441, 44697   2 rooms, 0 pb   Dinner arranged; wine
(216)-874-3133   Visa, MC   sitting room, piano
                        C-yes/S-ltd/P-yes
All year

The renovated 1863 "mill" features antique & gift shop, fine country accomodations. Professional Foodball Hall of Fame, Amish country, lakes, golf.

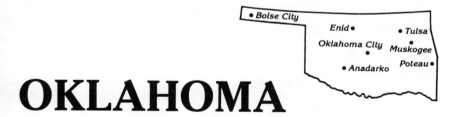

OKLAHOMA

YUKON ────────────────────────

Tulp House $20-30 B&B   Continental plus
1210 Kouba Dr., 73099 1 room, 1 pb   Afternoon tea
(405)-354-3280   sitting room
                        C-yes/S-no/P-no   travel & tourist advice
All year

Charming air-conditioned country-style home in suburban setting, adjacent to I-40, near Oklahoma City, featuring fresh-ground coffee, homemade bread.

Please mention this guide when you make your booking

OREGON

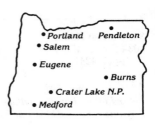

- •Portland   •Pendleton
- • Salem
- • Eugene
-          • Burns
- • Crater Lake N.P.
- • Medford

ASHLAND ————————————————————————————————————

Ashland's Main St. Inn $47-52 B&B   Continental breakfast
142 W. Main St., 97520   3 rooms, 3 pb
(503)-488-0969   sitting room, piano
                              C-yes/S-yes/P-no
All year

Period furnishings grace the 3 comfortable rooms in this charming Victorian style home. Close to the city plaza and theatres.

Chanticleer B&B Inn $48-59 B&B   Full breakfast
120 Gresham St., 97520   6 rooms, 6 pb   Complimentary wine
(513)-482-1919   sitting room
(503)-488-1011 RS   C-yes/S-ltd/P-no
All year

Antiques, fluffy comforters, air conditioned, brick patio and mountain views.

Coach House Inn $34-39 B&B   Complimentary breakfast
70 Coolidge St., 97520   3 rooms, 0 pb   complimentary wine
(503)-482-2257   none   claw foot tub
                              C-ltd/S-no/P-no   croquet, badminton
Feb. 20-Oct. 31   scenic tours

One of Ashland's original B&B's, still moderately priced. Lovingly restored 1890's farmhouse. Antiques and reproductions; mountain views.

Edinburgh Lodge $48-56 B&B   Full breakfast
586 E. Main St., 97520   6 rooms, 6 pb   Complimentary tea/sherry
(503)-488-1050   Visa, MC   sitting room
                              H-no
All year

Historic J.T. Currie Boarding House, 1908; B&B in British tradition; handmade quilts, period furniture, full breakfast and afternoon tea served.

Hersey House $55 B&B   Full breakfast
451 N. Main St., 97520   4 rooms, 4 pb   Complimentary tea, wine
(503)-482-4563   sitting room
                              S-ok/P-no   piano
May 1—October 1

Restored Victorian farmhouse in historic district. Six blocks from the theatres. Period furnishings, air conditioning, Afternoon tea or sherry.

Morical House
668 W. Main St., 97520
(503)-482-2254

All year

$45-59 B&B
5 rooms, 5 pb
Visa, MC
C-yes/S-ltd/P-no

Full breakfast
Complimentary tea, wine
sitting room, organ

An 1880's house, set in an acre of lawn and gardens, restored to the simple elegance of its Victorian heritage.

Neil Creek House
341 Mowetza, 97520
(503)-482-1334

All year

$65 B&B
2 rooms, 2 pb

C-no/S-ltd/P-no

Full breakfast
Complimentary wine
swimming pool, bicycles
entertainment
sitting room

European elegance on a 5-acre paradise: pool, duck pond, forest. Rustic outside, antiques inside, and gourmet breakfast by the creek.

Romeo Inn
295 Idaho St., 97520

Feb. 20-Oct. 31

$63 B&B
4 rooms, 4 pb
none
C-no/S-ltd/P-no/H-yes

Complimentary breakfast
comp. tea, fresh bread
hot tub, pool, piano
bicycles, sitting room
library

Charming Cape Cod, set amid big pines, overlooking the valley; elegant furnishings, outstanding food; your comfort is our specialty.

Shutes Lazy S
200 Mowetza Dr., 97520
(503)-482-5498

All year

$45 B&B
1 room, 1 pb

C-no/S-no/P-no

Full breakfast
Complimentary wine
Shakespearean library

Something special for non-smokers, a real farm experience. Organically home-grown breakfast feast. Down comforters. Many antiques. Double bed.

Winchester Inn
35 S. 2nd St., 97520
(503)-488-1113

Jan. 1—Dec. 15

$67 dbl B&B
7 rooms, 7 pb
Visa, MC, AmEx
C-yes/S-yes/P-no

Full breakfast
Gourmet restaurant
sitting room

Century-old historic home offering Victorian charm and sophisticated country living. Restaurant overlooks tiered gardens. 2 blks from Shakesperean theatres.

CORVALLIS

Madison Inn B & B
660 SW Madison Ave.
(503)-757-1274

All year

$35-40 B&B
5 rooms, 1 pb
Visa, MC
C-yes/S-yes/P-no

Full breakfast
Complimentary wine
2 sitting rooms
piano

Historic Madison Inn is ideally located one block from downtown Corvallis and two blocks from Oregon State campus.

198 Oregon

EUGENE

Campus Cottage
1136 E. 19th Ave., 97403
(503)-342-5346

$47-53 B&B
2 rooms, 2 pb

C-older/S-yes/P-no

Full breakfast
Complimentary wine
bicycles

All year

Completely renovated 1922 shingled cottage. Warm country atmosphere. Antiques, flowers, good conversation. Two blocks from University of Oregon.

Timewarp Inn
1006 Taylor St., 97402
(503)-344-5556

Except October

$35-65 B&B
2 rooms, 1 pb
Visa, MC
C-no/S-ltd/P-no

Continental plus
Afternoon tea
spa
parlor
cable TV movies

Local historic home—working costume shop on premises. Costume services available for special occasions (example—breakfast in bed).

FLORENCE

Johnson House
216 Maple St., 97439
(503)-997-8000

$34 B&B
4 rooms, 0 pb

S-no/P-no

Full breakfast
Afternoon tea
bicycles
sitting room

All year

Beautifully restored 1892 Victorian; down comforters; genuine antiques throughout; turn-of-the-century charm; in Old Town one block from bayfront.

GOLD BEACH

Tu Tu Tun Lodge
96550 North Bank, 97444
(503)-247-6664

May—October

$73 EP
18 rooms, 18 pb
Visa, MC
C-yes/S-yes/P-yes/H-yes

Full breakfast
Lunch, dinner, bar
swimming pool
library, sitting room
player piano

Secluded lodge nestled on the banks of the Rogue River with "Country Inn" hospitality, gourmet meals, white water excursions, fishing.

GRANTS PASS

Paradise Guest Ranch
7000 Monument Dr., 97526
(503)-479-4333

All year

$70-85 B&B
15 rooms, 15 pb
credit cards accepted
C-yes/S-yes/P-ltd/H-ltd

Full breakfast
Dinner (res.), bar
swimming, tennis
hot tub, bicycles
sitting room, piano

A picture book ranch nestled in the north end of the Rogue River Valley. An elegant ranch experience awaits your visit.

IDLEYLD PARK

Steamboat Inn
97447
(503)-496-3495
(503)-498-2411
All year

$44-50 EP
8 rooms, 8 pb
Visa, MC
C-yes/S-ltd/P-no/H-yes

Full breakfast
Lunch, dinner

A fishing lodge/country inn that serves excellent food. At night we close to the public and serve our famous fisherman dinner by reservation only!

Neil Creek House, Ashland, Oregon

JACKSONVILLE

Jacksonville Inn
175 E. California, 97530
(503)-899-7900

All year

$38-55 B&B
8 rooms, 8 pb
all major credit cards
C-yes/S-yes/P-small

Continental breakfast
Lunch, dinner, bar
entertainment (wknds)

Antique furnished Inn in historic Jacksonville. Gourmet food, early western atmosphere.

Judge Touvelle House
455 N. Oregon St., 97530
(503)-899-8223

All year

$35-55 B&B
6 rooms, 1 pb

C-no/S-no/P-no/H-yes

Continental plus
Complimentary wine
sitting room
swimming pool
hot tub

We're antique collectors—oriental rugs, silver, cut glass, antique dishes, walnut marble top furniture. One block from core area of landmark town.

Livingston Mansion Inn
4132 Livingston Rd., 97530
(503)-899-7107
(800)-872-4667 RS
All year

$55-75 B&B
3 rooms, 3 pb
credit cards accepted
C-yes/S-no/P-no/H-yes

Full breakfast
Complimentary tea, wine
sitting room
swimming pool

McCully House Inn
P.O. Box 387, 97530
(503)-899-1942

All year

$48-68 B&B
4 rooms, 4 pb

C-yes/S-ltd/P-no/H-yes

Full breakfast
Complimentary wine
sitting room
bicycles

Charming 1861 Classical Revival home on National Registry. Located in heart of Historic Jacksonville near Ashland's Shakesperean Festival, Rogue River.

JOSEPH

Wallowa Lake Lodge
97846
(503)-432-4082

mid-June—Labor Day

$20-26
20 rooms, 9 pb

C-yes/S-yes/P-no

Breakfast menu
Dinner, bar
piano, large lobby

Rustic 50-year-old lodge close to a glacial lake in the Wallowa Mts. Still has authentic Twenties flavor.

MERLIN

Morrison's Lodge
8500 Galice Rd., 97532
(503)-476-3825
(503)-476-3027
mid-May—mid-November

$45 pp MAP
13 rooms, 11 pb

C-yes/S-yes/P-no

Full breakfast
Dinner included
swimming, tennis
piano, sitting room
closed circuit movies

River lodge, with frontage and view of Rogue River. Long known as a headquarters for river runners and Steelhead fishermen. Reservations only.

OREGON CAVES

Oregon Caves Chateau
97523
Toll Sta. 1

mid-June—mid-Sept.

$37-49
23 rooms, 23 pb

C-yes/S-yes/P-no/H-yes

Continental plus
Lunch, dinner, bar
sitting room, piano

The Chateau located in the heart of the Siskiyou Mountains serving visitors to Oregon Caves National Monument since 1934.

SISTERS

Lake Creek Lodge
97759
595-6331

All year

$26-134
15 rooms, 15 pb

C-yes/S-yes/P-ltd/H-yes

Full breakfast
Dinner
swimming pool
tennis courts
sitting room

For rugged outdoor activities or relaxation, fishing, swimming, hiking, climbing, tennis, golf, skiing, & horseback riding.

STAYTON

Horncroft
42156 Kingston Lyons Dr.
(503)-769-6287

All year

$20-30 B&B
3 rooms, 1 pb

C-yes/S-no/P-no

Full breakfast
Afternoon tea
swimming pool
bicycles
piano, sitting room

Rural, private home, scenic area, one & half hours to ski & wilderness areas, or Pacific beaches.

WOLF CREEK ────────────────────────────

Wolf Creek Tavern
P.O. Box 97, 97497
(503)-866-2474

$26-34 EP
8 rooms, 8 pb
Visa, MC
C-yes/S-yes/P-no/H-yes

Breakfast menu
Lunch, dinner
sitting room

All year

Restored former stagecoach stop in the heart of the Oregon Siskiyou Mountains, close to the famous Rogue River.

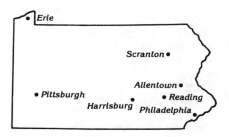

PENNSYLVANIA

AIRAVILLE ────────────────────────────

Spring House
Muddy Crk. Forks, 17302
(717)-927-6906

March—January

$42-48
3 rooms, 0 pb

C-yes/S-no/P-no

Full breakfast
Complimentary wine
sitting room, piano
bicycles
creek swimming

Restored 18th-Century stone house in pre-Revolutionary river-valley settlement near Lancaster, York. Featherbeds, gourmet country breakfast. Hiking, fishing.

ALLENTOWN ────────────────────────────

Coachaus
107-111 N. 8th St.,18102
(215)-821-4854

$38-54 EP
16 rooms, 14 pb
Visa, MC, AmEx
C-4 up/S-yes/P-no

Full breakfast
Complimentary wine
sitting room

Lovingly restored, graciously appointed, blessed with the amenities of the finest hotels. Olde Allentowne, shops, fine restaurants, theatre steps away.

Please mention this guide when you make your booking

BIRD IN HAND ───────────────────────────────────

Greystone Motor Lodge	$35	No food
P.O. Box 270, 17505	12 rooms, 12 pb	
(717)-393-4233	Visa, MC, AmEx	lobby
	C-yes/S-yes/P-no	
All year		

Victorian mansion and carriage house located on 2 acres close to Amish farms. Unique, air-conditioned rooms with private baths.

CANADENSIS ───────────────────────────────────

Dreamy Acres	$25-36 B&B	Continental plus
P.O. Box 7, 18325	8 rooms, 6 pb	
(717)-595-7115		sitting room, piano
	C-yes/S-yes/P-no	
All year		

Dreamy Acres is situated in "Heart of the Pocono Mountain Vacationland" close to stores, gift shops, churches and recreational facilities.

Nearbrook	$15-30 B&B	"Mountain Breakfast"
18325	4 rooms, 0 pb	
(717)-595-3152		library
	C-/S-no/P-yes/H-yes	

Great spot for summer and winter sports, hiking or just planning your sight- seeing of the Poconos from our maps & brochures.

Overlook Inn	$106-112 dbl MAP	Full breakfast
Dutch Hill Rd., 18325	20 rooms, 20 pb	Dinner, tea, wine inc.
(717)-595-7519	Visa, MC, AmEx	sitting room, piano
	C-12 up/S-yes/P-no	swimming pool
All year		

An outpost of personalized civility. Secluded turn-of-century inn. Superb food and service. Ski, swim, hike,or simply relax.

Pump House Inn	$45-55	Continental plus
18325	6 rooms, 6 pb	Dinner, bar
(717)-595-7501	Visa, MC, AmEx, DC	private sitting rooms
	C-yes/S-yes/P-no	piano
Except January		

Relax at this charming inn surrounded by the beauty and quietude that is the Poconos. Enjoy exquisite gourmet French dining.

CEDAR RUN ───────────────────────────────────

Cedar Run Inn	$12 pp	Full breakfast
17727	14 rooms, 4 pb	Dinner, bar
(717)-353-6241		sitting room
	C-yes/S-yes/P-yes/H-yes	trout streams
February—December		swimming, canoeing

Rustic country inn, situated along Pine Creek near the scenic Pennsylvania grand canyon. 1-1/2 hours north of Interstate 80.

COOKSBURG ────────────────────────────

Gateway Lodge
Rte. 36, 16217
(814)-744-8017

$30
8 rooms, 0 pb

C-/S-yes/P-no

All year

Full country breakfast
Dinner
sitting room, piano

Rustic log cabin inn nestled in mountains. Warm colonial charm, old-fashioned country style meals served by waitresses in colonial dress.

CRESCO ────────────────────────────

La Anna Guest House
R.D. 2, Box 1051, 18326
(717)-676-4225

$10 pp B&B
4 rooms, 0 pb

C-yes/S-yes/P-yes

All year

Continental plus

sitting room, piano

Private home nestled in Pocono Mt. village welcomes guests. Fishing, swimming, skating pond, cross-country skiing, waterfalls, woodland walks.

EPHRATA ────────────────────────────

Smithton
900 W. Main, 17522
(717)-733-6094

$35-65 B&B
4 rooms, 2 pb
Visa, MC
C-yes/S-yes/P-yes

All year

Full breakfast
Tea, bedtime snack
whirlpool bath
bicycles
sitting room, library

A picturesque Pennsylvania Dutch Country Inn, est. 1763. Fireplaces in parlor, dining & guest rooms. 4-poster beds, quilts, candles, etc.

ERWINNA ────────────────────────────

Evermay-on-the-
Delaware
18920
(215)-294-9100

$47-70 B&B
16 rooms, 16 pb
Visa, MC
C-12 up/S-yes/P-no/H-yes

All year

Continental plus
Complimentary tea/sherry
sitting room, piano

The inn is furnished with Victorian antiques which provide a romantic and peaceful atmosphere. Most rooms face the picturesque Delaware river.

Golden Pheasant Inn
River Rd., 18920
(215)-294-9595

$45
14 rooms, 1 pb
Visa, MC, AmEx
C-no/S-/P-no

Except January

Continental plus
Dinner, bar
sitting room

A 1857 Inn, serving International cuisine in a candlelit solarium. 2 intimate dining rooms in Victorian decor.

Advance reservations are essential at most inns during busy seasons and appreciated at other times

FAIRFIELD

Fairfield Inn
Main St., 17320
(717)-642-5410

$35 EP
6 rooms, 0 pb
Visa, MC
C-yes/S-/P-no

Full breakfast
Luncheon, dinner
sitting room

All year

Located in the rolling countryside near Gettysburg Battlefield. Original building dates from 1757, was the Miller Plantation.

HOLICONG

Barley Sheaf Farm
Box 66, 18928
(215)-794-5104

$45-80 B&B
9 rooms, 6 pb

C-8 up/S-yes/P-no/H-yes

Full farm breakfast

swimming pool
sitting room

March—December

30-acre working farm—raise sheep—rooms all furnished in antiques. Farm breakfast. Good antiquing & historic sights in area.

JAMESTOWN

Das Tannen-Lied
Rte. 1, 16134
(412)-932-5029

$20-30 B&B
2 rooms, 0 pb

C-8 up/S-yes/P-no

Full breakfast
Lunch/dinner on request
sitting room, library

April—October

1872 farm house overlooking 12 mile long lake, state park. All types of activities. Breakfast—whatever my guests would like!

KENNETT SQUARE

Mrs. K's Bed & Breakfast
404 Ridge Ave., 19348
(215)-444-5559

$18-35 B&B
2 rooms, 0 pb

C-yes/S-no/P-no

Full breakfast
Complimentary tea, wine

All year

Mrs. K's love of and interest in people provides the hospitality not usually found by travelers in commercial establishments.

KINZER

Groff Tourist Farm Home
R.D. 1, Box 36, 17535

$16-28 B&B
5 rooms, 1 pb
credit cards accepted
C-yes/S-no/P-no

No meals -
restaurants nearby
piano
bicycles

All year

Old-fashioned porched farmhouse, Amish neighbors, five carpeted single & family rooms; private and semi-private baths, picnic table, poultry and veal farm.

LANCASTER

Historic 1725 Witmer's
2014 Old Ph. Pike, 17602
(717)-299-5305

$50-70 B&B
5 rooms, 0 pb

C-yes/S-ltd/P-no

Continental breakfast

sitting room

All year

Lancaster's Pre-Revolutionary Inn still lodging travelers. Fireplaces, antiques. On National Register of Historic Places.

LITITZ

General Sutter Inn
14 E. Main St., 17543
(717)-626-2115

All year

$45-52
14 rooms, 12 pb
Visa, MC, AmEx
C-yes/S-yes/P-yes

All meals served
Lounge
sitting room, piano

Pennsylvania's oldest operating inn—founded in 1764. All rooms furnished w/ authentic Victorian furniture. Coffee shop, Gaslight Pub.

LUMBERVILLE

Black Bass Hotel
River Rd., 18933
(215)-297-5770

All year

$60-125 B&B
10 rooms, 3 pb
Visa, MC, AmEx, DC
C-/S-/P-yes

Continental breakfast
Lunch, dinner
Piano, entertainment

MILFORD

Cliff Park Inn
18337
(717)-296-6491

June—mid-October

$65 pp AP
20 rooms, 18 pb
Visa, MC, AmEx
C-yes/S-yes/P-no

Full breakfast
All meals included
sitting room, piano

Charming country inn surrounded by a golf course, with cliffs overlooking the Delaware River. American plan—superb continental cuisine.

MOUNT JOY

Cameron Estate Inn
R.D. 1, Box 305, 17752
(717)-653-1773

All year

$45-90 B&B
18 rooms, 16 pb
Visa, MC, AmEx
C-no/S-yes/P-no/H-yes

Continental plus
Lunch, dinner, bar
sitting room

Elegantly restored 1805 estate—listed on National Historic Register—center of Pennsylvania Dutch country.

NEW HOPE

Centre Bridge Inn
River Rd., 18938
(215)-862-2048
(215)-862-9139
All year

$55-100
9 rooms, 9 pb
Visa, MC
C-no/S-yes/P-no

Continental breakfast
Dinner, bar
sitting room

Charming country inn furnished with lovely period antiques—cozy old-world restaurant with open fireplace or patio dining, in season, by candlelight.

Hotel du Village
North River Rd., 18938
(215)-862-5164
(215)-862-9911
All year

$45-65
20 rooms, 20 pb
AmEx
C-yes/S-yes/P-no/H-yes

Continental plus
Dinner, bar
swimming pool
tennis courts
sitting room

Intimate country dining & lodging—pool, tennis. Relax with us in scenic Bucks County.

The Wedgewood Inn, New Hope, Pennsylvania

Inn at Phillips Mill
North River Rd., 18938

$49 EP
5 rooms, 5 pb

C-8 up/S-yes/P-no

Continental breakfast
Dinner
sitting room

Except Jan.—mid-Feb.

1750 renovated stone barn, 5 charming bedrooms, each with private bath. French cuisine, candlelit dining—by fire in winter, on flower-filled patio in summer.

Logan Inn
10 W. Ferry St., 18938
(215)-862-5134

10 rooms, 5 pb
Visa, MC, AmEx
C-ok/S-yes/P-no

Lunch, dinner, bar

February—December

1727 Logan Inn, oldest building in New Hope. Old York Road used 250 years. Antiques & paintings. Inn near village's square.

Pineapple Hill
Box 34C R.D. 2, 18938
(215)-862-9608

$45 B&B
4 rooms, 0 pb
AmEx
C-yes/S-yes/P-no/H-ltd

Continental plus
Tea, sherry, chocolates
sitting room
swimming

All year

Historic Bucks County farmhouse—primitive and Victorian antiques. Interesting stone ruins, five acres to roam. Shopping, restaurants & adventures nearby.

Wedgewood Inn
111 W. Bridge St., 18938
(215)-862-2570

$45-60 B&B
8 rooms, 3 pb

C-yes/S-ltd/P-no

Continental plus
Complimentary wine
sitting, breakfast rooms
bicycles
club: tennis, swimming

All year

Victorian manse near New Hope. Fresh flowers. Innkeepers on hand to make your stay as pleasant as the surroundings.

Whitehall Farm
R.D. 2, Box 250, 18938
(215)-598-7945

$50 up B&B
7 rooms, 3 pb
Visa, MC, AmEx
C-no/S-yes/P-no

Full breakfast
Complimentary tea, wine
swimming, tennis
bicycles

All year

sitting room, library

5 rooms with working fireplaces. 1794 stone manor house. Magnificent maple trees. Charm of famous Bucks County.

NEWFOUNDLAND

White Cloud
Rte. 447
(717)-676-3162

20 rooms, 7 pb
Visa, MC, AmEx, DC
C-yes/S-no/P-ltd/H-yes

Full breakfast
Lunch, dinner
outdoor swimming pool
tennis courts

All year

sitting room, piano

Country inn on fifty wooded acres, specializing in peace, quiet and good food. No TV; meatless, natural food meals.

ORTANNA

Hickory Bridge Farm Inn
17353
(717)-642-5261

$49 dbl B&B
7 rooms, 6 pb
credit cards accepted
C-yes/S-yes/P-no

Full breakfast
Saturday dinner
sitting room
bicycles, fishing,

All year

pond swimming

Hickory Bridge Farm is a quiet retreat at the foot of the South Mts. eight miles west of Gettysburg.

PARADISE

Maple Lane Farm
505 Paradise Ln., 17562
(717)-687-7479

$18-24 EP
4 rooms, 2 pb

C-yes/S-no/P-no

Continental plus

sitting room, piano

All year

Maple Lane Farm has air conditioning, antiques. Near Dutch wonderland, museums, flea markets. Farm guesthouse plus 120 cow dairy, streams & woodland.

Neffdale Farm
604 Strasburg Rd., 17562

$18-26
3 rooms, 1 pb

C-yes/S-no/P-no

No meals

sitting room

March—November

Stay on a real working farm—Amish neighbors—close to everything in the heart of Pennsylvania Dutch country.

PHILADELPHIA

Society Hill Hotel
3rd & Chestnut, 19106
(215)-925-1394

$56-90 B&B
12 rooms, 12 pb
Visa, MC, AmEx
C-yes/S-yes/P-no

Continental breakfast
Restaurant
piano bar

All year

An "Urban Inn" located in the midst of Philadelphia's Historic Park. Fresh flowers, chocolates and brass double beds grace each room.

208 Pennsylvania

POINT PLEASANT

Tattersall	$55 EP
18938	6 rooms, 6 pb
	C-/S-/P-

Beautiful old plastered fieldstone country house set among trees—sister inn to The Inn at Phillips Mill. Comfortable and romantic!

POTTSTOWN

Coventry Forge Inn	$36-54 B&B	Continental breakfast
R.D. 2, 19464	5 rooms, 5 pb	Dinner, bar
(215)-469-6222		swimming pool
	C-yes/S-yes/P-no	sitting room
All year		library

Coventry Forge Inn located in beautiful and historic Pennsylvania. Early Colonial furnishings, children accepted, continental breakfast.

QUAKERTOWN

Sign of the Sorrel Horse	$42-50 B&B	Continental plus
R.D. 3, 18951	6 rooms, 4 pb	Restaurant
(215)-536-4651	Visa, MC	swimming pool
	C-no/S-yes/P-no	bicycles
Except February		sitting room

The Sorrel Horse satisfies the yearning for comfortable, quiet vacations in a countryside steeped in history and covered with beauty.

RIEGELSVILLE

Riegelsville Hotel	$40-55 dbl B&B	Continental plus
10-12 Delaware Rd.,18077	12 rooms, 4 pb	Lunch, dinner, bar
(215)-749-2469	Visa, MC, AmEx	piano
	C-yes/S-yes/P-	
All year		

The Inn has been in continuous operation since 1838. Quaint, original, non-commercial atmosphere. family owned and operated. River view.

SHARTLESVILLE

Haag's Hotel	$10-15	Full breakfast
Main St., 19554	8 rooms, 5 pb	Lunch, dinner, bar
		sitting room, piano
	C-yes/S-no/P-yes	
All year		

Family style dinners a specialty. Building was built in 1915. Peaceful without modern facilities.

SMOKETOWN

Smoketown Village Tourist Home	$13-15	No meals
2495 Old Ph. Pike, 17576	5 rooms, 1 pb	
(717)-393-5975		sitting room
	C-yes/S-yes/P-no	
All year		

Beautiful Amish Country, colonial home in the heart of the Penn. Dutch area; refrigerator & picnic table available. Air conditioned; comfortable porch.

STARLIKE ————————————————————————————

Inn at Starlight Lake
18461
(717)-798-2519

Except 3/31-4/15

$35-49 pp MAP
29 rooms, 13 pb
Visa, MC
C-yes/S-yes/P-no

Full breakfast
Luncheon, dinner, bar
sitting room, piano
tennis courts
bicycles

A beautiful clear lake, setting of pastoral tranquility, excellent food and spirits, recreation for every season, congenial and informal atmosphere.

UPPER BLACK EDDY ————————————————————————

Upper Black Eddy Inn
Rt. 32-River Rd., 18972
(215)-982-5554

All year

$30 EP
6 rooms, 0 pb
Visa, MC, AmEx
C-yes/S-yes/P-no

Full breakfast
Lunch, dimmer, bar
river swimming

Overlooking picturesque Delaware River, this 1830 Inn, once a mule barge canal stop, now offers gourmet meals in rustic setting.

RHODE ISLAND

BLOCK ISLAND ————————————————————————————

Hotel Manisses
Spring Street, 02807
(401)-466-2421

April 1—Jan. 1

$70-125 B&B
17 rooms, 17 pb
Visa, MC, AmEx
C-ltd/S-yes/P-no/H-yes

Complimentary breakfast
lunch & dinner, full bar
bicycle rentals
nearby
elegant lobby

1872 Victorian hotel—fully restored—jacuzzi baths available—gourmet dining, High Tea served daily—Seafood Raw Bar.

The 1661 Inn
Spring St., 02807
(401)-466-2421

All year

$55-125 B&B
25 rooms, 12 pb
MC, Visa, AmEx
C-10-up/S-yes/P-no/H-yes

Complimentary breakfast
lunch & dinner, full bar
complimentary wine
ocean view deck
sitting room

Island country inn overlooking Atlantic Ocean—full buffet breakfast, wine & nibble hour—flaming coffees served on ocean view deck.

210 Rhode Island

NEWPORT ——————————————————————————

Admiral Benbow Inn $40-85 B&B Continental plus
93 Pelham St., 02840 15 rooms, 15 pb
(401)-846-4256 Visa, MC breakfast/conference rm.
(401)-846-1615 RS C-10 up/S-yes/P-no
All year

Brass Beds—Antiques & Atmosphere. Deck & spectacular view of Narragansett Bay. Sir Francis Chichester stayed here.

**Brinley Victorian Guest
House** $45-65 dbl. B&B Continental plus
23 Brinley St., 02840 17 rooms, 7 pb Afternoon tea
(401)-849-7645 sitting room, library
 C-12 up/S-yes/P-no

All year

Romantic Victorian uniquely decorated with antiques, fresh flowers and attention to detail. Park and walk to historic sites and beaches.

Ma Gallagher's $45-95 Full restaurant
348 Thames St., 02840 9 rooms, 9 pb full bar service
(401)-849-3975 Visa, MC, AmEx entertainment
(401)-849-7991 RS C-yes/P-no piano
All year

We have a European flair to our inn which is furnished in period antiques. Sailing, tennis, shopping nearby.

TIVERTON ——————————————————————————

Stone Bridge Inn $40-125 Lunch & dinner
1 Lawton Ave. 20 rooms, 20 pb full bar service
(401)-624-6601 MC, AmEx, Visa, CB entertainment
 C-yes/S-yes/P-no

All year

Right on the Sakonnet, sail boats abound—dock facilities and ocean beach. An inn on this site since 1682.

WAKEFIELD ——————————————————————————

Larchwood Inn $40-60 Full breakfast
176 Main St., 02879 18 rooms, 9 pb All meals, bar
(401)-783-5454 credit cards accepted sitting room, piano
 C-yes/S-yes/P-yes/H-yes entertainment

All year

Large mansion, nice rooms, pretty countryside. Food that benefits from off- shore fishing. Hearty farm products.

WESTERLY ——————————————————————————

Shelter Harbor Inn $48-58 dbl B&B Full breakfast
Post Rd., Shelter Harbor 18 rooms, 18 pb Lunch, dinner, bar
(401)-322-8883 Visa, MC, AmEx sitting room
 C-yes/S-yes/P-no entertainment

All year

18th-Century farmhouse just a mile from the R.I. shore offers a quiet, friendly atmosphere. Elegant country dining.

Woody Hill Guest House $40 B&B   Full breakfast
Woody Hill Rd.   2 rooms, 0 pb
(401)-322-0452   extensive library
                        C-yes/S-no/P-no
All year

Near beaches and Mystic seaport, yet secluded country atmosphere. Handmade quilts, antiques, wide-board floors,gardens, casual Colonial feeling.

SOUTH CAROLINA

BEAUFORT

Bay Street Inn $43-55   Full breakfast
601 Bay St., 29902   5 rooms, 5 pb   Sherry, fruit, chocolate
(803)-524-7720   Visa, MC   library
                        C-6 up/S-yes/P-no   bicycles
Jan.-July, Sept.-Dec.

Antebellum cotton planter's home furnished with antiques; beautiful water views and fireplaces in every room; nearby beaches and fine restaurants.

CHARLESTON

Elliott House Inn $77-97 B&B   Continental breakfast
78 Queen St., 29401   26 rooms, 26 pb   Room service, tea, wine
(803)-723-1855   Visa, MC, AmEx   hot tub
(800)-845-7638   C-yes/S-yes/P-no/H-yes   bicycles
All year   sitting room

Awake in the center of Historic Charleston. Enjoy your breakfast in bed or in our walled garden.

Hayne House $45-50 dbl   Continental plus
30 King St., 29401   2 rooms, 2 pb
(803)-577-2633
                        C-yes/S-yes/P-no
All year

Charleston single house built in 1775 with Victorian addition, located in the center of the historic district.

Holland's Guest House
15 New St., 29401
(803)-723-0090
(803)-722-6606 RS
All year

$50 B&B
1 room, 1 pb

C-no/S-yes/P-no

Private kitchen -
breakfast food provided

Renovated kitchenhouse of 100-year-old home in historic district; private entrance; private phone, TV.

Jasmine House
64 Hasell St., 29401
(803)-577-5900
(800)-845-763? RS
All year

$100
5 rooms, 5 pb
Visa, MC, AmEx
C-yes/S-yes/P-sm

Hunt breakfast

Jacuzzi in suite

A pre-Civil War (c. 1843) mansion. Beautiful authentic 19th-Century antiques. Located in Historic Charleston—easy walking distance to everything.

Sweet Grass Inn
23 Vendue Range, 29401
(803)-723-9980

All year

$55-78
8 rooms, 8 pb

C-ok/S-yes/P-no/H-yes

Full breakfast
Afternoon tea
sitting room
bicycles
roof terrace

Located in Old Historic Charleston. Distinctively furnished rooms, morning newspaper, fresh fruit, flowers with complimentary breakfast.

Sword Gate Inn
111 Tradd St., 29401
(803)-723-8518

All year

$50-78 B&B
6 rooms, 6 pb

C-6 up/S-yes/P-no/H-yes

Full breakfast
Complimentary wine
sitting room, piano
bicycles

Located in 18th-Century home in the center of the Historic District. Charleston's oldest inn. Continental breakfast, eggs, meat, pastries.

Two Meeting Street Inn
2 Meeting St., 29401
(803)-723-7322

All year

$50-85 B&B
7 rooms, 5 pb

C-older/S-yes/P-no

Continental breakfast
Complimentary sherry
bicycles

This Queen Anne mansion has welcomed guests since 1931. Given as a wedding gift in 1890, it features two "Honeymoon Suites". (Formerly Mrs. Carr's Guest House).

Vendue Inn
19 Vendue Range, 29401
(803)-577-7970
(800)-845-7900 RS
All year

$63-82 B&B
18 rooms, 18 pb
credit cards accepted
C-yes/S-yes/P-no/H-yes

Continental plus
Wine & cheese hour
sitting room, piano
chamber music
bicycles

Vendue Inn has oriental carpets, old Charleston wall coverings, chamber music during wine and cheese hours.

SOUTH DAKOTA

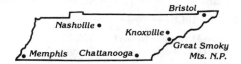

CANOVA ───────────────────────────────────

Skoglund Farm
57321
(605)-241-3445

$20 pp B&B
6 rooms, 0 pb

C-yes/S-ltd/P-yes

Full breakfast
Dinner
sitting room, piano
bicycles

All year

Return to your childhood, get away from it all at our farm—animals, horse riding, country walking—home-cooked delicious meals.

WEBSTER ───────────────────────────────────

Lakeside Farm
RR 2, Box 52, 57274
(605)-486-4430

$10 pp B&B
2 rooms, 0 pb

C-yes/S-no/P-no

Full breakfast
Other meals possible
sitting room, piano
bicycles

All year

A family-owned/operated Dairy Farm. Northeastern South Dakota lakes area. Fresh air. Open spaces. Fresh milk. Homemade cinnamon rolls.

TENNESSEE

CHATTANOOGA ───────────────────────────────────

Lookout Mts. Guest House $27 B&B
4415 Guild Tr.
(615)-821-8307

4 rooms, 0 pb

C-yes/S-yes/P-ltd/H-yes

Full breakfast
Dinner, bar
sitting room, piano

All year

GATLINBURG

LeConte Lodge	$30 pp B&B	Full breakfast
P.O. Box 350, 37738	16 rooms, 0 pb	Dinner
(615)-436-4473		sitting room
	C-yes/S-yes/P-no	
April—October		

On Mt. LeConte at 6,593' elevation. Spectacular views—breathtaking sunrises & sunsets. Forest trails. Atmosphere of friendliness and quiet simplicity.

Windhover	$49.50-58.30	No meals
Campbell Rd., 33738	5 rooms, 5 pb	
(615)-436-4068		swimming pool
	C-yes/S-yes/P-no	
All year		

Secluded, private condo cabins, each with woodburning fireplace, screened porch kitchen, color TV, unsurpassed view of mountains and village. Swimming pool.

MURFREESBORO

Clardy's Guest House	$12.50-17.50 B&B	Continental breakfast
435 E. Main St., 37130	9 rooms, 5 pb	
(615)-893-6030		sitting room
	C-yes/S-yes/P-yes	
All year		

Built in 1898 during opulent and decorative times, the house is completely furnished with beautiful antiques. Murfreesboro is the South's Antique Center.

ROGERSVILLE

Hale Springs Inn	$35-55 B&B	Continental breakfast
110 W. Main, 37857	10 rooms, 10 pb	Restaurant
(615)-272-5171	Visa, MC, AmEx	sitting room
	C-yes/S-yes/P-ok	
All year		

Restored 1824 Brick. Fronts Village Green with other Antebellum buildings. Antiques, poster beds, working fireplaces, plush large rooms—near Gatlinburg.

SEVIERVILLE

Kero Mountain Resort	$30-37	No meals served -
Rte. 11, Box 380, 37862	3 rooms, 3 pb	each cabin has kitchen
		Lake swimming
	C-yes/S-yes/P-yes	
All year		

Mountain fishing resort featuring privacy, views, fishing & swimming. 5 miles to restaurant and entertainment.

SHILOH

Leawood-Williams Estate	$40 up B&B	Full country breakfast
P.O. Box 24, 38376	18 rooms, 18 pb	Lunch, dinner
(901)-689-5106	AmEx, BA	swimming pool
	C-yes/S-yes/P-no	bicycles
All year		private sitting rooms

Huge English Tudor style estate with lovely natural woods, open to private guests and small meetings. Near Civil War Battleground.

TEXAS

BIG SANDY

Annie's B&B
106 N. Tyler, 75755
(214)-636-4307

All year

$45-100 B&B
13 rooms, 8 pb
Visa, MC
C-yes/S-no/P-no/H-yes

Complimentary breakfast
lunch, dinner
piano
sitting room
library

Restored Victorian home with antiques and inported rugs; handmade quilts. Some rooms feature balconies overlooking beautiful flower and water gardens.

CASTROVILLE

Landmark Inn
P.O. Box 577, 78009
(512)-538-2133

All year

$13-16
8 rooms, 4 pb

C-yes/S-ltd/P-no/H-ltd

No meals

lobby

Seven historic structures on five acres bordering the Medina River; includes grist mill, bathhouse, residences, main building, exhibit area, lobby.

DALLAS

Victor House
5123 Victor, 75215
(214)-821-9803

All year

$30-35 B&B
2 rooms, 2 pb

C-older/S-no/P-no

Continental breakfast

Unique Texas prairie-style home located in historic Munger Place in East Dallas Convenient to public transportation and downtown.

FAYETTEVILLE

Country Place Hotel
On the Square, 78940
(409)-378-2839

All year

$26.25-$31.50
8 rooms, 0 pb

S-no

Continental breakfast
Dinner (wknd)
sitting room

The Country Place Hotel is a 19th-Century small town inn. Explore Fayetteville and then relax on the second floor verandah or the back patio.

FORT DAVIS

Sutler's Limpia Hotel
P.O. Box 822, 79734

B&B
19 rooms, 19 pb

C-yes/S-yes/P-no/H-ltd

Full breakfast
Lunch, dinner, bar
sitting room
piano, entertainment

All year

GALVESTON

Victorian Inn
511 17th St., 77550
(409)-762-3235

$60-75 B&B
4 rooms, 0 pb
Visa, MC, AmEx
C-no/S-yes/P-no

Continental plus
Snack bar

All year

Victorian Mansion furnished in period antiques; spacious rooms provide comfort in a nostalgic environment. Generous continental breakfast.

JEFFERSON

Pride House
409 Broadway, 75657
(214)-665-2657

$37-56 B&B
6 rooms, 6 pb
Visa, MC
C-ltd/S-yes/P-ltd

Continental plus

sitting room

All year

An opportunity to experience the charm of the Victorian era and the traditional legendary hospitality of the deep South.

NEW BRAUNFELS

Prince Solms Inn
295 E. San Antonio, 78130

26 rooms, 26 pb

C-yes/S-yes/P-yes

Full breakfast
Lunch, dinner, bar
entertainment

Late 18th century converted to motel 1806, furnished with reproduction antique furnishings—turn of century; completely renovated and restored.

RIO GRANDE

La Borde House
601 E. Main St., 78582
(512)-487-5101

$40-55
21 rooms, 21 pb
Visa, MC, AmEx
C-yes/S-yes/P-no/H-yes

Full breakfast
Lunch, dinner, bar
sitting room
entertainment

All year

A faithful restoration dedicated to the proud past of all South Texas.

SAN ANTONIO

Cardinal Cliff
3806 Highcliff, 78218
(512)-655-2939

$18-25 B&B
3 rooms, 0 pb

C-yes/S-yes/P-no

Full breakfast

All year

Comfortable home on quiet street overlooking wooded river valley; easy access to airport and downtown attractions; we enjoy our guests!

Please mention this guide when you make your booking

VILLAGE MILLS

Big Thicket Guest House $40 B&B   Full breakfast
Box 91, 77663   2 rooms, 0 pb   Other meals, bar
(409)-834-2875   hot tub, bicycles
                           C-yes/S-yes/P-ltd   tennis courts
All year   sitting room

Country B&B—golf, tennis, bike riding and swimming—100 miles NE Houston. Big Thicket area. House furnished with county antiques.

La Borde House, Rio Grande City, Texas

WEIMAR

Weimar Country Inn
P.O. Box 782, 78962
(409)-725-8888

All year

$30-70
9 rooms, 7 pb
Visa, MC, AmEx
C-yes/S-yes/P-no

Full breakfast
Lunch, dinner, bar
upstairs lobby

A superbly furnished inn—antiques, wallpaper, ceiling fans and handmade quilts. Personalized service and good country cooking.

UTAH

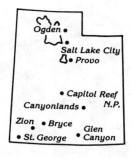

CEDAR CITY

Meadeau View Lodge
P.O. Box 356, 84720
(801)-648-2495

All year

$35-50 B&B
9 rooms, 9 pb

C-yes/S-yes/P-no

Full breakfast
Dinner (reservation)
sitting room

On scenic Hwy. 14 in Bryce, Zion, Cedar Breaks Triangle. Fantastic scenery, hiking, fishing, boating, X-C skiing, snowmobiling, pine/aspen forest.

LOGAN

Center Street B&B Inn
169 E. Center St., 84321
(801)-752-3443

All year

$15-60 B&B
3 rooms, 2 pb
none
C-yes/S-no/P-no

Complimentary breakfast
other meals served
games, piano
sitting room, library
Spanish spoken

1890 Victorian mansion with large ornate rooms. Bedrooms upstairs. Honeymoon/anniversary/anytime suite (3rd floor), hot tub, movies, games, king-sized bed.

MONROE

Mary Anne Peterson
PO Box 142
(801)-527-4830

All year

$35 pp
2 rooms, 1 pb
none
C-yes/S-ltd/P-no

Full breakfast
dinner
fresh homemade cookies
tennis nearby
pool nearby, bicycles

Monroe Hot Springs (olympic-sized pool), city park, mountains, golf, fishing and hunting just minutes away.

PARK CITY

Old Miner's Inn
615 Woodside Ave.

$60-120 B&B
6 rooms, 3 pb
major
C-yes/S-ltd/P-no

Complimentary breakfast
dinner by reservation
piano
sitting room, library

All year

French & Spanish spoken

An original miner's lodge—antique filled rooms, feather beds, full breakfast, complimentary cocktails and fine hospitality; an unforgettable experience!

PROVO

Sundance
PO Box 837, 84601

$85-500
14 rooms, 14 pb
C-yes/S-ltd/P-no

All year

Fourteen private cabins.

ST. GEORGE

Seven Wives Inn
217 N. 100 West, 84770
(801)-628-3737

$25-50 B&B
14 rooms, 14 pb
VISA, MC
C-yes/S-no/P-yes

Complimentary breakfast
Complimentary fruit
bicycles
sitting room, organ

All year

library, golf

One hundred and eleven-year-old pioneer home decorated throughout with antiques— quiet atmosphere—walking distance to town.

SALT LAKE CITY

Brigham Street Inn
1135 E. South Temple St.
(801)-364-4461

$60-125 B&B
9 rooms, 9 pb
AmEx, Visa, MC
C-yes/S-yes/P-no

Complimentary breakfast
comp. tea, bar set-ups
entertainment, piano
jacuzzi in 1 suite

All year

sitting room, library

National Historic Site, served as a designers' showcase in May 1982. Winner of several architectural awards. Seven major ski areas nearby.

Eller Bed & Breakfast
164 S. 900 E., 84012
(801)-533-8184

$20-35 B&B
5 rooms, 0 pb

C-yes/S-no/P-no

full breakfast

sitting room, piano
sauna

All year

1903 Victorian home redecorated and furnished with many antiques and family heirlooms. A delicious breakfast served family style.

We want this guide to be as complete as possible, so if you know of an inn (30 rooms or less), bed & breakfast or guesthouse we don't list, please send us their name on the form in the back of the book.

VERMONT

ARLINGTON

Hill's Farm Inn
05250
(802)-375-2269

$20-28 pp B&B
7 rooms, 2 pb
Visa, MC
C-yes/S-ltd/P-ltd

Full breakfast
Dinner, wine & beer
sitting room, piano

All year

An 1830 farmhouse; an inn since 1905; pleasant mountain views, hearty home cooking, fish the Battenkill, hike country roads.

West Mountain Inn
Off Rte. 313, 05250
(802)-375-6516

$36-50 EP
12 rooms, 7 pb
Visa, MC, AmEx
C-yes/S-ltd/P-no

Full breakfast
Dinner, bar
sitting room, piano

All year

Hillside estate with 150 acres to explore; fish the Battenkill, hike or X-C ski woodland trails; hearthside dining, charming rooms. Relax, enjoy.

BENNINGTON

Colonial Guest House
Rte. 7 North, 05201
(802)-442-2263

$15-18 EP
5 rooms, 0 pb

C-yes/S-yes/P-no

Full breakfast

sitting room

All year

A beautiful 100-year-old restored Colonial home, tastefully furnished, is yours to enjoy. Delicious family-style dining available.

BETHEL

Greenhurst Inn
05032
(802)-234-9474

$35-55
9 rooms, 2 pb
Visa, MC
C-yes/S-yes/P-yes

Continental plus
Dinner (res.), wine
sitting room, piano
tennis court

All year

National Register of Historic Places. 1891 Victorian elegance in a country setting on the White River. Near ski areas, fishing.

BOLTON VALLEY

Black Bear Lodge
05672
(802)-432-2126

$49-69 EP
20 rooms, 20 pb
Visa, MC
C-yes/S-yes/P-no

Full breakfast
Dinner, bar
swimming pool
entertainment
sitting room, piano

May-Oct., Dec.-April

Uniquely confortable mountaintop hideaway at the Bolton Valley Resort midst 6000 private acres of Vermont's beautiful green mountains.

BRADFORD

Merry Meadow Farm
Lower Plain, Rt 5, 05033
(802)-222-4412

$50 dbl B&B
4 rooms, 0 pb

C-yes/S-yes/P-yes

Full breakfast
Afternoon tea
swimming pool, bicycles
Sitting room, piano
Riding stable

September—June

Family-owned farm & stable with 60 horses. Excellent facility for entertaining & relaxing vacation. 20 min. to Dartmouth College. Canoeing on Connecticut Rvr.

BRANDON

Churchill House Inn
Rte. 73 East
(802)-247-3300

$48-60 pp MAP
9 rooms, 5 pb
Visa, MC
C-yes/S-ltd/P-no

Full breakfast
Dinner
swimming pool
bicycles
sitting room, piano

May-Oct., Dec.-March

Century-old farmhouse on the edge of the Green Mountain National Forest. Delicious home cooking, hiking, skiing, biking, inn to inn adventures.

BRIDGEWATER CORNERS

October Country Inn
Rte. 4, 05035
(802)-672-3412

$33-39 MAP
9 rooms, 0 pb

C-yes/S-yes/P-no

Full breakfast
Dinner (inc.), wine
sitting room, piano

All year

19th-Century Vermont farmhouse. Meals include garden vegetables, freshly baked breads, desserts. Fireplace, antique wood stove, comfortable rooms, grand piano.

BROOKFIELD

Green Trails Country Inn
05036

$42-48 B&B
15 rooms, 9 pb

C-yes/S-yes/P-no

Full breakfast
Dinner, tea
sitting room

All year

Located near the floating bridge.

BROWNSVILLE

Inn at Mt. Ascutney
Brook Rd., 05037
(802)-484-7725

$40-50 dbl
9 rooms, 5 pb
Visa, MC
C-yes/S-yes/P-dogs

Continental plus
Dinner, bar
sitting room, piano
swimming pond

Except April, November

High on a hilltop with magnificent views—yet close by to Historic Windsor, Woodstock & Hanover. Hiking, skiing, and just relaxing.

CHELSEA

Shire Inn
Main St., POB 222, 05038
(802)-685-3031

All year

$40-64 B&B	Full breakfast
6 rooms, 4 pb	Dinner (res), box lunch
Visa, MC	bicycles
C-10 up/S-yes/P-no	sitting room

1832 brick Federal country inn listed on National Historic Register with gracious fireplaced-bedrooms and period furnishings, on 17 private acres.

CHESTER

Hugging Bear Inn
Main St., 05143
(802)-875-2412

$30-60 B&B	Full breakfast
6 rooms, 6 pb	
Visa, MC	
C-yes/S-ltd/P-no	

A teddy bear in every bed. Located in a classic Victorian on the Village Green. Teddy Bear Shop on premises and guests get a discount.

Stone Hearth Inn
Rte. 11, 05143
(802)-875-2525

All year

$22-28 pp B&B	Full breakfast
8 rooms, 3 pb	Sandwich menu, bar
	sitting room
C-yes/S-ltd/P-no	game room
	pianos

Lovingly restored country inn built in 1810—beams, fireplaces, wide pine floors. Attached barn has game room, cozy pub. Family atmosphere.

CHITTENDEN

Tulip Tree Inn
Dam Rd., 05737
(802)-483-6213

Closed April, November

$45-52 MAP	Full breakfast
10 rooms, 2 pb	Dinner (inc.), bar
	sitting room, library
C-yes/S-yes/P-no	swimming pool, hot tub
	piano

Small, antique-filled country inn, hidden away in the Green Mountains. Gracious dining, homemade breads and desserts, liquor license, wine list.

CRAFTSBURY

Craftsbury Inn
05826
(802)-586-2848

All year

$45-65 dbl B&B	Full breakfast
10 rooms, 3 pb	Dinner, bar
Visa, MC	sitting room, piano
C-9 up/S-yes/P-no/H-ltd	lake swimming

Authentic Vermont Inn located in a quiet & picturesque hill town. Renowned dining, X-country skiing. Redecorated rooms with quilts.

CRAFTSBURY COMMON

Inn on the Common
05827
(802)-586-9619

All year

$70-140 B&B	Full breakfast
17 rooms, 13 pb	Dinner, bar
Visa, MC	swimming pool, sauna
C-older/S-yes/P-arr	tennis courts
	library, sitting rooms

Superbly decorated, meticulously appointed, wonderful cuisine, complete recreation facilities—for the inn connoiseur, everything you could want.

CUTTINGSVILLE

Maple Crest Farm
Box 120, 05738
(802)-492-3367

$15-30
6 rooms, 2 pb

C-yes/S-yes/P-no/H-ltd

Full breakfast
Afternoon tea
sitting room, piano
hiking, X-C skiing

All year

Dairy farm located in beautiful mountain town of Shrewsbury. Lovingly preserved for 5 generations of Vermont tradition. Original furnishings Rutland area.

Shrewsbury Inn
Rte. 103, 05738
(802)-492-3355

$23-30 pp B&B
7 rooms, 0 pb
Visa, MC
C-3 up/S-ltd/P-no

Full breakfast
Dinner, bar
sitting room

Closed May, November

Unusually esthetic ambiance; good food and drink; "An innkeeper's inn" says the Guide to Recommended Country Inns of New England.

DORSET

Barrows House
05251
(802)-867-4455

$110-138 dbl MAP
29 rooms, 27 pb

C-yes/S-yes/P-no/H-ltd

Full breakfast
Lunch, dinner, bar
swimming pool, sauna
tennis courts, bicycles
sitting room, piano

Except November

8 buildings on 6 parklike acres in picturesque Dorset. Close to golf, fishing, hiking, horseback riding, shopping, X-C ski shop.

Little Lodge at Dorset
Rte 30 Box 673, 05251
(802)-867-4040
(802)-362-3378 RS
All year

$39-55 dbl B&B
5 rooms, 3 pb

C-yes/S-yes/P-/H-yes

Continental plus
Afternoon tea
sitting room

Delightful old house on hillside near picturesque village. Lovely antiques, inviting barn-board den, guests' refrigerator, friendly atmosphere.

Maplewoods Guest House $25-35
Box 1019, Rt. 1, 05251
(802)-867-4470

5 rooms, pb

C-yes/S-ltd/P-ok

Full breakfast
Afternoon tea
hot tub, swimming pond
sitting room, piano

All year

Home is over 200 years old with 20 rooms, double living room with fireplace. Maintained trails through woods close by.

DUXBURY

Schneider Haus
Rte. 100
(802)-244-7726

$14-23 pp
10 rooms, 0 pb
Visa, MC
C-3 up/S-yes/P-no

Full breakfast
Dinner (winter)
hot tub, sauna
tennis courts
sitting room

6/1-10/15, 12/15-4/10

Built entirely by the innkeepers, its warmth is felt by everyone. Lots of balcony, quilts and friends.

EAST BARNET ───────────────────────────────────

Inwood Manor $23-35 B&B   Continental breakfast
Rte. 5, 05821   9 rooms, 0 pb   Dinner, wine & beer
(802)-633-4047   sitting room, piano
                          C-yes/S-ok/P-no   library
All year

*Tastefully restored country inn, period antiques in all rooms. Small, intimate and personal.
20 private acres with waterfalls.*

EAST MIDDLEBURY ───────────────────────────────

Waybury Inn $30-70 B&B   Full breakfast
Rte. 125, 05740   12 rooms, 8 pb   Lunch, dinner, pub
(802)-388-4015   Visa, MC   sitting room, piano
                          C-yes/S-yes/P-ltd   river swimming
All year

National Historic Building, 1810 stagecoach inn. A quiet atmosphere away from the city. Homemade breads and desserts. Fishing guides available.

FAIRHAVEN ─────────────────────────────────────

Victorian Marble Inn $50-80   Full breakfast
12 W. Park Place, 05743   12 rooms, 2 pb   Dinner, tea, wine, bar
(802)-265-4736   sitting room, piano
                          C-yes/S-yes/P-yes
All year

Walk back in time with us to a world of charm and elegance enhanced by a three story marble mansion.

FAIRLEE ───────────────────────────────────────

Aloha Manor   Full breakfast
Lake Morey, 05045   15 rooms, 16 pb   Afternoon tea
(802)-333-4478   sitting room, piano
                          C-yes/S-yes   tennis court
All year   lake swimming

C. 1785 farmhouse/inn (+ cabins June-Oct.) Swimming, canoeing, tennis, orchard, Sugarbush, antiques, near Dartmouth College.

GASSETTS ──────────────────────────────────────

Olde Town Farm Lodge $45-50 B&B   Full breakfast
Rte. 10, 05143   10 rooms, 2 pb   Dinner
(802)-875-2346   Visa, MC, AmEx   swimming pond
                          C-yes/S-yes/P-no   bicycles
All year   sitting room, piano

The handmade spiral staircase that curves to the second floor is beautiful, and it has been painstakingly restored to its original condition.

**Be sure to call the Inn to verify details and prices
and to make your reservation**

GOSHEN

Blueberry Hill
RFD 3, 05733
(802)-247-6735
(802)-247-6535
Closed April/May/Nov.

$56 pp MAP
9 rooms, 9 pb
credit cards accepted
C-yes/S-ltd/P-no/H-yes

Full breakfast
Dinner, tea, wine
sitting room
swimming pond

1800 charming inn, gourmet cooking, dining by candlelight. Relax in an atmosphere of elegance & leisure. Fishing, swimming, outdoor activities.

GRAFTON

Woodchuck Hill Farm
Middletown Road, 05146
(802)-843-2398

May—October

$40-80 B&B
8 rooms, 4 pb

C-8 up/S-yes/P-no

Continental plus
Dinner by reservation
sitting room
swimming pond

Colonial townhouse restored & furnished with antiques. Big open porch, fireplace in lounge area, antique shop in barn.

JAMAICA

Three Mountain Inn
R.R. 1, 05343
(802)-874-4140

Closed 4/15-5/15 and Nov

$45-60 pp MAP
8 rooms, 6 pb

C-yes/S-yes/P-no

Full breakfast
Dinner, bar
sitting room
bicycles
swimming pool

Small romantic 1780 Colonial Inn. Charming rooms and fine food, near skiing, hiking and fishing. Mid-week specials available.

JAY

Jay Village Inn
Rte 242, 05859
(802)-988-2643

All year

$32-42
14 rooms, 6 pb
Visa, MC, AmEx, DC, CB
C-yes/S-yes/P-no

Full breakfast
Dinner, bar
swimming pool
sitting room
player piano

Romantic Old World charm. Fine cuisine & wines in "Gallerie d'Art" dining room. Fireplace, bar, lounge; near shops & skiing.

KILLINGTON

Mountain Meadows Lodge
Sherbourne, 05751
(802)-775-1010

Except May

$28-38 pp MAP
18 rooms, 15 pb
Visa, MC
C-yes/S-yes/P-ltd

Full breakfast
Dinner
swimming pool
sitting room

A casual, friendly family lodge in a beautiful secluded mountain/lake setting. Complete cross-country ski center. Converted 1856 farmhouse and barn.

Vermont Inn
Rte. 41, 05751
(802)-773-9874

11/20-4/15, 6/1-10/30

$28-90
14 rooms, 8 pb
Visa, MC, AmEx
C-yes/S-ok/P-no/H-ltd

Continental plus
MAP (winter), bar
swimming pool, sauna
tennis courts, piano
sitting room, library

Fine dining, spectacular mountain views, secluded romantic stream. Minutes to Killington and Pico ski areas.

LANDGROVE

The Nordic Inn
Rt. 11, P.O. Box 96, 05148
(802)-824-6444

$32.00-69.50
3 rooms, 3 pb
Visa, MC, AmEx
C-yes/S-yes/P-no/H-yes

Full breakfast (winter)
Other meals, bar
piano
ski touring center

Summer-fall-winter

Charming inn serving continental food with a Scandinavian flair. Cross-country skiing right at the Inn (12 miles of trails.)

LONDONDERRY

Highland House
Rte 100, 05148
(802)-824-3019

$28-44 B&B
7 rooms, 0 pb
Visa, MC
C-yes/S-yes/P-no

Full country breakfast
Dinner, beer & wine
swimming pool
sitting room, fireplace

Except mid-April to
mid-May

Small country inn—fine dining, beautifully set on 26 acres of land. Hiking, horseback riding, tennis, golf, olympic size pool, alpine ski areas.

Village Inn
RFD Landgrove, 05148
(802)-824-6673

$30-55 dbl B&B
20 rooms, 14 pb
Visa, MC, AmEx
C-Yes!/S-yes/P-no

Full breakfast
Lunch, dinner, bar
hot tub, swimming pool
tennis courts
sitting room, piano

6/20-10/20, 12/20-3/31

Families welcome. A true country resort inn. Building dates 1840.

LOWER WATERFORD

Rabbit Hill Inn
05848
(802)-748-5168

$25-60
20 rooms, 20 pb
Visa, MC
C-yes/S-yes/P-yes

Full breakfast
Dinner, bar
sitting room, piano

Except April, November

An early 19th-Century Vermont inn, overlooking New Hampshire's White Mountains. X-C, nature trails. Canoeing. Swimming. Fishing.

LUDLOW

Combes Family Inn
RFD 1, 05149
(802)-228-8799

$36 dbl B&B
10 rooms, 6 pb
Visa, MC, AmEx
C-yes/S-yes/P-yes/H-yes

Full breakfast
Dinner
sitting room, piano
bicycles

Except 4/15-5/15

The Combes Family Inn is a century-old farmhouse located on a quiet country back road.

Governor's Inn
86 Main St., 05149
(802)-228-8830

$80 dbl B&B
8 rooms, 6 pb
Visa, MC, AmEx
C-no/S-/P-no

Full breakfast
Gourmet dinner, bar
sitting room
library

All year

A stylish, romantic, Victorian inn (c.1890). Furnished with family antiques. Beautiful fireplaces. Warm, generous hospitality in a quiet Vermont town.

Okemo Inn
Rte. 103, Box 4, 05149
(802)-228-8834

All year

$36
12 rooms, 10 pb
Visa, MC, AmEx, DC
C-yes/S-yes/P-no

Full breakfast
Dinner (res.), bar
swimming pool, sauna
sitting room, piano

Fine food and lodging—lovely 1810 country Inn where antiques set the mood. Convenient to all-season sports and activities.

Red Door
7 Pleasant St., 05149
(802)-228-2376

Labor Day—Ski Season

3 rooms, 0 pb

C-yes/S-yes/P-yes

Kitchen facilities

sitting room

Quaint 150-year-old house with real charm. 1 mile to Okems Mt. ski area & 1 block from Main St. with top quality restaurants.

MANCHESTER

Birch Hill Inn
Box 346, 05254
(802)-362-2761

5/20-10/28, 12/26-4/10

$28-44 pp B&B
6 rooms, 4 pb

C-6 up/S-ok/P-no

Full breakfast
Dinner, tea, wine
swimming pool
sitting room, piano

Small country inn, 15 km of private X-C trails thru woods; panoramic views; country cuisine; swimming pool; large fireplace.

1811 House
Box 207, 05254
(802)-362-1811

All year

$60-100 B&B
12 rooms, 12 pb
Visa, MC, AmEx
C-no/S-yes/P-no

Full breakfast
Bar
tennis courts
sitting room, library

Revolutionary building furnished with English & American antiques. Walk to golf, tennis, swimming. Near sailing, hiking, skiing. Unequalled charm.

Inn at Manchester
Rte. 7, 05254
(802)-362-1793

Dec.—Mar., May—Oct.

$40-55 B&B
15 rooms, 7 pb
AmEx
C-5 up/S-ltd/P-no

Full breakfast
Dinner (winter), wine
swimming pool
piano
3 lounge areas

Beautiful Victorian mansion restored by owners. Furnished with antiques. Delicious food served & made by chef/owner. Near everything. Skiing.

Reluctant Panther
05254
(802)-362-2568

Except May, November

$45-85
11 rooms, 11 pb
Visa, MC, AmEx
C-no/S-ltd/P-no

Full breakfast
Dinner, bar
sitting room

Enhance your romance with select lodging and elegant dining. Just eleven unusually decorated rooms—for adults. Six have working fireplaces.

Knoll Farm Inn, Waitsfield, Vermont

MARLBORO

Longwood Inn
Rte. 9, POB 86
(802)-257-1545

All year

$66-104 dbl B&B
13 rooms, 11 pb
Visa, MC
C-16 up/S-yes/P-no/H-yes

Full country breakfast
Lunch (seas.)/dinner/bar
swimming pool
bicycles, entertainment
sitting room

An inn for all seasons—tradition and charm for a unique lodging and dining experience in the heart of southern Vermont.

MENDON

Red Clover Inn
Woodward Rd., 05701
(802)-775-2290

6/1-10/16, 11/25-4/30

$22.50-$30.00 pp
14 rooms, 9 pb
Visa, MC, AmEx, DC, CB
C-yes/S-yes/P-no/H-yes

Full breakfast
Dinner, bar
swimming pool
sitting room, piano

Beautiful country inn nestled in a hidden mountain valley. Wonderful breakfasts and dinners served in warm, friendly, gracious atmosphere. Chef-owned.

MIDDLETOWN SPRINGS

Middletown Springs Inn
On-the-Green, 05757
(802)-235-2198

All year

$50-60 B&B
7 rooms, 1 pb
Visa, MC
C-yes/S-yes/P-no

Full breakfast
Complimentary wine, tea
sitting room, piano

Elegant-hundred-year old Victorian on Village Green. Antique dolls—heirlooms- unforgetable, restful retreat into the magical past!

MONTGOMERY VILLAGE

Black Lantern Inn	$35 EP	Full breakfast
05470	11 rooms, 9 pb	Dinner, bar
(802)-326-4507	Visa, MC, AmEx	sitting room, piano
	C-yes/S-yes/P-no	

All year

Winter: Cross-country skiing from door; 15 minutes from Jay Peak Ski Area. Summer: Swimming in natural waterfalls, near long trail, country auctions.

MONTPELIER

Lackey's Tourist Home		No food service
152 State St., 05602	9 rooms, 0 pb	
(802)-223-7292		sitting room
	C-yes/S-yes/P-no	

All year

1890 Victorian home, 1-4 guests. Antique shop in house. Short walk to capitol building, Vermont Historical Museum & numerous restaurants.

NEWFANE

Four Columns Inn	$50-75	Full breakfast
05345	13 rooms, 11 pb	Dinner, bar
(802)-365-7713	Visa, MC	swimming pool
	C-8 up/S-yes/P-arr	sitting room, piano

All year

Stately 1830's home converted to inn 1969. Furnished with beautiful antiques. Skiing, summer ativities. Fine French Nouvelle cuisine a specialty.

Old Newfane Inn	$65-85 B&B	Continental breakfast
Court St., 05345	10 rooms, 8 pb	Lunch, dinner, bar
(802)-365-4427		sitting room
	C-no/S-yes/P-no	

June-Oct., Jan.-March

1787 Colonial Inn, lovely rooms, exposed beams in dining room, brick fireplaces & classic French Suisse cuisine.

NORTH HERO

Charlie's Northland Lodge	$16-24 pp	Continental plus
Rte. 2, 05474	4 rooms, 0 pb	
(802)-372-8822		tennis courts
	C-yes/S-no/P-no/H-yes	sitting room

All year

Country Inn, North Hero village on Lake Champlain. A place to go to fish—even fall or winter. Separate guest houses available. Boating, hiking, swimming.

North Hero House	$30-65 EP	Full breakfast
Champlain Is., 05474	23 rooms, 22 pb	Lunch, dinner
(802)-372-8237		lounge, sitting room
	C-yes/S-ltd/P-no	tennis courts, sauna
Mid-June—Labor Day		bicycles

Gracious, intimate, old-fashioned (1870) island country inn overlooking magnificent Lake Champlain—with additional lakeside accomodations.

NORTH THETFORD

Stone House Inn
Rte. 5, 05054
(802)-333-9124

All year

$35 dbl B&B
6 rooms, 0 pb
Visa, MC
C-yes/S-yes/P-no

Continental plus
Wine & beer
sitting room, piano

Peaceful village location. Arrive by canoe as part of our unique canoeing Inn to Inn program; or arrive by car or train!

NORWICH

Inn at Norwich
05055

All year

$40-59 EP
23 rooms, 21 pb
Visa, MC, AmEx
C-yes/S-yes/P-yes/H-yes

Full breakfast
Lunch, dinner, bar
sitting room, piano

In town, country inn—excellent food, extensive wine list. 1 mile from Dartmouth College. A home away from home.

PERU

Johnny Seesaw's
Rte. 11, 05152
(802)-824-5533
(802)-824-5522
Closed Apr., Nov.

$20-55 pp
31 rooms, 26 pb
Visa, MC
C-yes/S-yes

Full breakfast
Dinner (winter), bar
swimming pool
tennis courts
sitting room, piano

Unique country lodge, rooms with private baths, cottages with king beds & fireplaces, licensed pub, game room, ¼ mile E. of Bromley Mountain.

PLYMOUTH UNION

Salt Ash Inn
05056
(802)-672-3748

Summer, Fall, & Winter

$31-36 EP
12 rooms, 4 pb
Visa, MC
C-yes/S-yes/P-no

Full breakfast
Dinner (fall), bar
sitting room, piano

Genuine old country inn whose furnishings reflect its rich past as an inn, general store, stagecoach stop, and post office.

PROCTORSVILLE

Castle Inn
Box 157, 05153
(802)-226-7222

Except April/May/Nov.

$50-60 pp MAP
13 rooms, 9 pb
Visa, MC, AmEx
C-yes/S-yes/P-no/H-ltd

All meals included

hot tub, sauna
tennis courts
sitting room, piano

Former Governor's mansion c. 1904, old world charm. Candlelight dinners, library lounge, piano. Hot tub, sauna, and pool and 2 clay tennis courts.

Golden Stage Inn
Rte 103, 05153
(802)-226-7744

Except Nov., April

$45-58 B&B
10 rooms, 2 pb
Visa, MC, AmEx
C-yes/S-yes/P-no/H-yes

Full breakfast
Dinner, tea, wine & beer
sitting room
bicycles

A 200-year-old stagecoach stop. Near six ski areas, golf, tennis. Large airy rooms, excellent food.

Okemo Lantern Lodge
Box 247, 05153
(802)-226-7770

All year

$28-33 B&B
7 rooms, 1 pb
Visa, MC, AmEx
C-yes/S-yes/P-no/H-yes

Full breakfast
Dinner, wine
sitting room, organ
bicycles

Elegant Victorian village inn decorated with antiques; gourmet meals served. Owned and operated by native Vermont family.

QUECHEE

Quechee Inn
Box 120, 05059
(802)-295-3133

Except April, part Dec.

$60-125 B&B
22 rooms, 22 pb
Visa, MC, AmEx
C-yes/S-yes/P-no

Continental plus
Dinner (Wed-Sun), bar
sitting room
club member (sauna,
swimming, tennis)

Country Inn, beautifully appointed rooms, private baths, TV. Fine dining in country elegance. Cocktails. Private club privileges, golf, swimming, tennis.

RANDOLPH

Three Stallion Inn
Green Mt. farm, 05060
(802)-728-5575

All year

$34-45 pp MAP
10 rooms, 2 pb

C-yes/S-ltd/P-no

Full breakfast
Lunch, dinner, bar
sauna, tennis
sitting room, piano
entertainment (wknds)

Charming country inn on 1300 beautiful acres. 35 km of groomed X-C ski trails. Hiking, biking, tennis, fishing, swimming, golfing, food/spirits/entertainment.

RIPTON VILLAGE

Chipman Inn
Rte. 125, 05766
(802)-388-2390

closed April, November

$50 pp MAP
10 rooms, pb
Visa, MC
C-yes/S-yes/P-no

Full breakfast
Dinner, tea, bar
sitting room, piano

Built in 1828, nestled in National Forest. Hearty country fare, pub with huge fireplace, piano, furnished with antiques. Hiking & skiing.

ROYALTON

Fox Stand Inn
Rte. 14, 05068

All year

$18-20 B&B
7 rooms, 0 pb

C-yes/S-yes/P-no/H-yes

Full breakfast
Lunch, dinner
sitting room
river swimming

Restored 1818 handsome brick building. Family-owned and operated inn. Economical rates include full breakfast.

SAXTONS RIVER

Saxtons River Inn
Main St., 05154
(802)-869-2110

April—December

$27.50-55.00 B&B
20 rooms, 11 pb

C-yes/S-yes/P-no

Continental breakfast
Dinner, bar
sitting room

Turn-of-century village inn restored by innkeeper, family & friends. Handsome guest rooms, varied cuisine with emphasis on FRESH!

SOUTH LONDONDERRY

Londonderry Inn		Full buffet breakfast
Rte. 100, 05155	25 rooms, 20 pb	Lunch, dinner ,bar
(802)-824-5226		swimming pool
	C-yes/S-yes/P-no/H-yes	sitting room
All year		game room

SOUTH WALLINGFORD

Green Mt. Guest House	$10-18 EP	Full breakfast
Rte. 7, 05773	5 rooms, 0 pb	Luncheon, tea
(802)-446-2611		sitting room, piano
	C-yes/S-yes/P-yes	
All year		

Rural charm in an old stagecoach stop. Canoe, fish, swim!

SOUTH WOODSTOCK

Kedron Valley Inn	$28-75 EP	Full breakfast
Rte. 106, 05071	31 rooms, 31 pb	Lunch, dinner, bar
(802)-457-1473	Visa, MC, DC	sitting room, piano
	C-yes/S-yes/P-ok/H-yes	swimming pond
All year		

Distinguished Country Inn built in 1822, in a gentle valley. Full riding stables, X-C skiing, hiking, swimming. Three meals daily.

STOWE

Anderson's Lodge	$20-38	Full breakfast
Rte. 108, 05672	17 rooms, 16 pb	Dinner
(802)-253-7336	credit cards accepted	swimming pool
	C-yes/S-yes/P-yes	sitting room, piano
Ski season		

Edson Hill Manor	$45-69 B&B	Full breakfast
RFD 1, 05672	15 rooms, 9 pb	Dinner, lunch (winter)
(802)-253-7371	Visa, MC	swimming pool
	C-yes/S-yes/P-no	sitting room
12/1-4/15, 6/1-10/31		horseback riding

Country estate on 400 secluded acres. Cross-country skiing; gorgeous swimming pool, outdoor games, barbeques, horseback riding, hiking in summer.

Fiddlers Green Inn	$19-21	Full breakfast
Mountain Rd., 05672	7 rooms, 4 pb	Supper (winter)
(802)-253-8124	Visa, MC, AmEx	sitting room
	C-yes/S-yes/P-no	
All year		

House was built in 1820—operated as an Inn since 1941. Vermont trout brook 15 feet from back door. Summer dining on terrace by brook.

Please mention this guide when you make your booking

Logwood Inn & Chalets
Box 2290, Rte. 1, 05672
(802)-253-7354

All year

$18-46 pp B&B
15 rooms, 8 pb
Visa, MC, AmEx
C-yes/S-yes/P-ltd/H-yes

Full breakfast
Dinner (in season)
swimming pool
tennis court, game room
sitting room, piano

A warm welcome, tree-filled quiet oasis by mt. stream in scenic Stowe. Main lodge, apt., 2 chalets, home cooking w/ Pennsylvania Dutch accent.

Ski Inn
Mountain Rd., 05672
(802)-253-4050

All year

$20-30 MAP; $10-15 EP
10 rooms, 4 pb

C-yes/S-yes/P-no

Full breakfast
Supper (Winter-MAP)
sitting room
piano

Charming Country Inn noted for good food and good conversation. Close to ski area. In winter, MAP; all other seasons, EP.

Spruce Pond Inn
05672
(802)-253-4828

All year

$25-75 EP
30 rooms, 30 pb
credit cards accepted
C-yes/S-yes/P-yes/H-yes

Full breakfast
Lunch, dinner, bar
swimming pool
sitting room

Cross-country skiing on our own trails, fireside dining in our 1827 Inn and swimming in our own lake.

Ten Acres Lodge
Luce Hill Rd., 05672
(802)-253-7638
(802)-253-7321 RS
All year

$35-58 EP
12 rooms, 0 pb
Visa, MC, AmEx, DC
C-yes/S-yes/P-ltd

Full breakfast
Dinner, bar
swimming pool
tennis courts
sitting room

Stowe's favorite country inn and restaurant for over forty years. Close to ski trails, hiking, golf in New England ski capital.

TYSON

Echo Lake Inn
Rte 100, 05149
(802)-228-8602

Except late April

$38-48 EPl B&B
25 rooms, 4 pb
Visa, MC, AmEx
C-yes/S-yes/P-no

Full breakfast
Dinner, bar
swimming, tennis
hot tub, bicycles
sitting room, grnd piano

Well-appointed rooms and hearty New England fare. Swimming and boating, skiing and tennis, fishing.

WAITSFIELD

Knoll Farm Country Inn
Bragg Hill Rd., 05783
(802)-496-3939

Except Nov., April

$20-34 MAP
4 rooms, 0 pb

C-5 up/S-ltd/P-no

Full farm breakfast
Lunch, dinner, wine, tea
sitting room, library
player piano, pump organ
swimming pond

Horseback riding, spectacular views from mountain pastures, delicious farm-grown meals, music, lasting friendships have made this Inn special since 1957.

Millbrook Inn
RFD Bx 62, Rte 17, 05673
(802)-496-2405

Closed May

$23-40 B&B
6 rooms, 1 pb
Visa, MC
C-yes/S-yes/P-no

Full breakfast
Dinner, beer & wine
sitting rooms (2)
piano

Charming hand-stencilled guest rooms with handmade quilts, country gourmet dining in our small candlelit restaurant, friendly, unhurried atmosphere.

Mountain View Inn
Rte 17, RFD Bx 69, 05673
(802)-496-2426

All year

$20 pp B&B
7 rooms, 7 pb

C-yes/S-no/P-no

Full breakfast
Dinner
sitting room, piano

An old Vermont farmhouse lovingly decorated & furnished with heirloom antiques. Homecooked meals served family style around large pine harvest table.

Tucker Hill Lodge
RFD 1, Box 147, 05673
(802)-496-3983
(800)-451-4580
All year

$43-54 pp MAP
20 rooms, 14 pb
Visa, MC, AmEx
C-yes/S-yes/P-no/H-ltd

Full breakfast
Dinner (inc.), bar
swimming pool
tennis courts
sitting room, piano

Inn nestled on wooded hillside. Spectacular flower gardens. Antiques, hand- made quilts. Extraordinary changing menu; fine wines. Hiking, X-C skiing.

WALLINGFORD

Wallingford Inn
Box 404, 05773
(802)-446-2849

All year

$35-55 B&B
6 rooms, 6 pb
Visa, MC
C-10 up/S-yes/P-no

Full breakfast
Restaurant, bar
piano

An 1876 Victorian mansion with high ceilings, wood floors, marble fireplaces & period decor. Located in a quaint tree-lined Vermont town.

WEST DOVER

Inn at Sawmill Farm
Box 8, 05356
(802)-464-8131

All year

$130-180 dbl MAP
22 rooms, 22 pb

C-12 up/S-yes/P-no/H-yes

Full breakfast
Dinner, bar
swimming pool
piano

200-year-old barn, rough hewn beams, old bricks, antique-filled w/highlights of brass & copper. American/continental menu, 15,000 bottle wine cellar.

Snow Den Inn
05356
(802)-464-9355
(802)-464-3333 RS

$35-70 B&B
8 rooms, 8 pb
Visa, MC, AmEx
C-yes/S-yes/P-no

Full breakfast
Dinner (winter)
sitting room

Lovely country inn filled with antiques. Fireplaces in three rooms. Close to golfing, swimming, tennis, skiing, hiking, antiqueing, skating, boating.

Weathervane Lodge $21-28 Full breakfast
Rte. 100, 05356 10 rooms, 4 pb
(802)-464-5426 sitting room, piano
C-yes/S-yes/P-no
All year

Mountainous country inn: Colonial antiques, lounge, recreation rooms with fireplaces; ski, cross-country, tennis, golf, swimming. Bring children.

WEST TOWNSHEND

Windham Hill Inn $43-47 MAP Full breakfast
Off Rte 30, 05359 10 rooms, 8 pb Dinner, bar
Visa, MC 3 sitting rooms
C-yes/S-yes/P-no library
Except April & November

Carefully restored 1825 farmhouse offering warm, distinctive guest and public rooms... elegant dining... secluded hilltop setting with spectacular view.

WESTON

Darling Family Inn $34-48 Full breakfast
Rte. 100, 05161 5 rooms, 3 pb Dinner, bar
(802)-824-3223 Visa, MC swimming pool
C-older/S-yes/P-ltd sitting room
All year

Nestled in a farmland and mountain setting with American and English country antiques. Closest inn to the famous Weston Priory.

Inn at Weston $46-62 B&B Full breakfast
Rte. 100 Box 56 BI, 05161 13 rooms, 8 pb Dinner, bar
(802)-824-5804 sitting room, piano
C-yes/S-yes/P-no/H-yes gameroom
May—Oct, Dec—Apr.

1848 converted farmhouse. Creative country cuisine. Featured Gourmet Magazine. Stroll to Weston shops. Ten years making memories. "Where Friendships Begin."

WILMINGTON

Darcroft's Schoolhouse $15-40 Continental plus
05363 3 rooms, 0 pb
(802)-464-2631 sitting room
C-yes/S-yes/P-no
All year

In heart of Mt. snow area, an 1837 schoolhouse tastefully remodeled to accomodate guests and small groups.

Hermitage $120-140 dbl MAP Full breakfast
Cold Brook Rd., 05363 16 rooms, 16 pb Lunch, dinner, bar
(802)-464-3511 tennis courts, sauna
(802)-464-8501 RS C-yes/S-yes/P-no/H-yes sitting room, piano
All year entertainment

A true working country inn—excellent continental dining, extensive wine list. Cross-country skiing. Homemade maple syrup, jam, jellies, bread.

Nutmeg Inn
Rte. 9, 05363
(802)-464-3351

May-Oct., Jan.-mid-April

$45-60 B&B
9 rooms, 4 pb
AmEx
C-9 up/S-ltd/P-no

Full breakfast
Dinner (ski season)
sitting room, piano

"Charming and cozy" early American farmhouse with informal home-like atmosphere—spotless guest rooms—delicious country-style meals.

White House
Rte 9, 05363
(802)-464-2135

All year

$49-88 B&B
12 rooms, 8 pb
credit cards accepted
C-yes/S-yes/P-no

Full breakfast
Dinner (inc.), bar
whirlpool bath, sauna
swimming pool
sitting room, piano

Turn-of-the-century inn offers elegance in the country; fireplace rooms, full spa facilities, indoor-outdoor pool, award-winning continental cuisine.

WOODSTOCK

3 Church Street B&B
3 Church St., 05091
(802)-457-1925

May—March

$40-52 B&B
10 rooms, 5 pb
Visa, MC
C-yes/S-yes/P-yes

Full breakfast
Other meals arranged
swimming pool
tennis courts
3 sitting rooms, piano

In walking distance to village of Woodstock—boutiques and restaurants. Listed in National Historic Registry, has many lovely antiques. Magnificent library.

Village Inn of Woodstock
41 Pleasant St., 05091
(802)-457-1255

All year

$40-50 EP
9 rooms, 3 pb
Visa, MC
C-yes/S-yes/P-sm

Full breakfast
Dinner, brunch, bar

A Victorian mansion (c. 1899) featuring many original furnishings. Simple yet superb New England fare. Five minutes walk to lovely village & shops.

VIRGINIA

CHARLOTTESVILLE

English Inn
316 14th St., NW, 22903
(804)-295-7707

All year

$30-45 B&B
8 rooms, 2 pb

C-ok/S-no/P-dogs

Continental plus

sitting room

Best in town, located in civilized surroundings, fairly priced, good clientele, close to restaurants, shops, etc.

CHINCOTEAGUE

Channel Bass Inn
100 Church St., 23336
(804)-336-6148

except December

$75-100
10 rooms, 10 pb
Visa, MC, AmEx, DC
C-no/S-yes/P-no

Full breakfast
Dinner, bar
sitting room

Near Assateague seashore; elegant Colonial atmosphere; all oversize beds; superb continental & classical cuisine. Expensive.

Miss Molly's Inn
23336
(804)-336-6686
(202)-232-8718 RS
April 1—December 1

$55 B&B
7 rooms, 1 pb

C-12 up/S-yes/P-no

Continental plus
Afternoon tea
sitting room

A charming old Victorian steeped in island history, gourmet breakfasts, afternoon tea, antique furnishings and magnificent sunsets over the bay.

FREDERICKSBURG

Fredericksburg Inn
1707 Prs. Anne St.,22401
(703)-371-8300

All year

$25-40 B&B
26 rooms, 15 pb
credit cards accepted
C-yes/S-yes/P-yes/H-yes

Continental breakfast

sitting room, piano
entertainment

Civil War era antiques; continental breakfast; southern hospitality; near antique & craft shops, 5 major Battlefields. 50 miles to Washington.

FRONT ROYAL

Constant Spring Inn
413 S. Royal Ave., 22630
(703)-635-7010

All year

$27.50 up MAP
9 rooms, 9 pb
Visa, MC
C-yes/S-yes/P-no

Full breakfast menu
Dinner, tea, cider
sitting room
bicycles

3 blocks from Skyline Drive; park-like setting; heart of history land. 80 min. to Washington D.C. Country cooking.

HILLSBORO

Sweetwater Farm
P.O. Box 143, 22132
(301)-694-2044

June-August

$50/cpl B&B
3 rooms, pb

C-yes/S-no/P-no

Continental breakfast

Swimming pool, hot tub
sitting room, piano

Log cabin on 65 acres, circa 1752, in Blue Ridge Mtns. Near antiques, restaurants, & historic. Drive to D.C., 1 hr. 45 min.

HOT SPRINGS

Vine Cottage Inn
Hwy. 220, POB 205, 24445
(703)-839-2422

All year

B&B
16 rooms, 8 pb
credit cards accepted
C-yes/S-yes/P-yes

Continental plus

sitting room

Summer sportsman's paradise—mountain trails—huge new lake (boating, fishing & swimming), golf courses, horseback riding; winter skiing at Homestead.

King Carter Inn	$35-55 B&B	Continental plus
P.O. Box 425, 22408	11 rooms, 7 pb	Afternoon tea
(804)-438-6053		tennis courts
	C-yes/S-yes/P-no	sitting room
All year		

An historic, comfortable tidewater Inn, where Southern breakfast breads from the Inn's ovens and a traditional Virginia welcome await you.

Laurel Brigade Inn	$21.20-31.80 EP	No meals
20 W. Market St., 22075	6 rooms, 6 pb	
(703)-777-1010		
	C-yes/S-yes/P-yes	
mid-February—December		

Alexander-Withrow		
House	$40-62	Juice/coffee/tea in room
3 W. Washington, 24450	23 rooms, 23 pb	Sherry/port/tea evenings
(703)-463-2044	Visa, MC	sitting room
	C-yes/S-yes/P-no/H-yes	
All year		

Country inn listed on the National Register of Historic Buildings, located in the center of Civil War history (Lexington, Va.)

McCampbell Inn	$40-62	No food service
11 N. Main St., 24450	16 rooms, 16 pb	Complimentary wine
(703)-463-2044	Visa, MC	sitting room
	C-yes/S-yes/P-no/H-yes	
All year		

Decorated in genuine antiques—located in historic section of downtown Lexington within walking distance of Washington & Lee University and VMI.

Welbourne	$40-50 pp B&B	Full breakfast
Rte. 743, 22117	6 rooms, 6 pb	Complimentary wine
(703)-687-3201		sitting room, piano
	C-yes/S-yes/P-yes/H-ltd	
All year		

Ante-bellum home occupied by the same family for seven generations. In heart of Virginia's fox-hunting country. Virginia Historic Landmark.

Wayside Inn since 1797	$45-90 EP	Full breakfast
7783 Main St., 22645	21 rooms, 21 pb	All meals, bar
(703)-869-1797	Visa, MC, AmEx, DC, CB	sitting room, piano
	C-yes/S-yes/P-no	
All year		

Serving the traveling public since 1797; all lodging rooms antique furnished. Virginia country fare served every day, breakfast, lunch and dinner.

MOUNT JACKSON

Sky Chalet
Star Rt, Box 28, 22842
(703)-856-2147

All year

$40-60
15 rooms, 15 pb
Visa, MC
C-yes/S-yes/P-ok/H-ltd

Full breakfast
Lunch, dinner, bar
swimming, tennis
sitting room, piano
mo-peds

Relax on our back porch where you can see clear to West Virginia. Enjoy our down home country style cooking.

NORFOLK

Cameron Residence
1605 Bill St., 23518
(604)-287-7446

All year

$28-49 B&B
30 rooms, 30 pb
Visa, MC
C-yes/S-yes/H-ltd

Continental breakfast
Lunch, dinner
hot tub, sauna
racquet courts
sitting room, piano

The big little "Inn" on the famous Campbell River. Rustic log rooms, restaurant & pub, racquets, sauna, whirlpool, experienced salmon guides. Est. 1948.

ONANCOCK

Colonial Manor Inn
POB 94, 23417
(804)-787-3521

All year

$22.88-28.08
15 rooms, 5 pb

C-yes/S-yes

sitting room

Family owned business since 1936. At-home kind of atmosphere in an historic little town on the water; fine restaurants.

ORANGE

Mayhurst Inn
Rte. 15, 22960
(703)-672-5597

All year

$45-75 B&B
7 rooms, 7 pb

C-yes/S-no/P-yes/H-no

Full breakfast
Complimentary tea, wine
sitting room
pond

Exciting Italianate villa on 36 acres of pasture land. Rooftop gazebo, balconies for guests. Antique furniture.

SPERRYVILLE

Conyers House
Slate Mills Rd., 22740
(703)-987-8025

All year

$70-100 B&B
8 rooms, 3 pb

S-ltd/H-yes

Hearty gourmet breakfast
Complimentary tea, wine
sitting room/library
fireplaces
piano

French, German, Italian spoken amidst gracious 18th century charm. Gastronomic and metaphysical delight. Breakfast on veranda or by a crackling fire.

Please Mention *The Complete Guide* **to the innkeeper when you reserve your room**

STRASBURG ────────────────────────────────────

Hotel Strasburg $30-60 B&B   Continental breakfast
201 Holliday St., 22657   18 rooms, 3 pb   All meals, bar
(703)-465-9191   Visa, MC, AmEx, CB, DC   sitting room, piano
    C-yes/S-yes/P-no

All year

Built in the 1890's, Victorian hotel with antiques and period art. Delicious Old Fashion recipes, homemade bread, and daily baked deserts.

VESUVIUS ────────────────────────────────────

Sugar Tree Lodge $59 B&B   Full breakfast
24483   5 rooms, 5 pb   All meals, bar
(703)-377-2197   Visa, MC   sitting room
    C-yes/S-yes/P-no/H-no

April—December

19th Century log lodge with 20th Century conveniences—Elegant garden & candlelight dining, fireplaces & rockers, near Geo. Washington Nat'l Forest.

**Be sure to call the Inn to verify details and prices
and to make your reservation**

Angie's Guest Cottage, Virginia Beach, Virginia

VIRGINIA BEACH

Angie's Guest Cottage
302 24th St., 23451
(804)-428-4690

All year

$38-48 B&B
6 rooms, 1 pb
Visa, MC, Choice
C-yes/S-yes/P-ok/H-no

Continental plus
Kitchens
sitting room, sundeck
BBQ pit, picnic tables
shaded porch

Located in the heart of the resort area, by Atlantic Ocean. Guests have the opportunity of meeting visitors from other countries staying at our Youth Hostel

WARM SPRINGS

Meadow Lane Lodge
Star Rt A Bx 110, 24484
(703)-839-5959

except Feb.-March

$65-85 B&B
8 rooms, 8 pb
Visa, MC, AmEx
C-yes/S-yes

Full breakfast

tennis courts
sitting room

In the midst of 1600 mountainous acres, scenic rivers stocked for trout fishing golf, horseback riding, etc., are all nearby.

WILLIAMSBURG

Fisher's Guest Home
23185
(804)-229-4320

All year

$30-35
2 rooms, 2 pb

C-yes/S-yes

No meals

player piano

City charm, close to Historic Area, churches, restaurants. Colonial furnishings & air conditioning. Walk to points of interest.

Harper's /Guest Home
724 Bypass Road, 23185

All year

$14-18 EP
3 rooms, 0 pb

C-yes/S-yes/P-no

Coffee

hot tub
sitting room
piano

Located on Rt. 60 Bypass Road, within walking distance to Colonial Williamsburg Information Center & 6 miles to Bush Gardens.

We want this guide to be as complete as possible, so if you know of an inn (30 rooms or less), bed & breakfast or guesthouse we don't list, please send us their name on the form in the back of the book.

WASHINGTON

ANACORTES ─────────────────────────────

Nantucket Inn　　　　$26-40 EP
3402 Commercial, 98221　5 rooms, 2 pb
(206)-293-6007　　　　　　　　　　　　sitting room
　　　　　　　　　　　　S-no/P-no

All year

One of the finest old homes in the area, furnished in antiques, handmade quilts & petit-point pieces done by innkeeper.

ASHFORD ─────────────────────────────

Alexander's Manor　　$32.50-65.00 B&B　　Continental plus
98304　　　　　　　　　　12 rooms, 5 pb　　　Lunch, dinner
(206)-569-2300　　　　　Visa, MC　　　　　　hot tub
　　　　　　　　　　　　S-ltd/P-no　　　　　sitting room
　　　　　　　　　　　　　　　　　　　　　　fishing, nature trails

Established 1912, newly renovated Spring '83, large lodge room, big fireplace, critically acclaimed restaurant, hiking, cc. skiing (Nov. thru May).

CATHLAMET ─────────────────────────────

Cathlamet Hotel　　　$20-30 B&B　　　　Continental breakfast
67-69 Main St., 98612　12 rooms, 2 pb　　　Dinner, bar
(206)-795-8751　　　　　Visa, MC, DC　　　　sitting room
　　　　　　　　　　　　C-yes/S-yes/P-yes

All year

Return to the Roaring Twenties with us. Beautiful antiques and memorabilia. Tennis, golf and swimming nearby.

CLINTON ─────────────────────────────

Home by the Sea　　　$55　　　　　　　　Full breakfast
2388 E. Sunlight Beach　2 rooms, 2 pb　　　Complimentary sherry
(206)-221-2964　　　　　　　　　　　　　　hot tub
　　　　　　　　　　　　C-10 up/S-ltd/P-no　sitting room
All year　　　　　　　　　　　　　　　　　piano

Whidbey Island, Washington—a year-round waterfront bed & breakfast surrounded by a natural bird sanctuary. A blend of international elegance, natural beauty.

COUPEVILLE

Captain Whidbey	B&B	Continental breakfast
98239	24 rooms, 16 pb	All meals, bar
		sitting room, piano
	C-yes/S-yes/P-yes	bicycles

Historic log Inn, est. 1907. On the shores of Penn Cove. Antique furnished. Fine restaurant and quaint bar. Sailboats, rowboats & bikes.

Penn Cove Inn	$39-51 B&B	Continental plus
P.O. Box 628, 98239	3 rooms, 0 pb	
(206)-678-6868	Visa, MC	sitting room
	S-yes/P-no	
All year		

Early 1900 residence converted to a small, intimate inn. 1 block from waterfront.

The Victorian House	$45-50 B&B	Full breakfast
602 N. Main St., 98239	2 rooms, 0 pb	
(206)-678-5305		bicycles
	C-16 up/S-no/P-no	sitting room
All year		piano

Quiet, intimate inn (1889) furnished in heirlooms and antiques. Listed on National Register. Gift shop, cozy Victorian parlor with fireplace.

DEER HARBOR

Palmer's Chart House	$30 pp B&B	Full breakfast
P.O. Box 51, 98243	2 rooms, 2 pb	Dinner (inc.)
(206)-376-4231		library
	C-no/S-ltd/P-no	travel slideshows
All year		

Fishing, hiking, golf, biking available nearby. Complimentary sailing available on the owner's 33' sloop, Amante, when the skipper is available.

EASTSOUND

North Beach Inn	$35-75 EP	Full breakfast
P.O. Box 80, 98245	11 rooms, 11 pb	Dinner
(206)-376-2660		
	C-yes/H-yes	
All year		

Secluded older rustic cabins along ⅓ mile of sand & gravel beach, no frills, just peace.

FREELAND

Cliff House	$85 B&B	Continental plus
5440 S Grigware Rd, 98249	1 room, 1 pb	Complimentary wine
321-1566		hot tub
	C-no/S-no/P-no	sitting room
All year		piano

A stunningly beautiful house, for one couple. Complete privacy in this forested hideaway with miles of beach.

GREENBANK

Guest House
835 E Cristenson, 98253

$25-80 B&B
6 rooms, 4 pb
Visa, MC
C-14 up/S-no/P-no

Full breakfast
Complimentary wine
library

All year

Country hideaway, secluded cottages, large doghouse, around private pond. Farmhouse with guest bedrooms on 25 wooded acres, charming antique decor.

HARBOR

San Juan Hotel
P.O. Box 776, 98250
(206)-378-2070

$38 dbl B&B
10 rooms, 0 pb
Visa, MC
C-no/S-ltd/P-no

Continental breakfast

bicycles
sitting room

All year

A "Delightfully Different" hotel (or inn) with a Friday Harbor View Parlor which is not just another place to stay, but a place to stay another day!

LA CONNER

La Conner Country Inn
Old Town, 98257
(206)-466-3101

$43-51 B&B
21 rooms, 21 pb
Visa, MC, AmEx, DC, CB
C-yes/S-yes/P-yes/H-yes

Continental breakfast
Lunch, dinner, bar
library

All year

In the charming village of La Conner. All rooms have fireplaces & brass beds. Continental breakfast served around the fireplace in the library.

LANGLEY

Sally's Bed & Breakfast
P.O. Box 459, 98260
(206)-221-8709

$55 dbl B&B
2 rooms, 2 pb
Visa, MC
C-no/S-no/P-no

Full breakfast

hot tub

A turn of the century legend beckons nature lovers and shoppers alike.

The Orchard
619 3rd St.
(206)-221-7880

$32-40
2 rooms, 0 pb

C-yes/S-no/P-yes

Full breakfast

bicycles
sitting room
piano

All year

Country farmhouse antique furnished; full breakfast in family atmosphere; walk to quaint seaside village, wooded walks and horseback trail riding.

Whidbey House
106 First St., 98260
(206)-321-7115

$55 B&B
3 rooms, 3 pb
Visa, MC
C-no/S-no/P-no

Continental breakfast
Complimentary wine

Apr.-Dec./wknds all year

A beautiful Whidbey Island hideaway. Three rooms, each with private bath and a dramatic water view. Close to antique shops.

LEAVENWORTH

Haus Rohrbach
12882 Ranger Rd., 98826
(509)-548-7024

$44
14 rooms, 2 pb
Visa, MC
C-yes/S-ltd/P-no

Full breakfast

hot tub, swimming pool
sitting room

All year

One of a kind, European-style country inn, unequaled in the Pacific Northwest. Alpine setting—pool & hot tub. Year round outdoor activities.

LONGMIRE

National Park Inn

(206)-569-2565
(206)-569-2275 RS
All year

$36.50-49.50 EP
16 rooms, 7 pb
Visa, MC
C-yes/S-yes/P-no/H-ltd

Full breakfast
Lunch, dinner, wine
sitting room

Comfortable rustic hotel located within Mt. Ranier Nat'l Park offering daily lodging, food service, gift shop and a service station.

PORT TOWNSEND

James House
1238 Washington, 98368
(206)-385-1238

$48-80
12 rooms, 4 pb
Visa, MC
C-12 up/S-ltd/P-no

Continental plus

sitting room, piano

All year

Old Victorian house built in 1889 on bluff above Port Townsend, a historical seaport. Overlooking Cascade Mtns. and Puget Sound.

Lizzie's
731 Pierce St., 98368
(206)-385-4168

$42-79 B&B
7 rooms, 3 pb
Visa, MC
C-ok/S-yes/P-no

Full breakfast

sitting room, piano

The most intriguing and civilized accomodations anywhere; an excellent base to explore Olympic National Park & Puget Sound.

Palace Hotel
1004 Water St., 98368
(206)-385-0773

$28-54 EP
10 rooms, 7 pb
Visa, MC
C-yes/S-ltd/P-no

No meals

1900 pump organ

All year

Beautifully restored Victorian building, in historic downtown Port Townsend—Major Victorian Historic District in U.S. Close to restaurants, shops.

Quimper Inn
1306 Franklin St., 98368
(206)-385-1086

All year

$43-64 B&B
6 rooms, 2 pb

C-arr./S-no!/P-no

Continental plus

hot tub, bicycles
sitting room, library
jugglers & artist

An adventure in creative and magical filled nooks and crannies, this bed and breakfast borders on whimsey and surprise.

Starrett House
744 Clay St., 98368
(206)-385-2976

$50-75 B&B
9 rooms, 1 pb
Visa, MC
C-8 up/S-yes/P-no/H-ltd

Full champagne breakfast
Dinner (F,S,S,M)
Baby grand, electric,
player pianos;

All year

sitting room; Jaccuzi

Port Townsend's only full service Victorian Inn. Full champagne breakfast and the most spectacular architectural achievement in the Pacific Northwest.

POULSBO —————————————————————————————

Fjord House
18290 Fjord Dr. NE, 98370
(206)-779-4582

$29-35 B&B
1 room, 1 pb

C-yes/S-no/P-no

Full breakfast
Afternoon tea
living room

All year

Affordable stay in pre-1900 waterfront home with bay and mountain view. Breakfast awaits you in the morning.

ROCHE HARBOR —————————————————————————

Roche Harbor Resort
98250
(206)-378-2155

$35-80 EP
20 rooms, 4 pb
Visa, MC, AmEx
C-yes/S-yes/P-no

Full breakfast
Full dining, bar
swimming pool, bicycles
tennis courts

All year

entertainment

Seaward hideaway furnished in the original antiques. Beautiful garden and water view. Fine dining at the Inn.

SEATTLE ———————————————————————————————

Burton House
P.O. Box 9902, 98109
(206)-285-5945

$25-35 B&B
3 rooms, 0 pb

Continental breakfast

sitting room, piano

All year

Comfortable, casual & quiet with buffet breakfast.

———————————————————————————————————————

College Inn Guest House
4000 Univ. Wy. NE, 98105
(206)-633-4441

$25-45 B&B
27 rooms, 0 pb
Visa, MC, AmEx
C-yes/S-ltd/P-no

Continental plus

sitting room, piano

All year

Next door to University of Washington; historic building on National Register; easy walking for shopping and dining; excellent public transportation.

———————————————————————————————————————

Emerald City Inn
1521 Bellevue Av., 98122
(206)-587-6565

$45-110
9 rooms, 9 pb
Visa, MC, AmEx
C-no/P-no

Continental plus
Complimentary wine
hot tub
gym

All year

Centrally located within easy walking distance to all restaurants, shopping & tourist attractions, full baths, wet bars all units.

Galer Place
318 W. Galer St., 98119
(206)-282-5339

$35-45 B&B
3 rooms, 0 pb
Visa, MC
C-no/S-ok/P-no

Continental plus

hot tub
sitting room

All year

Turn of the century inn, parking. Afternoon tea, fresh ground coffee & baked goods at breakfast. Hot tub. Seattle Center near.

Seattle B&B
2442 NW Market 300,98107
(206)-784-0539

$18-35 B&B
4 rooms, 2 pb
credit cards accepted
S-no/P-no/H-yes

Full breakfast
Complimentary tea, wine
sitting room

All year

Relaxed atmosphere, near downtown, parks, University. Hostess knowledgable about the area—a most hospitable home.

SEAVIEW

Shelbourne Inn
Pac.Hwy. 103 & J St.
(206)-642-2442

$29-53 EP
14 rooms, 1 pb
Visa, MC
C-yes/S-yes/P-no/H-yes

Restaurant -
all meals
lobby w/fireplace
organ

All year

Vintage Country Inn furnished in genuine antiques, features nationally acclaimed gourmet restaurant. Short walk from the Pacific Ocean.

STEHEKIN

North Cascades Lodge
98852
(509)-682-4711

$41-77 EP
26 rooms, 26 pb
Visa, MC
C-yes/S-yes/P-no

Full service restaurant,
bar
hot tub
bicycles
sitting room

All year

A remote & isolated mountain resort. There are no roads that lead to the North Cascades Lodge. You must travel by boat or plane.

TACOMA

Keenan House
2610 N. Warner, 98407
(206)-752-0702

$25-30 B&B
5 rooms, 0 pb

C-yes/S-ltd/P-no

Full breakfast
Dinner (with notice)
sitting room, piano

All year

Modeled after the English Bed & Breakfast homes—breakfast is generous—with homemade breads, etc. Warm, friendly atmosphere.

TOKELAND

Tokeland Hotel
P.O. Box 117, 98590
(206)-267-7700

$28-30 EP
14 rooms, 0 pb
Visa, MC
C-12 up/S-ltd/P-no

Continental breakfast
Dinner, bar
sitting room, piano

May—December

A National Historic Site featuring exquisite family dining. All rooms furnished in antiques. A step into yesteryear.

The Swan Inn, Vashon Island, Washington

USK

River Bend Inn
Rte. 2, 99180

$30-35 EP
7 rooms, 7 pb
Visa, MC
C-yes/S-yes/P-no/H-yes

Full breakfast
Meals, ice cream
bicycles
piano

All year

Country home built in 1912 and converted to a lodge w/dining room decorated and furnished in that era. On the Beautiful Pend Orielle River.

VASHON

Swallow's Nest
Rt. 3 Box 221, 98070

$30-40 EP
2 rooms, 2 pb
Visa, MC
C-yes/S-no/P-no/H-yes

Continental plus

All year

Get away to comfortable country cottages overlooking Puget Sound and Mt. Ranier.

**Enter your favorite inn in our "Inn of the Year" contest
(entry form is in the back of the book).**

Swan Inn
Rte. 5 Box 454, 98070
(206)-463-3388

$40-55 B&B
3 rooms, 1 pb
Visa, MC
C-8 up/S-yes/P-no

Full breakfast
Complimentary tea, wine
sitting room, piano

All year

Small Country Inn patterned after a 14th Century English Inn—furnished with English Antiques, farm setting.

WHIDBEY ISLAND ──────────────────────────────

Saratoga Inn
4850 Langley, 98260
(206)-221-7526

$55-70 B&B
5 rooms, 5 pb
credit cards accepted
C-no/S-no/P-no

Continental plus

sitting room

All year

A Cape Cod Inn set on 25 acres with spectacular view of Saratoga Passage. Furnished with antique quilts, country pine furniture.

WASHINGTON, D.C.

Connecticut-Woodley
2647 Woodley Rd.NW,20008
(202)-667-0218

$19-33
14 rooms, 9 pb
no
C-yes/S-yes/P-no

All year

Less than ½ block to Connecticut Avenue subway, buses and restaurants, free parking, children, open all year.

Kalorama Guest House
1854 Mintwood Pl., 20009
(202)-667-6369

$30-45 B&B
13 rooms, 2 pb
Visa, MC, AmEx
C-yes/S-yes/P-no

Continental plus
Complimentary wine
sitting room

All year

Victorian gentility in the Embassy district of the nation's capitol. Our historic townhouse is charming, convenient and remarkably inexpensive.

Kalorama Guest House, Washington, D.C.

The Manse
1307 R.I. Ave. NW, 20005
(202)-232-9150
(202)-328-3510 RS
All year

$26.40-41.00
4 rooms, 0 pb

C-yes/S-yes/P-yes

Continental plus
Complimentary wine
sitting room
library
piano

Spacious rooms with wood-burning fireplaces and crystal chandeliers bring a bit of the nineteenth century to historic downtown Washington.

WEST VIRGINIA

Wheeling
Parkersburg
Martinsburg
Charleston
Huntington

LEWISBURG

General Lewis Motor Inn
301 E. Washington, 24901

All year

$35-65 EP
27 rooms, 25 pb
Visa, MC, AmEx
C-yes/S-yes/P-yes/H-yes

Full breakfast
Lunch, dinner, bar
sitting room

An old country inn (c. 1834) furnished with genuine antiques, in the 200 year old town of Lewisburg with over 50 antebellum structures.

SUMMIT POINT

Summit Point B&B
P.O. Box 57, 25446
(304)-725-2614
(717)-762-2722 RS
All year

$30-35 B&B
2 rooms, 2 pb

S-ltd/P-yes

Continental plus
Afternoon tea
sitting room
bicycles

Near historic Harper's Ferry, area surrounding this cozy country inn provides splendid hiking, bicycling, antiquing, sightseeing opportunities.

WISCONSIN

ALMA

Laue House
1111 S. Main, 54610
(608)-685-4923

March 1—December 15

$15.75-24.00
7 rooms, 0 pb

C-yes/S-yes/P-yes

Continental breakfast
Afternoon tea
sitting room, piano
canoes

Plain small town—good food—good scenery—good fishing—and friendly folks

BAYFIELD

Old Rittenhouse Inn
301 Rittenhouse, 54814
(715)-779-5765

May—October

$40-70
5 rooms, 3 pb

C-yes/S-no/P-no/H-ltd

Full breakfast
Dinner, wine
bicycles
sitting room
piano, entertainment

Beautiful 21-room Victorian mansion, antiques & seven working fireplaces. Guests can relax on the porch. Overlooking Lake Superior.

BIRNAMWOOD

Old Birnamwood Inn
425 Maple St., 54114
(715)-449-2883

All year

$13.50-24.00 B&B
14 rooms, 0 pb

C-yes/S-yes/P-no

Continental breakfast
Lunch, gourmet dinner
tennis courts
sitting room
fireplace, piano

Breakfast amid antiques, fresh flowers and small print wallpaper is only a part of the nostalgic charm of this 1901 hotel.

FISH CREEK ————————————————————————————————————

Proud Mary
P.O. Box 193, 54212
(414)-868-3442

$44/cpl
8 rooms, 8 pb
credit cards accepted
C-5 up/S-yes/P-no

Just coffee

Victorian porch, foyer

May—October

A hundred year old restored Victorian Inn with seven shops. Original furnishings, crystal chandeliers, wicker-lined sitting porch.

STRUM ————————————————————————————————————

Lake House
RR 2, Box 217, 54770
(715)-695-3519

$15-20 B&B
2 rooms, 1 pb

C-yes/S-yes/P-yes

Continental plus

sitting room
tennis courts
bicycles

June—August

Village home on small lake overlooking hills—breakfast served on deck overlooking lake, weather permitting.

Please Mention *The Complete Guide* **to the innkeeper
when you reserve your room**

Old Rittenhouse Inn, Bayfield, Wisconsin

WYOMING

• *Yellowstone N.P.*

• *Devil's Tower*

• *Grand Teton N.P.*
• *Jackson*

Casper •

Laramie •

• *Evanston*

Cheyenne •

EVANSTON

Pine Gables Inn
1049 Center St., 82930
(307)-789-2069

All year

$28.50 up B&B
6 rooms, 2 pb
Visa, MC, DC
C-yes/S-ok/P-small

Continental breakfast

sitting room
antique piano
Edison phonograph

1883 Pine Gables Inn furnished in 1880 antiques carefully chosen for the comfort and enjoyment of our guests. Located in the historical district.

JACKSON HOLE

Capt. Bob Morris
Teton Vlg. Box 261, 83025
(307)-733-4413

June-Sept, Thsgvg-Easter

$20-25 B&B
2 rooms, 1 pb

C-yes/S-yes/P-yes/H-yes

Continental plus

sitting room

400 yards from longest tram in U.S. 56-foot greenhouse and Mass Wall. Five restaurants within walking distance.

MORAN

Fir Creek Ranch
P.O. Box 190, 83013
(307)-543-2416

All year

donation (B&B)
7 rooms, 7 pb

C-yes/S-no/P-no

Full breakfast
Lunch, dinner
sitting room, piano

Christian retreat center. Write or call for details.

Jenny Lake Lodge
P.O. Box 240, 83013
(307)-733-4677

June 9 - September 9

$178-195 MAP
30 rooms, 30 pb
Visa, MC, AmEx
C-yes/S-yes/P-yes

Full breakfast
Dinner (included)
bicycles
piano
horseback riding

Delightful Lodge has a special charm and relaxing atmosphere. Borders on an alpine meadow directly under the towering peaks of Grand Tetons.

Prices quoted are the most current available. However, due to increases and seasonal fluctuations, they may have changed. Be sure to check when you make your reservations.

RAWLINS

Ferris Mansion
607 West Maple, 82301
(307)-324-3961

All year

$25 B&B
2 rooms, 2 pb
credit cards accepted
C-no/S-ltd/P-no

Continental breakfast

sitting room
piano

Elegant Victorian mansion (1903), antique furnishings, National Register of Historic Places. Frontier prison, museums, hot pool, golfing close by.

WILSON

Heck of a Hill Homestead
P.O. Box 105, 93014
(307)-733-8023

All year

$60/cpl B&B
1 room, 1 pb

C-yes/S-yes/P-yes

Full breakfast
Dinner available
steam bath
sitting room
piano, fireplace

Private mountain homestead in Jackson Hole. Congenial hosts offer homegrown meals, variety of farm animals, beautifully restored home furnished w/antiques.

Snow Job
P.O. Box 371, 83014
(307)-73909695

December 1—April 15

$22-25 B&B
2 rooms, 0 pb

C-no/S-no/P-no

Full breakfast
Other meals (req.)
sitting room

Ski chalet convenient to Jackson Hole, Targhee, and Snow King ski areas. Take sleigh ride to elk feeding grounds.

PUERTO RICO

VEGA ALTA ──────────────────────────────

Villa Elaine　　　　　$55-65 EP　　　　　Full breakfast
Buzon 330-A, 00762　　9 rooms, 1 pb　　　Meals, bar
(809)-883-2138　　　　　　　　　　　　　sitting room
　　　　　　　　　　C-ltd/S-ltd/P-no/H-yes　bicycles
All year

Villa Elaine on Cerro Gordo Bay, one of the finest resorts in the world. Golf, tennis, beautiful beaches, dancing at casino.

ALBERTA

HINTON ──────────────────────────────

Black Cat Guest Ranch　$55-80 MAP　　　　Full breakfast
P.O. Bos 542, T0E 1B0　　16 rooms, 16 pb　　Lunch, dinner
(403)-866-2107　　　　　Visa　　　　　　　sitting room, piano
　　　　　　　　　　C-yes/S-yes/P-yes
All year

A year round lodge facing the front range of the Rockies, featuring trail rides & hiking in summer, cross-country skiing in winter.

NANTON ──────────────────────────────

Timber Ridge Lodge　　$12 pp EP　　　　Full breakfast
P.O. Box 94, T0L 1R0　　5 rooms, 0 pb　　　Lunch, supper
(403)-646-5683　　　　　　　　　　　　　hot tub
　　　　　　　　　　C-yes/S-ltd/P-ltd　　sitting room, piano
June—September　　　　　　　　　　　　horseback riding

Friendly, informal atmosphere—good food—horseback riding in beautiful foothills country with wildflowers and great views of the Rockies.

Rams Head Inn, Rossland, British Columbia

BRITISH COLUMBIA

CAMPBELL RIVER

Campbell River Lodge
176 Island Hwy.
(604)-287-7446

All year

$28-49 B&B
30 rooms, 30 pb
Visa, MC
C-yes/S-yes/H-ltd

Continental breakfast
Lunch, dinner
hot tub, sauna
sitting room, piano
racquet courts

The BIG little "Inn" on the famous Campbell River. Rustic log rooms, restaurant, pub, racquets, sauna, whirlpool, experienced salmon guides.

Riverbend Inn
Box 633, V9W 6J3
(604)-287-4231
(604)-688-0044 RS
Dec. 15—Sept. 30

$9.95-19.95 pp B&B
5 rooms, 1 pb

C-10 up/S-ltd

Full breakfast
Lunch, Dinner
sauna, hot tub
sitting room, bicycles

B&B house located on the river near Discovery Passage Resort and Campbell River Lodge, and guests receive special rates or coupons for all their attractions.

Seascape House
Box 633, V9W 6J3
287-4231
(604)-688-0044 RS
Dec. 15—Sept. 30

$9.95-24.95 (US) B&B
4 rooms, 2 pb

C-yes/S-ltd/P-yes

Full breakfast
Lunch, Dinner
rock seawater pool
sauna, gazebo
sitting room, bicycles

Classic cedar chalet on beautiful beachfront—we specialize in personal touches you will remember—near best fishing, skiing, diving, beachcombing.

COBBLE HILL —————————————————————————————

Wilcuma Resort
RR 3, V0R 1L0
(604)-748-8737

All year

$40-59 EP
14 rooms, 14 pb
Visa
C-ltd/S-yes/P-yes

Full breakfast
Lunch, dinner
swimming pool
sitting room

English country estate by the sea. Beautiful views and sunsets. Seafood fresh from Cowichan Bay. Moorage and boat rentals.

DENMAN ISLAND ————————————————————————————

Denman Isl. Guesthouse
P.O. Box 9, V0R 1T0
(604)-335-2688

All year

$20-30
5 rooms, 0 pb

C-yes/S-yes/P-yes

Full breakfast

Country charm—19th-Century farm house in the Gulf Islands, hourly ferry, ocean, beach, recreational activities, hearty country breakfast.

EAGLE CREEK ————————————————————————————

Bradshaw's Minac Lodge
On Canim Lake, V0K 1L0
(604)-397-2416

All year

$25 EP
4 rooms, 4 pb
Visa
C-yes/S-yes/P-no/H-ltd

Full breakfast

sitting room

Quiet family-run informal operation—on lake—cross-country skiing in winter—canoes— boats & motors—sitting room.

FORT ST. JOHN ————————————————————————————

Gimmy's Farm
SS2, Site 13, Comp. 11
(604)-787-9104

All year

$20-25 B&B
6 rooms, 2 pb

C-yes/S-yes/P-yes

Full breakfast
Other meals on request
hot tub
bicycles
sitting room

A home away from home. Peaceful, in beautiful British Columbia. Come visit our farm. Snow & water sports.

We want to hear from you — any comments regarding the inns or our publication may be noted on the form at the end of the book.

FRASER LAKE ──────────────────────────────

Lynn's Lodge $30 dbl EP Full breakfast
Box 253, V0J 1S0 4 rooms, 2 pb Meals (res.), bar
(604)-699-6982 sitting room, piano

  C-yes/S-yes/P-dogs

All year

Colonial-style log house, 58 acres of evergreens, creek and river, lakes nearby for fishing. Hunting in season. Sun deck and fireplaces.

GABRIOLA ISLAND ──────────────────────────

Surf Lodge $45-50 EP Full breakfast
RR 1, Berry Pt. Rd. 18 rooms, 18 pb Tea, dinner, bar
(604)-247-9231 Visa, MC sitting room, piano

  C-4 up/S-yes/P-no/H-ltd swimming pool
May—October tennis courts, bicycles

Situated on 15 acres by the shores of the Straits of Georgia. Incomparable sunsets. 9 hole golf course nearby.

HORNBY ISLAND ────────────────────────────

Sea Breeze Lodge AP Full breakfast
V0R 1Z0 12 rooms, 8 pb All homecooked meals
  sitting room, piano
  C-yes/S-yes/P-yes/H-ltd grass tennis courts
April 15—Sept. 30 ocean swimming

Sea Breeze Lodge—mentioned in '83 edition of West World. Near the ocean. Breakfast, homemade pastries.

LADYSMITH ─────────────────────────────────

Manana Lodge $30-45 B&B Continental plus
4760 Brenton Pg. Rd. 5 rooms, 1 pb Dinner
(604)-245-2312 Visa, MC fireside lounge area
  C-yes/P-no

Except January

Manana Lodge is a unique old style country inn—Canadiana origin. A warm & friendly atmosphere—furnished in antiques & homey memorabilia.

NORTH DELTA ───────────────────────────────

Dastar's $22.50-29.50 B&B Full breakfast
10356 Skagt Dr., V4C 2K9 rooms, pb
(604)-588-8866

  C-yes

All year

Complete privacy in a homey atmosphere. Separate entrance, color TV, host available to act as tour guide or make airport pickup for a small fee.

NORTH VANCOUVER ──────────────────────────

Katie's Bed & Breakfast $25-35 Full breakfast
217 Keith Rd., V7L 1V4 4 rooms, 0 pb
(604)-987-1092 Roman tub
  C-yes/S-yes/P-no sitting room

All year

Vancouver's first B & B. Comfortable and popular — be sure to reserve!

PARKSVILLE

Earl & Eugenia Taggart	$25-40 B&B	Full breakfast
RR1, Site 116-C71,V0R 2S0	2 rooms, 2 pb	Afternoon tea
(604)-248-2585		sitting room
	C-yes/S-ltd/P-no	piano & pump organ
All year		bicycles

Unique West Coast cedar country location—walking distance to town & Provincial Park—outstanding beaches—centrally situated on Vancouver Island.

QUILCHENA

Quilchena Hotel	$35-45 EP	Full breakfast
	14 rooms, 0 pb	Lunch, dinner, bar
(604)-378-2611	Visa, MC	golf, lake swimming
	C-yes/S-yes/P-no	riding, boating, fishing
May-October		sitting room, piano

If you're looking for a friendly atmosphere, good home cooking, old fashioned comfort, then come stay at the Quilchena Hotel.

ROSSLAND

Ram's Head Inn	$36-40 EP	Full breakfast
Red Mt. Ski Area	8 rooms, 8 pb	Family style dinner
	Visa, MC	hot tub, sauna
	C-yes/P-no	sitting room
All year		

A quality well remembered from little inns and guest houses in Europe.

SECHELT

Lord Jim's Lodge	$44-48	Full breakfast
Ole's Cove Rd.	23 rooms, 23 pb	Lunch, dinner, bar
(604)-885-2232	yes	swimming pool, saunas
	C-yes/S-yes/P-no	sitting room, piano
All year		entertainment

Located right on the ocean, very secluded. Excellent salmon fishing charter service. Excellent view.

SOOKE

Sooke Harbour House	$27-78	Full breakfast
RR 4, V0S 1N0	5 rooms, 1 pb	Dinner, bar
(604)-642-3421	Visa, MC, AmEx, DC	sitting room, piano
	C-yes/S-yes/P-yes/H-ltd	entertainment
Closed November		

Country hideaway right by the ocean with an internationally known restaurant specializing in FRESH seafood and local produce. Children accepted.

TOFINO

Clayoquot Lodge	$65-85	Full breakfast
P.O. Box 188, V0R 2Z0	9 rooms, 9 pb	Restaurant, bar
(604)-725-3284	Visa, MC	sitting room, piano
	C-yes/S-yes/P-yes	
April 1—October 15		

One of the prettiest little resorts in Canada. Located on 150 acre Stubb's Island (private) only 10 min. from Tofino B.C. by our boat.

VICTORIA ──────────────────────

Battery St. Guesthouse	$20-35 B&B	Full breakfast
670 Battery St., V8V 1E5	6 rooms, 2 pb	
		sitting room
	C-yes	
April—October		

Heritage guesthouse near downtown Victoria. Easy walking distance to downtown; one block from park & beaches. Dutch second language.

Captain's Palace	$95 B&B	Full breakfast
309 Belleville, V8V 1X2	2 rooms, 2 pb	Complimentary wine
(604)-388-9191	Visa, MC, AmEx	
All year		

1897 mansion, crystal chandeliers, stained glass, antiques, restaurant, breakfast included, near heart of Victoria, full view of Inner Harbor.

WHISTLER ──────────────────────

Kieth & Dorothy Sabey	$25 (Can) pp B&B	Full breakfast
Box 341, V0N 1B0	5 rooms, 0 pb	Dinner, tea
(604)-932-3498		hot tub, sauna
	C-14 up/S-no/P-no	sitting room
All year		

Large cedar home with hand-paved driveway, much carving in the inside beams & loaded with antiques—across the highway from Green Lake. Private & dorm rooms

Margit Abt	$20-45 (US)	Full breakfast
Box 466, V0N 1B0	2 rooms, 0 pb	Afternoon tea
(604)-932-5974		whirlpool
	C-yes/S-no/P-no	sitting room, organ
All year		

Unique handcrafted Alpine Chalet. Deluxe rooms. Comfortable and cozy atmosphere. Whirlpool and Swiss-style dining area available for our guests.

MANITOBA

MORRIS ──────────────────────

Deer Bank Farm	$28/cpl B&B	Full breakfast
Box 23, RR 2, R0G 1K0	3 rooms, 0 pb	Supper
(204)-746-8395		sitting room, piano
	C-yes/S-ltd/P-yes	
All year		

There is nothing like a quiet night on the farm and a hearty, full breakfast to start you on your day.

TREHERNE ───────────────────────────────

Beulah Land $15 pp B&B   Full breakfast
Box 26, R0G 2V0   3 rooms, 0 pb   All meals
(204)-723-2828   hot tub
                       C-yes/S-yes/P-no   sitting room
All year

Beulah Land Farm is situated in the beautiful valley of the Assiniboine, in the centre of Manitoba. All meals are home-grown and home-cooked.

NEW BRUNSWICK

GRAND MANAN ───────────────────────────

Compass Rose $20-35 B&B   Full breakfast
North Head   9 rooms, 0 pb   Lunch, tea, dinner
(506)-662-8570   Visa   sitting room
                      C-yes/S-yes/P-yes/H-ltd
June 1—October 10

The Compass Rose consists of two old houses on an island overlooking a fishing harbour—isolated, restful and charming! Antiques.

Grand Harbor Inn $22-35 B&B   Continental breakfast
E0G 1X0   6 rooms, 0 pb   Dinner
(506)-662-8681   sitting room
(506)-662-3698 RS   C-yes/P-yes
May—October

Turn-of-the-century 3-story inn, furnished with antique beds, wash stands, and old style quilts. Local fish our specialty.

ROTHESAY ─────────────────────────────────

Shadow Lawn Inn $24-32 EP   Full breakfast
                      12 rooms, 8 pb   Dinner, bar
(506)-847-7539   tennis courts
                      C-yes/S-yes/P-yes/H-yes piano
All year   sitting room

Shadow Lawn in the village of Rothesay—Next to golf, tennis, sailing.

SACKVILLE ─────────────────────────────────

Different Drummer $26.50-$30.00 B&B   Full breakfast
Box 188, E0A 3C0   4 rooms, 4 pb
(506)-536-1291   Visa, MC   sitting room
                      C-yes/S-yes   pump organ
All year (RS)

Victorian house set in lovely garden. Four poster and spool beds in sunny bay-windowed rooms, all with private baths.

SAINT-ANDREWS-BY-THE-SEA ————————————————

Shiretown Inn	$40-44	Continental breakfast
Town Square	26 rooms, 26 pb	Lunch, dinner, bar
(506)-529-8877	Visa, MC, AmEx	sitting room, piano
(800)-268-8993 RS	C-yes/S-yes/P-yes/H-yes	salt water beach
All year		

Enjoy our old-fashioned hospitality (built 1881). Patio restaurant overlooking market wharf, Passamaquoddy Bay and town steeped in history. Open all year.

NEWFOUNDLAND

LEWISPORTE ————————————————

Chaulk's Tourist Home	$25-30 EP	Breakfast
P.O. Box 339	6 rooms, 1 pb	
(709)-535-6305		sitting room
	C-yes/S-yes/P-no	
All year		

Sit and relax in our garden. Also we have a patio overlooking the Harbour.

TRINITY ————————————————

Village Inn	$24-30 EP	Full breakfast
A0C 2S0	5 rooms, 0 pb	Other meals, bar
(709)-464-3269	credit cards accepted	sitting room, library
	C-yes/S-yes/P-yes	piano, entertainment
All year		whale watching trips

Possibly the finest geographic location worldwide to see and study the GREAT WHALES. Trinity is the oldest village in North America.

NOVA SCOTIA

ANNAPOLIS COUNTY ————————————————

Shining Tides	$18-22 B&B	Continental plus
RR2, Granville Ferry	3 rooms, 0 pb	
(902)-532-2770		sitting room
(902)-532-5769 RS	C-yes/S-yes	library
June 1—October 15		

Large veranda—wilderness walk toward North Mountain—trout stream—wild flowers and native trees—view of Annapolis River.

ANNAPOLIS ROYAL

Bread and Roses
P.O. Box 177, B0S 1A0
(902)-532-5727

$32-38 EP
7 rooms, 7 pb
Visa, MC
C-yes/S-no/P-yes

Continental plus

sitting room
bicycles

May—October

Restored Victorian home in heart of Canada's oldest permanent European settlement. Walk to Historic Gardens, Fort Anne, Tidal Power Project.

Garrison House Inn
Box 108
(902)-532-5750

$32-40 dbl B&B
7 rooms, 5 pb
Visa, MC
C-yes/S-yes/P-no

Full breakfast
Tea, dinner, bar
sitting room
bicycles

All year

Restored 1854 Heritage House, early Canadiana antiques, hooked rugs, quilts, & folk art treasures. Near all major attractions. Golfing, canoeing, bicycling.

CAPE BRETON

Hart and Hart's T. H.
N.E. Margaree, B0E 2H0

$20 dbl EP
10 rooms, 6 pb

C-yes/S-yes/P-yes

Full breakfast

hot tub
sitting room
piano

May—November

Central location, daily trips to places of interest, trout & salmon fishing on property, golf course close by. "Home away from home."

Blomidon Inn, Wolfville, Nova Scotia

Kilmuir Place
NE Margaree, B0E 2H0
(902)-248-2877

$45 pp MAP
5 rooms, 3 pb

C-yes/S-yes/P-yes/H-yes

Full breakfast
Dinner
piano, sitting room

mid-June—mid-October

Quiet country home located near Margaree River. Salmon fishing arranged. Hiking—scenic drives nearby.

Riverside Inn
Margaree Hrb., B0E 2B0
(902)-235-2002

$25 dbl B&B
2 rooms, 0 pb

C-yes/S-yes/P-yes

Full breakfast

sitting room, piano

July—mid-October

Victorian home on Gulf of St. Lawrence. Great fishing area for salmon and trout. Breakfast specialty blueberry pancakes.

DIGBY COUNTY

Lovett Lodge Inn
Bx. 19, Bear R., B0S 1B0
(902)-467-3917
(800)-341-6096 RS
May—October

$17-23 (US) EP
4 rooms, 0 pb

C-yes/S-yes/P-yes

Full breakfast
Afternoon tea
sitting room, piano
fireplaces
verandas

A Victorian inn, furnished with comfortable antiques, in an Alpine setting on a tidal river. Nova Scotia—artists' and poets' paradise.

HEBRON

Manor Inn
P.O. Box 56, B0W 1X0
(902)-742-2487
(902)-742-7811
May—October

$55-115 EP
29 rooms, 29 pb
Visa, MC, AmEx
C-yes/S-yes/P-yes/H-yes

Full breakfast
Lunch, dinner, bar
entertainment

Nine acres of landscaped grounds, formal rose garden, 3000 feet of lake front. Magnificent old mansion and 20 unit motel.

LORNEVILLE

Amherst Shore Inn
Hwy. 366
(902)-667-4800

$34-49 EP
5 rooms, 3 pb
Visa, MC
C-yes/S-ok/P-yes

Full breakfast
Gourmet dinner, bar
sitting room
baby grand piano
bicycles

All year

Seaside country inn—spacious grounds, 600 ft. private beach (red sand), average summer water temp 71 degrees F. Four course gourmet dinner.

MUSQUODOBOIT HARBOUR

Camelot
Rt 7, Box 31, B0J 2L0
(902)-889-2198
(800)-565-7105 RS
All year

$26-38 EP
5 rooms, 0 pb

C-yes/S-ltd/P-yes

Full breakfast
Dinner (res), beer/wine
sitting room
library

Charming old home where strangers become friends. Excellent meals, oversized fireplace—an enchanting and relaxing escape from the "other" world.

PUGWASH

Blue Heron Inn
Box 405, B0K 1L0
(902)-243-2900
(902)-243-2020 RS
June—September

$24-36 B&B
5 rooms, 1 pb
Visa
C-yes/S-yes/P-no

Continental plus
Lunch, dinner
sitting room, piano
canoes

A renovated home in the Village of Pugwash furnished with many antiques. Close to beaches, golf course & lobster pounds.

WALLACE

Senator Guest Home
Sunrise Trail, Route 6
(902)-257-2417
June 1—October 15

$15-18
5 rooms, 2 pb
Visa
C-yes/S-yes/P-no

Continental breakfast
Dinner
sitting room, piano

Traditional architecture highlights historical aspect of this early 18th-Century home— high ceiling, marble fireplace, original stone, dutch oven.

WOLFVILLE

Blomidon Inn
P.O. Box 839, B0P 1X0
(902)-542-9326
(800)-341-6069
May—December

$30-55 B&B
11 rooms, 9 pb
Visa, MC
C-yes/P-no/H-ltd

Full breakfast
Lunch, dinner, bar
library
sitting rooms
baby grand piano

Elegant 19th-Century sea captain's mansion on two acres of shaded lawn in university town. Seven fireplaces, poster beds, fine mahogany furniture.

Historic Inn of Wolfville
416 Main St.
(902)-542-5744
May 1—September 30

$29-49 EP
12 rooms, 14 pb
credit cards accepted
C-yes/S-yes/P-yes/H-yes

Full breakfast
Lunch, dinner, bar
sitting room

Victorian Inn in beautiful Nova Scotia. Interesting fireplaces in each room, antiques, soft music, Acadians' 'Cajun cuisine. Traditional dining room.

Victoria's Historic Inn
Box 819, B0P 1X0
(902)-542-5744
(902)-422-9651 RS
May—September

$29-49 EP
17 rooms, 12 pb
MC, AmEx
C-yes/S-ok/P-ltd/H-yes

Full breakfast
Lunch, dinner, bar
sitting room

The Inn is filled w/ antiques, fireplaces of fruitwood, oak & marble mantels. New Orleans Cajun Cuisine available in The Inn.

We want to hear from you — any comments regarding the inns or our publication may be noted on the form at the end of the book.

ONTARIO

BAYFIELD ————————————————————————————

Little Inn
P.O. Box 102, N0M 1G0
(516)-565-2611

All year

$40-64
23 rooms, 13 pb
credit cards accepted
C-yes/S-yes/P-no

Full breakfast
Lunch, dinner, bar
sitting room
sauna

Ontario's oldest continuously operating inn—since 1832. Antique-filled bedrooms and quiet parlors. Award-winning dining room. X-C ski trails.

BLACKSTOCK ————————————————————————

Landfall Farm
RR 1, L0B 1B0
(416)-986-5588

May 15—October 15

4 rooms, 0 pb

C-yes/S-yes/P-no

Full breakfast
Lunch, dinner
swimming pool
bicycles
sitting room

1868 fieldstone country home near Toronto. Large lawns, swimming pool, pond, bicycles, billiards, table tennis, lawn games. Home cooking and baking.

BRACEBRIDGE ————————————————————————

Holiday House Inn
17 Dominion St., P0B 1C0
(705)-645-2245

All year

$40-120
17 rooms, 17 pb
Visa, MC, AmEx
C-yes/S-yes/P-no

Full breakfast
Lunch, dinner, bar
swimming pool
sitting room, pianos
entertainment

Over 100 years old, this historic Muskoka landmark combines the charm of old-fashioned hospitality and decor with modern comfort.

BRADFORD ————————————————————————————

Country Guest Home
RR 2, L0G 1C0
(416)-775-3576

All year

$17-28
6 rooms, 0 pb

C-yes/S-no/P-no/H•yes

Full breakfast
Dinner
sitting room, piano

Century-old farm home, large lawn, shady maples, scenic view. Enjoy good night's rest and hearty home-cooked meals.

BRAESIDE ————————————————————————————

Glenroy Farm
RR 1, K0A 1G0
(613)-432-6248

All year

$18-25 B&B
4 rooms, 1 pb

C-yes/S-yes/P-no

Full breakfast

sitting room, piano
bicycles

Century-old Stone farmhouse on the Ottawa River, 50 miles to Canada's Capitol. Reservations 8 am or 6 pm. Rafting, full breakfast.

CALEDON EAST

Caledon Inn	$45	Continental plus
L0N 1E0	4 rooms, 4 pb	Lunch, tea, dinner
(416)-584-2891	Visa, MC	sitting room
	P-no/H-ltd	

Except January

180-year-old stone inn nestled in the Caledon Hills, furnished in antiques, on 25 acres.

COBOURG

Northumberland Heights	$47.50	Full breakfast
RR 5, K9A 4J8	12 rooms, 12 pb	Lunch, dinner, bar
(416)-372-7500	Visa, MC, AmEx	hot tub, sauna
	C-yes/S-yes/P-no/H-yes	swimming pool
All year		sitting room, piano

Situated on 100 acres of rolling countryside. Relaxing patio areas, miniature golf, outdoor checkers, trout pond, X-C skiing, skating.

COOKSTOWN

Chestnut Inn	$42-52	Full breakfast
9 Queen St., L0L 1L0	4 rooms, 2 pb	All meals, bar
	all credit cards	sitting room, piano
	C-yes/S-yes/P-yes/H-yes	
All year		

Experience rural Ontario, Canada in heart of village of Cookstown and stay in cottage with its antique and original furnishings.

EAGLE LAKE

Sir Sam's Inn	$75 dbl B&B	Full breakfast
	20 rooms, 15 pb	All meals, bar
(705)-754-2188	Visa, MC, AmEx	hot tub, swimming pool
	C-yes/S-yes/P-no	tennis courts
Except April, November		sitting room, piano

Full facility country inn. Windsurfing, tennis, whirlpool, waterskiing, classic charm, magnificent setting, superb food.

FENWICK

Lucky Lancione's	$25-35 B&B	Full breakfast
635 Metler Rd., L0S 1C0	3 rooms, 0 pb	All meals
(416)-892-8104		sitting room
	C-yes/S-yes/P-yes	bicycles
All year		

Large old house situated in a small village in the middle of the Niagara Peninsula, near Niagara Falls, St. Catherines.

FERGUS

Breadelbane Inn	$40-65 EP	Full breakfast
486 St.Andrew W., N1M 1P2	10 rooms, 0 pb	Dinner
(519)-843-4770	Visa, MC	sauna
	C-yes/P-no/H-yes	bicycles
All year		

Fine Scottish architecture, sip wine in the Victorian garden, country cooking.

GANANOQUE

Athlone Inn
250 King St.W.
(613)-382-2440

$32-66 EP
10 rooms, 10 pb
Visa, MC
C-yes/S-yes/P-yes

Full breakfast
Dinner, bar

All year

A typical Victorian inn, built 1874, well known for its fine continental and French cuisine throughout North America.

KINGSTON

Prince George Hotel
200 Ontario St., K7L 2Y9
(613)-549-5440

$36-58 EP
22 rooms, 22 pb
Visa, MC, AmEx
C-yes/S-yes/P-yes

Full breakfast
Lunch, dinner
sauna
entertainment

All year

KIRKFIELD

Kirkfield MacKenzie Home
Highway 48, K0M 2B0
(705)-438-3158

$45-65 EP
12 rooms, 12 pb
Visa, MC, AmEx, DC, CB
C-yes/S-yes/P-yes

All meals, bar
sitting room
piano, entertainment

All year

Historic and peaceful country inn, surrounded by magnificent Norway Spruce in rural Ontario, only 85 miles from Metro Toronto.

MINDEN

Minden House
P.O. Box 789, K0M 2K0
(705)-286-3263

$20-28 B&B
5 rooms, 2 pb

C-yes/S-no/P-ltd

Full breakfast
Afternoon tea
tennis courts
sitting room
bicycles

May—October

Historic home quietly situated on Gull River, steps from quaint Village of Minden in beautiful Haliburton Highlands.

NEWBORO

Sterling Lodge
K0G 1P0
(613)-272-2435

$32-48 B&B
34 rooms, 30 pb
Visa, MC
C-yes/S-yes/P-no/H-yes

Full breakfast
Lunch, dinner, bar
swimming pool
bicycles
sitting room, piano

Mid-May—Mid-October

Country hideaway on beautiful Newboro Lake. A wonderful place to enjoy genuine "old fashioned" hospitality amongst a haven of flowers.

NEW HAMBURG

Waterlot Restaurant
17 Huron St., N0B 2G0
(579)-662-2020

$50-75
3 rooms, 1 pb
Visa, MC, AmEx
C-no/S-no/P-no

Continental breakfast
Lunch, dinner, bar

All year-closed Mondays

Just the place for a Romantic Gourmet!

NIAGRA-ON-THE-LAKE ─────────────────────────────

Gate House $45 Coffee only
142 Queen St. 9 rooms, 9 pb
(416)-468-2205 Visa, MC
  C-yes/S-yes/P-yes
All year

Small inn (9 rooms) built in late 18th Century as Wilson's Hotel. Victorian and traditional furniture. Private bathrooms.

───

Advance reservations are essential at most inns during busy seasons and appreciated at other times

Union Hotel, Normandale, Ontario

NORMANDALE

Union Hotel
Box 38, RR 1, N0E 1W0
(519)-426-5568
May-Dec. 7 days
Jan.-Apr. wknds only

$30
3 rooms, 0 pb

C-yes/S-ltd/P-no

Full breakfast
Luncheon, dinner (res)
sitting room

NORWICH

Willi-Joy Farm
RR 3, N0J 1P0
(519)-424-2113

All year

$12 pp B&B
4 rooms, 0 pb

C-yes/S-ltd/P-ltd

Full breakfast
Afternoon tea
swimming pool
bicycles
sitting room

Our 1850 farm home is on a quiet road in western Ontario. Holstein cows and many more interesting sights on the farm.

PORT CARLING

Sherwood Inn
P.O. Box 400, P0B 1J0
(705)-765-3131

All year

$80-125 pp MAP
16 rooms, 16 pb
Visa, MC, AmEx, DC
C-yes/S-yes/P-no/H-ltd

Full breakfast
Lunch, dinner, bar
tennis court
sitting room, piano

We have given every consideration to your leisure and recreational needs. All for your enjoyment, full breakfast, children welcome.

PORT COLBORNE

Rathfon Inn
Box 14, Lakeshore, L3K 5V7
(416)-834-3908

All year

$35-55
18 rooms, 17 pb
credit cards accepted
C-yes/S-yes/P-yes

Continental breakfast
Lunch, dinner, bar
swimming pool, bicycles
sitting room, piano
entertainment

Historic country inn on Lake Erie, 9 acres beautiful lawn, outdoor patio bar, fine swimming, golf nearby—living room with fireplace.

ST. JACOBS

Jakobstettel Guest House
16 Isabella St., W0B 2W0
(519)-664-2208

All year

$40-85 B&B
12 rooms, 12 pb
Visa, MC, AmEx
C-yes/S-yes/P-no

Continental plus
Tea, coffee, snacks
swimming pool
tennis courts, bicycles
sitting room

Luxurious privacy set amidst 5 treed acres. Deluxe B&B. Each bedroom offers charm & unique features—decorated in keeping with the Victorian style house.

VIOLET HILL

Mrs. Mitchell's
L0N 1S0
(819)-925-3672

All year

7 rooms, pb
Visa, MC
C-yes/S-yes/P-no/H-yes

Lunch, dinner, bar
Entertainment (wknds)

1889 schoolhouse converted into a 17th-Century diningroom with two fireplaces, authentic artifacts, oil paintings to create a memorable ambiance.

WORKWORTH ——————————————————————————

Dartford $30 dbl. EP Full breakfast
RR 5, K0K 3K0 2 rooms, 0 pb lunch, dinner
(705)-924-2992 none complimentary wine
  C-yes/S-yes/P-yes sitting room, library

All year

Century old renovated church in a scenic hamlet in rural southern Ontario. Gourmet meals and home baking using our own produce. Reservations essential.

YOUNG'S POINT ——————————————————————————

Old Bridge Inn $35-45 B&B Full breakfast
K0L 3G0 6 rooms, 0 pb French restaurant, bar
(405)-652-8507 Visa, MC
  C-yes/S-yes

All year

120-year-old country inn on Trent Canal System, north of Peterborough. Licensed French Restaurant, delightful rooms, patio, full breakfast.

PRINCE EDWARD ISLAND

BONSHAW ——————————————————————————

Churchill Farm T.H. $16-18 Full breakfast
RR3, C0A 1C0 5 rooms, 0 pb Afternoon tea
(902)-675-2481   piano
  C-yes/S-yes/P-no

All year

Near a lot of attractions, including golf courses, harness racing, children's playground, swimming, fishing, shopping, restaurants.

BRACKLEY BEACH ——————————————————————————

Shaw's Hotel & Cottages $45-60 pp MAP Full breakfast
C0A 2H0 24 rooms, 9 pb Dinner, bar
(902)-672-2022 Visa sitting room, piano
  C-yes/S-yes/P-yes

June 15—Sept. 7

Shaw's Hotel, est. 1860, has developed a special charm that has come from four generations of Shaw family management.

CHARLOTTETOWN

Dundee Arms Motel & Inn
200 Pownal St.
(902)-892-2496
(800)-565-7105 RS
All year

$45-72 B&B
6 rooms, 6 pb
Visa, MC, AmEx, EnRoute
C-yes/S-yes/P-no

Continental breakfast
Luncheon, dinner, pub

A gracious Victorian inn furnished in antiques. Famous for fine dining, charming atmosphere, and warm hospitality.

Just Folks B & B
RR 5
(902)-569-2089

All year

$16 B&B
4 rooms, 0 pb

C-yes/S-ok/P-yes

Full breakfast

hot tub
sitting room, library

94-year-old farm home, quiet location, large lawn, 10 km. from Confederation Centre of the Arts, library, centrally located, games.

KENSINGTON

Sherwood Farm Tourist Home
RR 1, C0B 1M0
(902)-836-5430

All year

$20 pp MAP
8 rooms, 0 pb

C-yes/S-yes/P-yes/H-yes

Full breakfast
Dinner (inc.)
sitting room
piano

Near lovely sandy beaches, clam digging, country walks. Food is all homemade including the bread and butter. Quiet way of life and pleasant atmosphere.

LITTLE YORK

Dalvay by the Sea Hotel
National Park
(902)-672-2048

June 20—September 10

$49-53 pp MAP
26 rooms, 26 pb
Visa, MC, AmEx
C-yes/S-yes/P-yes

Full breakfast
Lunch, dinner
bicycles
tennis courts
sitting room, piano

Old time country hotel, 200 yards from beautiful beach. Excellent cuisine. Tennis, canoes, deep sea fishing, lawn bowling. 16 miles from Charlottetown.

MURRAY HARBOUR

Harbourview B&B
RR 1, C0A 1V0
(902)-962-2565

June—September

$20 EP
5 rooms, 0 pb

C-yes/P-no

Full breakfast

sitting room

Rural setting with beautiful view, overlooking the harbour and village. Home away from home. Homecooked food. Breakfast. Beaches nearby.

Prices quoted are the most current available. However, due to increases and seasonal fluctuations, they may have changed. Be sure to check when you make your reservations.

NORTH RIVER ───────────────────────────────

Obanlea Farm Tourist
Home $15-16 EP   Full breakfast
York Point Rd.   2 rooms, 0 pb   Other meals, tea
(902)-566-3067   sitting room
                          C-yes/S-yes/P-sm
All year

Two large bedrooms, baths, private entrance, kitchen privileges, breakfast, ocean beaches, fishing, golf, shopping centers. Family farm.

STANLEY BRIDGE ───────────────────────────────

Gulf Breeze T.H. $16-20 EP   Full breakfast
RR 1, C0A 1E0   4 rooms, 0 pb
(902)-886-2678   sitting room, piano
                          C-yes/S-yes
June—October

Home, near stores, restaurants, golf course, fishing. Children, large play area. Picnic tables. Open May to October. Lobster suppers.

VERNON RIVER ───────────────────────────────

Lea's Bed & Breakfast $16-20 EP   Full breakfast
C0A 2E0   5 rooms, 1 pb
(902)-651-2501   hot tub
                          C-yes/S-yes/P-no   sitting room, piano
All year

Small farm with beef cattle, pheasants, rabbits and a bird dog called "Tipsy". Bedrooms with 2 double beds, some with one double bed. Country breakfasts.

QUEBEC

CAP-A-L AIGLE ───────────────────────────────

Auberge La Pinsonniere   Full breakfast
124 R. St. Raphael, G0T 1B0 26 rooms, 15 pb   Dinner, bar
                          credit cards accepted sitting rooms (3)
                          C-yes/S-yes/P-no   piano

St. Lawrence River inn. Exclusive wild beach, golf, ski, wine cellar, gourmet food, beautiful view, fresh air, conference rooms.

CO. LOTBINIERE

Auberge Manoire de Tilly $30 EP
3854 Chemin Tilly,G0S 2C0
(418)-477-2407
6 rooms, 1 pb
Visa, MC, AmEx
C-yes/S-yes/P-no

Spring—Fall

Full breakfast
Lunch, dinner, bar
swimming pool
bicycles
sitting room, piano

1786 Manor built by the Seigneur (King's Representative) on the shore of the beautiful St. Lawrence River. 15 minutes from Quebec Bridge Gate to Quebec City.

COIN DU BANC-PERCE

Auberge Le Coin Du Banc $25-40 EP
Rte. 132
(418)-645-2907
9 rooms, 3 pb

C-yes/S-yes/P-no

All year

All meals, bar
sitting room
beachcombing

Country inn just like your great-grandmother's house, full of antiques. Beautiful beach, sailing school.

COMO

Willow Inn $35-40
208 Main Rd., J0P 1A0
(514)-458-7006
8 rooms, 8 pb
Visa, MC, AmEx
C-yes/S-yes/P-no

All year

Continental breakfast
Lunch, dinner, bar
swimming pool

Thirty-five miles from Montreal, on the lake of two mountains, in a world of peaceful countryside.

COMTE DE MANTANE

Auberge La Matre $20-25
G0E 2H0
(418)-288-5533
6 rooms, 0 pb
credit cards accepted
C-yes/S-yes/P-small/H-yes

All year

Full breakfast
Dinner, supper, bar
hot tub
entertainment

Homemade bread, specialty is fish. Middle of hamlet of 450, 25 km east of Ste. Anne des Monts.

DUNHAM

Maplewood $20-30 B&B
Malenfant Rd., J0E 1M0
(514)-295-2519
4 rooms, 0 pb

C-8 up/S-yes/P-no

All year

Full breakfast (winter)
Continental (summer)
sitting room

Unique 1855 mansion features quiet charm, elegant furnishings, gracious hospitality, modern comforts, antique setting—20 minutes to skiing.

HUBERDEAU

Outer Lake Haus $36-45 EP
J0T 1G0
(819)-687-2767
20 rooms, 8 pb
credit cards accepted
C-yes/S-ltd

Except November

Full breakfast
Lunch, dinner, bar
tennis courts, bicycles
sitting room, piano
lake swimming

65 km. x-country ski trails, lake & boats, cozy family atmosphere, home-cooked meals.

HUDSON

Auberge Willow Inn
208 Main St., J0P 1A0
(514)-458-7006

$25-40 EP
8 rooms, 8 pb
Visa, MC, AmEx
C-yes/S-yes/P-no

Full breakfast
Lunch, dinner, bar
swimming pool
sailing, swimming
riding

All year

Peaceful, cozy, 19th-Century country inn; settled on lake surrounded by rolling hills. Fireplace, bar, dining room, recreational activities.

ILE D'ORLEANS

Manor De L'Anse
22 Av. du Quai, G0A 4C0
(418)-828-2248

$40-58 B&B
33 rooms, 18 pb
Visa, MC, AmEx
C-yes/S-yes/P-no

Continental plus
French & Canadian meals
swimming pool
sitting room
2 pianos

All year

Situated on the river. Fantastic for seeing the boats for the World sailing rendezvous, this is the most charming place, good sleep, good meals, personal.

KNOWLTON

Auberge Laketree
RR 2. J0E 1V0
(514)-243-6604

$23 B&B
10 rooms, 3 pb

C-yes/S-ltd/P-no/H-yes

Full breakfast

bicycles
sitting room
piano

Food organic, varied and plenty. Artistic the inn and spacy, fits 20, unique the view over mountains and lake, Gemutlichkeit, ski trails-here is your break!

LAC SAQUAY

Auburg du Pain Chaud

(819)-278-3226

$14-20 EP
14 rooms, 4 pb
Visa, MC
C-yes/S-yes/P-no

Bar service
sitting room, piano

All year

On Highway and Lake. Marvellous view whole year around. Lake, good clear water, drinkable. Quiet for a good rest.

MONT TREMBLANT

Auburg Saugivnon
J0T 1Z0
(819)-425-2658

$25 B&B
8 rooms, 1 pb
Visa, MC, AmEx
C-yes/S-yes/P-no

Full breakfast
Dinner ala carte
sitting room

June-Oct, Dec.-April

Old World Inn, ski package at world famous Mt. Tremblant. After breakfast, start from our back yard. Relax by fireplace after dinner.

Chateau Beauvallon
Montee Ryan
(819)-425-7275

$27 pp MAP
14 rooms, 7 pb

C-yes/S-yes/P-no/H-yes

Full breakfast
Dinner, bar
sitting room, piano
bicycles
lake swimming

Nov-April, May-October

Country inn with home cooking, on a clear quiet mountain lake. Cycling, golf, tennis, windsurfing, all available within two mile proximity.

MONTREAL ————————————————————————————————

Armor Tourist Lodge $15-40
151 R. Sherbrooke, H2X 1C7 15 rooms, 7 pb
(514)-285-0894

C-yes/S-yes/P-no
All year

Once a fine Victorian townhouse in downtown Montreal. Fine woodwork in foyer and some guest rooms.

MORIN HEIGHTS ————————————————————————————

Auberge Hollandaise $33 EP   Full breakfast
Rte. 329   10 rooms, 8 pb   Dinner, bar
(514)-226-2009   Visa, MC, AmEx   sitting room, piano
                         C-yes/S-yes/P-no
All year

Rustic country inn with carved ceiling supports, tables and chairs. Large stone fireplace. View of pine woods and gently meandering river.

NORTH HATLEY ————————————————————————————

Hovey Manor $45-70 (US)   Full breakfast
Box 60, J0B 2C0   28 rooms, 28 pb   Lunch, dinner, bar
(819)-842-2421   Visa, MC, AmEx   tennis courts, 2 beaches
                         C-yes/S-yes/P-no/H-yes piano, sitting room
All year   entertainment

Formerly a private estate. All rooms with private bath. Water sports, tennis, cross-country skiing.

POINTE AU PIC ————————————————————————————

Auberge Au Petit Berber $45-90 EP   Full breakfast
1 Cote Bellevue   20 rooms, 10 pb
(418)-665-4182   Visa, MC   hot tub
                         C-yes/S-yes/P-no/H-yes entertainment
Except November   sitting room

Enjoy the charm of a French country inn situated in magnificent countryside. Tennis and nearby skiing for the sports-minded.

QUEBEC CITY ————————————————————————————

Auberge La Chouette $45-60 dbl B&B   Full breakfast
71 R. d'Auteuil   8 rooms, 8 pb
(418)-694-0232   Visa, MC, AmEx
                         C-yes/S-yes/P-no
All year

We are at the doorstep of points of interest of the historical area and enjoy a priviledged view over the Esplanade Park.

Chateau de la Terrasse $38-62
6 Terrassee Dufferin   18 rooms, 18 pb
(418)-694-9472   hot tub
                         C-yes/S-yes/P-no
February—December

Located inside the walls of Old Quebec, on the boardwalk. Front rooms overlook St. Lawrence River.

Le Chateau De Pierre $55-75   No meals
17 Av.St.Genevieve, G1R   15 rooms, 15 pb
4A8   Visa, MC
(418)-694-0429   C-yes/S-ok/P-no
All year

Old English colonial mansion, of colonial charm. With fine appointments and a distinctive atmosphere. Prominently located in Old Quebec Uppertown.

Maison Marie Rollet $44-60 EP
81 R. Ste. Anne, G1R 3X4   10 rooms, 10 pb
(418)-694-9271   Visa
                             C-yes/S-yes/P-no
All year

Well-situated, in the center of Old Quebec facing the City Hall. Parking across the street. Quiet Victorian house.

Manoir Ste. Genevieve $45-60 EP
13 Av.S.Genevieve,G1R 4A7   9 rooms, 9 pb
(418)-694-1666   MC
                             C-yes/S-yes/P-no
All year

Manor with modern facilities, furnished with antiques. Located behind Chateau Frontenac, on the St. Lawrence River. Walk to all points of interest.

SAINTE ANNE DES MONTS ————————————————————

Gite Du Mont Albert $22-70 EP
Rte 299, CP 1150, G0E 2G0   21 rooms, 8 pb
(418)-763-2288   all credit cards   piano
                             C-yes/P-no   hiking trails

Excellent food—four forks for the region—specialty: lobster thermidor, smoked salmon, fresh fish. Nicely rustic decor. Open only in summer.

VAL DAVID ————————————————————————————————

Auberg Du Vieux Foyer $35-47 MAP   Breakfast & dinner inc.
3167 Don Caster, J0T 2N0   21 rooms, 5 pb
                             Visa, MC, AmEx   sitting room, piano
                             C-yes/S-yes/P-no   bicycles
All year

Charming Swiss Chalet close to slope. Country hideaway surrounded by mountains and private lake. Excellent cuisine. Cozy and relaxing atmosphere.

Auberge Le Rucher $42-47 MAP   Full breakfast
2368 L'Eglise, J0T 2N0   13 rooms, 12 pb   Supper, bar
(819)-322-2507   Visa, MC, AmEx   hot tub, sauna
                             C-yes/S-yes/P-yes   swimming pool
June 22-Nov. 1, Dec. 1-Apr.
10   sitting room, piano

Unique French Auberge built by the owner, many hidden corners, rooms with poster beds and fireplace, country pine furniture, French cuisine.

Parker's Lodge
1340 Lac Paquin, J0T 2N0
(819)-322-2026

All year

$25-50 AP
18 rooms, 11 pb

C-yes/S-yes/P-yes/H-yes

Full breakfast
All meals
tennis courts
entertainment
sitting room, piano

SASKATCHEWAN

BURSTALL

Tiger Lily Farm
Box 135, S0N 0H0
(306)-679-4709

All year

B&B
3 rooms, 2 pb

C-yes/S-yes/P-yes/H-yes

Full breakfast
All meals if ordered
hit tub, bicycles
sitting room
library

Plenty of Canadian Geese in the Fall. Good meals.

Part III

Reservation Service Organizations

Reservation Service Organizations

These are businesses through which you can reserve a room in thousands of private homes across the country. RSO's can represent a single city, a state, or the entire country. Some require a small membership fee, others sell a list of their host homes. Many will attempt to match you with just the type of accomodation you're seeking. Please note: The RSO listings that follow are annotated as information was available. • = *National and Regional RSO's*.

ALABAMA ———————————————————————————

Bed & Breakfast Birmingham
P.O. Box 31328
Birmingham, AL 35222

Bed & Breakfast Mobile	(205)-473-2939	Free brochure
P.O. Box 66261	$24-40	Alabama only
Mobile, AL 36606	Cash	24 hours

Brunton's Bed & Breakfast
P.O. Box 1066
Scottsboro, AL 35768

ALASKA ———————————————————————————

Alaska Private Lodgings	(907)-345-2222	Free brochure
P.O. Box 110135 South Station	$25-50	Alaska only
Anchorage, AK 99511	Cash	8:30am-8:00pm

Bed & Breakfast International
1823 Bunker St.
Anchorage, AK 99503

Stay with a Friend	(907)-274-6445	Brochure SASE
3605 Arctic Blvd. No. 173	$29-56	Alaska only
Anchorage, AK 99503	Cash	9:00am-6:00pm

Fairbanks Bed & Breakfast
Box 74573
Fairbanks, AK 99707

Alaska Bed & Breakfast
114 S. Franklin., No.102
Juneau, AK 99801

ARIZONA ———————————————————————————

Bed & Breakfast in Arizona	(602)-995-2831	Brochure SASE
8433 N. Black Canyon Hwy No. 160P		Arizona only
Phoenix, AZ 85021	Visa/MC	8:00am-5:00pm

Mi Casa—Su Casa
1456 N. Scottsdale Rd No. 110
Tempe, AZ 85281

(602)-990-0682
$35-50
$25 dep, Cash

Brochure $2
Arizona only
8:00am-8:00pm

Scottsdale / San Diego B & B
P.O. Box 995
Scottsdale, AZ 85258

Desert Hospitality B & B
416 W. Eighteenth St.
Tuscon, AZ 85701

ARKANSAS ───────────────────────────────

Ozark B & B
1567 Porter
Bakesville, AR 72501

CALIFORNIA ───────────────────────────────

Visitors Advisory Service
1516 Oak Street No. 327
Alameda, CA 94501

Eye Openers Bed & Breakfast
P.O. Box 694
Altadena, CA 91001

(213)-684-4428
$40-60
MC/BA

Free brochure
California only
10:00am-6:00pm

Digs West
8191 Crowley Circle
Buena Park, CA 90621

(714)-739-1669
$40-69
Cash

Brochure SASE
California only
24 hours

Homestay
P.O. Box 326
Cambria, CA 93428

(805)-927-4613
$35-50
Visa/MC

Brochure SASE
California only
24 hours

Bed & Breakfast West Coast
4744 Third Street
Carpinteria, CA 93013

B & B of San Diego
P.O. Box 1006
Coronado, CA 93103

California B & B Inn Service
P.O. Box 1256
Chico, CA 95927

● **New Age Travel**
839 Second Avenue
Encinitas, CA 92024

(619)-436-9977

50% Dep., Cash

Brochure $4
Worldwide
10:00am-5:00pm

B & B of Southern California
P.O. Box 218
Fullerton, CA 92632

(714)-819-2568
$30-55
Cash

Free brochure
S. California
9:00am-5:00pm

Bed & Breakfast Inns of Amador
P.O. Box 10
Jackson, CA 95462

• **Bed & Breakfast International** 151 Ardmore Rd. Kensington, CA 94707	(415)-527-8836 $44-58 Visa/MC/AmEx	Free brochure Nationwide 8:30am-5:30pm
Seaview Reservations P.O. Box 1355 Laguna Beach, CA 92652	(714)-494-8878 $50-85 Cash	Free brochure California only 9:00am-5:00pm
Houseguests Inc. 672 South Lafayette Park Pl. No. 42 Los Angeles, CA 90057		
Megan's Friends 1611 9th St. Los Osos, CA 93402	(805)-528-6645 $20-55 Cash	Free brochure California
Accomodation Referral Service 105 Hennessey Dr. Napa, CA 94559		
Napa Valley B & B Reservations 1834 1st St. Napa, CA 94559	(707)-257-1051 $55-150 Visa/MC	Brochure ($) California only 9:00am-9:00pm
California Bed & Breakfast P.O. Box 1551 Sacramento, CA 95807		
Sacramento Innkeepers Association 2209 Capitol Avenue Sacramento, CA 95816		
Carolyns Bed & Breakfast Homes P.O. Box 84776 San Diego, CA 92138	(619)-435-5009 $40-95 50% Dep., Cash	Free brochure California only 9:00am-7:00pm
American Family Inn 2185 A Union St. San Francisco, CA 94123	(415)-931-3083	
University Bed & Breakfast 66 Clarendon Avenue San Francisco, CA 94114	(415)-661-8940 $32-55 Cash	Free brochure California only daily
Bed & Breakfast San Francisco 2185 A Union Street San Francisco, CA 94123	(415)-931-3083 $50-100 Visa/MC/AmEx	Free brochure California only 9:00am-5:00pm

- **American Historic Homes B & B** (714)-496-7050 Brochure $1
  P.O. Box 388 $35-47 Nationwide
  San Juan Capistrano, CA 92693 Cash 9:00am-5:00pm

- **Christian Bed & Breakfast** (714)-496-7050 Brochure $1
  Box 388 $25-40 Nationwide
  San Juan Capistrano, CA 92693 Cash 9:00am-5:00pm

Educators' Vacation Alternatives (805)-687-2947 Directory $5.50
317 Piedmont Road $17-30 U.S., Canada
Santa Barbara, CA 93105

Wine Country Bed & Breakfast
P.O. Box 3211
Santa Rosa, CA 95403

Bed-by-the-Bay
P.O. Box 902
Sausalito, CA 94966

The Intern'l Spare Room
Box 518
Solana Beach, CA 92075

Bed & Breakfast Exchange (707)-963-7756 Free brochure
P.O. Box 88 $45-100 California only
St. Helena, CA 94574 Cash 9:00am-5:00pm

Little Lodgings Booking Services
1321 Allyn Avenue
St. Helena, CA 94558

- **Home Suite Homes** (408)-733-7215 Free brochure
  1470 Firebird $25-60 Nationwide
  Sunnyvale, CA 94087 Cash 8:00am-5:00pm

- **California Houseguests Intl.** (213)-344-7878 Brochure SASE
  6051 Lindley Ave. No. 6 $45-75 CA/International
  Tarzana, CA 91356 Cash 9:00am-5:30pm

Mona's Bed & Breakfast Homes (714)-676-4729
P.O. Box 1805
Temecula, CA 92390

Bed & Breakfast Approved Hosts (805)-647-0651 Free brochure
10890 Galvin $45-100 California only
Ventura, CA 93004 Cash 8:00am-12:30pm

Bed & Breakfast of Los Angeles (213)-889-8870 Brochure SASE
32127 Harborview Lane $35-50 California only
Westlake Village, CA 91361 20% Dep., Cash 8:00am-8:00pm

Teacher's Co-op Travel Club
P.O. Box 729
Windsor, CA 95492

COLORADO

B & B of Boulder, Inc. Box 6061 Boulder, CO 80302	(303)-442-6664 $22.50-40.00 Visa/MC	Free info Boulder only 8:00am-dark
• **Bed & Breakfast Rocky Mtns.** P.O. Box 804 Colorado Springs, CO 80901	(303)-630-3433 $20-35 20% Dep., Cash	List $1 & SASE CO/MT/NM/WY 9:00am-6:00pm
Bed & Breakfast Colorado P.O. Box 20596 Denver, CO 80220	(303)-333-3340 $33-40 Visa/MC	Free brochure Colorado only 8:00am-4:00pm
Bed & Breakfast Durango 862 Main St., Suite 222 Durango, CO 81301		
Steamboat Springs Chamber P.O. Box 773377 Steamboat Springs, CO 80477		
Vail Bed & Breakfast P.O. Box 491 Vail, CO 81658	(303)-476-1225	

CONNECTICUT

• **Nautilus Bed & Breakfast** 133 Phoenix Drive Groton, CT 06340	(203)-448-1538 $35-50 Cash	Free brochure CT/RI 7:00am-10:00pm
Bed & Breakfast Guide 10 Fenway North Milford, CT 06460		
B & B Ltd. in New Haven P.O. Box 216 New Haven, CT 06513	(203)-469-3260 $22.50-45.00 Cash	Brochure $2 Connecticut daily
Seacoast Landings 21 Fuller Street New London, CT	(203)-442-1940 $40-80 Cash	Free brochure Connecticut 8:00am-8:00pm
American Shakespeare Theatre 1850 Elm St. Stratford, CT 06497		
• **Covered Bridge Bed & Breakfast** West Cornwall, CT 06796	(203)-672-6052 $45-72 Cash	Free brochure CT/MA 9:00am-6:00pm
Nutmeg Bed & Breakfast 56 Fox Chase Lane West Hartford, CT 06107	(203)-236-6698 Visa/MC	Broch. $2 SASE Connecticut 9:00am-6:00pm

DELAWARE

• **Bed & Breakfast of Delaware**
1804 Breen Lane
Wilmington, DE 19810

(302)-475-0340
$30-35
20% Dep., Cash

Brochure
DE/PA
3:00pm-6:00pm

FLORIDA

B & B Registry of Florida
Box 322
Jupiter, FL 33458

Tropical Isles B & B Co.
P.O. Box 490382
Key Biscayne, FL 33149

Suncoast Accomodations
P.O. Box 8334
Madeira Beach, FL 33738

B & B of the Florida Keys, Inc
5 Man-O-War Drive
Marathon, FL 33050

(305)-743-4118
$25-40
Cash

Free brochure
Florida only
8:00am-11:00pm

Bed & Breakfast Company
1205 Mariposa Ave. No. 233
Miami, FL 33146

(305)-661-3270
$30-50
Cash

Brochure SASE
Florida only
24 hours

Florida Suncoast B & B
P.O. Box 12
Palm Harbor, FL 33563

(813)-784-5118
$28-40
Cash

Brochure $3
Florida/England
8:00am-6:00pm

Florida Lifestyles B & B
445 S.W. 2nd St. No. 30
Pompano Beach, FL 33060

Sarasota Bed & Breakfast
3230 South Tamiami Trail
Sarasota, FL

Tallahassee Bed & Breakfast
3023 Windy Hill Lane
Tallahassee, FL 32308

(904)-385-3768

Cash

Free brochure
Florida only
6:30am-11:00pm

AAA Bed & Breakfast of Florida
P.O. Box 1316
Winter Park, FL 32790

(305)-628-3733

Cash

Free brochure
Florida only
9:00am-5:00pm

GEORGIA

At Home in Athens
120 Cedar Circle
Athens, GA 30605

Bed & Breakfast Atlanta
1221 Fairview Road N.E.
Atlanta, GA 30306

378-6026
$24-52
20% Dep., Cash

Free brochure
Georgia only
10:00am-5:00pm

Southern Home Hospitality
2472 Lauderdale Dr. NE
Atlanta, GA 30345

(404)-493-1930

Hideaway Bed & Breakfast
Star Route Box 76
Blue Ridge, GA 30513

(404)-623-3663

Home Hospitality
1111 Clairmont Road, Suite D4
Decatur, GA 30030

Bed & Breakfast-Savannah
117 West Gordon Street
Savannah, GA 31401

(912)-238-0518
$24-48
Visa/MC/AmEx

Free brochure
Georgia only
24 hours

Savannah Historic Inns R.S.
1900 Lincoln Street
Savannah, GA 31401

(912)-233-7666
$28-88
Visa/MC/AmEx

Free brochure
Georgia only
9:00am-9:00pm

Intimate Inns of Savannah
19 W. Perry Street
Savannah, GA 31401

Savannah Area Visitors Bureau
801 Broad Street
Savannah, GA 31499

(912)-236-1774
$65-80
Cash

Free brochure
Georgia only
24 hours

Quail Country Bed & Breakfast
1104 Old Monticello Road
Thomasville, GA 31792

(912)-226-7218

Visa/MC

Free brochure
Georgia only
24 hours

HAWAII ———————————

Pacific—Hawaii B & B
19 Kai Nani Place
Kailua, Oahu, HI 96734

Bed & Breakfast Hawaii
P.O. Box 449
Kapia, HI 96746

(808)-822-1582
$25-40
15% Dep., Cash

Directory $5
Hawaii only
8:30am-4:30pm

ILLINOIS ———————————

• **Bed & Breakfast Chicago, Inc.**
P.O. Box 14088
Chicago, IL 60614

(312)-951-0085
$45-70
Visa/MC

Free brochure
IL/WI/IN
9:00am-5:00pm

Bed & Board/America Inc.
7308 W. Madison Ave.
Forest Park, IL 60130

(312)-771-8100

Bed & Breakfast Quad Cities
2530 29 ½ Street
Rock Island, IL 61201

INDIANA

- **Inn Review Newsletter**   (317)-742-0252   Subscript'n $12
  P.O. Box 1345   Nationwide
  Lafayette, IN 47902   Visa/MC/AmEx   8:00am-5:00pm

Tammy Galm B & B
P.O. Box 546
Nashville, IN 47448

IOWA

Bed & Breakfast in Iowa, Ltd.   (515)-277-9018   Brochure $1
7104 Franklin Avenue $20-55   IA/SD
Des Moines, IA 50322   Visa/MC   9:00am-5:00pm

KANSAS

Kansas City Bed & Breakfast   (913)-268-4214   Free brochure
P.O. Box 14781 $32-50   KS/MO
Lenexa, KS 66215   Cash   5:00pm-10:00pm

Kansas City B & B
15416 Johnson Drive
Shawnee, KS 66217

KENTUCKY

Kentucky Homes Bed & Breakfast
1431 St. James Court
Louisville, KY 40208

LOUISIANA

- **Southern Comfort B & B**   (504)-346-1928   Brochure $1
  2856 Hundred Oaks $30-90   LA/MS
  Baton Rouge, LA 70808   Cash   8:00am-8:00pm

Bed & Breakfast Inc.   (504)-525-4640   Free brochure
1236 Decatur Street $25-35   Louisiana only
New Orleans, LA 70116   20% Dep., Cash   24 hours

Bed & Breakfast New Orleans
3658 Gerfilly, Blvd.
New Orleans, LA 70122

- **New Orleans Bed & Breakfast**   (504)-949-6705   Brochure SASE
  P.O. Box 8163 $30-125   LA/MS
  New Orleans, LA 70182   Cash   8:00am-8:00pm

MAINE _____

B & B Down East Box 547 Eastbrook, ME 04634	(207)-565-3517 $15-40 Visa/MC	Brochure $1 Maine 8:00am-8:00pm
B & B Registry of Maine 32 Colonial Village Falmouth, ME 04105	(207)-781-4528 $25-40 Visa/MC	Free list Maine only nights/wknds

The Maine Publicity Bureau
97 Winthrop Street
Hallowell, ME 04347

Chamber of Commerce
142 Free Street
Portland, ME 04101

Nova Scotia Tourist Information Office
129 Commercial Street
Portland, ME 04101

B & B Accomodations
P.O. Box 805
Rockland, ME 04841

MARYLAND _____

Sharp-Adams Inc. 8 Gentry Court Annapolis, MD 21403	(301)-269-6232 $40-165 $25 dep., Cash	Free brochure Maryland only 9:00am-5:00pm

MASSACHUSETTS _____

● **Bed & Breakfast Associates** P.O. Box 166 Babson Pk. Branch Boston, MA 02157	(617)-872-6990 $25-55 Visa/MC	Free brochure MA/ME/VT/NH 10:00am-5:00pm

Elder Hostels
100 Boylston, Suite 200
Boston, MA 02116

B & B Brookline/Boston
Box 732
Brookline, MA 02146

Greater Boston Hospitality P.O. Box 1142 Brookline, MA 02146	(617)-734-0807 $30-100 Cash	Free brochure Massachusetts 24 hours

Bed & Breakfast Cambridge
73 Kirkland Street
Cambridge, MA 02138

City Cousins Inc.
111Lakeview Ave.
Cambridge, MA 02138

Cape Cod Chamber of Commerce
Hyannis 96
Cape Cod, MA 02601

Hampshire Hill Bed & Breakfast
P.O. Box 17
Chesterfield, MA 01012

House Guests, Cape Cod
85 Hokum Rock Road
Dennis, MA 02638

B & B in Minuteman Country
8 Linmoor Terrace
Lexington, MA 02173

● **Educators Inn**   (617)-334-6144   Directory
P.O. Box 663 $20-100   Most States
Lynnfield, MA 01940   Memb. fee

Christian Hospitality   (617)-947-2356   Free brochure
P.O. Box Drawer D $30-45   Nationwide
Middleboro, MA 02346   Cash   7:00am-9:00pm

Pineapple Hospitality, Inc. (617)-990-1696   Brochure ($)
384 Rodney French Blvd. $26-35   New England
New Bedford, MA 02744   Cash   9:00am-5:00pm

Host Homes of Boston   (617)-244-1308   Free brochure
P.O. Box 117 $32-45   Massachusetts
Newton, MA 02168   Visa/MC/AmEx   8:00am-6:00pm

New England Bed & Breakfast
1045 Centre Street
Newton, MA 02159

Be Our Guest B & B   (617)-746-1208   Free brochure
P.O. Box 1333 $39-45   Massachusetts
Plymouth, MA 02360   Visa/MC/AmEx   8:30am-10:30pm

Berkshire Bed & Breakfast   (413)-783-5111   Brochure $1
141 Newton Road $20-50   MA/NY
Springfield, MA 01118 $20 dep., Cash   9:00am-5:00pm

Pioneer Valley Bed & Breakfast
84 Agnes Street
Springfield, MA 01108

Sturbridge Bed & Breakfast   (413)-783-5111   Brochure $1
141 Newton Road $25-50   Massachusetts
Springfield, MA 01118 $20 dep., Cash   9:00am-5:00pm

Bed & Breakfast Cape Cod
Box 341
West Hyannisport, MA 02672

(617)-775-2772
$35-55
25% Dep., Cash

Free brochure
Massachusetts
9:30am-5:30pm

MICHIGAN

Betsy Ross Bed & Breakfast
3057 Betsy Ross Drive
Bloomfield Hills, MI 48013

646-5357
$25-40
Cash

Free brochure
Michigan only
9:00am-9:00pm

B & B of Grand Rapids
344 College S.E.
Grand Rapids, MI 49503

(616)-451-4849
$35-40
$20 dep., Cash

Free brochure
Michigan
9:00am-5:00pm

Hometels of Michigan
8019 Hendrie Street
Huntington Woods, MI 48070

MINNESOTA

• **Bed & Breakfast Upper Midwest**
P.O. Box 28036
Crystal Lake, MN 55428

(612)-535-7135
$20-54
Cash

Free brochure
MN/SD/WI
24 hours

Uptown-Lake District B & B
2000 Aldrich Avenue S.
Minneapolis, MN 55405

Bed & Breakfast Registry
P.O. Box 80174
St. Paul, MN 55108

(612)-646-4238
$30-55
Visa/MC

Brochure $1

8:30am-10:00pm

MISSISSIPPI

Lincoln Ltd. Bed & Breakfast
Box 3479
Meridian, MS 39301

(601)-482-5483
$45-75
$25 dep., Cash

Free brochure
Mississippi
8:30am-5:30pm

Pilgrimage Garden Club
P.O. Box 347
Natchez, MS 39120

446-6631
$80
Visa/MC/AmEx

Free brochure
Mississippi
8:30am-5:30pm

MISSOURI

• **Ozark Mountain Country B & B**
Box 295
Branson, MO 65616

334-5077
$25-38
$20 dep., Visa/MC

Free brochure
MO/AR
24 hours

Truman Country Bed & Breakfast
Rt. 2 Box 763K
Independence, MO 64050

(816)-796-8653

Lexington Bed & Breakfast
115 N. 18th Street
Lexington, MO 64067

(816)-259-4163

• **Midwest Host Bed & Breakfast** P.O. Box 27 Saginaw, MO 64846	(417)-782-9112 $15-20 pp Cash	Brochure SASE International Mail only
• **Bed & Breakfast of St. Louis** 1 Grandview Heights St. Louis, MO 63131	(314)-965-4328 $25-189 MC	Directory $3 MO/IL 24 hours
Bed & Breakfast St. Louis 16 Green Acres St. Louis, MO 63137	(314)-868-2335 $20-45 Cash	Free list St. Louis area 24 hours
River Country Bed & Breakfast No 1 Grandview Heights St. Louis, MO 63131	(314)-965-4328	

MONTANA

Western Bed & Breakfast Hosts P.O. Box 322 Kalispell, MT 59901	(406)-257-4476 $20-38 Cash	Free brochure Montana only 9:00am-5:00pm

NEBRASKA

B & B of Nebraska
1464 28th Ave.
Columbus, NE 68601

NEVADA

B & B/Ski America & Canada
P.O. Box 5246
Incline Village, NV 89450

NEW HAMPSHIRE

New Hampshire B & B RFD 3, Box 53 Laconia, NH 03246	(603)-279-8348 $15-45 Cash	Brochure $1 New Hampshire noon-8:00pm

NEW JERSEY

B & B of New Jersey (201)-444-7409
103 Godwin Avenue, Suite 132
Midland Park, NJ 07432

B & B By-the-Sea
600 Mercer Avenue
Spring Lake Heights, NJ 07762

NEW MEXICO

B & B Directory of New Mexico
P.O. Box 26866
Albuquerque, NM 87125

Bed & Breakfast Sunbelt
1310 Calle de Ranchero, N.E.
Albuquerque, NM 87106

Bed & Breakfast of Santa Fe 218 E. Buena Vista Street Santa Fe, NM 87501	(505)-982-3332 $30-60 Visa/MC	Brochure SASE New Mexico only 24 hours

NEW YORK —————————————————————————

Travelers Retreat
RD 3, Melvin Lane
Baldwinsville, NY 13027

Bed & Breakfast USA Ltd. P.O. Box 528 Croton-on-Hudson, NY 10521	(914)-271-6228 $30-50 Visa	Free brochure New York 7:30am-9:00pm

Alternative Lodging P.O. Box 1782 East Hampton, NY 11937	(516)-324-9449 Visa/MC	Free brochure New York only 9:00am-9:00pm

Hampton Hosts
P.O. Box 507
East Hampton, NY 11937

Lodgings Plus Bed & Breakfast
P.O. Box 279
East Hampton, NY 11937

Hampton Bed & Breakfast Registry
Box 695
East Moriches, NY 11940

Cherry Valley Ventures
6116 Cherry Valley Turnpike
Lafayette, NY 13084

● **No. Country B & B Res. Svce.** Box 286-B Lake Placid, NY 12946	(518)-523-3739 $12-100 Cash	Free brochure NY/VT 11:00am-8:00pm

New Yorkers at Home 301 E. 60th St. New York, NY 10022	(212)-838-7015 $35-55 Cash	Brochure SASE New York only 9:00am-5:00pm

Urban Ventures 322 Central Park West New York, NY 10025	(212)-662-1234 $44-135 VISA/MC	Free brochure New York City 9:00am-5:00pm

Rainbow Hospitality B & B 9348 Hennepin Avenue Niagara Falls, NY 14304	(716)-283-4794 $25-60 $7 dep., Cash	Brochure $1 New York only 8:00am-5:00pm

Bed & Breakfast Guide
Rd. 2, Box 64
Rhinebeck, NY 12572

● **Tobin's Bed & Breakfast Guide**   Brochure $5
Rd. 2, Box 64 $25-45   East Coast
Rhinebeck, NY 12572   Cash   Mail only

Bed & Breakfast of Central New York
1846 Belleview Ave.
Syracuse, NY 13204

East End Bed & Breakfast Inc.   (516)-288-4488
P.O. Box 178
West Hampton, NY 11977

NORTH CAROLINA ─────────────────────────────────────

Charlotte B & B—The Chimneys   (704)-366-0979
1700-2 DeLane Avenue $20-30   North Carolina
Charlotte, NC 28211   Cash   10:00am-5:00pm

Bed & Breakfast/Greensboro   (919)-272-6248
210 W. Bessemer Ave.
Greensboro, NC 27410

OHIO ──

Chillicothe Bed & Breakfast
189 North High St.
Chillicothe, OH 45601

Friendly Way Stays Division   (216)-321-3213
530 Hanna Bldg.
Cleveland, OH 44118

Private Lodgings, Inc.   (216)-321-3213 Free info
P.O. Box 18590   Cleveland area
Cleveland, OH 44118   Cash   9:00am-5:00pm

Columbus Bed & Breakfast   (614)-444-8888 Free brochure
769 S. Third Street   Ohio only
Columbus, OH 43206   Cash   24 hours

Buckeye Bed & Breakfast
P.O. Box 130
Powell, OH 43065

OREGON ──

Bend Bed & Breakfast
19838 Ponderosa Drive
Bend, OR 97707

Galluci Hosts, Hostels, B & B
P.O. Box 1303
Lake Oswego, OR 97034

Bed & Breakfast Oregon 5733 S.W. Dickinson St. Portland, OR 97219	(503)-245-0642 $19-35 Visa/MC	Brochure SASE Oregon only 9:00am-7:00pm
● **P T International** 1318 S.W. Troy St. Portland, OR 97219	(800)-547-1463 Visa/MC/AmEx	Free brochure International 8:00am-5:00pm
● **Northwest Bed & Breakfast** 7707 S.W. Locust Street Portland, OR 97223	(503)-246-8366 $20-40 Cash	Directory $5 Northwest 9:00am-7:00pm

PENNSYLVANIA ─────────────────────

B & B of Southeast Penn. Box 278, RD 1 Barto, PA 19504	(215)-845-3526 $25-40 20% Dep., Cash	Brochure $1 Pennsylvania 24 hours
B & B of Southeast Pennsylvania Box 278, RD. 1 Barto, PA 19504	(215)-845-3526	
Bed & Breakfast Pocono Northeast P.O. Box 115 Bear Creek, PA 18602	(717)-472-3145	
Nassly's Old Home Inns 624 West Chestnut St. Lancaster, PA 17602		
B & B of Philadelphia P.O. Box 101 Oreland, PA 19075	(215)-884-1084 $18-85 Visa/MC	List $3 Pennsylvania 9:00am-12am
Bed & Breakfast/Center City 1908 Spruce Street Philadelphia, PA 19103		
Rest & Repast B & B Service P.O. Box 126 Pine Grove Mills, PA 16868	(814)-238-1484 $30-37 $20 dep., Cash	Free brochure Pennsylvania after 5:00pm
Pittsburgh Bed & Breakfast P.O. Box 25353 Pittsburgh, PA 15242	(412)-241-5746 $32-65 Cash	Brochure SASE Pennsylvania 9:00am-11:00pm

Please Mention *The Complete Guide* **to the innkeeper when you reserve your room**

● **Country Cousins B & B**   (717)-762-2722   Brochure SASE
228 W. Main Street $35-48   PA/WV
Waynesboro, PA 17268   Cash   1:00pm-6:00pm

RHODE ISLAND ——————————————————————————

Narragansett Chamber of Commerce
Box 742
Narragansett, RI 02882

Bed & Breakfast Registry   (401)-846-0362
Castle Keep, 44 Everett
Newport, RI 02840

Guest House Association
23 Brinley Street
Newport, RI 02840

At Home in New England
P.O. Box 25
Saunderstown, RI 02874

Charletown Chamber of Commerce
154 Main St.
Westerly, RI 02891

SOUTH CAROLINA ——————————————————————

Bay Street Accomodations
601 Bay Street
Beaufort, SC 29902

Charleston Society B & B   (803)-723-4948   Free brochure
84 Murray Blvd.   South Carolina
Charleston, SC 29401   Cash   9:00am-6:00pm

Historic Charleston B & B   (803)-722-6606   Free brochure
23 Wentworth Street $50-100   South Carolina
Charlestown, SC 29401   Cash   1:00pm-6:00pm

TENNESSEE ——————————————————————————————

Grinders Switch B & B
Reseveration Agency   (615)-729-5002
Rt. 2, Box 44
Centerville, TN 37033

Hospitality at Home
Rt. 1, Buttermilk Road
Lenoir City, TN 37771

● **Bed & Breakfast in Memphis** (901)-726-5920   Brochure $2.50
P.O. Box 41621   Mid-South
Memphis, TN 38104   Visa/MC   8:00am-7:00pm

River Rendezvous
P.O. Box 240001
Memphis, TN 38124

Nashville Bed & Breakfast
P.O. Box 15651
Nashville, TN 37215

Nashville Host Homes	(615)-331-5244	Free brochure
P.O. Box 110227	$26-45	Tennessee only
Nashville, TN 37222-0227	Visa/MC	24 hours

Bed & Breakfast Nashville
1101 17th Avenue
South Nashville, TN 37215

TEXAS ————————————————————————

Sand Dollar Hospitality	(512)-853-1222	Free directory
3605 Mendenhall	$20-50	Texas
Corpus Christi, TX 78415	Cash	7:00am-7:00pm

Bed & Breakfast Texas Style	(214)-298-8586	Brochure $2
4224 W. Red Bird Lane	$20-40	Texas
Dallas, TX 75237	Cash	8:30am-6:00pm

Dallas Hosts at Home
LBJ Freeway, Suite 180
Dallas, TX 75234

• **Bed & Breakfast Society**	(512)-997-4712	membership
330 W. Main Street	$15-25 memb.	International
Fredericksburg, TX 78624	Visa/MC	10:00am-5:00pm

Gasthaus B & B Lodging	(512)-997-4712	Free brochure
322 East Main Street		Fredericksburg
Fredericksburg, TX 78624	Visa/MC	9:30am-5:00pm

B & B Society of Houston	(713)-666-6372	Free brochure
4432 Holt	$25-85	Houston area
Houston, TX 77401	Cash	9:00am-5:00pm

Bed & Breakfast of Dallas/Fort Worth
1701 W. Greenville Ave. No. 304
Richardson, TX 75081

B & B Hosts of San Antonio	(512)-824-8036	Free brochure
166 Rockhill	$36-58	Texas
San Antonio, TX 78209		9:00am-5:00pm

UTAH ————————————————————————

Eller B & B
164 S. 900 East
Salt Lake City, UT 84102

Bed & Breakfast Assoc. of Utah (801)-532-7076
P.O. Box 81602   Utah only
Salt Lake City, UT 84108   Cash   9:00am-5:00pm

VERMONT

- **American B & B in New England**   Brochure $3
  Box 983   NH/VT/MA/NY
  St. Albans, VT 05478   Cash   9:00am-4:00pm

VIRGINIA

Bed & Breakfast—Alexandria
819 Prince Street
Alexandria, VA 22314

Princely Bed & Breakfast   (703)-683-2159   Free list
819 Prince Street $53 average   Alexandria only
Alexandria, VA 22314   Cash   9:00am-6:00pm

Blue Ridge B & B   (703)-955-3955   Brochure SASE
Rte. 1, Box 517 $25-40   VA/WV
Bluemont, VA 22012   Cash   24 hours

Guest Houses B & B   (804)-979-7264   Brochure SASE
P.O. Box 5737   Virginia only
Charlottesville, VA 22903   VISA/MC   1:00pm-6:00pm

Sojourners Bed & Breakfast   (804)-384-1655
3609 Tanglewood Lane
Lynchburg, VA 24503

Bed and Breakfast of Tidewater   (804)-627-1983   Free brochure
P.O. Box 3343 $35-90   Virginia only
Norfolk, VA 23514   Cash   24 hours

Bensonhouse of Richmond   648-7560   Brochure SASE
P.O. Box 15131 $32-66   Virginia only
Richmond, VA 23227   Visa/MC   1:00pm-5:00pm

The Travel Tree   (804)-229-4037   Free brochure
P.O. Box 83 $25-60   Virginia only
Williamsburg, VA 23187   Cash   5:00pm-9:00pm

WASHINGTON

- **B & B Service (BABS)**   (206)-733-8642   Book $3.75
  P.O. Box 5025 $18-28   Nationwide
  Bellingham, WA 98227   Cash   8:00am-10:00pm

RSVP Bed & Breakfast Res. Stn.   (206)-384-6586   Free brochure
P.O. Box 778 $30-36   Washington only
Ferndale, WA 98248   Cash   9:00am-5:00pm

Guest House Bed & Breakfast
835 E. Christenson Road
Greenback, WA 98253

Whidbey Island B & B Ass'n P.O. Box 259 Langley, WA 98260	(206)-221-8709 $35-85 Visa/MC	Free brochure Washington only 24 hours

Travellers' Bed & Breakfast
P.O. Box 492
Mercer Island, WA 98040

• **Pacific Bed & Breakfast** 701 N.W. 60th Street Seattle, WA 98107	(206)-784-0539 $28-40 $20 dep., Cash	Free brochure WA/ID 7:00am-7:00pm

West Coast Bed & Breakfast Club
11304 20th Pl. S.W.
Seattle, WA 98146

• **INNterlodging Bed & Breakfast** P.O. Box 7044 Tacoma, WA 98407	(206)-756-0343 $45 membership Cash	Listing International 8:00am-6:00pm

WASHINGTON, D.C.

Bed & Breakfast of Washington
P.O. Box 12011
Washington, DC 20005

• **Sweet Dreams & Toast, Inc.** P.O. Box 4835-0035 Washington, DC 20008	(202)-483-9191 $35-50 Visa, MC	Free brochure DC/VA/MD 11:00am-6:00pm

The Bed & Breakfast League
2855 29th Street N.W.
Washington, DC 20008

WISCONSIN

Bed & Breakfast in Door Country
Route 2
Algoma, WI 54201

Bed & Breakfast of Milwaukee 3017 N. Downer Avenue Milwaukee, WI 53211	(414)-342-5030 $30-50 Visa/MC	Wisconsin 9:00am-9:00pm

WYOMING

B & B of Columbia Comsy
P.O. Box 122
Spencertown, WY 12165

Canada

ALBERTA ─────────────────────────────────────

Banff/Jasper Central Reservation (403)-762-5561
204 Caribou, P.O. Box 1628 $20 up Alberta only
Banff, AB Canada T0L 0C0 Cash 9:00am-5:00pm

AAA Bed West (403)-240-1151
3 Willow Cresc., S.W. $20-30 Alberta only
Calgary, AB Canada T3G 3B8 $20 dep., Cash 10:00am-10:00pm

Alberta Bed & Breakfast
5209-27 Grier Place N.E.
Calgary, AB T2K 5Y5

Jasper/Banff Central Reservation
626 Connaught Avenue
Jasper, AB T0L 0C0

Mountain Travellers Jasper Nat'l Park

Jasper, AB T0E 1E0

BRITISH COLUMBIA ──────────────────────────

Born Free Bed & Breakfast Agency (604)-298-8815
4390 Frances St.
Burnaby, BC V5C2R3

Bed & Breakfast in B.C.
Box 24492
Vancouver, BC V5T HCS

Canadian Bed & Breakfast
726 Richards
Vancouver, BC V6B 3L2

Canadian Bed & Breakfast (604)-321-1265
664-West 71st Ave.
Vancouver, BC V6P3A1

Greater Vancouver Convention Bureau
650 Burrard St.
Vancouver, BC V6C 2L2

Town & Country B & B in B.C. 731-5942 Book $5.95
P.O. Box 46544, Stn. G B.C. only
Vancouver, BC Canada V6R 4G6 Cash

Vancouver & Vicinity B&B 731-5942
Box 24492 Station CG
Vancouver, BC V5T VE1

AAA Bed & Breakfast Canada
P.O. Box 6010, Station C
Victoria, BC V8P S3M

Tourism British Columbia
1117 Wharf St.
Victoria, BC V8W 272

Traveller's Bed & Breakfast	(604)-477-3069	
1840 Midgard		
Victoria, BC V8P 2Y9		

Victoria Hospitality Club	(604)-477-5604	
1240 Gladstone		
Victoria, BC V8T 1G6		

VIP Bed & Breakfast	(604)-477-5604	Free info
1786 Teakwood Road		BC only
Victoria, BC, Canada V8N 1G2	Cash	7:00am-10:00pm

MANITOBA ——————————————————————

Canadian B & B
Box 5
Petersfield, MB R0C 2L0

Canadian B & B in Manitoba
35 Pontiac Bay
Winnipeg, MB R3K 0S6

NEW BRUNSWICK ——————————————————————

New Brunswick Tourism
P.O. Box 12345
Frederick, NB E3B 5C3

NEWFOUNDLAND ——————————————————————

Tourist Services Division
Box 2061
St. John's, NF A1C 5R8

NORTHWEST TERRITORIES ——————————————————

Travel Arctic
Yellowknife, NW X1A 229

Please mention this guide when you make your booking

NOVA SCOTIA

Halifax Metro Bed & Breakfast
Box 1613, Station M
Halifax, NS B3J 2Y3

ONTARIO

Beachburg & Area Bed & Breakfast
Box 146
Beachburg, ON K0J 1C0

The Bruce Trail Association
Box 857, 680 Plains Rd. W.
Hamilton, ON L8N 3N9

Bed & Breakfast Kingston Area 10 Westview Rd. Kingston, ON Canada K7M 2C3	(613)-542-0214 $23-34 Cash	Brochure $1 Ontario 7:30am-11:00pm

London & Area Bed & Breakfast 720 Headley Dr. London, ON Canada N6N 3V6	(519)-471-6228 $22-30 Cash	Brochure SASE Ontario daily

Shaw Festival Theatre
Box 774
Niagra-on-Lake, ON L0S 1J0

Information Orillia
18 Peter Street North
Orillia, ON L3V 4Y7

Downtown Ottawa Bed & Breakfast
478 Albert Street
Ottawa, ON K1R 5B5

Ottawa Area Bed & Breakfast
Box 4848 Station E
Ottawa, ON K1S 5J1

Country Host
RR 1
Palgrave, ON L0N 1P0

Information Paris
63 Grand River Street North
Paris, ON N3L 2M3

Paris Bed & Breakfast
63 Grand River, Station N
Paris, ON N3L 2M3

Penetanguishene CP 1270 Penetanguishene, ON L0K 1P0	(705)-549-3116 $25-30 Cash	 Ontario 9:00am-5:00pm

Bed & Breakfast Prince Edward County
Box 1500
Picton, ON K0K 2T0

St. Catherines
Box 3025
St. Catherines, ON L2R 7E9

Stratford Area Bed & Breakfast
38 Albert Street
Stratford, ON N5A 3K3

Stratford Bed & Breakfast 123 Waterloo St. Stratford, ON Canada N5A 4B3	(519)-273-4840 $25-30 Visa/AmEx	Ontario 24 hours	

Stratford Festival Accomodations
Box 520
Stratford, ON N5A 6V2

Ontario Travel
900 Bay Street, Queen's Park
Toronto, ON M7A 2E5

Toronto Bed & Breakfast P.O. Box 74, Station M Toronto, ON Canada M6S 4T2	(416)-233-3887 $40 average Cash	Booklet $3 Toronto area evenings/wknds	

Metropolitan Bed & Breakfast
12 Danzig Street
West Hill, ON M1E 2K8

PRINCE EDWARD ISLAND ———————————————

Visitors Services Division
P.O. Box 940
Charlottetown, PE C1A 7MJ

Kensington Area Tourist Assn RR 1 Kensington, PEI Can C0B 1M0	(902)-836-5418 $12-27 Cash	Free brochure Pr. Edward Is. 24 hours	

QUEBEC ———————————————

Agricotours
525 Ave. Viger
Montreal, QB H2L 2P1

Bed & Breakfast Montreal
4692 Kent St.
Montreal, QB 3W1 H1

Montreal Area B & B 5020 St. Kevin St. No.8 Montreal, QB Canada H3W 1P4	(514)-735-7493 $35-65 Cash	Free brochure Quebec 8:30am-9:00pm	

Tourism Quebec
CP 20 000
Quebec, QB G1K 7X2

Les Gites L'Estrie
2883 West King Street
Sherbrooke, QB G1L 1C6

Gite Quebec	(418)-651-1860	Free brochure
3729 Avenue leCorbusier		Quebec only
St-Foy, QB Canada G1W 4R8	Cash	24 hours

Montrealers-at-Home	(514)-932-9690	Free brochure
331 Clarke, Ste. 29	$25-50	Montreal/Quebec
Westmount, Mont., QB CAN H3Z 2E7	Cash	9:00am-6:00pm

SASKATCHEWAN

Sask Travel
3211 Albert Street
Regina, SK S4S 5W6

YUKON

Tourism Yukon
Box 2703
Whitehorse, YU Y1A 2C6

PUERTO RICO

Puerto Rico Tourist Co.
1290 Avenue of the Americas
New York, NY 10104

VIRGIN ISLANDS

U.S. Virgin Islands Gov't Travel Service
1270 Ave. of the Americas
New York, NY 10020

Part IV

B & B Inns
With
Special Amenities

FISHING

Nothing like a good catch. These inns are near the haunts of the really big ones. Fishing over, head back to the inn and tell tall tales to fellow enthusiasts.

Sierra Shangri-La
Downieville, CA

River Rock Inn
Placerville, CA

James Creek Ranch Lodging
Pope Valley, CA

Outlook Lodge
Green Mountain Falls, CO

Harbour Inne
Mystic, CT

The 1735 House
Amelia Island, FL

Eden House
Key West, FL

Redfish Lake Lodge
Stanley, ID

Grey Rock Inn
Northeast Harbor, ME

The Inn at 77 Shore Rd.
Ogunquit, ME

The Squire Tarbox Inn
Wiscasset, ME

Dockside Guest Quarters
York, ME

Bay Breeze Guest House
Cape Cod, MA

Blue Lake Lodge
Mecosta, MI

Izaak Walton Inn
Essex, MT

Broken Drum Guest Ranch
Pecos, NM

The Hedges
Blue Mountain Lake, NY

Garnet Hill Lodge
North River, NY

Pine Hill Arms
Pine Hill, NY

Stonehearth Inn
Bat Cave, NC

Folkstone Lodge
Bryson City, NC

Blue Boar Lodge
Robbinsville, NC

Tu Tu Tun Lodge
Gold Beach, OR

Steamboat Inn
Idleyld Park, OR

Morrison's Lodge
Merlin, OR

Lake Creek Lodge
Sisters, OR

Kero Mountain Guest Resort
Sevierville, TN

Churchill House Inn
Brandon, VT

Black Lantern Inn
Montgomery Village, VT

Fishing, *Cont'd*

Cameron Residence
Norfolk, VA

Black Cat Guest Ranch
Hinton, AB   CAN

Campbell River Lodge
Campbell River, BC   CAN

Riverbend Inn
Campbell River, BC   CAN

Wilcuma Resort
Cobble Hill, BC   CAN

Gimmy's Farm & Guest House
Fort St. John, BC   CAN

Quilchena Hotel
Quilchena, BC   CAN

Lord Jim's Lodge
Sechelt, BC   CAN

The Compass Rose
Grand Manan, NB   CAN

Shiretown Inn
St. Andrews By-the-Sea, NB   CAN

Shining Tides
Annapolis, NS   CAN

Kilmuir Place
Cape Breton, NS   CAN

Riverside Inn
Cape Breton, NS   CAN

Camelot
Musquodoboit Harbor, NS   CAN

Sterling Lodge
Newboro, ON   CAN

Outer Lake Haus
Huberdeau, QB CAN

Auberge Le Coin Du Banc
Huberdeau, QB   CAN

SPAS

Hot mineral waters are nature's own relaxant. These inns have a close proximity to, or are, spas.

Williams House Inn
Hot Springs, AR

Scarlett's Country Inn
Calistoga, CA

St. Elmo Hotel
Ouray, CO

Weisbaden Hot Spr. Spa & Lodging
Ouray, CO

Jackson Hotel
Poncha Springs, CO

Idaho City Hotel
Idaho City, ID

Idaho Rocky Mountain Ranch
Stanley, ID

Mary Anne Peterson B&B
Monroe, UT

LOW PRICE

The following lodgings are particularly noted for modest pricing. It is possible to obtain a room for $30 or less.

Kraft Korner
Mobile, AL

The Cochise Hotel
Cochise, AZ

Casa Arguello
San Francisco, CA

Clementina's Bay Brick Inn
San Francisco, CA

Hotel Edward II
San Francisco, CA

Pension San Francisco
San Francisco, CA

Little Red School Haus
Aspen, CO

The Imperial Hotel
Cripple Creek, CO

St. Elmo Hotel
Ouray, CO

The Alma House
Silverton, CO

Idaho City Hotel
Idaho City, ID

Hobson's Bluffdale
Eldred, IL

Doe Run Inn
Brandenburg, KY

Weld Inn
Weld, ME

Governor's Inn
Lexington, MI

Blue Lake Lodge
Mecosta, MI

Lake Shore Farm
Northwood, NH

Los Alamos B & B
Los Alamos, NM

The Plum Tree
Pilar, NM

Casa Sibella
Santa Fe, NM

Elmshade Guest House
Ithica, NY

Agnes Hall Tourist Home
Oneonta, NY

Mountain High
Glenville, NC

La Anna Guest House
Cresco, PA

Smoketown Village Tourist Home
Smoketown, PA

Landmark Inn
Castroville, TX

Seven Wives Inn
St. George, UT

Low Price, *Cont'd*

Fox Stand Inn
Royalton, VT

Fiddlers Green Inn
Stowe, VT

Palmer's Chart House
Deer Harbor, WA

The College Inn
Seattle, WA

Pine Gables Inn
Evanston, WY

Timber Ridge Lodge
Nanton, AB   CAN

Deer Bank Farm
Morris, MB   CAN

The Village Inn
Trinity, NF   CAN

The Blue Heron Inn
Pugwash, NS   CAN

Hart & Hart's Tourist Home
Cape Breton, NS   CAN

The Senator Guest Home
Wallace, NS   CAN

Churchill Farm Tourist Home
Bonshaw, PEI   CAN

Gay Breeze Tourist Home
Stanley Bridge, PEI   CAN

Auberge La Matre
Comte de Mantane, QB   CAN

Auberge Laketree
Knowlton, QB   CAN

Auberge du Pain Chaud
Lac Saquay, QB   CAN

Armor Tourist Lodge
Montreal, QB   CAN

COMFORT

Old fashioned comfort and friendly staff are important to every lodging. These inns have these qualities in abundance.

Glass Beach B&B Inn
Fort Bragg, CA

Big River Lodge
Mendocino, CA

Dunbar House
Murphys, CA

The Morey House
Placerville, CA

The Bed and Breakfast Inn
San Francisco, CA

The Monte Cristo
San Francisco, CA

Cobweb Palace
Westport, CA

The Alma House
Silverton, CO

The Inn at Chester
Chester, CT

The Kenwood Inn
St. Augustine, FL

Clefstone Manor
Bar Harbor, ME

The 1802 House
Kennebunkport, ME

Old Fort Inn
Kennebunkport, ME

Charmwoods
Naples, ME

The Gosnold Arms
New Harbor, ME

Walker House
Lenox, MA

Rocky Shores Inn and Cottages
Rockport, MA

Coach House
Salem, MA

The Rosemont Inn
Douglas, MI

Haverhill Inn
Haverhill, NH

The Queen Victoria
Cape May, NJ

Seventh Sister Guest House
Cape May, NJ

Normandy Inn
Spring Lake, NJ

The Pines Country Inn
Pisgah Forest, NC

Los Alamos Bed & Breakfast
Los Alamos, NM

Romeo Inn
Ashland, OR

The Hill Farm Inn
Arlington, VT

The 1811 House
Manchester Village, VT

Stone House Inn
North Thetford, VT

Nutmeg Inn
Wilmington, VT

The English Inn
Charlottesville, VA

The King Carter Inn
Irvington, VA

The Swallow's Nest
Vashon, WA

The Saratoga Inn
Whidbey Island, WA

Katie's B & B
North Vancouver, BC   CAN

Quilchena Hotel
Quilchena, BC   CAN

Shiretown Inn
St. Andrews By-the-Sea, NB   CAN

Lovett Lodge Inn
Digby County, NS   CAN

Comfort, *Cont'd*

Camelot
Musquodoboit Harbor, NS   CAN

Holiday House Inn
Bracebridge, ON   CAN

The Kirkfield Mackenzie Historic Home
Kirkfield, ON   CAN

Sherwood Inn
Port Carling, ON   CAN

Just Folks Bed & Breakfast
Charlottetown, PEI   CAN

Le Chateau de Pierre
Quebec City P.Q., QB   CAN

GOLF

Tee off, walk and relax, then head back to your cozy inn. What could be nicer?

The Napa Inn
Napa, CA

Hotel Manning
Keosauqua, IA

Grane's Fairhaven Inn
Bath, ME

The Green Heron
Kennebunkport, ME

Harbourside Inn
Northeast Harbour, ME

The Squire Tarbox Inn
Wiscasset, ME

Holiday Inn
Intervale, NH

Birchwood Inn
Temple, NH

Brae Loch Inn
Cazenovia, NY

The Inn on the Library Lawn
Westport, NY

Mary Anne Peterson's
Monroe, UT

Surf Lodge
Gabriola, BC   CAN

Quilchena Hotel
Quilchena, BC   CAN

Shadow Lawn Inn
Rothesay, NB   CAN

The Garrison House Inn
Annapolis Royal, NS   CAN

The Blue Heron Inn
Pugwash, NS   CAN

Auberge La Pinsonniere
Cap-a-l'Aigle, QB   CAN

Chateau Beauvallon
Mont Tremblant, QB   CAN

DECOR

Distinctive decor and unusual architecture are always a pleasure. Enjoy them in these inns.

The Union Hotel
Benicia, CA

Carter House Inn
Eureka, CA

Hope-Merrill House
Geyserville, CA

Saint Orres
Gualala, CA

Blackthorne Inn
Inverness, CA

Green Gables Inn
Pacific Grove, CA

The James Blair House
Placerville, CA

Morning Glory
Sacramento, CA

Fay Mansion Inn
San Francisco, CA

The Inn at Union Square
San Francisco, CA

Inn on Castro
San Francisco, CA

Willows Bed and Breakfast Inn
San Francisco, CA

Casa Madrona
Sausalito, CA

Bradley House
Truckee, CA

Bordeaux House
Yountville, CA

Oleander House
Yountville, CA

The Imperial Hotel
Cripple Creek, CO

The Bailey House
Fernandina Beach, FL

Deloffre House
Columbus, GA

Mintmere Plantation House
New Iberia, LA

The Columns
New Orleans, LA

Lamothe House
New Orleans, LA

The Captain Jeffers' Inn
Kennebunkport, ME

The Captain Jefferds Inn
Kennebunkport, ME

The Captain Lord Mansion
Kennebunkport, ME

The Stephen Daniels House
Salem, MA

The Marlborough Inn
Woods Hole, MA

White Swan Tavern
Chestertown, MD

The Burn
Natchez, MS

Anchuca
Vicksburg, MS

Nevada City Hotel
Nevada City, MT

Decor, *Cont'd*

Bel-Horst Inn
Belgrade, NB

Colonial Inn
Brevard, NC

The Brass Bed
Cape May, NJ

Benn Conger Inn
Groton, NY

Ashland's Main St. Inn
Ashland, OR

Golden Pheasant Inn
Erwinna, PA

Annie's Bed & Breakfast
Big Sandy, TX

Weimar Country Inn
Weimar, TX

Brigham Street Inn
Salt Lake City, UT

Victorian Marble Inn
Fairhaven, VT

Mayhurst Inn
Orange, VA

The Different Drummer
Sackville, NB   CAN

The Senator Guest Home
Wallace, NS   CAN

The Breadalbane Inn
Fergus, ON   CAN

GOURMET

An excellent meal can add a lot to your stay. The inns listed here are particularly celebrated for their fine cuisine.

The Union Hotel
Benicia, CA

Mt. View Hotel
Calistoga, CA

Madrona Manor
Healdsburg, CA

The Pelican Inn
Muir Beach, CA

Ingleside Inn
Palm Springs, CA

Casa Madrona
Sausalito, CA

Tall Timber
Durango, CO

The Peck House
Empire, CO

The Inn at Chester
Chester, CT

The Homestead Inn
Greenwich, CT

Copper Beech Inn
Ivorytown, CT

The Inn on Lake Waramaug
New Preston, CT

Chalet Suzanne
Lake Wales, FL

Smith House
Dahlonega, GA

The Duneland Beach Inn
Michigan City, IN

The Inn at Stone City
Anamos, IA

Hotel Manning
Keosauqua, IA

Old Talbott Tavern
Bardstown, KY

Blue Hill Inn
Blue Hill, ME

Thistle Inn
Boothbay Harbor, ME

Tarry-a-While
Bridgton, ME

Aubergine
Camden, ME

Camden Harbour Inn
Camden, ME

Le Domaine
Hancock, ME

White Barn Inn
Kennebunkport, ME

Bramble Inn
Brewster, MA

Inn of the Golden Ox
Brewster, MA

The Old Manse Inn
Brewster, MA

The Turning Point
Great Barrington, MA

Haus Andreas
Lee, MA

The Country Inn at Princeton
Princeton, MA

Inn at Duke Creeke
Wellfleet, MA

Schumacher's New Prague Hotel
New Prague, MN

Der Klingerbau
Herman, MO

Bel-Horst Inn
Belgrade, NB

Highlands Inn
Highlands, NC

Maplehurst Inn
Antrim, NH

David's Inn
Bennington, NH

Indian Shutters Inn
North Charlestown, NH

Stonehurst Manor
North Conway, NH

Troutbeck
Amenia, NY

Hedges House
East Hampton, NY

Interlaken Lodge
Lake Placid, NY

Taughannock Farms Inn
Trumansburg, NY

Jamieson House
Poynette, OH

Steamboat Inn
Idleyd Park, OR

Overlook Inn
Canadensis, PA

Cedar Run Inn
Cedar Run, PA

Black Bass Hotel
Lumberville, PA

Centre Bridge Inn
New Hope, PA

The Inn at Phillips Mill
New Hope, PA

White Cloud
Newfoundland, PA

Haag's Hotel
Shartlesville, PA

Hotel Manisses
Block Island, RI

Shelter Harbor Inn
Westerly, RI

Old Miner's Inn
Park City, UT

The Inn at Mt. Ascutney
Brownsville, VT

Blueberry Hill
Goshen, VT

Longwood Inn
Marlboro, VT

Red Clover Inn
Mendon, VT

Old Newfane Inn
Newfane, VT

Tucker Hill
Waitsfield, VT

The Inn at Weston
Weston, VT

The Shelbourne Inn
Seaview, WA

Ram's Head Inn
Rossland, BC   CAN

Sooke Harbour House
Sooke, BC   CAN

The Captain's Palace
Victoria, BC   CAN

Amherst Shore Country Inn
Lorneville, NS   CAN

Historic Inn of Wolfville
Wolfville, NS   CAN

Victoria's Historic Inn
Wolfville, NS   CAN

The Little Inn
Bayfield, ON   CAN

Athlone Inn
Gananoque, ON   CAN

The Sir William MacKenzie Inn
Kirkfield, ON   CAN

Auberge la Pinsonniere
Cap-A-L'Aigle, QB   CAN

Gite du Mont Albert
Sainte Anne des Monts, QB   CAN

Auberge du Vieux Foyer
Val David, QB   CAN

Auberge Le Rucher
Val David, QB   CAN

HISTORIC

Inns situated in historic buildings or locales hold a special appeal for many people. The following is a sampling.

Mullins House
Juneau, AK

Kay El Bar Ranch
Wickenburg, AZ

French Gulch Hotel
French Gulch, CA

Hope-Merrill House
Geyserville, CA

The Heirloom Inn
Ione, CA

The Victorian Farm House
Little River, CA

The Headlands Inn
Mendocino, CA

The Olema Inn
Olema, CA

Crown Bed & Breakfast
Pasadena, CA

Morey House
Placerville, CA

The Ink House
St. Helena, CA

The Washington Square Inn
San Francisco, CA

Bed & Breakfast San Juan
San Juan Bautista, CA

Thistle Dew Inn
Sonoma, CA

Oak Hill Ranch
Tuolunme, CA

Teller House Hotel
Silverton, CO

New Sheridan Hotel
Telluride, CO

The Manse
Washington, DC

Island Hotel
Cedar, FL

The Bailey House
Fernandina Beach, FL

Mason House Inn
Bentonsport, IA

Hotel Manning
Keosauqua, IA

Old Talbott Tavern
Bardstown, KY

Mintmere Plantation House
New Iberia, LA

Estorge House
Opelousas, LA

The 1780 Egremont Inn
South Egremont, MA

Merrell Tavern Inn
South Lee, MA

Gibson's Lodgings
Annapolis, MD

White Swan Tavern
Chestertown, MD

The Inn at Perry Cabin
St. Michaels, MD

Lincoln House
Dennysville, ME

The Captain Lord Mansion
Kennebunkport, ME

Homeport Inn
Searsport, ME

Borgman's Bed & Breakfast
Arrow Rock, MO

Cedar Grove
Vicksburg, MS

The Inn at Christian Shore
Portsmouth, NH

Captain Mey's Inn
Cape May, NJ

Ashling Cottage
Spring Lake, NJ

The Ray House
Asheville, NC

The Cider Mill
Zoar, OH

Edinburgh Lodge
Ashland, OR

McCully House Inn
Jacksonville, OR

Historic 1725 Witmer's Tavern
Lancaster, PA

Cameron Estate Inn
Mount Joy, PA

The Wedgewood Inn
New Hope, PA

Stone Bridge Inn
Tiverton, RI

Hale Springs Inn
Rogersville, TN

Brigham Street Inn
Salt Lake City, UT

Seven Wives Inn
St. George, UT

Shire Inn
Chelsea, VT

Old Newfane Inn
Newfane, VT

Golden Stage Inn
Proctorsville, VT

Miss Molly's Inn
Chincoteague, VA

Alexander-Withrow House
Lexington, VA

Mayhurst Inn
Orange, VA

The Victorian House
Coupeville, Whidbey Is., WA

San Juan Hotel
Friday Harbor, WA

The College Inn
Seattle, WA

The Shelbourne Inn
Seaview, WA

Pine Gables Inn
Evanston, WY

Ferris Mansion
Rawlins, WY

Historic, *Cont'd*

Shiretown Inn
St. Andrews By-the-Sea, NB   CAN

Bread and Roses
Annapolis Royal, NS   CAN

Victoria's Historic Inn
Wolfville, NS   CAN

The Sir William MacKenzie Inn
Kirkfield, ON   CAN

Sterling Lodge
Newboro, ON   CAN

The Dartford Church
Warkworth, ON   CAN

FAMILY FUN

Children aren't welcome at all B&B's, so be sure to check this list if you're traveling with your brood of six. The inns below are ideal for a family fun vacation.

LaPrade's Camp
Clarksville, GA

The Gosnold Arms
New Harbor, ME

Bay Breeze Guest House
Cape Cod, MA

Lone Mountain Ranch
Big Sky, MT

Loch Lyme Lodge
Lyme, NH

Snow Village Lodge
Snowville, NH

Broken Drum Guest Ranch
Pecos, NM

All Breeze Guest Farm
Barryville, NY

Tanglewood Manor House and Lodge
Clemmons, NC

The Piedmont Inn
Waynesville, NC

Morrison's Lodge
Merlin, OR

Lake Creek Lodge
Sisters, OR

Knoll Farm Country Inn
Waitsfield, VT

Jenny Lake Lodge
Moran, WY

Sea Breeze Lodge
Hornby Island, BC   CAN

Clayoquot Lodge
Tofino, BC   CAN

Sherwood Inn
Port Corling, ON   CAN

SPORTS

Sports are an integral part of many people's vacation plans. These inns are noted for their sporting facilities or locales. Be sure to call ahead to see if they have the specific facilities you require.

Howard Creek Ranch Inn
Westport, CA

Outlook Lodge
Green Mountain Falls, CO

Harbour Inne
Mystic, CT

The Inn on Lake Waramaug
New Preston, CT

The 1735 House
Amelia Island, FL

The Duneland Beach Inn
Michigan City, IN

Ship's Knees Inn
Chatham, MA

Westmoor Inn
Nantucket Island, MA

Tarry-a-While
Bridgton, ME

Center Lovell Inn
Center Lovell, ME

Charmwoods
Naples, ME

The Raymond House Inn
Port Sanilac, MI

Loch Lyme Lodge
Lyme, NH

Cranmore Mountain Lodge
North Conway, NH

Snow Village Lodge
Snowville, NH

The Hedges
Blue Mountain Lake, NY

Pine Hill Arms
Pine Hill, NY

The Inn on the Library Lawn
Westport, NY

Folkestone Lodge
Bryson City, NC

Morrison's Lodge
Merlin, OR

Mary Ann Peterson's
Monroe, UT

Churchill House Inn
Brandon, VT

Red Clover Inn
Mendon, VT

Sky Chalet
Mount Jackson, VA

Palmer's Chart House
Deer Harbor, WA

Sports, *Cont'd*

Wilcuma Resort
Cobble Hill, BC   CAN

Quilchena Ranch
Quilchena, BC   CAN

Sir Sam's Inn
Eagle Lake, ON   CAN

Sterling Lodge
Newboro, ON   CAN

Rathfon Inn
Port Colborne, ON   CAN

Jakobstettel Guest House
St. Jacobs, ON   CAN

Dalvay by the Sea
Little York, PEI   Canada

Auberge du Pain Chaud
Lac Saquay, QB   CAN

ANTIQUES

Many of the inns we list are graced by antiques. These inns have put a
special emphasis on antiques and period decor.

The City Hotel
Columbia, CA

Carter House
Eureka, CA

Whitegate Inn
Mendocino, CA

Blue Quail Inn
Santa Barbara, CA

The Peck House
Empire, CO

Jesse Mount House
Savannah, GA

Stillman Inn
Galena, IL

Lamothe House
New Orleans, LA

The Captain Lorenz Perkins
Ogunquit, ME

The Strawberry Inn
New Market, MD

Addison Choate Inn
Rockport Grove, MA

Borgman's Bed & Breakfast
Arrow Rock, MO

Oak Square
Port Gibson, MS

Cedar Grove
Vicksburg, MS

Nevada City Hotel
Nevada City, MT

The Mainstay
Cape May, NJ

Ashling Cottage
Spring Lake, NJ

Poor Richard's Summit Inn
Franklin, NC

The Cider Mill
Zoar, OH

Judge Touvelle House
Jacksonville, OR

Greystone Motor Lodge
Bird in Hand, PA

Historic 1725 Witmer's Tavern
Lancaster, PA

Ma Gallagher's
Newport, RI

Annie's Bed & Breakfast
Big Sandy, TX

The Country Place
Fayetteville, TX

Seven Wives Inn
St. George, UT

Woodchuck Hill Farm
Grafton, VT

The Governor's Inn
Ludlow, VT

The Village Inn of Woodstock
Woodstock, VT

Mayhurst Inn
Orange, VA

The Victorian House
Coupeville, Whidbey Island, WA

Lizzie's
Port Townsend, WA

Pine Gables Inn
Evanston, WY

Ferris Mansion
Rawlins, WY

Wilcuma Resort
Cobble Hill, BC   CAN

Manana Lodge
Ladysmith, BC   CAN

The Captain's Palace
Victoria, BC   CAN

Grand Harbour Inn
Grand Manan, NB   CAN

Lovett Lodge Inn
Digby County, NS   CAN

The Blue Heron Inn
Pugwash, NS   CAN

Historic Inn of Wolfville
Wolfville, NS   CAN

Auberge Willow Place Inn
Como, QB   CAN

Maplewood
Dunham, QB   CAN

CONFERENCE

Small conferences can be very productive when held in the inns listed below, all of which have the facilities you need and the quiet and opportunity, too, for the fellowship you require.

Fairview Manor
Ben Lomond, CA

Stillwater Cove Ranch
Jenner, CA

La Residencia Inn
Napa, CA

The Briggs House
Sacramento, CA

The Archbishop's Mansion
San Francisco, CA

Jackson Court
San Francisco, CA

Spreckels Mansion
San Francisco, CA

The Darling House
Santa Cruz, CA

Wanek's Lodge
Estes Park, CO

Susina Plantation Inn
Thomasville, GA

Beaumont Inn
Harrodsburg, KY

Pine Edge Inn
Little Falls, MN

Las Palomas Conference Center
Taos, NM

Troutbeck
Amenia, NY

Lincklaen House
Cazenovia, NY

Lake Creek Lodge
Sisters, OR

Ten Acres Lodge
Stowe, VT

Tucker Hill
Waitsfield, VT

Wallingford Inn
Wallingford, VT

The McCampbell Inn

Lexington, VA

Sky Chalet
Mount Jackson, VA

Holiday House Inn
Bracebridge, ON   CAN

Northumberland Heights
Coboury, ON   CAN

Sherwood Inn
Port Carling, ON   CAN

Jakobstettel Guest House
St. Jacobs, ON   CAN

Auberge la Pinsonniere
Cap-A-L'Aigle, QB   CAN

Auberge Hollandaise
Morin Heights, QB   CAN

LUXURY

These establishments are famed for their luxurious appointments, special attention to creature comforts and style.

Dairy Hollow House
Eureka Springs, AR

Gramma's Bed and Breakfast Inn
Berkeley, CA

Carriage House
Laguna Beach, CA

Ingleside Inn
Palm Springs, CA

Jackson Court
San Francisco, CA

The Foxes in Sutter Creek
Sutter Creek, CA

Magnolia Hotel
Yountville, CA

Molly Gibson
Aspen, CO

West Lane Inn
Ridgefield, CT

Ballastone Inn
Savannah, GA

Charlton Court
Savannah, GA

The Foley House
Savannah, GA

17 Hundred 90 Inn
Savannah, GA

Lamothe House
New Orleans, LA

The Soniat House
New Orleans, LA

The Captain Lord Mansion
Kennebunkport, ME

Dunelawn
Ogunquit, ME

Deerfield Inn
Deerfield, MA

The Country Inn at Princeton
Princeton, MA

The Burn
Natchez, MS

Linden
Natchez, MS

Oak Square
Port Gibson, MS

Stonehurst Manor
North Conway, NH

Mainstay Inn
Cape May, NJ

Preston House
Santa Fe, NM

Brae Loch Inn
Cazenovia, NY

Luxury, *Cont'd*

Trent River Plantation
Pollocksville, NC

Romeo Inn
Ashland, OR

Overlook Inn
Canadensis, PA

The Elliot House Inn
Charleston, SC

Sundance
Provo, UT

Brigham Street Inn
Salt Lake City, UT

Emerald City Inn
Seattle, WA

The Captain's Palace
Victoria, BC   CAN

The Manor Inn
Hebron, NS   CAN

Northumberland Heights Country Inn
Coboury, ON   CAN

Jacobstettel Guest House
St. Jacobs, ON   CAN

Le Chateau De Pierre
Quebec City, P.Q., QB   CAN

Manoir Ste. Genevieve
Quebec City, P.Q., QB   CAN

NATURE

Nature lovers, alert! Be your fancy ornithology or whale watching, these inns will speak to your heart.

Elk Cove Inn
Elk, CA

The Grey Whale Inn
Ft. Bragg, CA

Shadow Mountain Ranch
Julian, CA

The Olema Inn
Olema, CA

River Rock Inn
Placerville, CA

The House of Yesteryear
Ouray, CO

Lake Rabun Inn
Lakemont, GA

Little St. Simons Island
St. Simons, GA

The Home Place
Meridian, ID

Manor House Inn
Bar Harbor, ME

Eggemoggin Inn
Little Deer Isle, ME

Breezemere Farm
South Brooksville, ME

Nature, *Cont'd*

Lone Mountain Ranch
Big Sky, MT

Izaac Walton Inn
Essex, MT

David's Inn
Bennington, NH

Cascade Lodge
North Woodstock, NH

La Puebla House
Espanola, NM

La Casita
Glenwood, NM

Genesee Falls Hotel
Portageville, NY

LeConte Lodge
Gatlinburg, TN

Merry Meadow Farm
Bradford, VT

Mountain View Inn
Waitsfield, VT

Sally's Bed & Breakfast Manor
Langley, WA

Jenny Lake Lodge
Moran, WY

Black Cat Guest Ranch
Hinton, AB   CAN

Timber Ridge Lodge
Nanton, AB   CAN

Lynn's Lodge
Fraser Lake, BC   CAN

The Compass Rose
Grand Manan, NB   CAN

The Village Inn
Trinity, NF   CAN

GARDENS

Ah, to while away an hour in a lovely garden. What could be more relaxing? These inns are renowned for their lush gardens.

Holiday House
Carmel, CA

The Sandpiper Inn at the Beach
Carmel By-the-Sea, CA

The Shacklefords
El Cajon, CA

The Gingerbread Mansion
Ferndale, CA

Casa del Noyo
Fort Bragg, CA

The Jabberwock
Monterey, CA

Arbor Guest House
Napa, CA

Union Street Inn
San Francisco, CA

Sutter Creek Inn
Sutter Creek, CA

Blue Sky Inn
Buena Vista, CO

Butternut Farm
Glastonbury, CT

Eaton Lodge
Key West, FL

St. Francis Inn
St. Augustine, FL

Liberty Inn 1834
Savannah, GA

Stoddard-Cooper House
Savannah, GA

The Thurlows
Wakerfield, KS

Manor House Inn
Bar Harbor, ME

Seekonk Pines
Great Barrington, MA

Garden Gables Inn
Lenox, MA

Bradford Gardens Inn
Provincetown, MA

Hargood House
Provincetown, MA

Martin Hill Inn
Portsmouth, NH

Sixteen Firs
Staten Island, NY

The Ray House
Asheville, NC

Annie's Bed & Breakfast
Big Sandy, TX

The Inn on the Common
Craftsbury, VT

Tucker Hill Lodge
Waitsfield, VT

Roche Harbor Resort
Roche Harbor, WA

Chaulk's Tourist Home
Lewisporte, NF   CAN

The Manor Inn
Hebron, NS   CAN

The Breadelbane Inn
Fergus, ON   CAN

Sterling Lodge
Newboro, ON   CAN

ROMANCE

Ah, romance! These inns offer a hideaway, a peaceful space in which to be together and let the world go by.

Dairy Hollow House
Eureka Springs, AR

Edwardian Inn
Helena, AR

Inn of the Happy Landing
Carmel, CA

The Gingerbread Mansion
Ferndale, CA

Murphy's Jenner by the Sea
Jenner, CA

Big River Lodge
Mendocino, CA

The Pelican Inn
Muir Beach, CA

East Brother Light Station
Point Richmond, CA

Stewart-Grinsell House
San Francisco, CA

Glenborough Inn and Cottage
Santa Barbara, CA

Cliff Crest
Santa Cruz, CA

The Old Seal Beach Inn
Seal Beach, CA

Sonoma Hotel
Sonoma, CA

The Foxes in Sutter Creek
Sutter Creek, CA

Webber Place
Yountville, CA

Tall Timber
Durango, CO

Liberty Inn 1834
Savannah, GA

The Inn at Stone City
Anamos, IA

Mason House Inn
Bentonsport, IA

The Cornstalk Hotel
New Orleans, LA

Clefstone Manor
Bar Harbor, ME

Ledgelawn Inn
Bar Harbor, ME

Aubergine
Camden, ME

Chebeague Inn
Chebeague Island, ME

Charmwoods
Naples, ME

Old Sea Pines Inn
Brewster, MA

Westmoor Inn
Nantucket Island, MA

The Stephen Daniels House
Salem, MA

The Victorian
Whittinsville, MA

Romance, *Cont'd*

The Victorian Villa
Union City, MI

Schumacher's New Prague Hotel
New Prague, MN

Ravennaside
Natchez, MS

Oak Square
Port Gibson, MS

The Barnard-Good House
Cape May, NJ

The Gingerbread House
Cape May, NJ

Chestnut Hill on the Delaware
Milford, NJ

The Inn At Shaker Mill
Canaan, NY

Folkestone Lodge
Bryson City, NC

Chateau Madeleine
LaPointe, OH

The Brinley Victorian Guest House
Newport, RI

Jasmine House
Charleston, SC

Two Meeting Street Inn
Charleston, SC

Channel Bass Inn
Chincoteague, VA

The Inn at Manchester
Manchester, VT

The Captain's Palace
Victoria, BC   CAN

FOREIGN LANGUAGE

Attention international travelers: it's doubly nice to stay in a small, intimate lodging where they speak your language. The following inns have staff members who can converse with you.

Forest Manor
Angwin, CA
Thai & Spanish

Mangels House
Aptos, CA
French, Spanish

Red Castle Inn
Blue Hill, CA
German, Spanish

Toll House Inn
Booneville, CA
Portuguese, Spanish, Italian, U.K.

Scarlett's Country Inn
Calistoga, CA
Spanish

Sea View Inn
Carmel, CA
French

The Old Crocker Inn
Cloverdale, CA
Greek

Vintage Towers
Cloverdale, CA
French, Italian

Eagle House Bed & Breakfast
Eureka, CA
Spanish

Mill Rose B & B Inn
Half Moon Bay, CA
French & Spanish

Belle de Jour Farm
Healdsburg, CA
French

The Grape Leaf Inn
Healdsburg, CA
German

Murphy's Jenner by the Sea
Jenner, CA
German, French

Arbor Guest House
Napa, CA
Spanish

Ingleside Inn
Palm Springs, CA
French, German

The Rupley House
Placerville, CA
French

Rosi's of Rutherford
Rutherford, CA
Spanish

Bear Flag Inn
Sacramento, CA
German

Albion House
San Francisco, CA
French, German, Italian

Casa Arguello
San Francisco, CA
Spanish

Hermitage House
San Francisco, CA
Italian, French, Spanish

Hotel Edward II
San Francisco, CA
Spanish, Dutch, Italian

The Inn at Union Square
San Francisco, CA
Portuguese, French, German, Spanish

Lyon Street Bed & Breakfast
San Francisco, CA
French

Petite Auberge
San Francisco, CA
French

Riley's Bed & Breakfast
San Francisco, CA
French

Wamsley Bed & Breakfast Art Center
San Francisco, CA
Finnish

Bed & Breakfast San Juan
San Juan Bautista, CA
Spanish, Mandarin

The Olive House
Santa Barbara, CA
German, French, Dutch

The Parsonage
Santa Barbara, CA
German

The Babbling Brook Inn
Santa Cruz, CA
French & Greek

Chateau Victorian
Santa Cruz, CA
German

Jameson's
Sonora, CA
Spanish

Lulu Belle's
Sonora, CA
German

The Ryan House
Sonora, CA
French

Bartels Ranch
St. Helena, CA
Spanish

Bell Creek B & B
St. Helena, CA
Greek, French, Spanish

Erika's Hillside
St. Helena, CA
German

Judy's Bed & Breakfast
St. Helena, CA
Italian

Oak Hill Ranch
Tuolumne, CA
Spanish & Japanese

La Maida House
West Hollywood, CA
Afrikaans

Hearthstone House
Aspen, CO
French, German

Molly Gibson
Aspen, CO
Spanish

Snow Queen Lodge
Aspen, CO
French, Spanish

Ullr Lodge
Aspen, CO
Dutch

Blue Sky Inn
Buena Vista, CO
French, Spanish

The Peck House
Empire, CO
French, Spanish

Sky Valley Lodge
Steamboat Springs, CO
French, Spanish

New Sheridan Hotel
Telluride, CO
Spanish

Hopkins Inn
New Preston, CT
German

Sunshine
Pensacola, FL
German

Four Seventeen
Savannah, GA
German, Norwegian, Spanish, French

Pacific Hawaii Bed & Breakfast
Oahu, HI
German, Spanish

The Ellsworth Inn
Hailey, ID
French, German, Norwegian

The Columns
New Orleans, LA
Spanish, French

Altehofen House
Blue Hill, ME
German, Italian, French

Kemp House
St. Michaels, MD
German

Seafarer Motel
Chatham, MA
Greek

Addison Choate Inn
Rockport Grove, MA
German

Inn at Duke Creeke
Wellfleet, MA
French

The Sjoholm B & B Inn
West Falmouth, MA
French

The Marlborough House
Woods Hole, MA
French

Schmidt's Guesthouse
Herman, MO
German

Der Klingerbau
Hermann, MO
German

Lazy K Bar Ranch
Big Timber, MT
Spanish

Tokfarm Inn
Rindge, NH
German, French, Spanish, Dutch

The Johnson House
Spring Lake, NJ
Finnish, Hungarian

Lincklaen House
Cazenovia, NY
French

Jamieson House
Poynette, OH
French, German, Italian, Norwegian

Centre Bridge Inn
Centre Bridge, PA
German

Pineapple Hill
New Hope, PA
German

Landmark Inn
Castroville, TX
German

The Country Place
Fayetteville, TX
German, Spanish, Italian

Old Miners Inn
Park City, UT
French, Spanish

The Conyers House
Sperryville, VA
French, German, Italian

Golden Stage Inn
Proctorsville, VT
German

Palmer's Chart House
Deer Harbor, WA
Spanish, French

Seattle Bed & Breakfast
Seattle, WA
German

Jenny Lake Lodge
Moran, WY
Spanish, French, German

Battery Street Guest House
Victoria, BC   CAN
Dutch

Auberge Laketree
Knowlton, QB   CAN
German

Le Chateau de Pierre
Quebec City P.Q., QB   CAN
French, Spanish

Tiger Lily Farm
Burstall, SK   CAN

INNKEEPERS

Innkeepers are special people with large stores of warmth and patience. The following are a few inns with extra-special innkeepers.

Norm & Jeri Brunton
The Brunton House
Scottsboro, AL

Pat & Jim Wanek
Wanek's Lodge
Estes Park, CO

Julie Bishop
Bishopsgate Inn
East Haddam, CT

Marsha & Judie
Ellie's Nest
Key West, FL

Jim & Ginny Austin
Mostly Hall
Falmouth, MA

Margaret Lobenstine
The Wildwood Inn
Ware, MA

Marge & Alden Fellows
Captain Isaiah's House
Bass River, MA

Margot & Brad Sweet
Addison Choate Inn
Rockport, MA

Marie & Harold Coats, innkeepers
St.Rita Hotel
Beach Haven, NJ

Ingram Paperny
The Inn At Shaker Mill
Canaan, NY

Wally & Sherry Lossing, innkeepers
Livingston Mansion Inn
Jacksonville, OR

Nadine Silnatzer & Carl Glassman
The Wedgewood Inn
New Hope, PA

Steve & May Darlington
Pineapple Hill
New Hope, PA

Majine & Don Palmer
Palmer's Chart House
Deer Harbor, WA

Thelma Scudi
Lizzie's
Port Townsend, WA

The Shaw Family
Shaw's Hotel
Brackley Beach, PE   CAN

SPECIAL

These inns all have an extra special, out of the ordinary something which distinguishes them. We hope you'll agree.

Dairy Hollow House
Eureka Springs, AR
Antique bathtub "big enough for two".

The French Hotel
Berkeley, CA
Directly across from world famous Chez Panisse restaurant.

Saint Orres
Gualala, CA
Incredibly beautiful handwrought fantasy building.

Anne Marie's Lodgin & Gallery
Jackson, CA
Artist in residence and children very welcome.

East Brother Light Station
Point Richmond, CA
On an island in the middle of San Francisco Bay!

The Mansion Hotel
San Francisco, CA
Magic shows and a resident "spirit."

Country House Inn
Templeton, CA
Near Hearst Castle.

The Home Ranch
Clark, CO
Sleigh rides and a herd of llamas.

The Imperial Hotel
Cripple Creek, CO
Cabaret style "melodrama" theatre.

The Balloon Ranch
Del Norte, CO
Hot air balloon trips & balloon pilots school.

Ellie's Nest
Key West, FL
Especially for women.

Susina Plantation Inn
Thomasville, GA
Pretend you're Scarlett O'Hara.

Patchwork Quilt Bed & Breakfast
Middlebury, IN
Take a tour of Amish farm country.

The Inn at Stone City
Anamos, IA
Moonlight surrey serenade.

Rosalea's Hotel
Harper, KS
Hotel as an art form on the Kansas plains.

Holbrook Inn
Bar Harbor, ME
Large doll collection.

Greenville Inn
Greenville, ME
Largest seaplane base on the East Coast.

The Old Manse Inn
Brewster, MA
During the Civil War, a link to the underground railroad.

Deerfield Inn
Deerfield, MA
Located in the center of Historic Deerfield

Seekonk Pines
Great Barrington, MA
Fresh vegetables for sale in the garden.

The Turning Point
Great Barrington, MA
Natural foods and environment.

The Wildwood Inn
Ware, MA
Refreshing "Norman Rockwell" brook-fed swimming hole.

Lazy K Bar Ranch
Big Timber, MT
Exclusive use of a horse for your holiday on working dude ranch.

Fort Robinson Inn
Crawford, NB
Buffalo dishes in a real forte.

The Inn at Shaker Mill Farm
Canaan, NY
Vegetarian meals available in an informal environment.

The Golden Eagle
Garrison's Landing, NY
Film location for the movie "Hello Dolly."

Cedar Hill Inn
Ghent, NY
Natural foods.

Trent River Plantation
Pollocksville, NC
Animal petting farm.

Hugging Bear Inn
Chester, VT
Teddy bears of every description.

Inwood Manor
East Barnet, VT
Canoeing on the Connecticut River from the inn.

Fox Stand Inn
Royalton, VT
Special herd of polled Hereford cattle.

Knoll Farm Country Inn
Waitsfield, VT
Organically grown vegetables and a herd of Scotch Highland cattle.

Fjord House
Poulsbo, WA
"Little Norway" near Seattle and the Olympic Peninsula.

The Swan Inn
Vashon Island, WA
A little bit of Merrie Olde England.

Beulah Land
Treherne, MB   CAN
Homegrown, homecooked meals.

The Village Inn
Trinity, NF   CAN
Ocean expeditions to view whales.

The Waterlot
New Hamburg, ON   CAN
Just the place for a romantic gourmet.

Auberge Le Rucher
Val David, QB   CAN
Hand built by the owner, Luc Invernizzi.

Part V

Some Favorite
B & B Recipes

Some Favorite B&B Recipes

From the bustling kitchens of Bed & Breakfasts across the country comes this list of distinctive recipes. Some are simple and quick, others are VERY gourmet. All are delicious. Hope you enjoy them as much as we did.

Drinks

Grant Corner Inn, Santa Fe, New Mexico

ORANGE FRAPPE

4 cups fresh squeezed orange juice
1 lemon, squeezed
1 large banana

6 strawberries, fresh or frozen
¼ cup whipping cream
6 ice cubes

Mix ingredients in electric blender on high speed for approximately 1 minute. Serve in frozen stemmed goblets with fresh sprig of mint garnish. Serves 6.

The Okemo Inn, Ludlow, Vermont

HOT SPICED TEA

Combine the following and boil for 5 minutes:
2 cups sugar
2 cups water
2 inch stick of cinnamon

1 tsp. ground allspice
12 whole cloves or
1 ½ tsp. ground cloves

ADD:
4 tsps. loose tea or use 12 tea bags
Let stand for 10 minutes and
strain.

ADD:
1 ½ cups orange juice (4 oranges)
¾ cup lemon juice (2 lemons)
4 quarts hot water

Serve hot in mugs or cups. The spices and tea can be brewed and stored in glass jar in the refrigerator ahead of time... when ready to use, mix with the juices and water, and heat. Serves 50.

Deerfield Inn, Deerfield, Massachussetts

CHRISTMAS WASSAIL

1 cup water	½ tsp. allspice
4 cups sugar	1 stick cinnamon or
1 Tbsp. nutmeg	2 Tbsps. powdered cinnamon
2 tsps. ginger	4 quarts/liters dry sherry
½ tsp. mace	2 cups brandy
6 whole cloves	1 dozen eggs

Combine water, sugar and spices in a saucepan. Bring to full boil for 5 minutes. Heat sherry and brandy almost to boiling, in separate pans. Separate eggs. Beat whites until stiff. Beat yolks until light in color and well mixed. Fold whites into yolks in a large bowl. Mixing quickly, strain sugar/spice mixture into folded eggs. Use a whisk if available. Very gradually, add hot sherry to egg mixture, stirring constantly. Add brandy, stirring. Serves 25-30.

Appetizers

The Lyme Inn, Lyme, New Hampshire

STUFFED MUSHROOMS

Large Mushrooms	¼ tsp. pepper
¼ cup melted butter	½ tsp. chopped onions
1 tsp. salt	1 cup minced clams

Remove stems and prepare mushrooms for stuffing. Chop the stems and add minced clams. Add butter, salt, pepper and onions. Stuff into mushroom caps. Sprinkle with bread crumbs and paprika. Bake at 400⁰ F. for 20 minutes. Serves 12.

The Bramble Inn, Brewster, Cape Cod, Massachussetts

ANGELS ON HORSEBACK

Wrap raw oysters with strips of bacon. Secure each oyster with a toothpick. Broil until bacon is crisply browned, turning once. Allow 3 oysters for each serving as an hors d'oeuvre.

The Parsonage, Santa Barbara, California

HOT CLAM DIP

2 pkg. 8 oz. cream cheese
4 heaping Tbsps. sour cream
4 Tbsps. mayonnaise
1 tsp. onion powder

2—8 oz. cans minced clams, drained
parmesan cheese
dehydrated chives

Spray pie plate or quiche pan. Mix cream cheese, sour cream and mayonnaise. Blend well. Add clams. Pour in pan—sprinkle heavily with parmesan cheese / lightly with chives. Bake in 325⁰ F. oven for 30 minutes. Serve with wheat thins.

Northfield Country House, Northfield, Massachussetts

SQUASH FLOWER FRITTERS

5 Yellow Squash Flowers
  (Summer Squash)
1 ⅓ cups flour
1 tsp. salt

2 eggs
½ cup milk
1 tsp. salad oil

Rinse flowers, pat dry (well) and break into pieces. Combine with all other ingredients. Drop level tablespoonfuls into 3-4 in. heated oil in deep fat fryer or kettle. Fry 5 mins. Serve hot with maple syrup. Serves 5.

Cereal

Breezemere Farm, So. Brooksville, Maine

BREEZEMERE GRANOLA

5 cups uncooked oatmeal
1 cup safflower oil
1 cup honey
1 cup raisins
1 cup other dried fruit pieces
  (Such as currants or apple)

1 cup each:
  sliced almonds
  broken walnuts
  sesame seeds
  unsalted sunflower seeds
  wheat germ
  shredded coconut

Combine oatmeal, nuts, seeds, wheat germ and coconut well. Meld together oil and honey, pour over dry ingredients and mix well. Bake at 325° F. for one hour or until nicely brown. When cool, add raisins and other dried fruit. Serves 12.

Folkestone, Bryson City, North Carolina

GRANDMA'S OATMEAL

2 ½ cups water	½ tsp. cinnamon
1/8 tsp. salt	5 oz. can condensed milk
2 cups oatmeal	3 Tbsp. butter
2 heaping Tbsps. sugar	5 tbsps. brown sugar

Bring water to a boil. Add salt. Stirring constantly, add dry oatmeal gradually. Continue stirring. Add sugar, cinnamon. Cook 1 minute, add condensed milk and reheat to boiling. Pour into serving dish, add butter and brown sugar.

Fruit Dishes

Grane's Fairhaven Inn, Bath, Maine

BANANAS "GRANE"

MIX:

½ cup sour cream	1 Tbsp. sugar or honey
2 Tbsps. Kirsch	2 Tbsps. whipping cream

SERVE atop fresh-cut sliced bananas and serve with fresh strawberry on top. Serves 8.

The Okemo Inn, Ludlow, Vermont

FRESH FRUIT COMPOTE

3 medium-large cantaloupes	whipped cream
1 quart fresh blueberries	sliced almonds—toasted
1 quart fresh red raspberries	sugar to taste
1 cup Amaretto liqueur	

Cut each cantaloupe in half crosswise. Trim a sliver from the bottom of each half so they sit flat. Scoop out melon rounds (after removing seeds) leaving a clean smooth "cup" for serving. Put halves in nice serving bowls or on nice small plates and set in refrigerator to chill well. Meanwhile, rinse and drain all berries and place them in a large bowl with the cantaloupe balls. Sprinkle enough sugar over fruit to sweeten slightly (strictly optional) and then pour 1 cup Amaretto liqueur over all. Mix all ingredients well but gently—cover and set in refrigerator to chill.

When ready to serve, fill each cantaloupe shell with fruit mixture. Garnish with a healthy serving of whipped cream and then sprinkle the toasted sliced almonds over all. A sprig of fresh mint adds color and zest!

TO TOAST ALMONDS: Spread sliced almonds thinly on a small cookie pan and toast in 350⁰ F. oven until light golden brown—about 8-10 minutes. Serves 6.

Chalet Suzanne, Lake Wales, Florida

BAKED GRAPEFRUIT

½ grapefruit per person
butter (melted)
sugar
cinnamon
chicken livers

flour
salt
pepper

Cut out small center of each grapefruit half and loosen sections. Fill center cavity with melted butter. Sprinkle top with a mixture of cinnamon and sugar (generously). Place under broiler until well browned. To serve, garnish with a chicken liver or two that have been dusted with flour, salt and pepper and sauteed on a hot grill or skillet in butter.

Muffins

Preston House, Santa Fe, New Mexico

ZUCCHINI MUFFINS

3 eggs
2 cups sugar
1 cup vegetable oil
1 Tbsp. vanilla
2 cups loosely packed
   grated zucchini

2 cups flour
1 Tbsp. cinnamon
2 tsps. soda
1 tsp. salt
½ tsp. baking powder
1 cup chopped nuts

Beat eggs until frothy. Beat in sugar, oil and vanilla until mixture is thick or lemon colored. Stir in zucchini. Add flour, cinnamon, soda, salt, and baking powder. Fold in nuts. Pour mix into 2 oiled and floured 8" x 4 ½ " x 3" pans or muffin tins. Fill only half-full as it bubbles and puffs up during baking. Bake at 350° F, 1 hour for large pans or 30 minutes for muffins. Cool in pans 10 minutes. Serves 12.

Deep Creek Inn, Bonners Ferry, Idaho

ENGLISH TEA MUFFINS

2 cups boiling water
5 tsps. soda
2 cups sugar
1 cup shortening
4 eggs
1 quart buttermilk

2 cups chopped dates
1 cup nuts
5 cups flour
4 cups All Bran
1 cup bran flakes
1 tsp. salt

Add eggs to sugar and shortening and beat well. Add buttermilk, dates and nuts, and mix. Add flour, All Bran, bran flakes, and salt. Add soda and water. You can keep in gallon jar for up to 2 weeks in refrigerator—don't stir—dip out as needed. Pour in muffin or cup cake papers—half-full. Bake at 400° F. for 25 minutes. Serves 35-40.

Wildwood Inn, Ware, Massachussetts

WILDWOOD'S TEA SCONES

2 cups sifted flour	⅓ cup butter
2 Tbsp. sugar	1 egg, beaten
3 tsps. baking powder	Approx. ½ - ¾ cup milk
½ tsp. salt	

Preheat oven to 425° F. Sift flour, sugar, baking powder and salt together. Chop in butter with a pastry blender until the flour-coated particles of butter are the size of coarse cornmeal. Add the egg and about ½ cup milk. Stir quickly and lightly until no flour shows. The less milk the better, but add a little if needed to make a soft dough. Grease your hands and turn the dough out onto a floured dish towel. Knead gently 15 times. Cut dough in half. Shape each half into a ball, and press down each one into a round approx. ¼" thick. Cut each into 8 wedges, like a pie — use a floured knife. Place wedges on a greased cookie sheet or pie tin, not allowing sides to touch. Bake for 10-15 min. If you wish them to shine, glaze with lightly beaten egg before baking. Scones should be golden brown when done. Serves 6.

Pancakes

The Inn at Manchester, Vermont

COTTAGE PANCAKES WITH HOT BLUEBERRY SAUCE

1 cup cottage cheese	6 Tbsps. melted butter
4 fresh eggs	1 cup unbleached flour

Mix cottage cheese, eggs and butter with a wisk. Fold in flour. Bake on a medium griddle. Serves 3.

Sauce:

2 cups blueberries	1 tsp. lemon juice
½ cup sugar	1 cup water
1 tsp. cornstarch	

Combine blueberries, sugar, lemon juice and ½ cup water. Cook for four minutes. Add another ½ cup water mixed with cornstarch. Heat to boiling and serve.

Elk Cove Inn, Elk, California

EIERKUCHEN
(German Egg Cakes)

½ cup flour	½ cup buttermilk
¾ tsp. baking powder	6 egg whites
1 Tbsp. sugar	cream of tartar
dash salt	sweet butter
6 egg yolks	flavoring (vanilla, almond)

Put flour, baking powder, sugar, salt, egg yolks, flavoring and buttermilk in a large bowl. Beat. In a separate bowl beat egg whites quite stiff with cream of tartar. Carefully fold into yolk mixture. Preheat griddle to 275-300⁰ F. with a small amount of butter. Spoon onto griddle (spreading dough slightly with side of spoon) making small round pancakes. Flip over when golden brown to bake other side. Top with any kind of fresh berries or applesauce. Fresh huckleberries taste delicious folded into the mixture just before baking. Serves 4.

B & B in Minuteman Country, Lexington, Massachusetts

SWEDISH PANCAKES

2 eggs	¾ cup milk
½ tsp. salt	⅔ cup flour
¼ cup sugar	1 large Tbsp. oil

Beat eggs. Add remaining ingredients (oil last). Mix until smooth. Bake on moderately hot griddle. Serve with butter and syrup. Serves 2.

Egg Dishes

Edison Hill Manor, Stowe, Vermont

L'OMELET HOMARD FORESTIERE
(Omelette with Lobster and Mushrooms)

4 oz. sliced mushrooms	¼ cup heavy cream
1 oz. clarified butter	1 fresh lobster tail, poached,
salt and pepper to taste	shelled and diced
¼ cup good port	freshly grated Parmesan cheese

Saute the mushrooms in butter, season with salt and pepper, stir in port and cream and reduce 50%. Add the lobster and simmer until the meat is hot. In a prepared omelette pan, add some clarified butter, heat pan and add two beaten eggs. Stir briskly with a fork. Add lobster mixture. Fold, sprinkle with Parmesan, garnish plate and serve quickly. Serves 4.

City Hotel, Columbia, California

EGGS WARHOL

(Poached Eggs in Tomato Halves with Avocado Sauce)

8 poached eggs	1 Tbsp. horse radish sauce
4 ripe tomatoes, halved	salt and pepper to taste
3 ripe Haas avocados	1 ½ cups whipped cream
½ to ¾ cup sour cream	chopped pimento for garnish

Shake the seeds and moisture out of the tomato halves, scoop some of the pulp out of each and discard. Place the tomatoes on a baking sheet and sprinkle with salt and pepper, dot each with olive oil. Broil for 4 minutes, or until lightly brown. Set aside and keep warm. Poach the eggs in a large skillet with one tablespoon of salt and one tablespoon of white vinegar in the water. When done, put one egg in each tomato half. Cover with avocado mousseline sauce and garnish with chopped pimento.

Avocado Mouseline Sauce

Add the 3 avocados, sour cream, lemon juice and horse radish in a mixing bowl and whip until smooth. Add salt and pepper to taste. Run the mixture through a food mill or fine wire mesh to remove avocado pulp and lumps. Fold in whipped cream to make the mousseline. Serves 4.

Dairy Hollow House, Eureka Springs, Arkansas

APPLE-BRIE CHEESE OMELETTE

1 Tbsp. melted butter	1 tbsp. light cream or milk
½ crisp, well-flavored apple,	dash salt
peeled, cored, sliced thinly	dash white pepper
2 eggs	2 Tbsps. brie cheese, diced

Saute apple slices gently in butter until soft but not mushy. Prepare an omelette using eggs, cream or milk, salt and white pepper. Cook in omelette pan, pulling up undersides with spatula to allow uncooked egg to run onto the exposed pan and cook. When omelette is no longer runny but not quite done, scatter brie cheese over its surface. Cook a few seconds longer, then scatter cooked apple slices over the cheese. Roll omelette, and serve on warmed plate. Garnish with a fresh strawberry or a slice of raw apple with the peel still on, and a sprig of fresh mint. Serve with homemade bread (we often use wholewheat butterhorns), butter, and homemade jam. Serves 1 (easily doubled or tripled).

Coffee Cakes

Valley View Citrus Ranch, Orosi, California

5 MINUTE COFFEE CAKE

4 Tbsps. butter	1 tsp. cinnamon
½ cup sugar	salt
1 cup flour	½ cup milk
3 tsps. baking powder	1 egg
chopped nuts or coconut	cinnamon sugar

Preheat oven to 375° F. Put butter in pie pan or square baking pan. Sift together sugar, flour, baking powder, cinnamon and salt. Measure milk, drop in egg, stir and add to flour mixture. Add melted butter last, stir, pour into pan. Sprinkle top with chopped nuts (or coconut) and cinnamon sugar. Bake about 25 minutes. Serve warm. Reheats quite well. Serves 6.

Innwood Manor, East Barnet, Vermont

FLORENTINE CORNMEAL CAKE

⅔ cup soft butter	1 egg yolk
2 ⅔ cups powdered sugar	1 ¼ cups cake flour
1 tsp. vanilla	⅓ cup corn meal
2 whole eggs	

Beat butter with sugar until creamy. Beat in vanilla. Add eggs one at a time. Sift and measure cake flour and then mix with corn meal. Add to batter a portion at a time. Blend well after each addition. Grease and dust decorative deerback pan or 4 cup tube pan. Spoon batter into pan—spread evenly. Bake at 325° F. for 1 hr. 15 min. Cool in pan for a few minutes—turn out to wire rack. Sift some powdered sugar over warm cake. Thinly sliced, serves 15.

Pudding Creek Inn, Fort Bragg, California

PUDDING CREEK INN COFFEE CAKE

2 ½ cups flour	½ tsp. salt
1 cup melted butter	6 Tbsps. sugar
2 tsps. baking powder	2 beaten eggs
½ tsp. baking soda	4 Tbsps. flour
1 cup buttermilk	2 Tbsps. butter
2 tsps. vanilla	⅓ cup fruit jam or
1 cup sugar	drained fruit or pie filling

In medium size bowl stir together the flour, sugar, baking powder, baking soda and salt. Make a well in center of dry ingredients. In small bowl combine eggs, melted butter, buttermilk and vanilla. Add to dry ingredients and mix well. Turn batter into greased rectangular pan (approx. 9" x 13"). Drop jam, drained fruit or pie filling by teaspoons atop batter.

In small bowl combine 6 Tbsps. sugar, 4 Tbsps. flour and 2 tsps. butter. Cut until crumbly. Sprinkle crumb mix atop batter. Serves 18.

Quick Bread

Baker's Manor, Ouray, Colorado

POPPY SEED BREAD

2 eggs	1 cup oil
1 cup milk	2 cups flour
1 cup sugar	½ tsp. salt
1 tsp. vanilla	2 tsps. baking powder
poppy seeds	

Beat together eggs, milk, sugar, vanilla and oil until well blended. Then add flour, salt and baking powder. Beat well and add several tablespoons poppy seeds. Pour into 9" x 4" greased and floured pan. Bake at 350⁰ F. for 45-60 minutes.

Country Inn, Harwich Port, Massachussetts

COUNTRY INN LEMON BREAD

⅓ cup butter	½ cup milk
1 cup sugar	¼ tsp. almond extract
2 eggs	1-½ cup flour
rind of 11 lemons, grated	1 tsp. baking powder

Glaze:

Juice of one lemon	⅓ cup sugar

Preheat oven to 350° F. Grease one loaf pan. Cream butter and sugar until light. Add eggs and beat until well combined. Mix milk, grated rind and almond extract together in measuring cup. Mix flour and baking powder together in small bowl. Add dry ingredients and milk mixture. Beat until well mixed. Bake in loaf pan at 350⁰ F. for one hour or until done when tested with a toothpick. Serves 6.

Woodchuck Hill Farm, Grafton, Vermont

BLUEBERRY BOY BAIT
(Blueberry Bread)

2 cups flour	1 cup milk
1 ½ cups sugar	2 eggs
2 tsps. baking powder	2 to 3 cups blueberries
1 tsp. salt	1 cup sugar
⅔ cup margerine or oil	1 tsp. cinnamon

Combine first 7 ingredients and beat 3 minutes. Pour into greased and floured 9" x 13" pan. Arrange on top of batter at least 2 cups of blueberries. Combine sugar with cinnamon and sprinkle on top. Bake 40-50 minutes at 350°F. Can be reheated. Serve with whipped cream as desert or plain for breakfast. Serves 8.

Toppings

The Inn at Weston, Weston, VT.

APPLE BUTTER

5 lbs. apples	1 ½ tsp. ground cloves
2 cups cider	¼ tsp. ground allspice
1 cup sugar	dash of nutmeg
3 tsp. cinnamon	

Wash, stem and core apples; peel and cut into ¼" wedges. Cook apples in cider with sugar. Season with cinnamon, cloves, allspice and nutmeg. Continue cooking till apples are soft but still hold their shape a bit. Cool and refrigerate.
Besides being a delicious addition to toast or muffins, try mixing with sour cream or mayonnaise for a fruit salad dressing.

Trent River Plantation, Pollocksville, North Carolina

PLANTATION FRUIT SPREAD

8 oz. cream cheese, softened	½ pint strawberries, blueberries, bananas, or cranberries (add some sugar)

Beat cream cheese and fruit until creamy. Chill overnight to develop flavor. Spread on fruit bread.

Briar Rose Bed & Breakfast, Boulder, Colorado

LEMON CURD

juice of 6 lemons	12 beaten eggs
grated rind of 6 lemons	2 ½ cups sugar

Combine all ingredients in double boiler. Stir CONSTANTLY over moderate heat until thick. Cool. Store in refrigerator. Good on hot scones, muffins or biscuits.

Sweet Endings

The Lyme Inn, Lyme, New Hampshire

MAPLE MOUSSE

1 Tbsp. gelatin	½ cup light brown sugar
½ cup water	4 egg whites, whipped
4 egg yolks	2 cups heavy cream, whipped
1 cup maple syrup	

Combine gelatin, water, egg yolks and maple syrup over heat (in a double boiler). Use a wire whip to stir out the lumps. Add the brown sugar and continue to whip. Take off heat and allow to cool slightly. Fold in the beaten egg whites and the whipped cream. Pour into champagne glasses and chill. Serves 4.

The Inn at April Point, Campbell River, British Columbia

CARROT CAKE

2 cups sugar	2 cups flour
1 cup Wesson oil	2 tsps. soda
4 eggs	½ tsp. salt
3 cups grated carrots	1 tsp. cinnamon
1 cup shopped nuts	

Beat eggs, add oil and sugar. Mix nuts with flour, soda and other dry ingredients. Add to egg mixture. Add carrots and beat well. Bake in three layers at 350° F. 35-40 minutes.

FROSTING:

1 cube butter	1 8 oz. pkg. cream cheese
1 lb. packed sugar	1 tsp. vanilla

Combine above ingredients until smooth and creamy. Serves 8.

Garland's Oak Creek Lodge, Sedona, Arizona

GARLAND'S FRESH PEAR CREAM SHERBET

2 lbs. very ripe pears, peeled, cored & chopped	1 ½ cups heavy cream
1 cup sugar	1 tsp. vanilla
1 ½ cups milk	2 Tbsps. Pear William liqueur
	2 Tbsps. lemon juice

Mix milk and cream together, add sugar, and stir until dissolved. Pour into a tray and freeze until firm. Puree pears in processor until smooth. Process frozen cream mixture and pear puree; add vanilla and Pear William. Process briefly. Add lemon juice to taste, to freshen the mixture. Pour back into tray. Refreeze until firm, but still yielding, about 1 ½ hours. Serves 8.

On Becoming an Innkeeper

Do you dream of being an innkeeper, meeting and making friends with interesting guests and regaling them with your own special brand of hospitality? Make no mistake, innkeeping is hard work (especially if you have more than two rooms) but it can be very rewarding.

Many people prefer to buy an established inn. If you are interested in buying an inn you may wish to contact the editor of this guide regarding the information we have on inns for sale.

Our address: The Complete Guide to Bed & Breakfasts
P.O. Box 20467
Oakland, CA 94620 0467

Vote for Your Choice of "Inn of the Year"

To the editors of *The Complete Guide to Bed & Breakfasts, Inns and Guesthouses of the U.S. and Canada*:

I cast my vote for "Inn of the Year" for:

Name of Inn _____

Address _____

_____

Phone _____

Reasons _____

_____

_____

I would also like to (please check one):

___**Recommend a new Inn**   ___**Comment**

___**Critque**   ___**Suggest**

Name of Inn _____

Address _____

_____

Phone _____

Comment _____

_____

_____

Please send your entries to:

The Complete Guide to Bed & Breakfast Inns
P.O. Box 20467
Oakland, CA 94620 0467

Travel Guides from
John Muir Publications

I'd like to order the terrific travel guides checked below . . .

Quantity		Each	Total
	Europe Through the Back Door	$8.95	
	The Complete Guide to Bed & Breakfasts, Inns & Guesthouses In the U.S. & Canada	$9.95	
	Free Attractions USA	$10.95	
	The People's Guide to Mexico (Revised)	$10.50	
	The People's Guide to Camping in Mexico	$10.00	
	The On & Off the Road Cookbook	$8.50	
	Subtotal	$	
	Shipping	1.50	
	Total Enclosed	$	

Send order to:
John Muir Publications
P.O. Box 613
Santa Fe, NM 87504

ALLOW 4 TO 6 WEEKS FOR DELIVERY

Please send my order to:
Name _____
Street _____
City _____ State _____ ZIP _____

☐ I'm not ready to order yet. Send me your FREE descriptive catalog.